Shojo Beat

Natsume's BOOK of FRIENDS

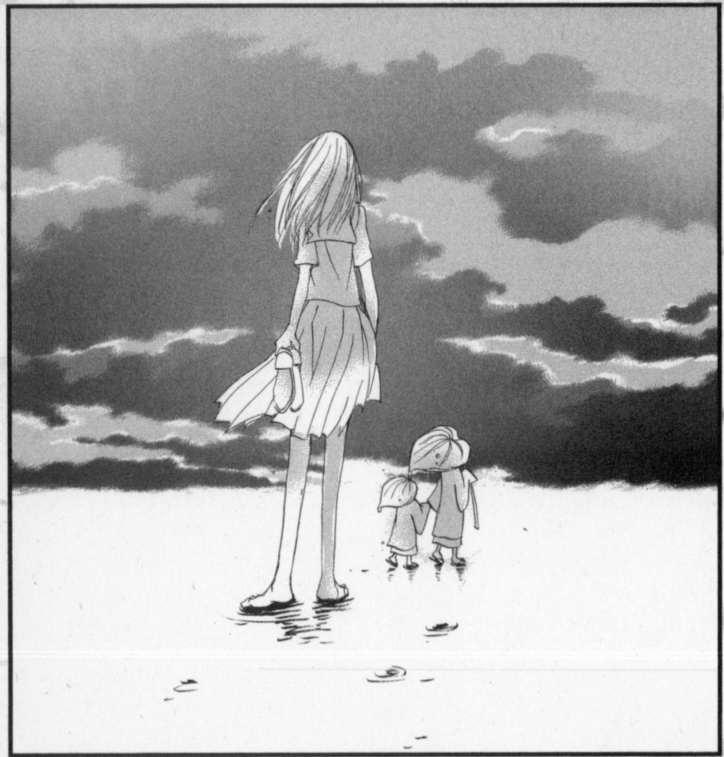

STORY and ART by
Yuki Midorikawa

VOLUME 12

Natsume's
BOOK of FRIENDS
VOLUME 12 CONTENTS

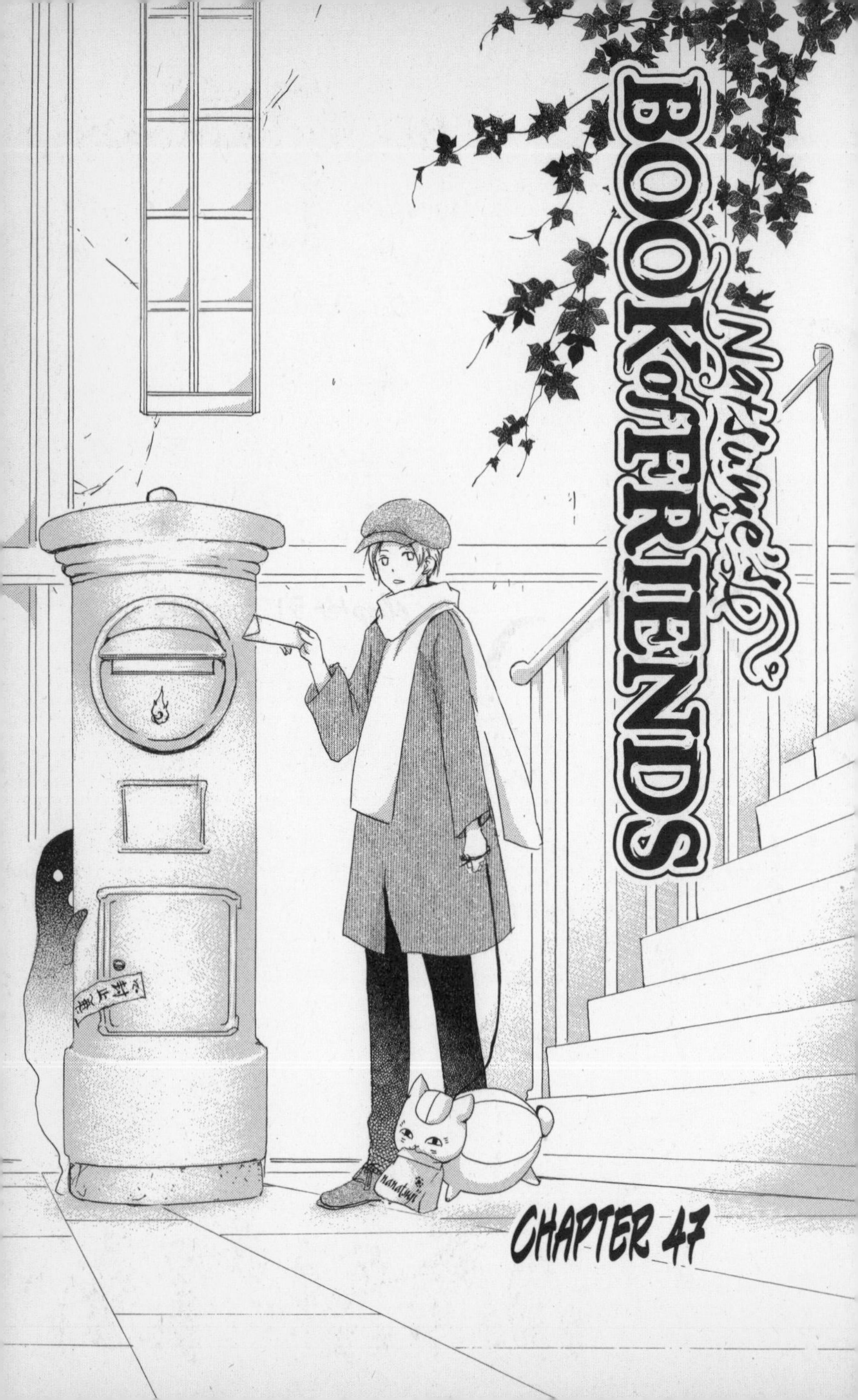
Natsume's BOOK of FRIENDS
CHAPTER 47

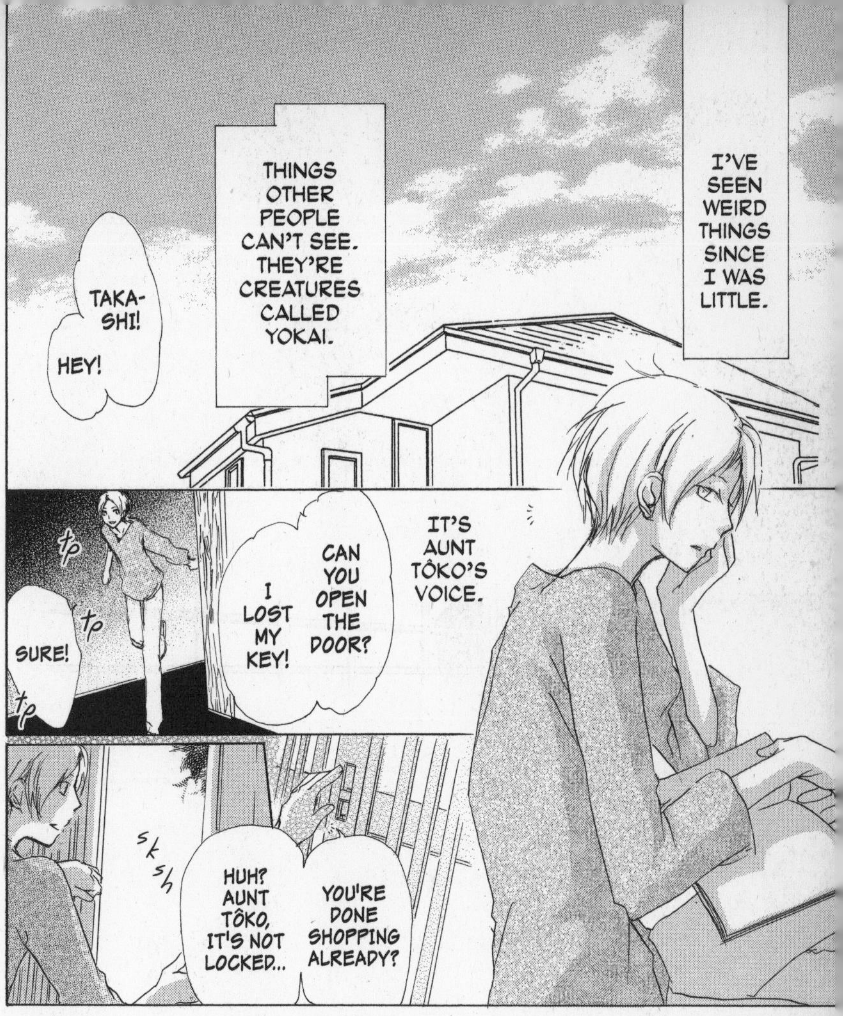
I'VE SEEN WEIRD THINGS SINCE I WAS LITTLE.
THINGS OTHER PEOPLE CAN'T SEE. THEY'RE CREATURES CALLED YOKAI.
TAKA-SHI!
HEY!
IT'S AUNT TÔKO'S VOICE.
CAN YOU OPEN THE DOOR?
I LOST MY KEY!
tp
tp
SURE!
tp
sksh
YOU'RE DONE SHOPPING ALREADY?
HUH? AUNT TÔKO, IT'S NOT LOCKED...

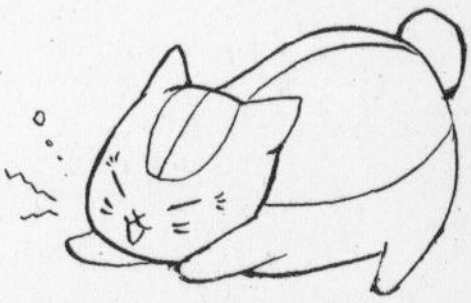

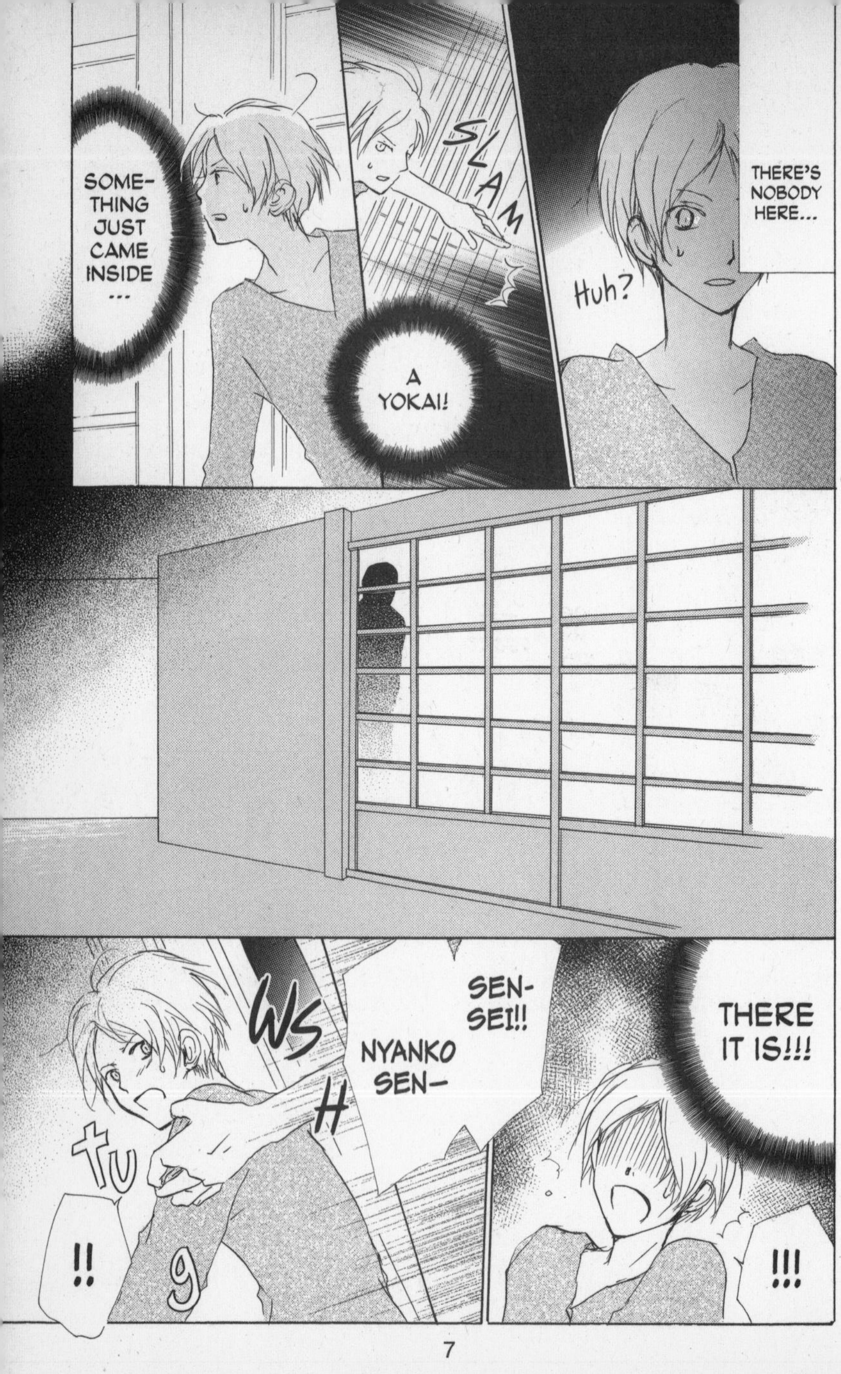
SOME-THING JUST CAME INSIDE...
SLAM
A YOKAI!
Huh?
THERE'S NOBODY HERE...
tug
!!
WSH
NYANKO SEN-
SEN-SEI!!
THERE IT IS!!!
!!!

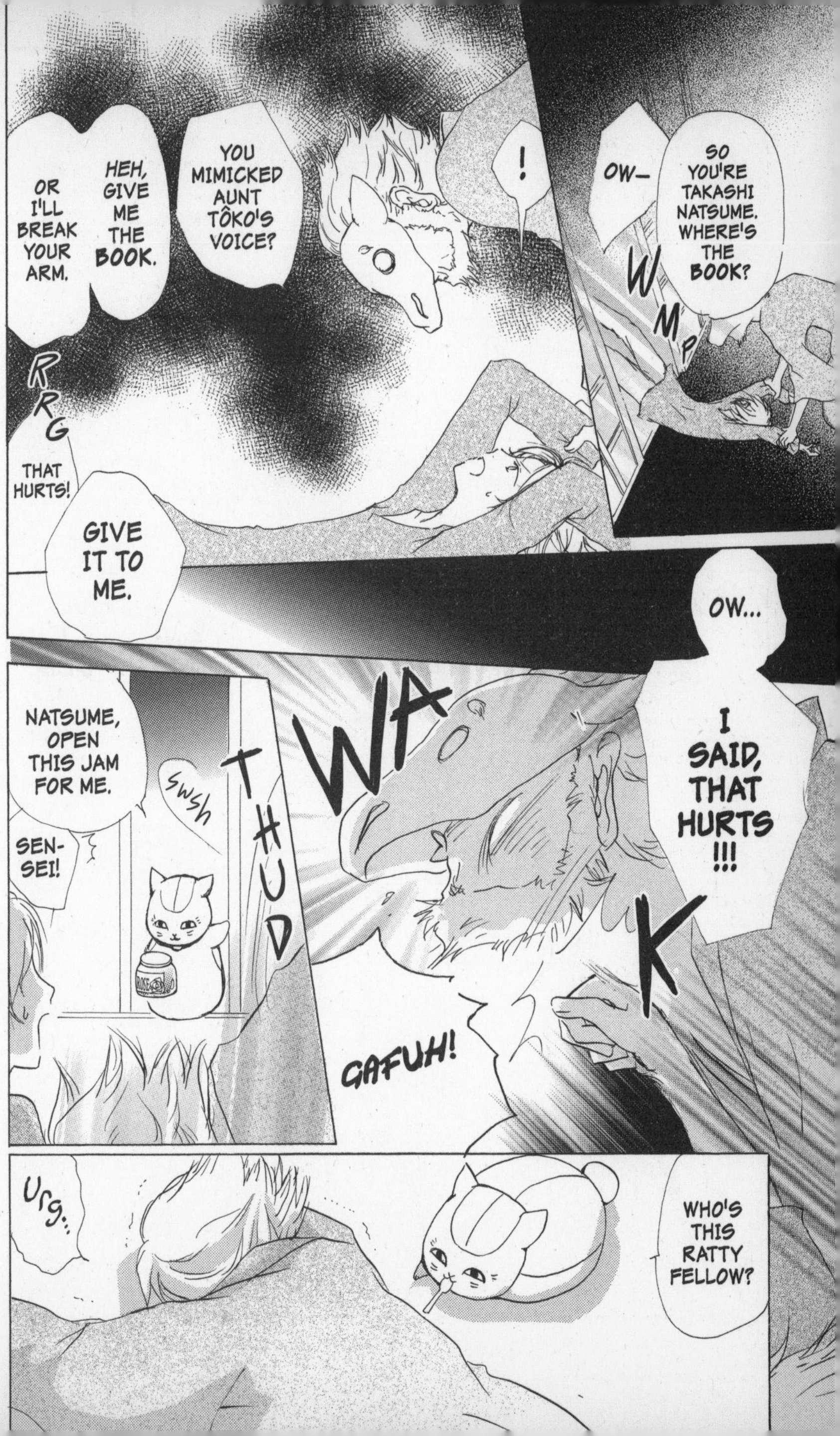
SO YOU'RE TAKASHI NATSUME. WHERE'S THE BOOK?
OW—
WMP
!
YOU MIMICKED AUNT TÔKO'S VOICE?
HEH, GIVE ME THE BOOK.
OR I'LL BREAK YOUR ARM.
RRG
THAT HURTS!
GIVE IT TO ME.
OW...
I SAID, THAT HURTS!!!
WAK
GAFUH!
NATSUME, OPEN THIS JAM FOR ME.
swsh
THUD
SEN-SEI!
ROSE
WHO'S THIS RATTY FELLOW?
Urg...

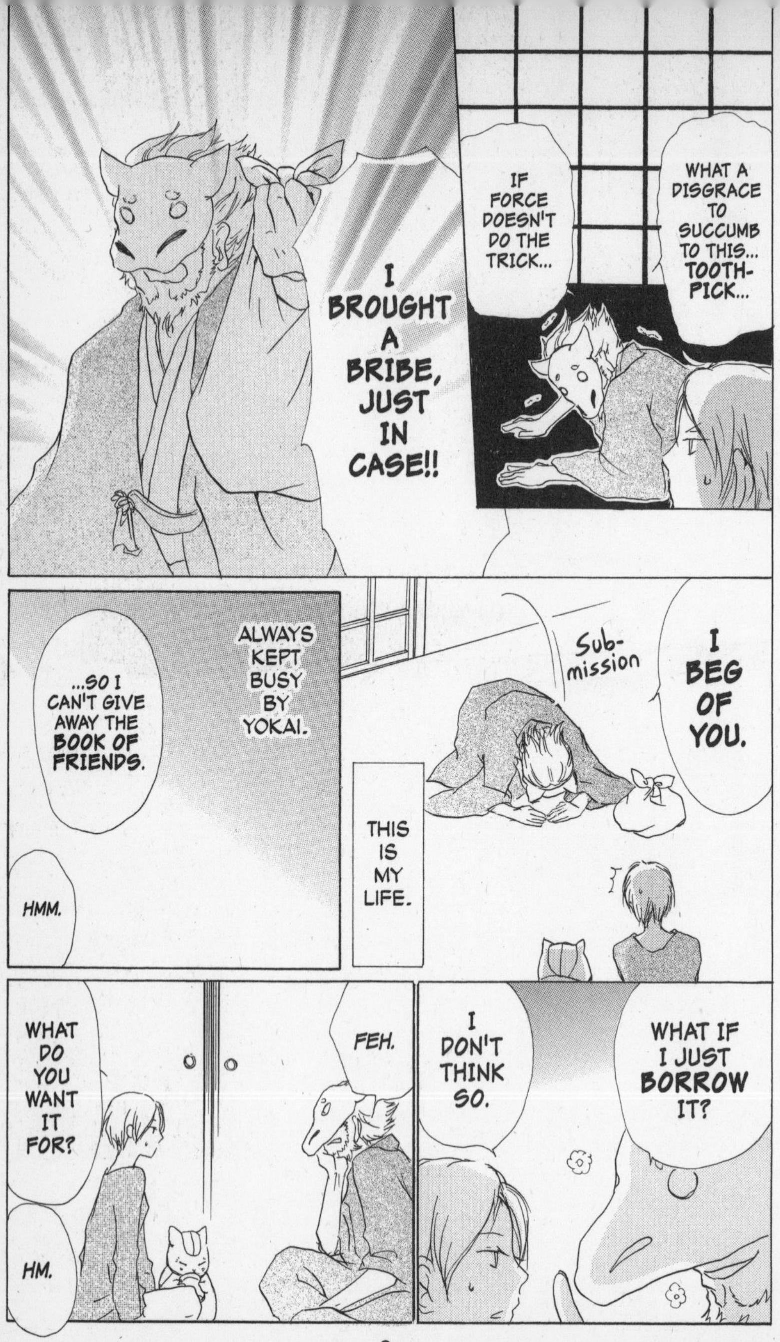
WHAT A DISGRACE TO SUCCUMB TO THIS... TOOTH-PICK...
IF FORCE DOESN'T DO THE TRICK...
I BROUGHT A BRIBE, JUST IN CASE!!
I BEG OF YOU.
Sub-mission
THIS IS MY LIFE.
ALWAYS KEPT BUSY BY YOKAI.
...SO I CAN'T GIVE AWAY THE BOOK OF FRIENDS.
HMM.
WHAT IF I JUST BORROW IT?
I DON'T THINK SO.
FEH.
WHAT DO YOU WANT IT FOR?
HM.

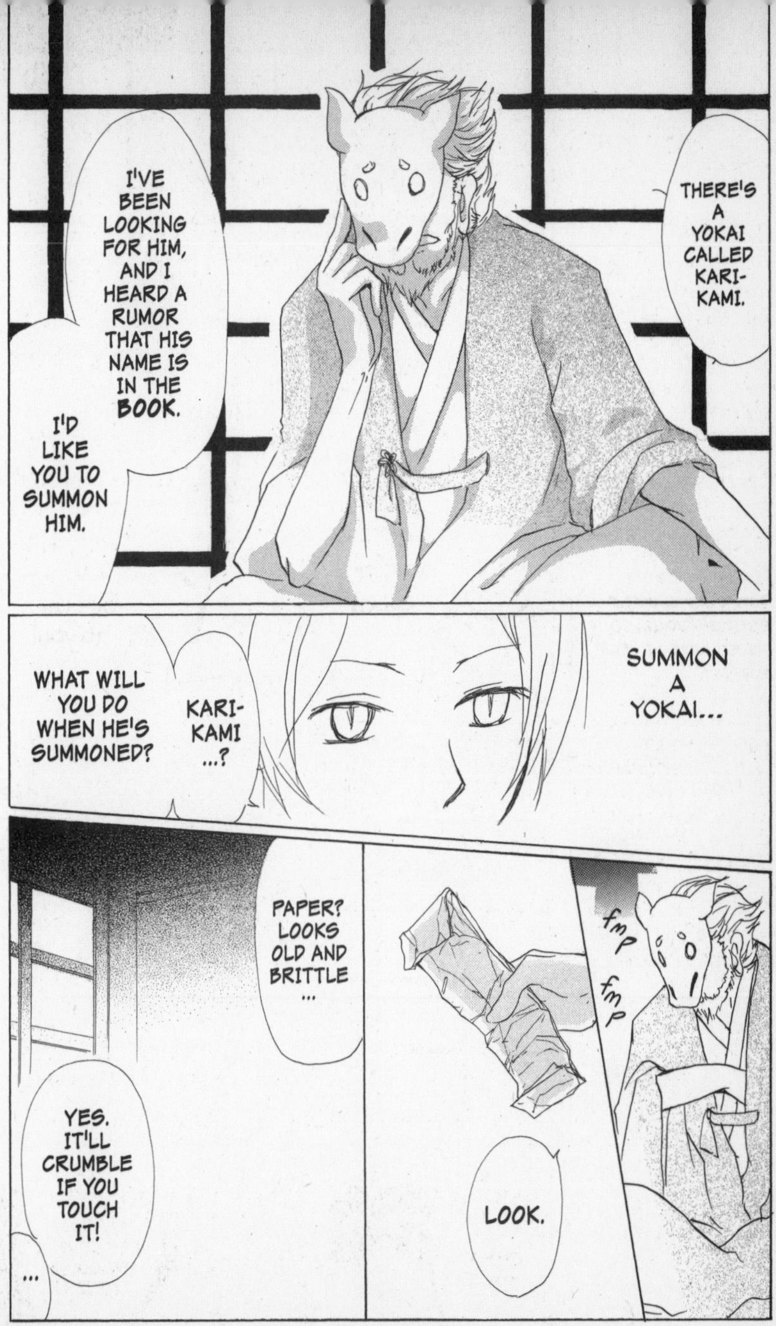
THERE'S A YOKAI CALLED KARI-KAMI.
I'VE BEEN LOOKING FOR HIM, AND I HEARD A RUMOR THAT HIS NAME IS IN THE BOOK.
I'D LIKE YOU TO SUMMON HIM.
SUMMON A YOKAI...
KARI-KAMI ...?
WHAT WILL YOU DO WHEN HE'S SUMMONED?
fmp fmp
LOOK.
PAPER? LOOKS OLD AND BRITTLE ...
YES. IT'LL CRUMBLE IF YOU TOUCH IT!
...

01

Hello, I'm Midorikawa. This is my 20th total graphic novel. I'm so happy I get to mark another milestone as a manga artist.

Thank you to everyone who has followed along on my journey. I'd like to continue having fun making interesting manga, so please keep up your support.

In March 2011 there was a great and terrible earthquake in Japan. I would like to express my deepest sympathy to everyone who has lost loved ones. May the dead rest in peace and those left behind find some solace.

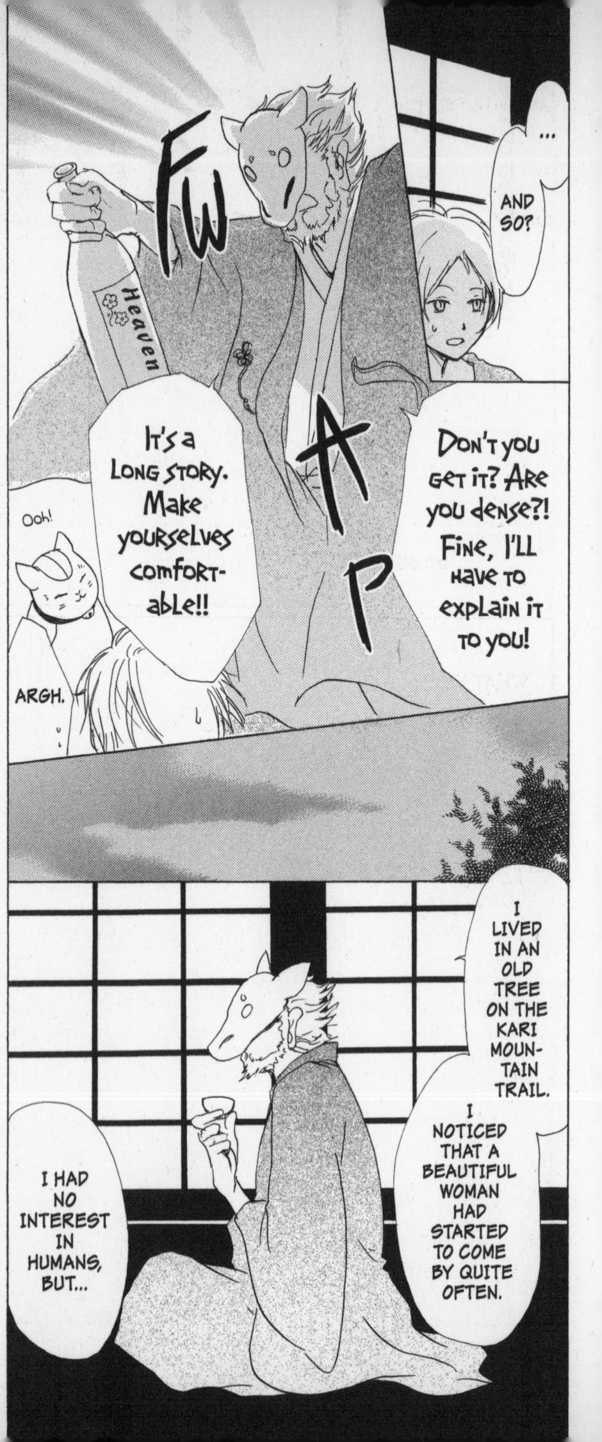
...
AND SO?
Don't you get it? Are you dense?! Fine, I'll have to explain it to you!
FWAP
Heaven
It's a long story. Make yourselves comfortable!!
Ooh!
ARGH.
I LIVED IN AN OLD TREE ON THE KARI MOUNTAIN TRAIL.
I NOTICED THAT A BEAUTIFUL WOMAN HAD STARTED TO COME BY QUITE OFTEN.
I HAD NO INTEREST IN HUMANS, BUT...

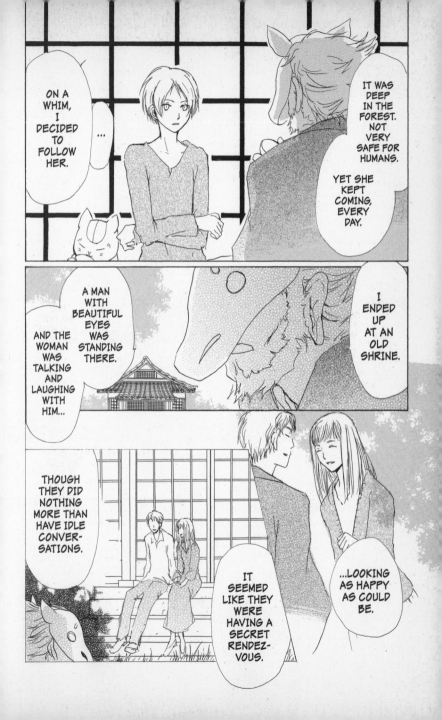

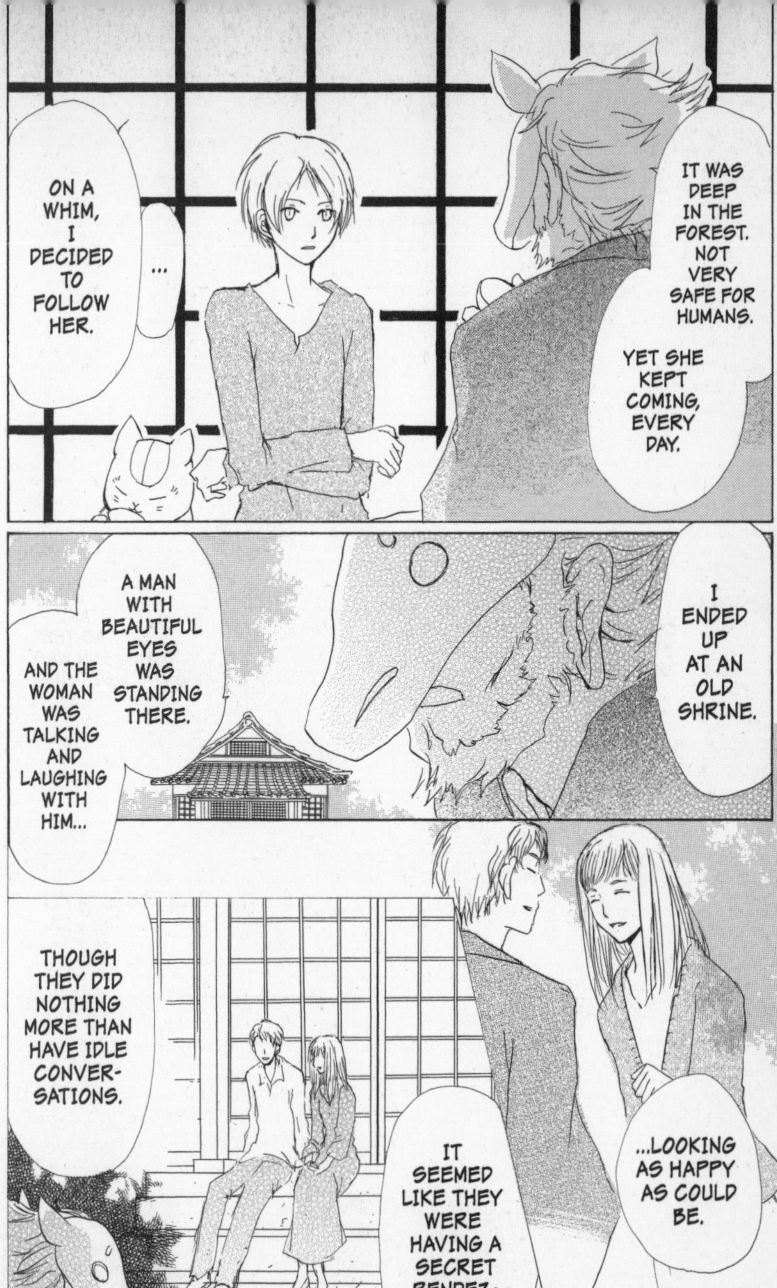
IT WAS DEEP IN THE FOREST. NOT VERY SAFE FOR HUMANS.
YET SHE KEPT COMING, EVERY DAY.
...
ON A WHIM, I DECIDED TO FOLLOW HER.
I ENDED UP AT AN OLD SHRINE.
A MAN WITH BEAUTIFUL EYES WAS STANDING THERE.
AND THE WOMAN WAS TALKING AND LAUGHING WITH HIM...
...LOOKING AS HAPPY AS COULD BE.
IT SEEMED LIKE THEY WERE HAVING A SECRET RENDEZ-VOUS.
THOUGH THEY DID NOTHING MORE THAN HAVE IDLE CONVER-SATIONS.

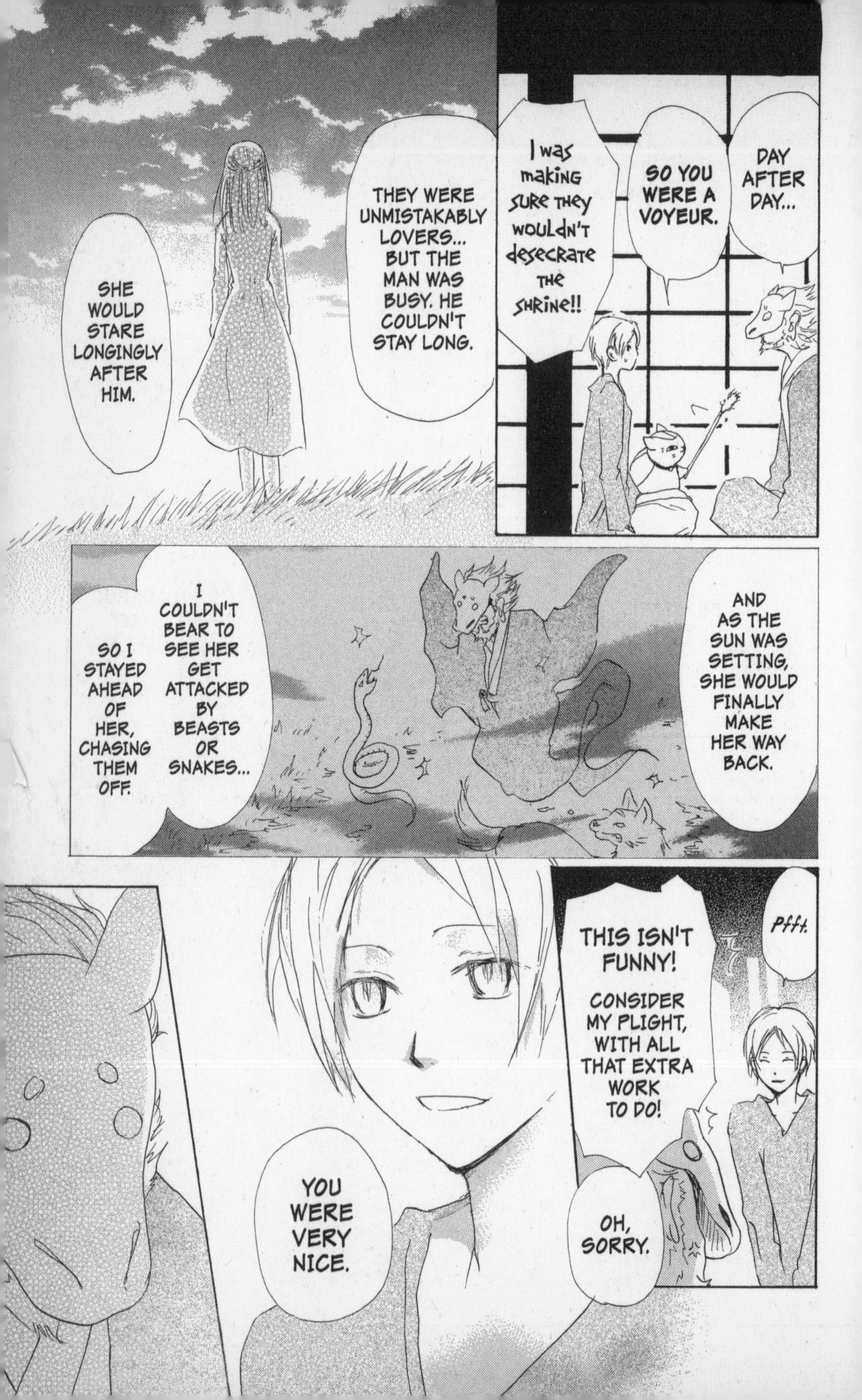
DAY AFTER DAY...
SO YOU WERE A VOYEUR.
I was making sure they wouldn't desecrate the shrine!!
THEY WERE UNMISTAKABLY LOVERS... BUT THE MAN WAS BUSY. HE COULDN'T STAY LONG.
SHE WOULD STARE LONGINGLY AFTER HIM.
AND AS THE SUN WAS SETTING, SHE WOULD FINALLY MAKE HER WAY BACK.
I COULDN'T BEAR TO SEE HER GET ATTACKED BY BEASTS OR SNAKES...
SO I STAYED AHEAD OF HER, CHASING THEM OFF.
Pfft.
THIS ISN'T FUNNY!
CONSIDER MY PLIGHT, WITH ALL THAT EXTRA WORK TO DO!
OH, SORRY.
YOU WERE VERY NICE.

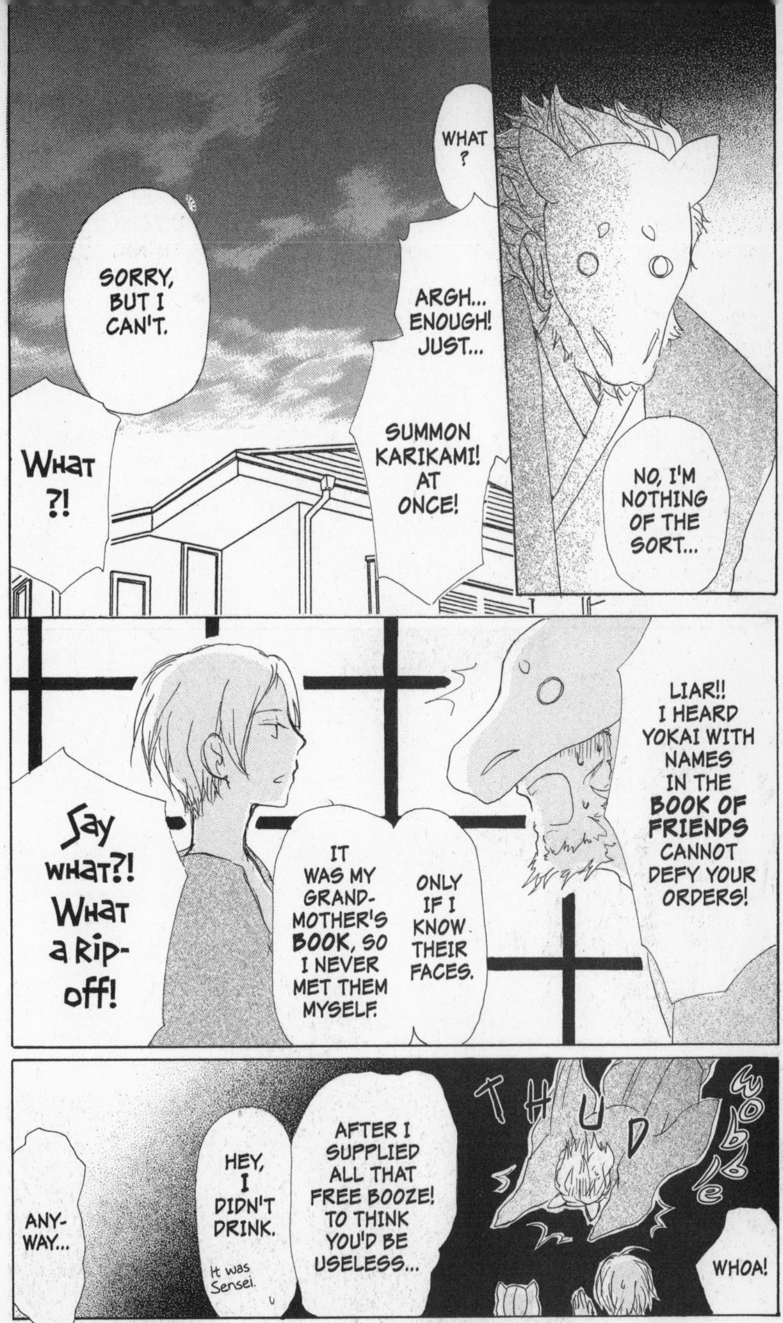
NO, I'M NOTHING OF THE SORT...
WHAT?
ARGH... ENOUGH! JUST...
SUMMON KARIKAMI! AT ONCE!
SORRY, BUT I CAN'T.
WHAT?!
LIAR!! I HEARD YOKAI WITH NAMES IN THE BOOK OF FRIENDS CANNOT DEFY YOUR ORDERS!
ONLY IF I KNOW THEIR FACES.
IT WAS MY GRAND-MOTHER'S BOOK, SO I NEVER MET THEM MYSELF.
Say what?! What a rip-off!
wobble
THUD
WHOA!
AFTER I SUPPLIED ALL THAT FREE BOOZE! TO THINK YOU'D BE USELESS...
HEY, I DIDN'T DRINK.
It was Sensei.
ANY-WAY...

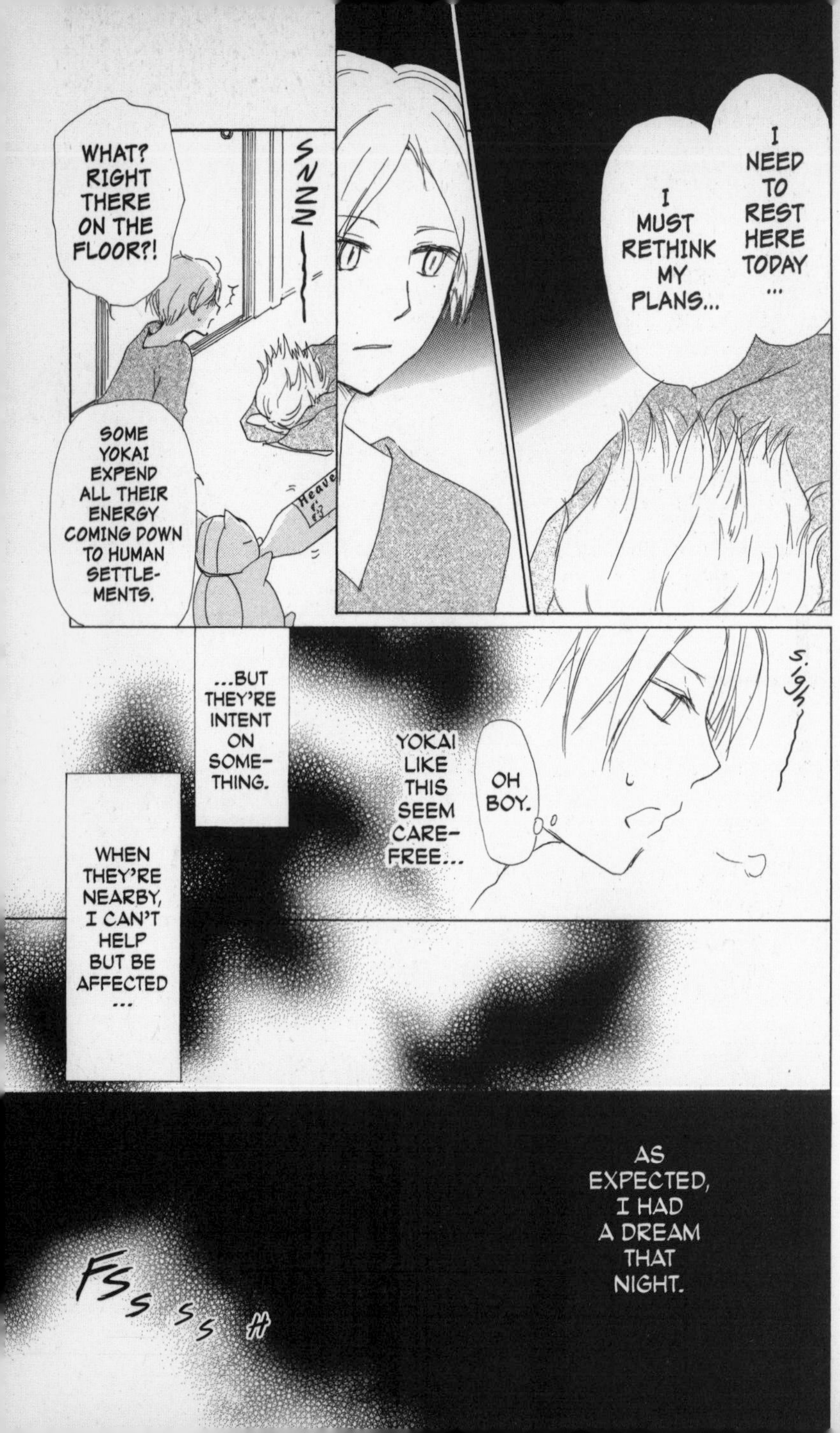
I NEED TO REST HERE TODAY...
I MUST RETHINK MY PLANS...
SNZZ——
WHAT? RIGHT THERE ON THE FLOOR?!
SOME YOKAI EXPEND ALL THEIR ENERGY COMING DOWN TO HUMAN SETTLEMENTS.
sigh
OH BOY.
YOKAI LIKE THIS SEEM CAREFREE...
...BUT THEY'RE INTENT ON SOMETHING.
WHEN THEY'RE NEARBY, I CAN'T HELP BUT BE AFFECTED...
AS EXPECTED, I HAD A DREAM THAT NIGHT.
FSSSSH

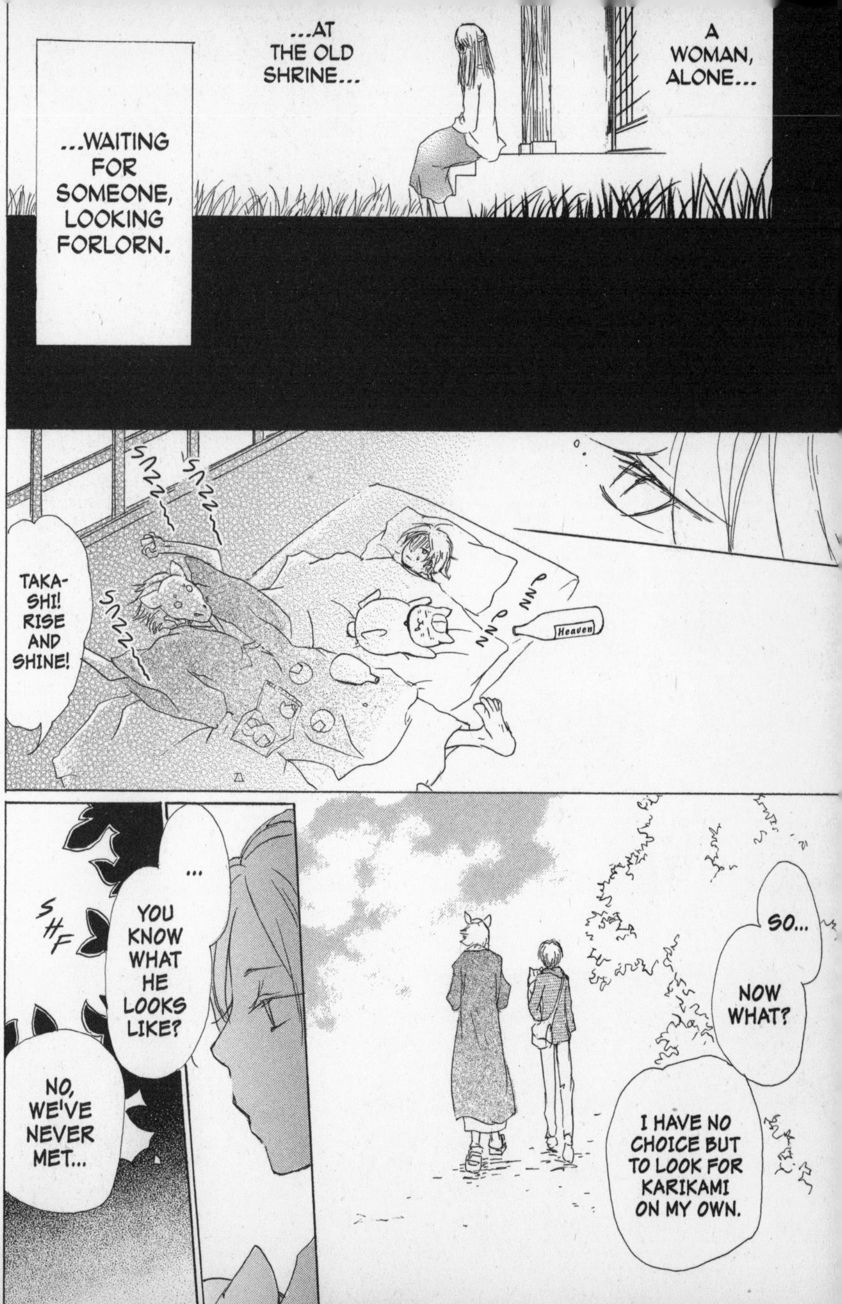
A WOMAN, ALONE...
...AT THE OLD SHRINE...
...WAITING FOR SOMEONE, LOOKING FORLORN.
SNZZZ
SNZZZ
Heaven
TAKASHI! RISE AND SHINE!
SNZZZ
SO...
NOW WHAT?
I HAVE NO CHOICE BUT TO LOOK FOR KARIKAMI ON MY OWN.
...
YOU KNOW WHAT HE LOOKS LIKE?
SHF
NO, WE'VE NEVER MET...

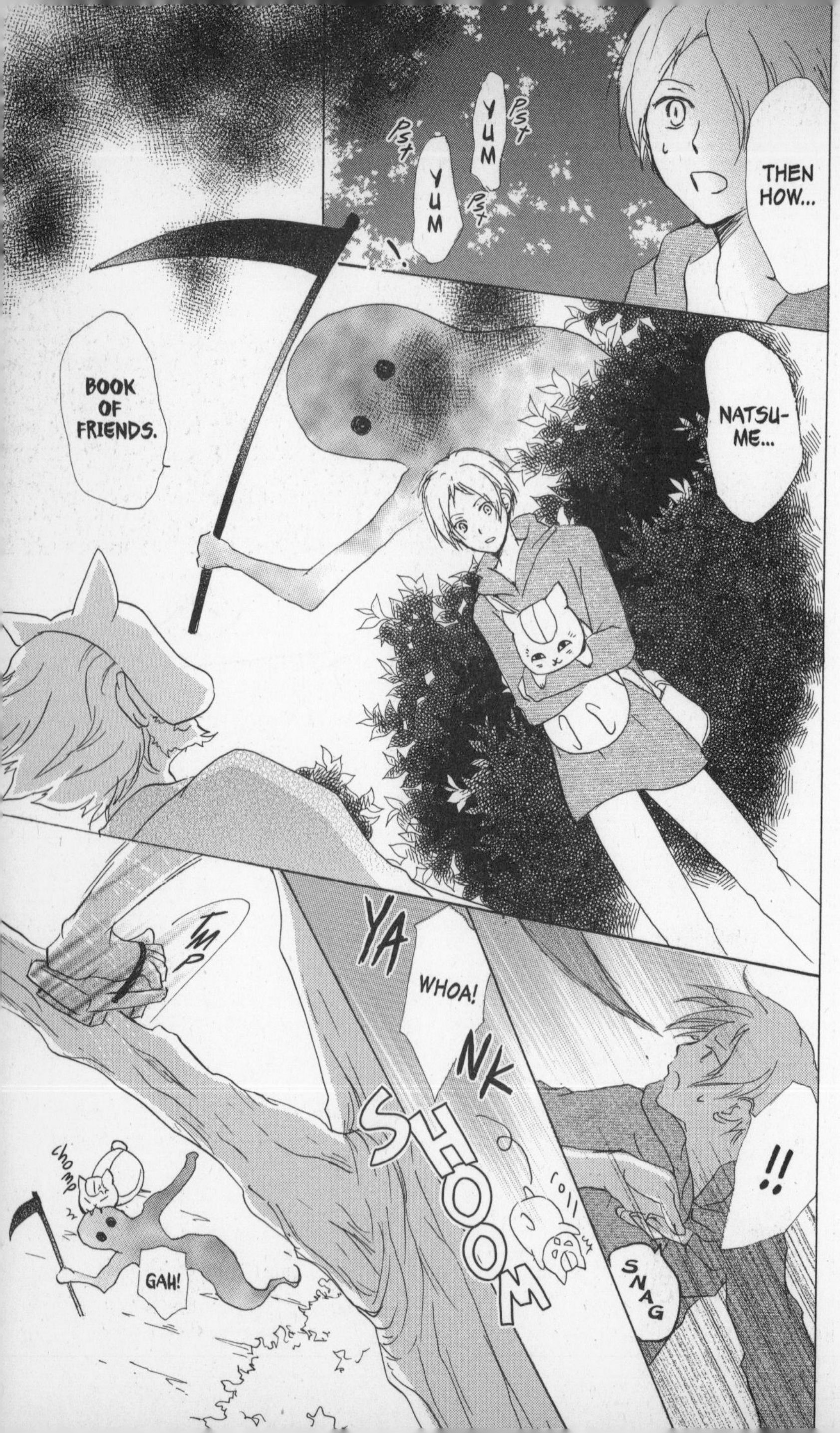
THEN HOW...
PST
YUM
PST
YUM
!
NATSU-ME...
BOOK OF FRIENDS.
!!
YANK
WHOA!
TMP
SNAG
roll
SHOOM
chomp
GAH!

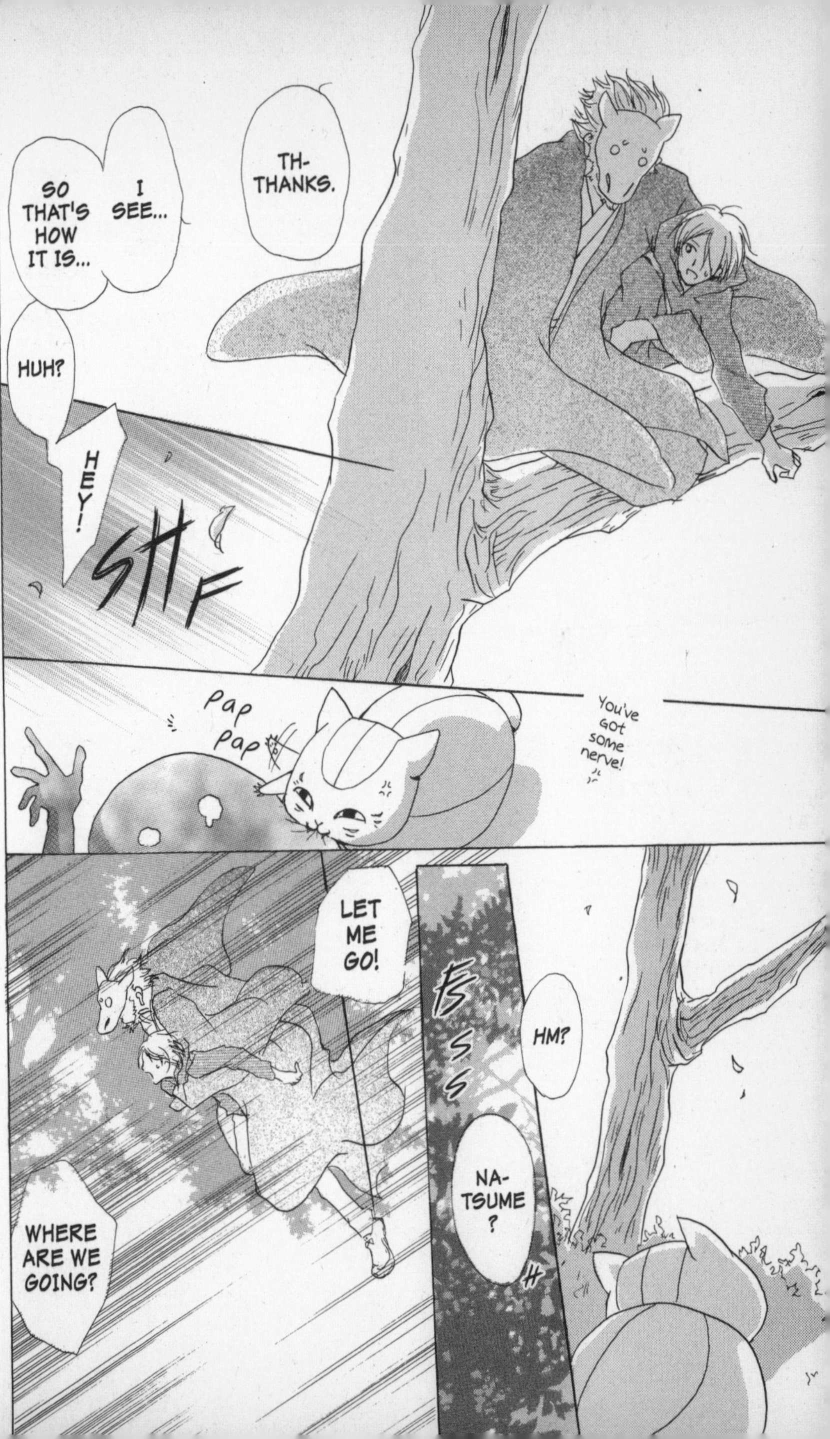
TH-THANKS.
I SEE...
SO THAT'S HOW IT IS...
HUH?
HEY!
SHF
You've got some nerve!
Pap pap
FSSS
HM?
NA-TSUME?
LET ME GO!
WHERE ARE WE GOING?

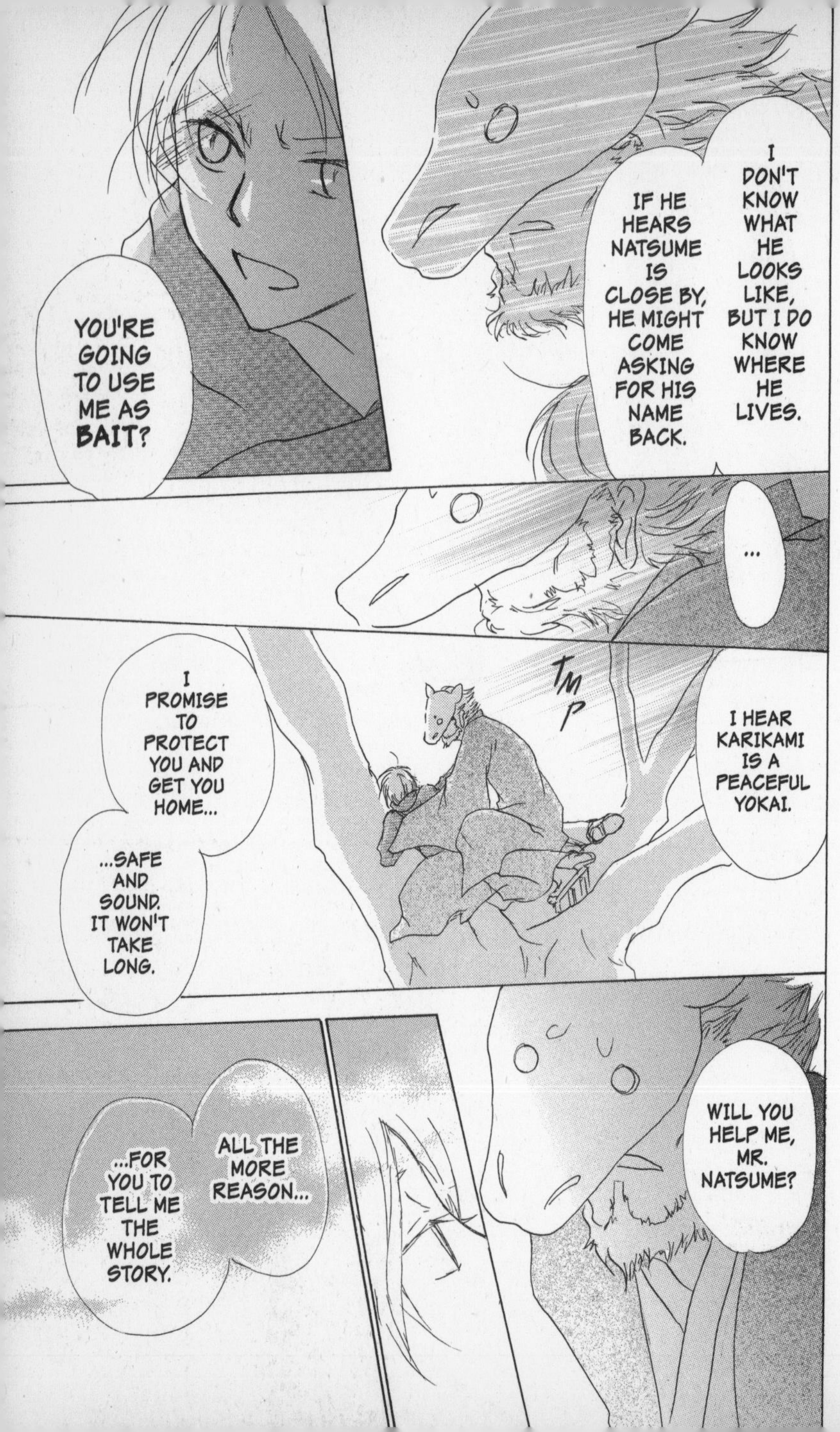
I DON'T KNOW WHAT HE LOOKS LIKE, BUT I DO KNOW WHERE HE LIVES.
IF HE HEARS NATSUME IS CLOSE BY, HE MIGHT COME ASKING FOR HIS NAME BACK.
YOU'RE GOING TO USE ME AS **BAIT**?
...
I HEAR KARIKAMI IS A PEACEFUL YOKAI.
TMP
I PROMISE TO PROTECT YOU AND GET YOU HOME...
...SAFE AND SOUND. IT WON'T TAKE LONG.
WILL YOU HELP ME, MR. NATSUME?
ALL THE MORE REASON...
...FOR YOU TO TELL ME THE WHOLE STORY.

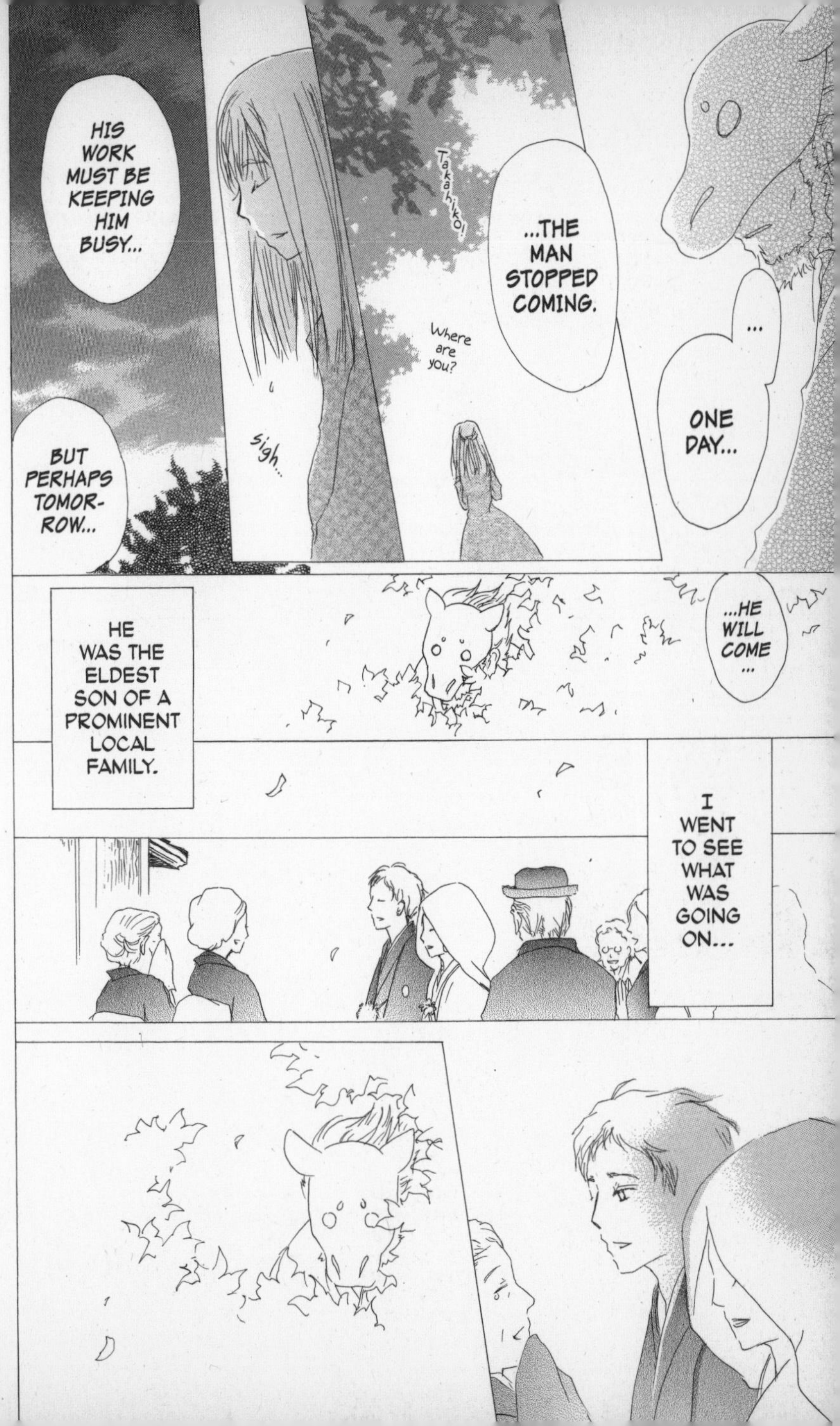
...
ONE DAY...
...THE MAN STOPPED COMING.
Takahiko!
Where are you?
HIS WORK MUST BE KEEPING HIM BUSY...
sigh...
BUT PERHAPS TOMORROW...
...HE WILL COME...
HE WAS THE ELDEST SON OF A PROMINENT LOCAL FAMILY.
I WENT TO SEE WHAT WAS GOING ON...

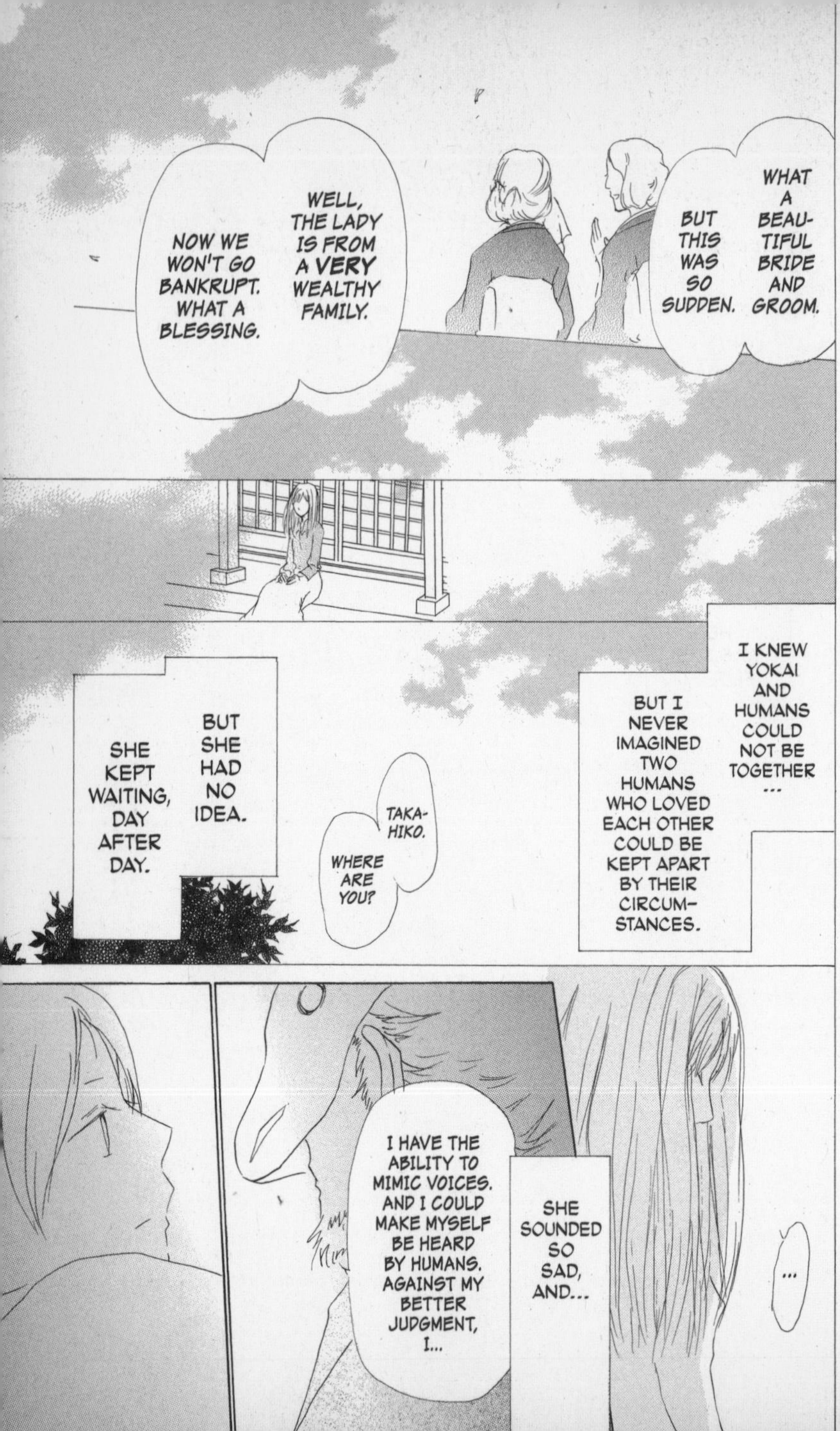
WHAT A BEAU-TIFUL BRIDE AND GROOM.
BUT THIS WAS SO SUDDEN.
WELL, THE LADY IS FROM A **VERY** WEALTHY FAMILY.
NOW WE WON'T GO BANKRUPT. WHAT A BLESSING.
I KNEW YOKAI AND HUMANS COULD NOT BE TOGETHER...
BUT I NEVER IMAGINED TWO HUMANS WHO LOVED EACH OTHER COULD BE KEPT APART BY THEIR CIRCUM-STANCES.
TAKA-HIKO.
WHERE ARE YOU?
BUT SHE HAD NO IDEA.
SHE KEPT WAITING, DAY AFTER DAY.
...
SHE SOUNDED SO SAD, AND...
I HAVE THE ABILITY TO MIMIC VOICES. AND I COULD MAKE MYSELF BE HEARD BY HUMANS. AGAINST MY BETTER JUDGMENT, I...

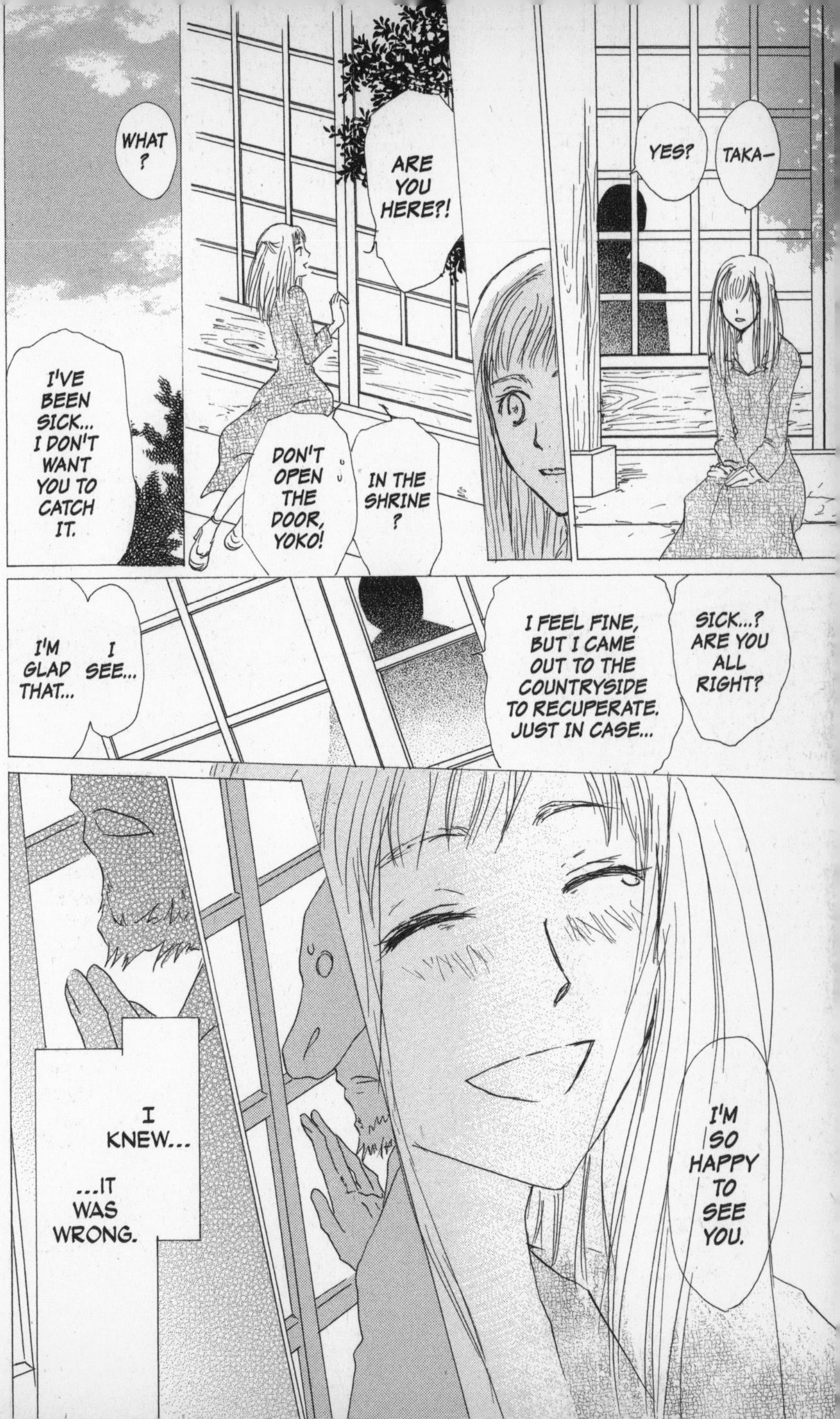
TAKA-
YES?
ARE YOU HERE?!
IN THE SHRINE?
DON'T OPEN THE DOOR, YOKO!
WHAT?
I'VE BEEN SICK... I DON'T WANT YOU TO CATCH IT.
SICK...? ARE YOU ALL RIGHT?
I FEEL FINE, BUT I CAME OUT TO THE COUNTRYSIDE TO RECUPERATE. JUST IN CASE...
I SEE...
I'M GLAD THAT...
I'M SO HAPPY TO SEE YOU.
I KNEW...
...IT WAS WRONG.

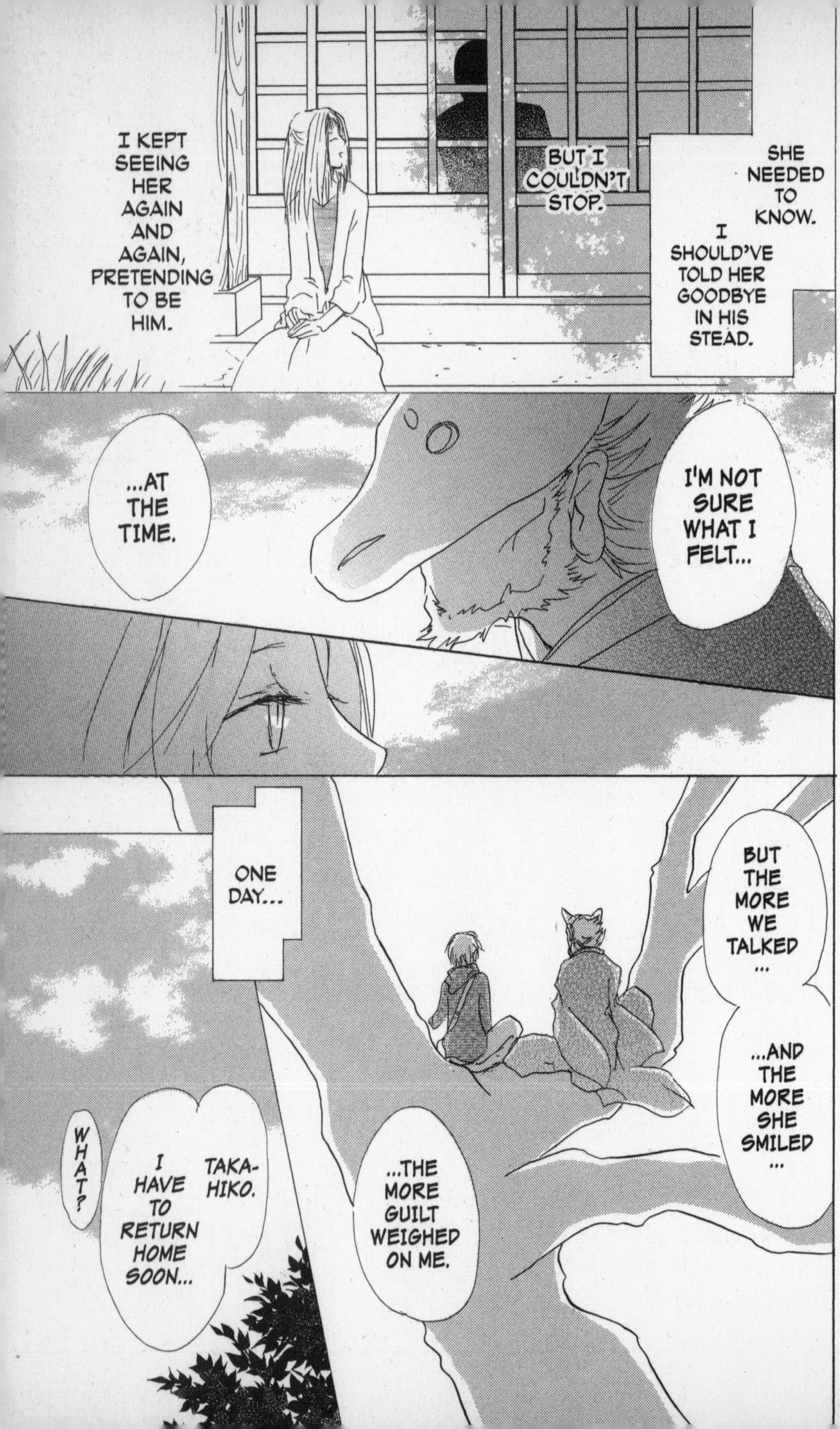
SHE NEEDED TO KNOW.
I SHOULD'VE TOLD HER GOODBYE IN HIS STEAD.
BUT I COULDN'T STOP.
I KEPT SEEING HER AGAIN AND AGAIN, PRETENDING TO BE HIM.
I'M NOT SURE WHAT I FELT...
...AT THE TIME.
BUT THE MORE WE TALKED...
...AND THE MORE SHE SMILED...
...THE MORE GUILT WEIGHED ON ME.
ONE DAY...
TAKAHIKO. I HAVE TO RETURN HOME SOON...
WHAT?

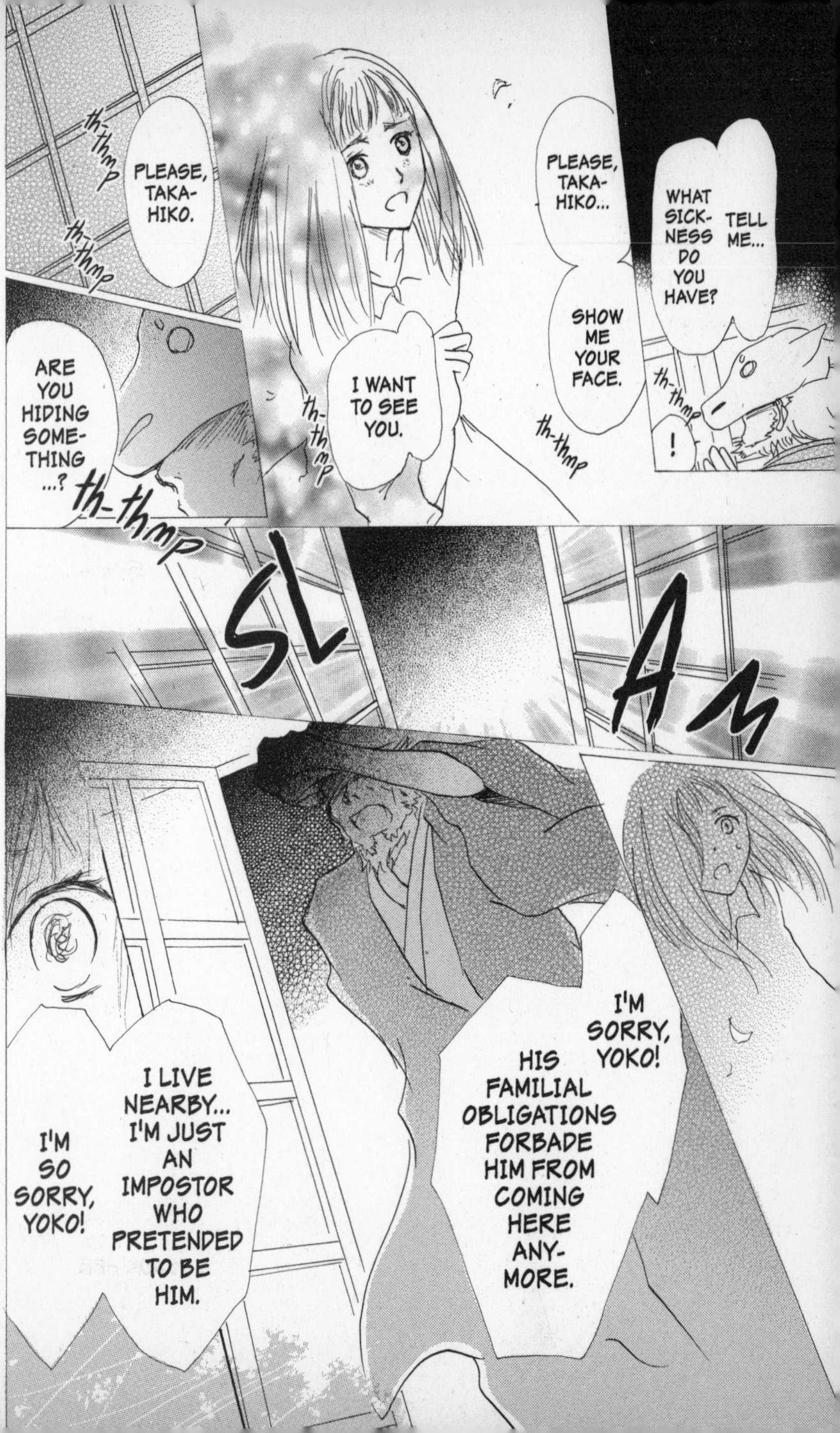
TELL ME...
WHAT SICKNESS DO YOU HAVE?
th-thmp
!
PLEASE, TAKA-HIKO...
SHOW ME YOUR FACE.
th-thmp
I WANT TO SEE YOU.
th-thmp
PLEASE, TAKA-HIKO.
th-thmp
th-thmp
ARE YOU HIDING SOME-THING ...?
th-thmp
SLAM
I'M SORRY, YOKO!
HIS FAMILIAL OBLIGATIONS FORBADE HIM FROM COMING HERE ANY-MORE.
I LIVE NEARBY... I'M JUST AN IMPOSTOR WHO PRETENDED TO BE HIM.
I'M SO SORRY, YOKO!

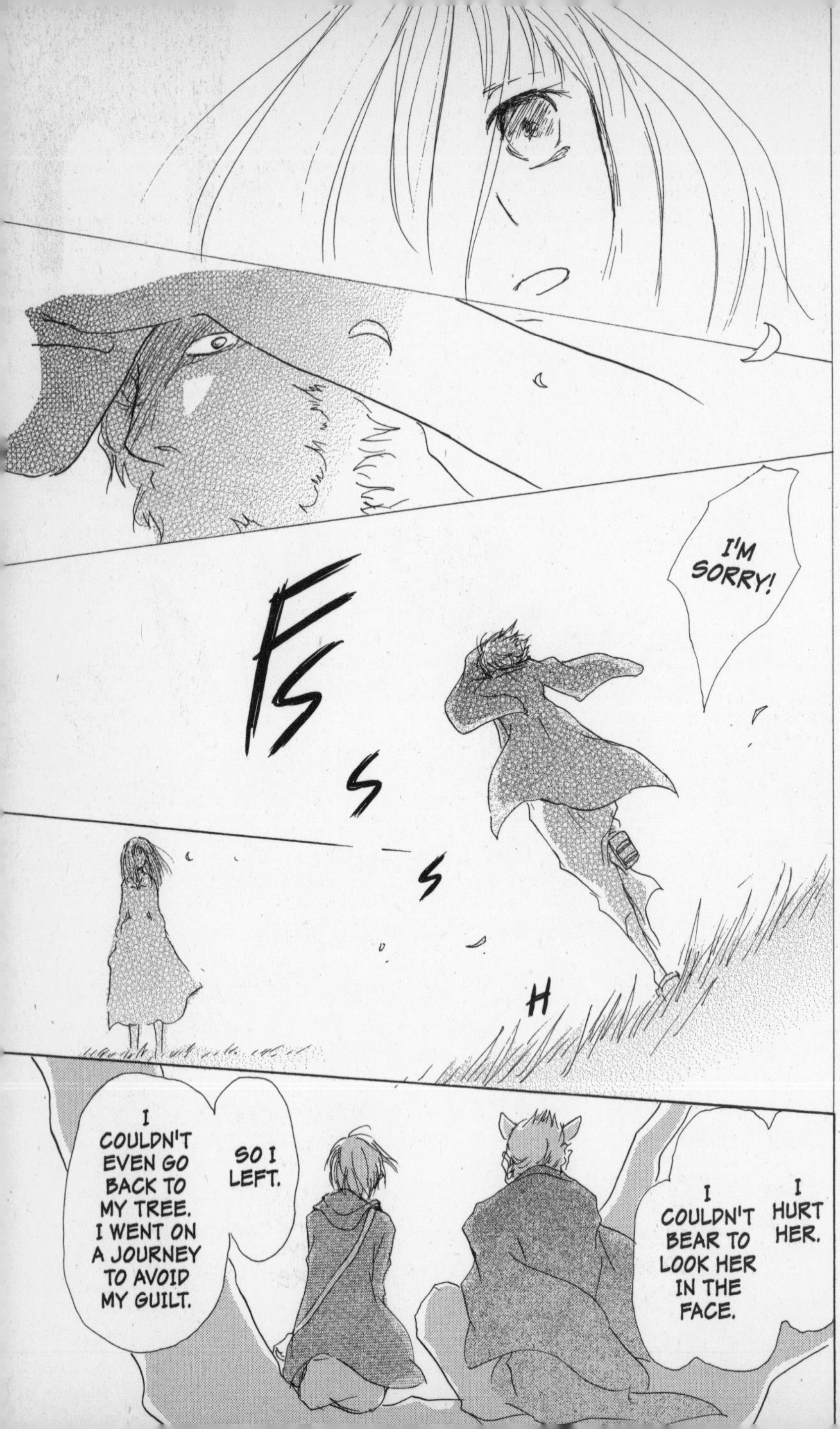
I'M SORRY!
FSSSH
I HURT HER.
I COULDN'T BEAR TO LOOK HER IN THE FACE.
SO I LEFT.
I COULDN'T EVEN GO BACK TO MY TREE. I WENT ON A JOURNEY TO AVOID MY GUILT.

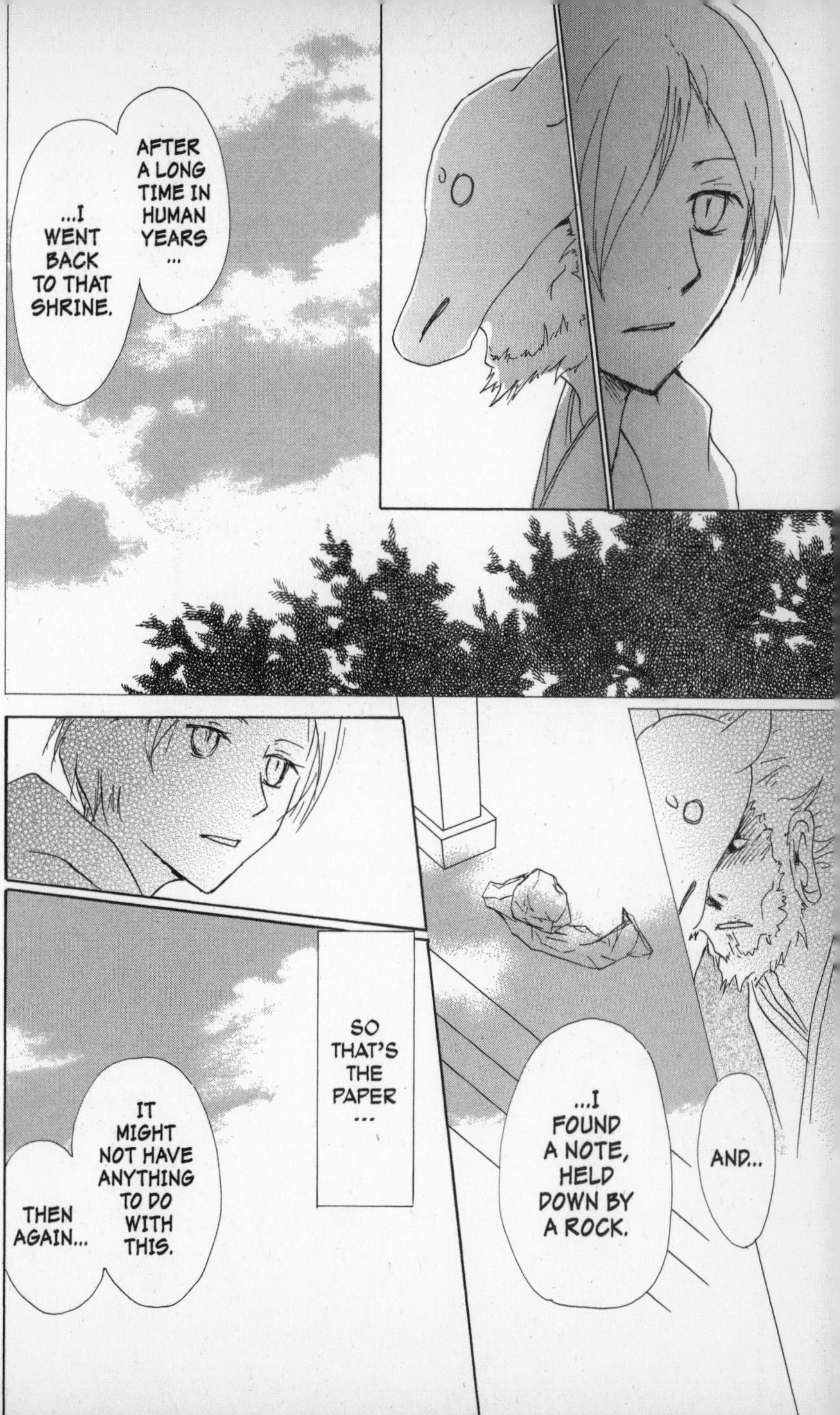
AFTER A LONG TIME IN HUMAN YEARS ...
...I WENT BACK TO THAT SHRINE.
AND...
...I FOUND A NOTE, HELD DOWN BY A ROCK.
SO THAT'S THE PAPER ...
IT MIGHT NOT HAVE ANYTHING TO DO WITH THIS.
THEN AGAIN...

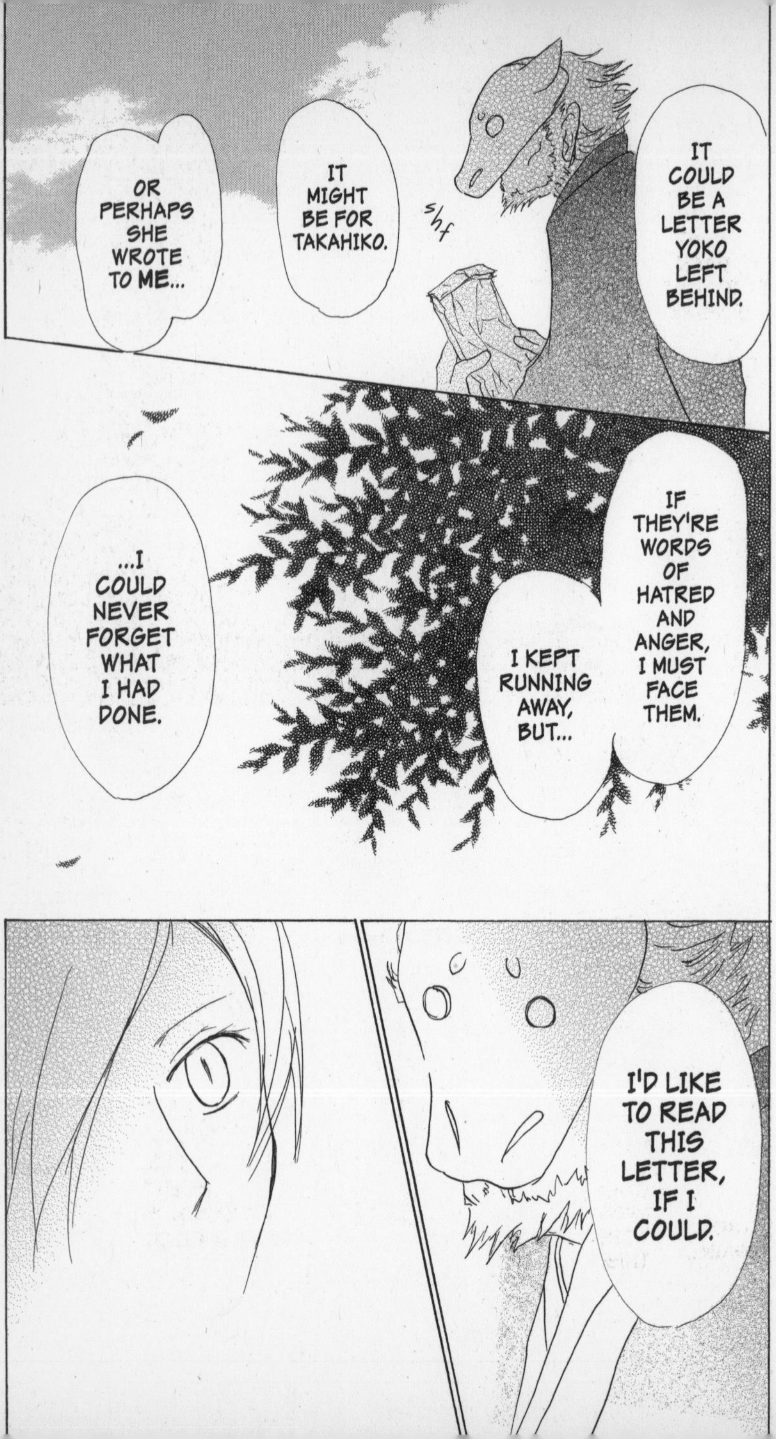
IT COULD BE A LETTER YOKO LEFT BEHIND.
shf
IT MIGHT BE FOR TAKAHIKO.
OR PERHAPS SHE WROTE TO ME...
IF THEY'RE WORDS OF HATRED AND ANGER, I MUST FACE THEM.
I KEPT RUNNING AWAY, BUT...
...I COULD NEVER FORGET WHAT I HAD DONE.
I'D LIKE TO READ THIS LETTER, IF I COULD.

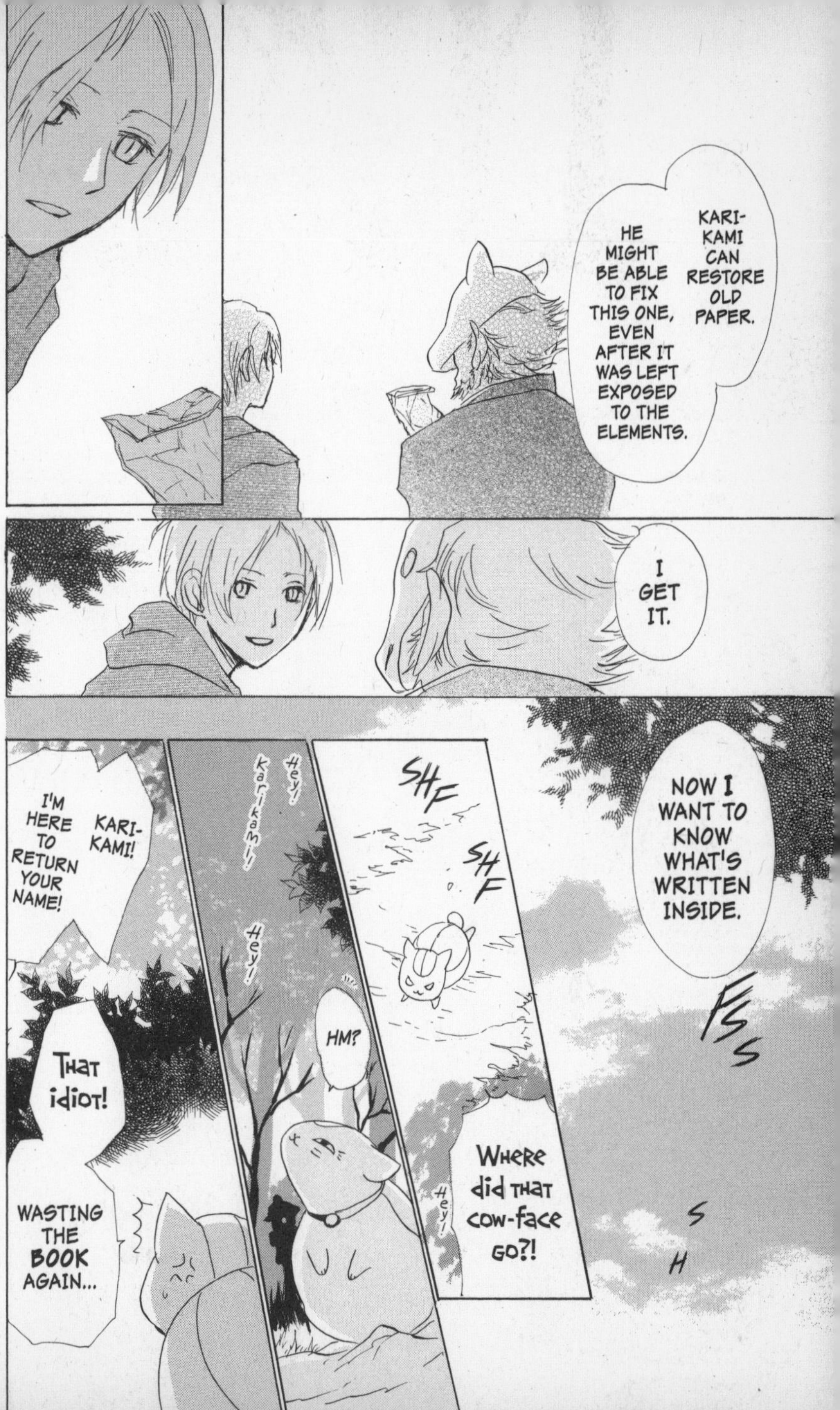
KARI-KAMI CAN RESTORE OLD PAPER.
HE MIGHT BE ABLE TO FIX THIS ONE, EVEN AFTER IT WAS LEFT EXPOSED TO THE ELEMENTS.
I GET IT.
NOW I WANT TO KNOW WHAT'S WRITTEN INSIDE.
FSSS
SH
SHF
SHF
HM?
Where did that cow-face go?!
Hey!
Hey! Karikami!
Hey!
KARI-KAMI!
I'M HERE TO RETURN YOUR NAME!
That idiot!
WASTING THE BOOK AGAIN...

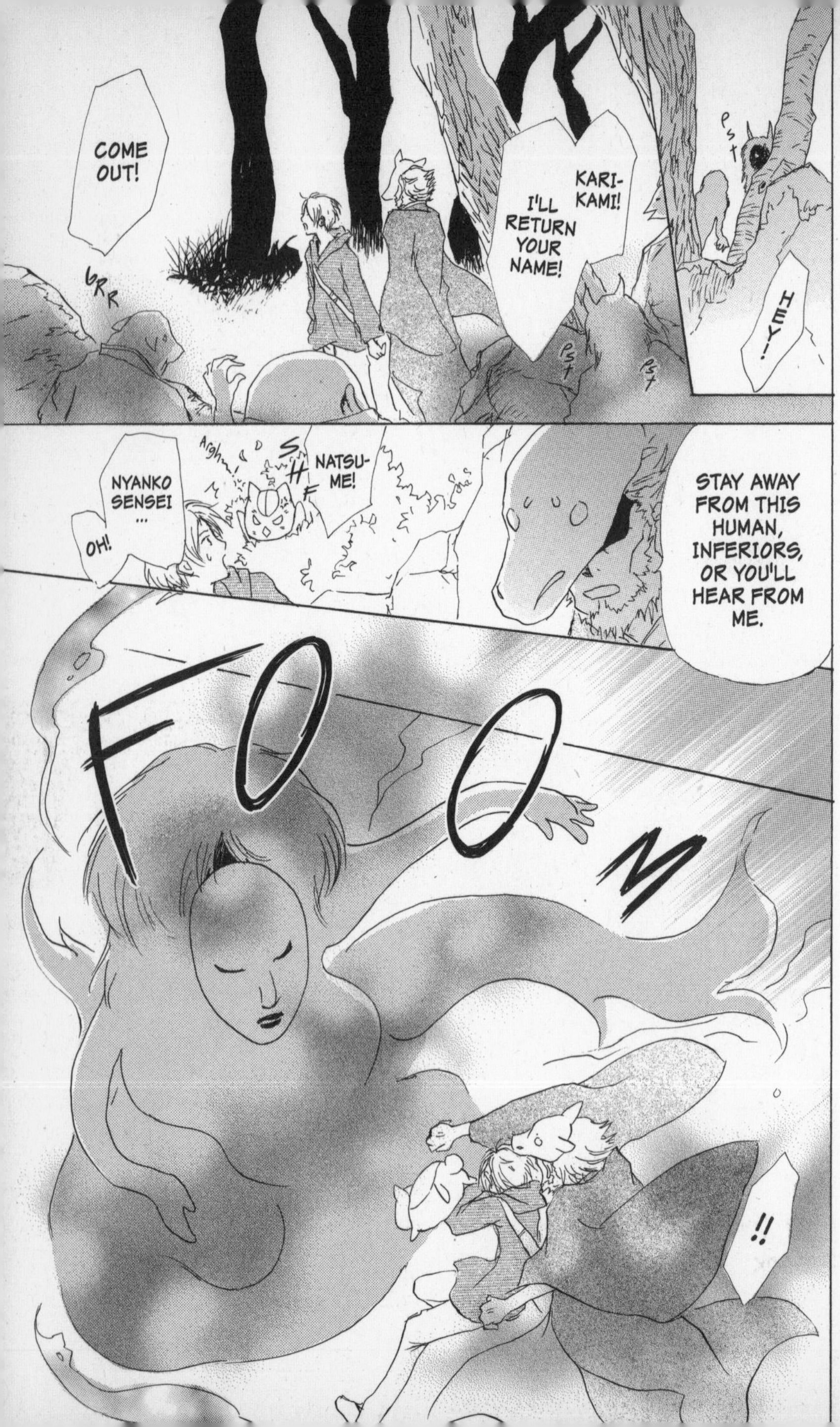
pst
HEY!
KARI-KAMI! I'LL RETURN YOUR NAME!
COME OUT!
GRR
pst
pst
STAY AWAY FROM THIS HUMAN, INFERIORS, OR YOU'LL HEAR FROM ME.
NATSU-ME!
SHF
Argh
NYANKO SENSEI ...
OH!
FOOM
!!

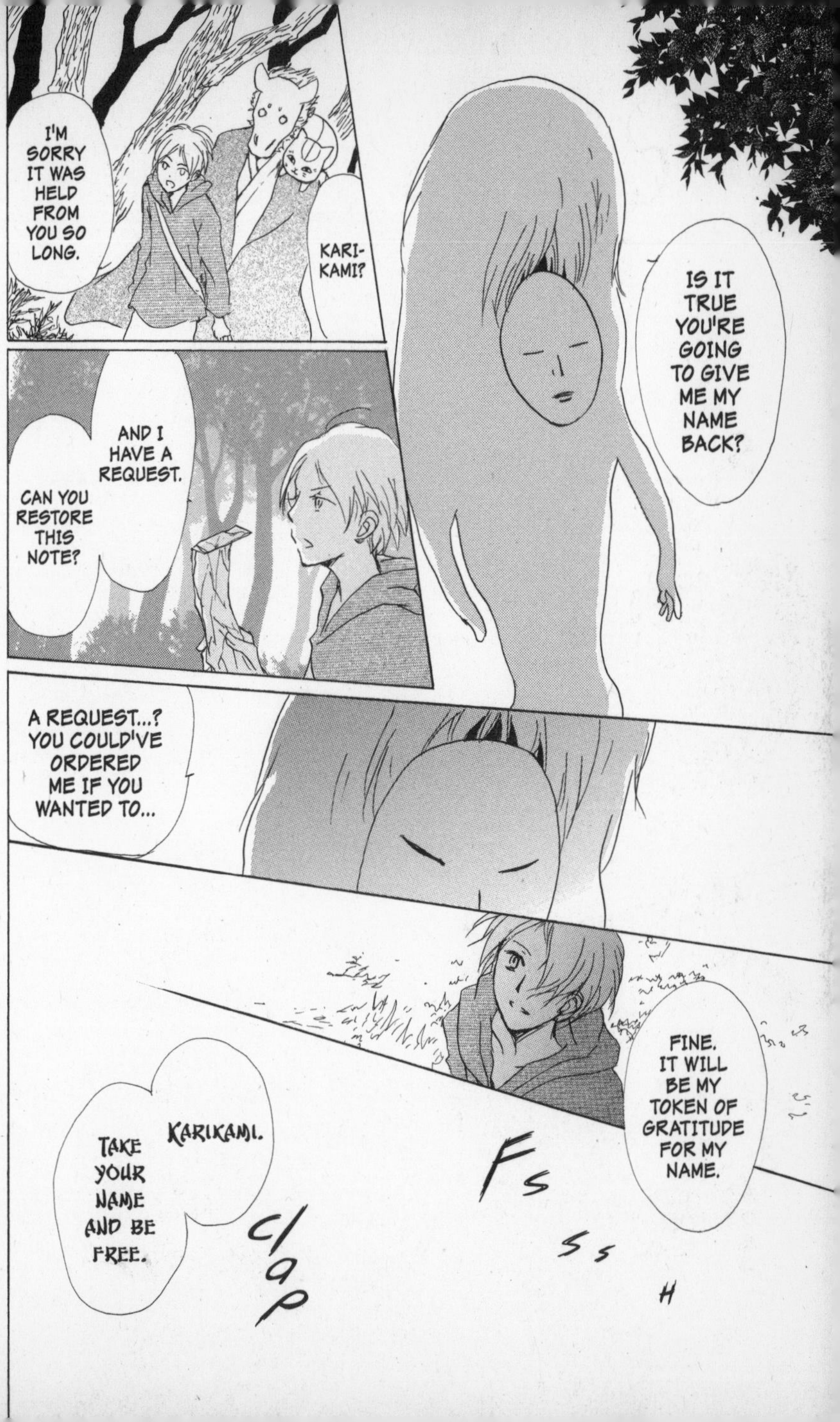
IS IT TRUE YOU'RE GOING TO GIVE ME MY NAME BACK?
KARI-KAMI?
I'M SORRY IT WAS HELD FROM YOU SO LONG.
AND I HAVE A REQUEST.
CAN YOU RESTORE THIS NOTE?
A REQUEST...? YOU COULD'VE ORDERED ME IF YOU WANTED TO...
FINE. IT WILL BE MY TOKEN OF GRATITUDE FOR MY NAME.
FSSSH
KARIKAMI.
TAKE YOUR NAME AND BE FREE.
CLAP

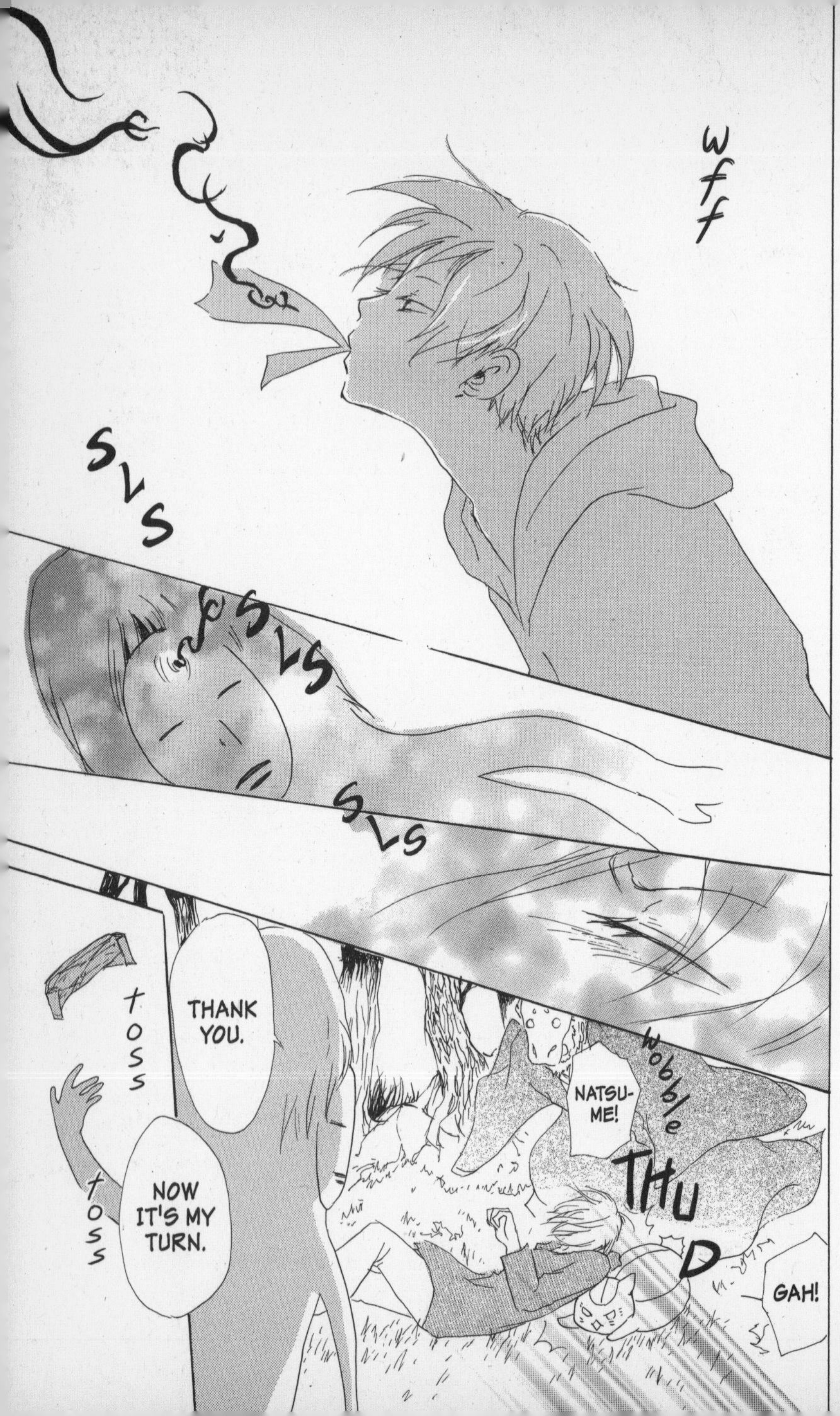

WFF
SVS
SVS
SVS
WOBBLE
NATSU-
ME!
THUD
GAH!
THANK YOU.
TOSS
NOW IT'S MY TURN.
TOSS

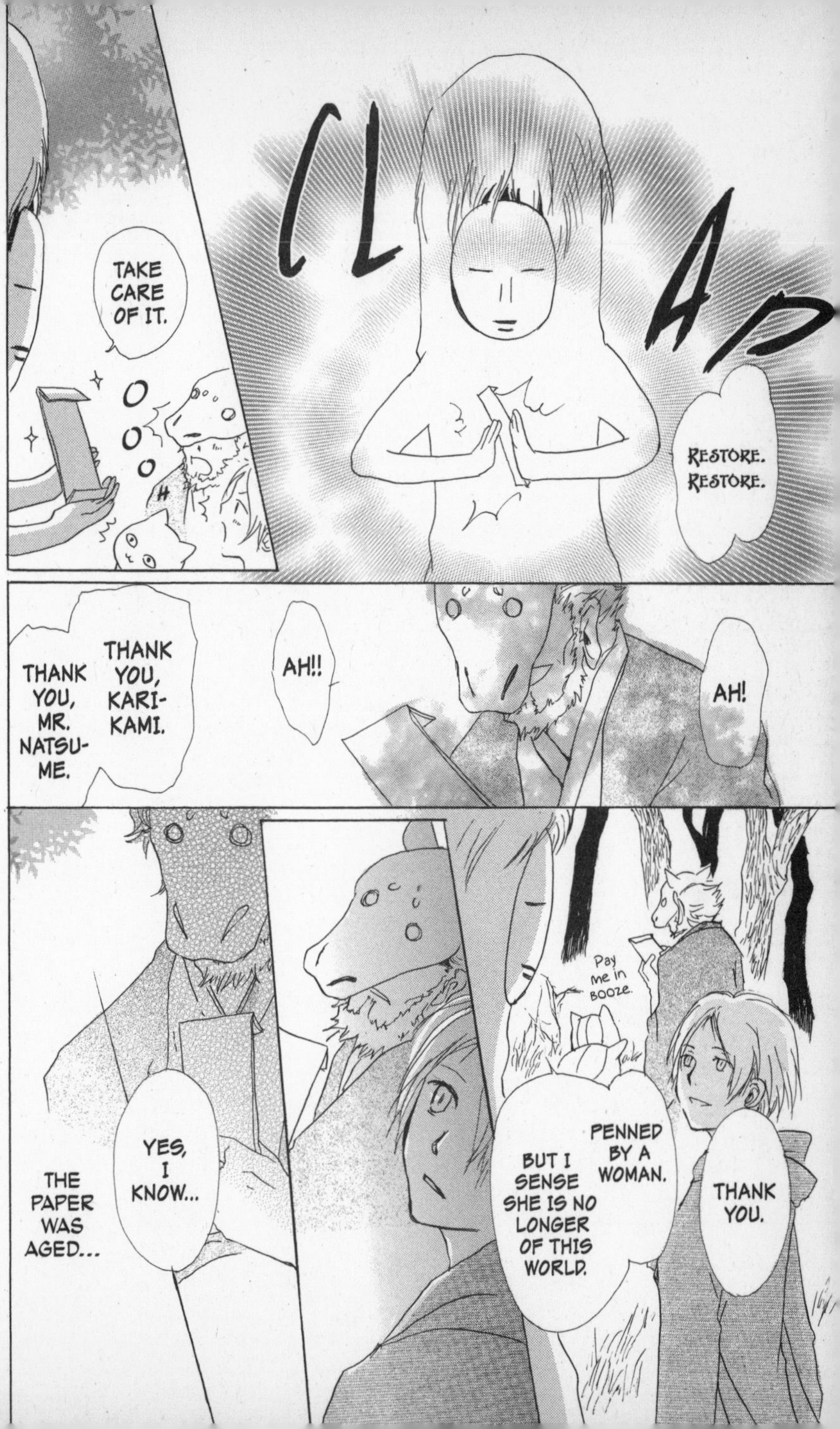
CLAP
RESTORE. RESTORE.
TAKE CARE OF IT.
OOOH
AH!
AH!!
THANK YOU, KARI-KAMI.
THANK YOU, MR. NATSU-ME.
Pay me in booze.
THANK YOU.
PENNED BY A WOMAN.
BUT I SENSE SHE IS NO LONGER OF THIS WORLD.
YES, I KNOW...
THE PAPER WAS AGED...

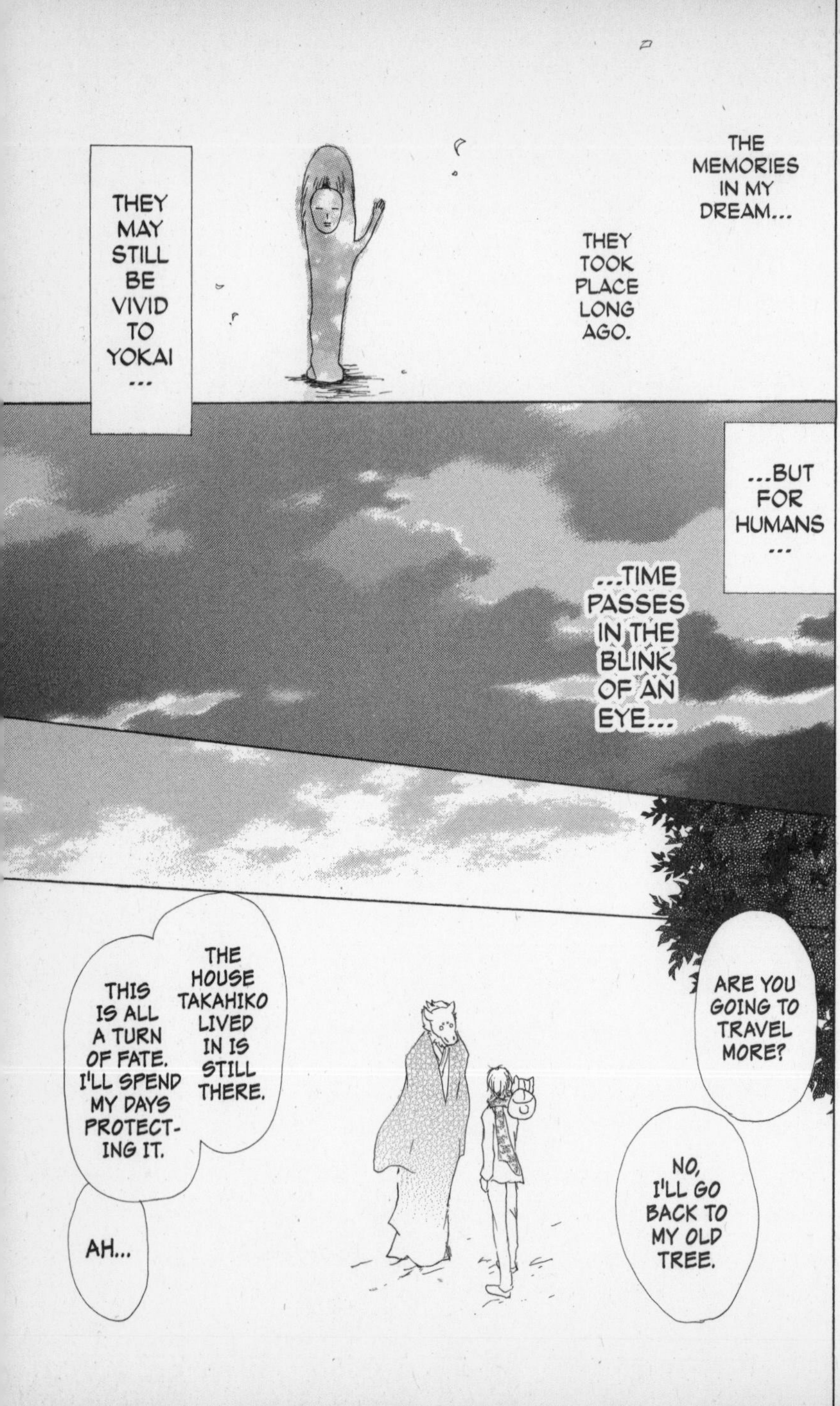
THE MEMORIES IN MY DREAM...
THEY TOOK PLACE LONG AGO.
THEY MAY STILL BE VIVID TO YOKAI...
...BUT FOR HUMANS...
...TIME PASSES IN THE BLINK OF AN EYE...
ARE YOU GOING TO TRAVEL MORE?
NO, I'LL GO BACK TO MY OLD TREE.
THE HOUSE TAKAHIKO LIVED IN IS STILL THERE.
THIS IS ALL A TURN OF FATE. I'LL SPEND MY DAYS PROTECTING IT.
AH...

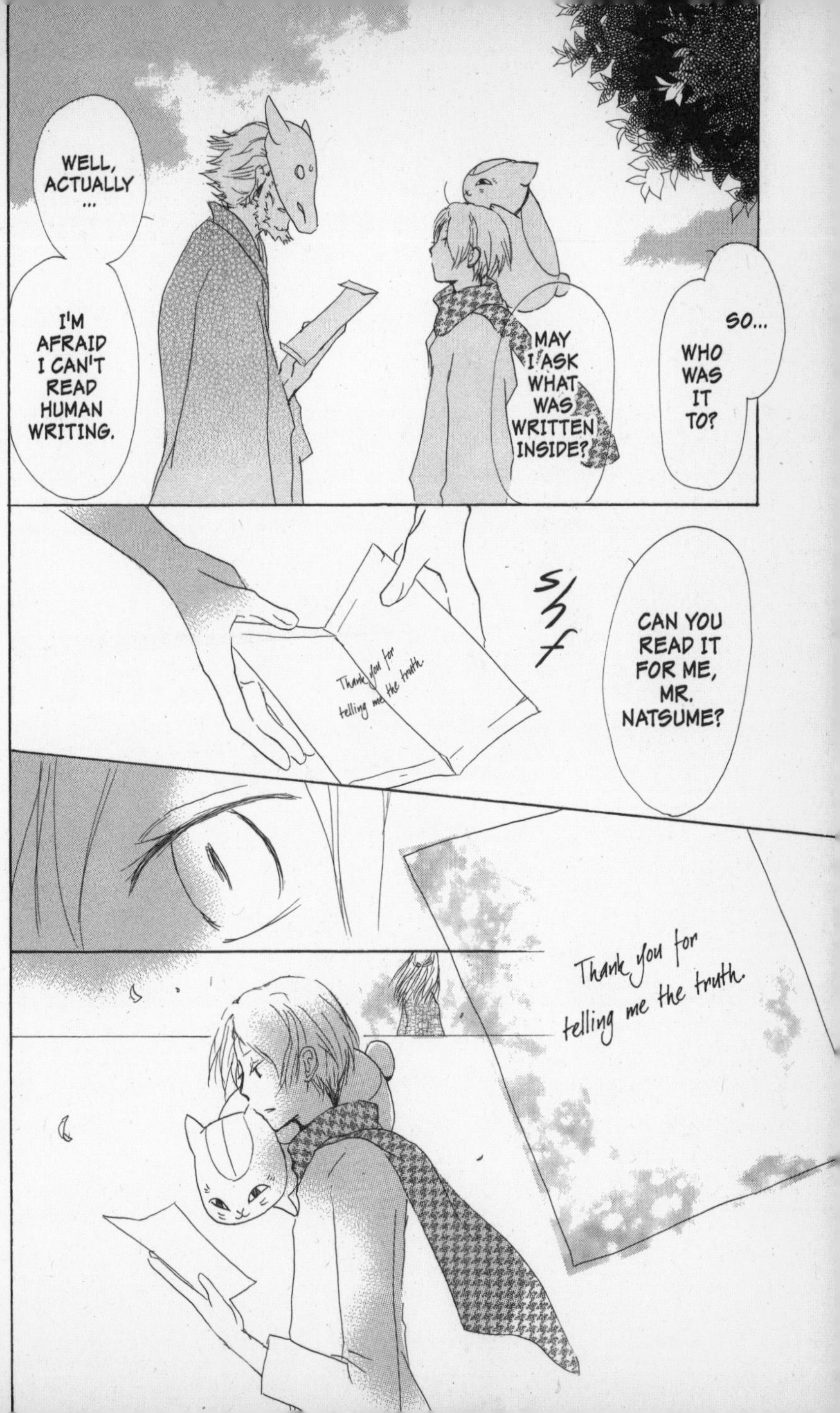

SO... WHO WAS IT TO?
MAY I ASK WHAT WAS WRITTEN INSIDE?
WELL, ACTUALLY ...
I'M AFRAID I CAN'T READ HUMAN WRITING.
CAN YOU READ IT FOR ME, MR. NATSUME?
shf
Thank you for telling me the truth.
Thank you for telling me the truth.

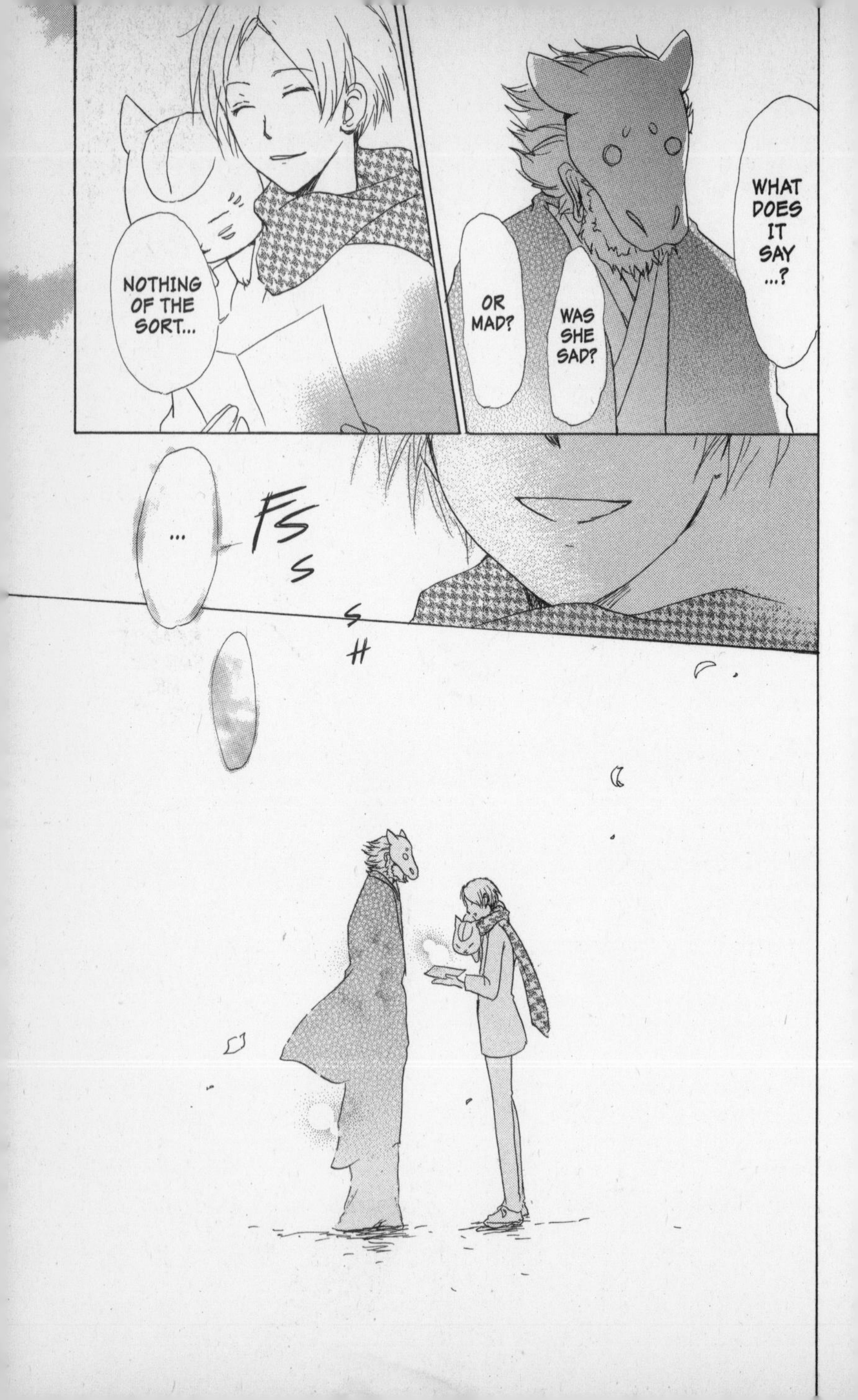
WHAT DOES IT SAY ...?
WAS SHE SAD?
OR MAD?
NOTHING OF THE SORT...
...
FSSSH

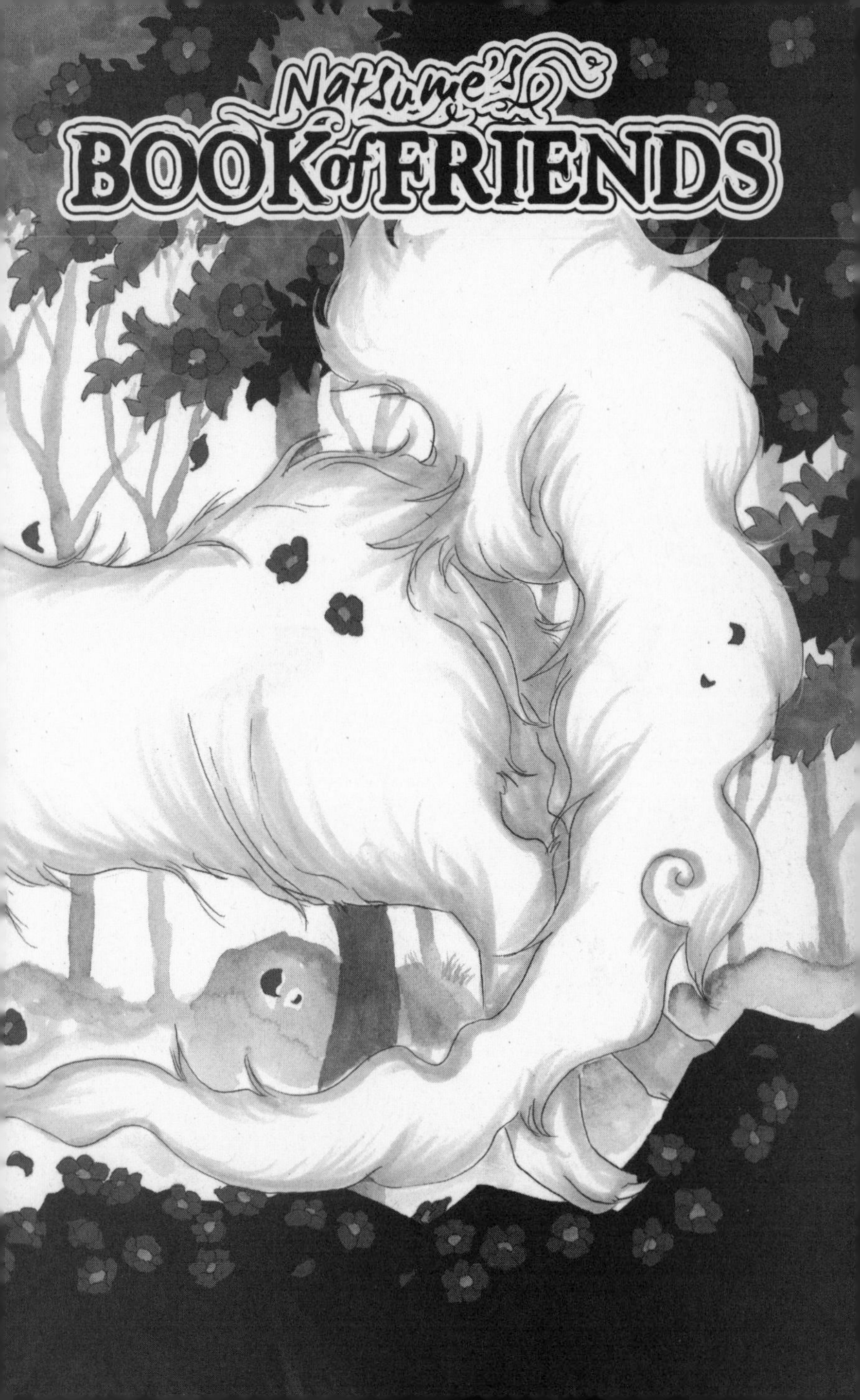
Natsume's
BOOK of FRIENDS

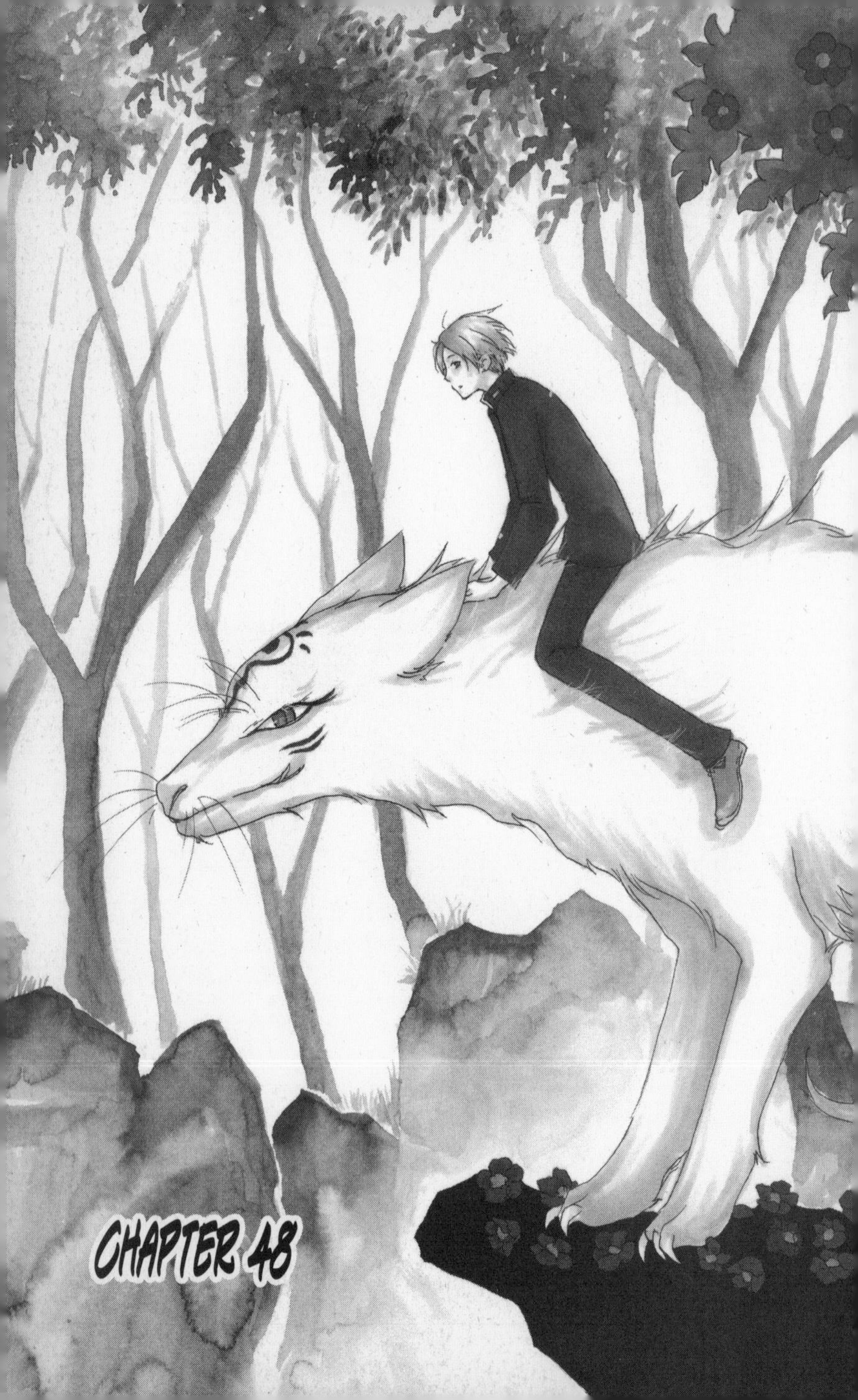
CHAPTER 48

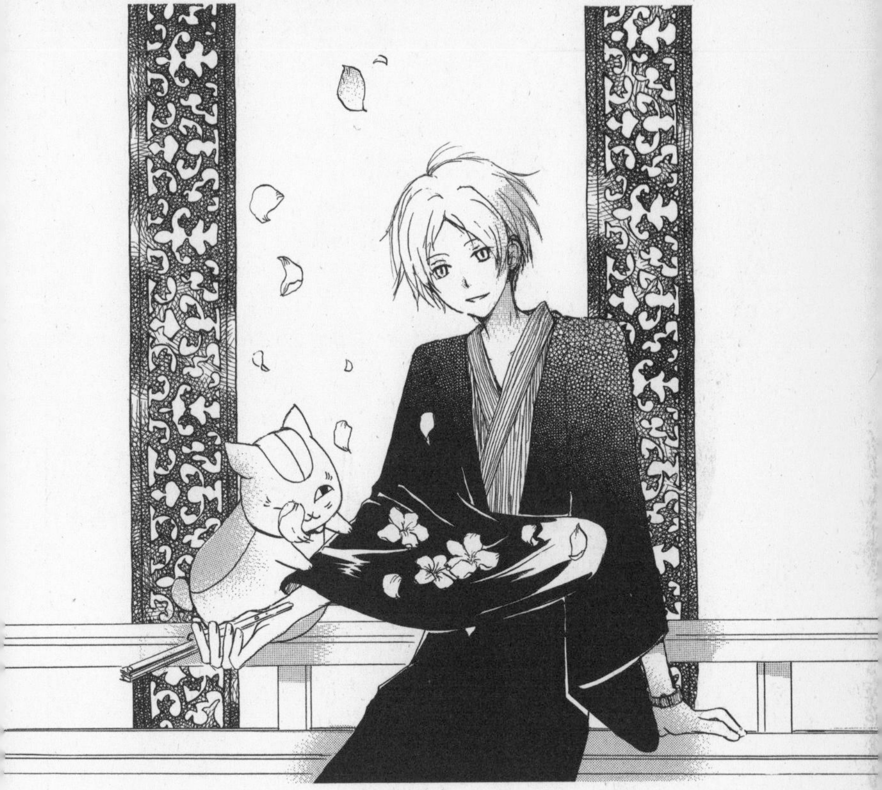

I'VE SEEN WEIRD THINGS SINCE I WAS LITTLE.

THINGS OTHER PEOPLE CAN'T SEE. THEY'RE CREATURES CALLED YOKAI.

HEY.

ZGG

EEK!

ZG

NO BITES TODAY.

LET'S GO PICK SOME AKEBI...

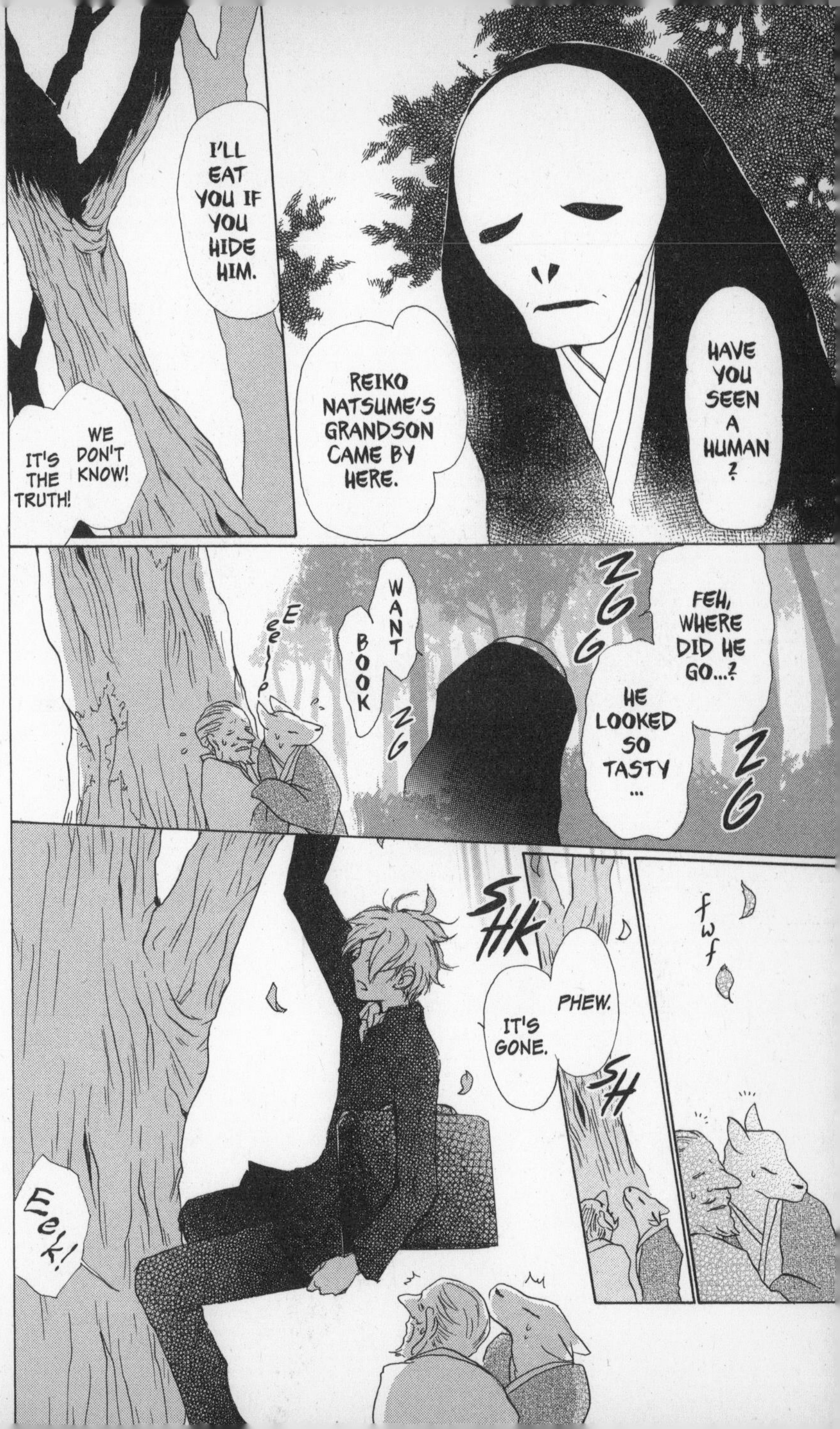
HAVE YOU SEEN A HUMAN?
REIKO NATSUME'S GRANDSON CAME BY HERE.
I'LL EAT YOU IF YOU HIDE HIM.
WE DON'T KNOW!
IT'S THE TRUTH!
ZG
FEH, WHERE DID HE GO...?
HE LOOKED SO TASTY...
ZG
ZG
WANT BOOK
Eee--p
fwf
SHK
SH
PHEW.
IT'S GONE.
Eek!

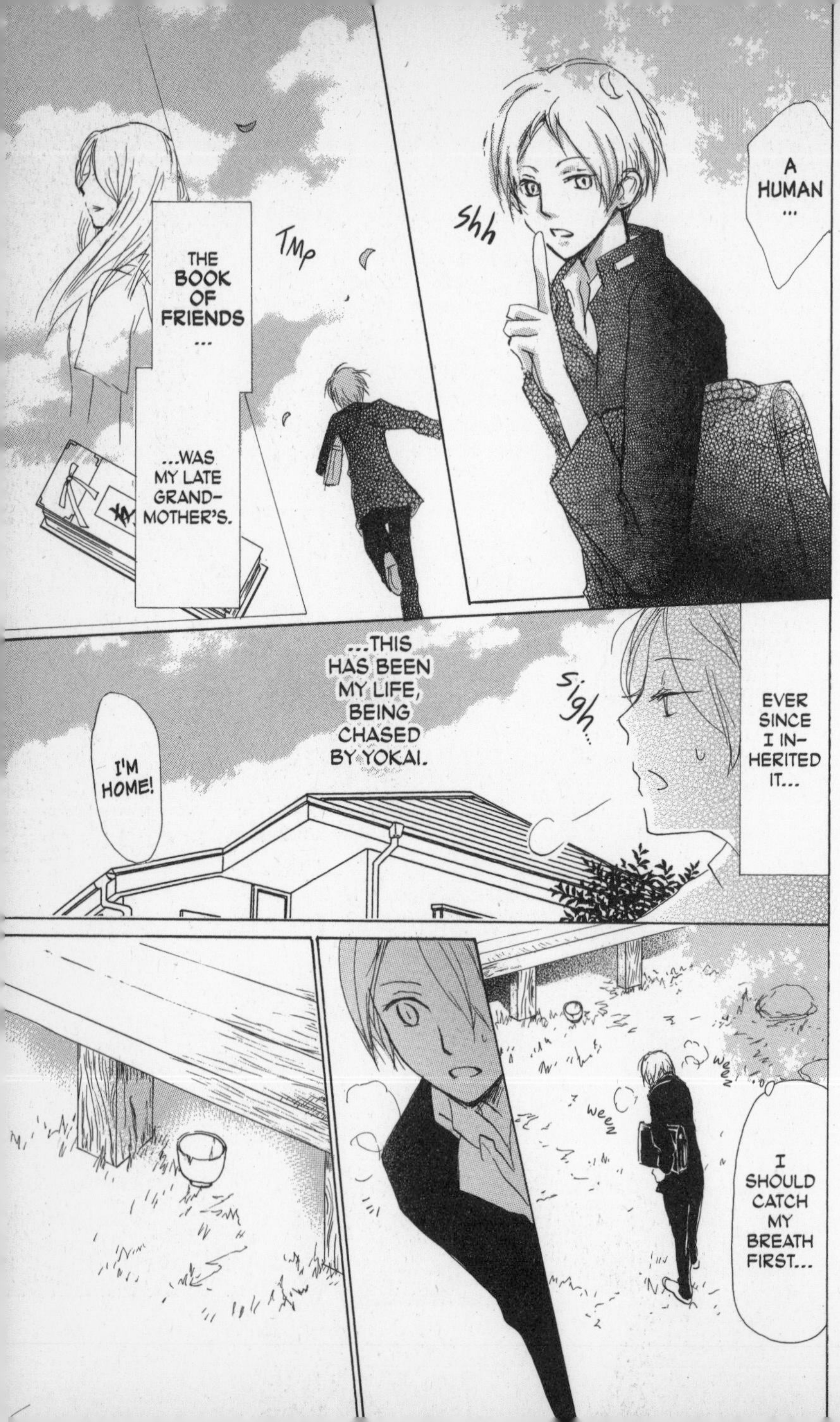
A HUMAN ...
Shh
TMp
THE BOOK OF FRIENDS ...
...WAS MY LATE GRAND-MOTHER'S.
EVER SINCE I IN-HERITED IT...
sigh...
...THIS HAS BEEN MY LIFE, BEING CHASED BY YOKAI.
I'M HOME!
I SHOULD CATCH MY BREATH FIRST...
ween
ween
ween

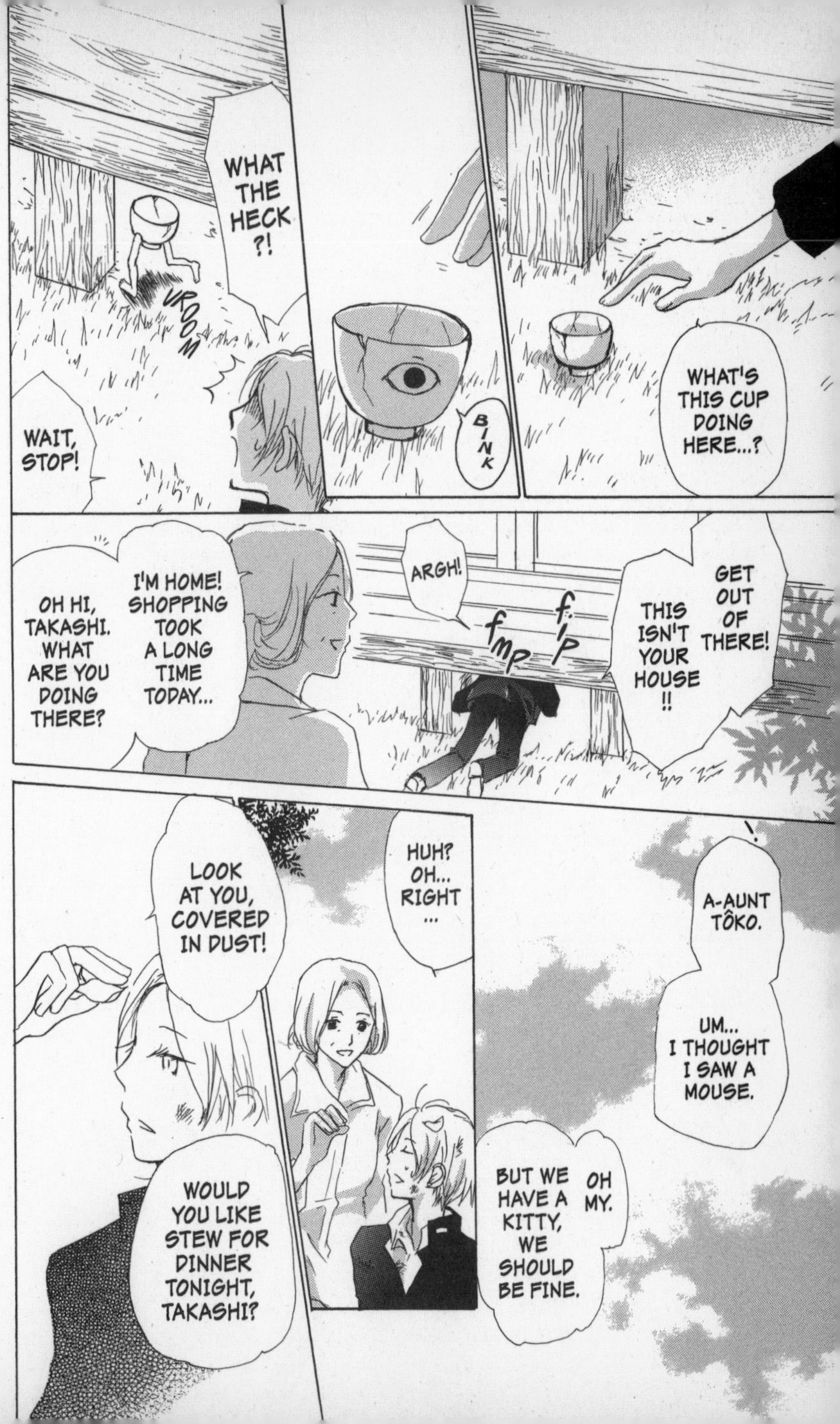
WHAT'S THIS CUP DOING HERE...?
BINK
WHAT THE HECK ?!
UROOOM
WAIT, STOP!
GET OUT OF THERE!
THIS ISN'T YOUR HOUSE !!
fip
fmp
ARGH!
I'M HOME! SHOPPING TOOK A LONG TIME TODAY...
OH HI, TAKASHI. WHAT ARE YOU DOING THERE?
A-AUNT TÔKO.
UM... I THOUGHT I SAW A MOUSE.
HUH? OH... RIGHT ...
OH MY.
BUT WE HAVE A KITTY, WE SHOULD BE FINE.
LOOK AT YOU, COVERED IN DUST!
WOULD YOU LIKE STEW FOR DINNER TONIGHT, TAKASHI?

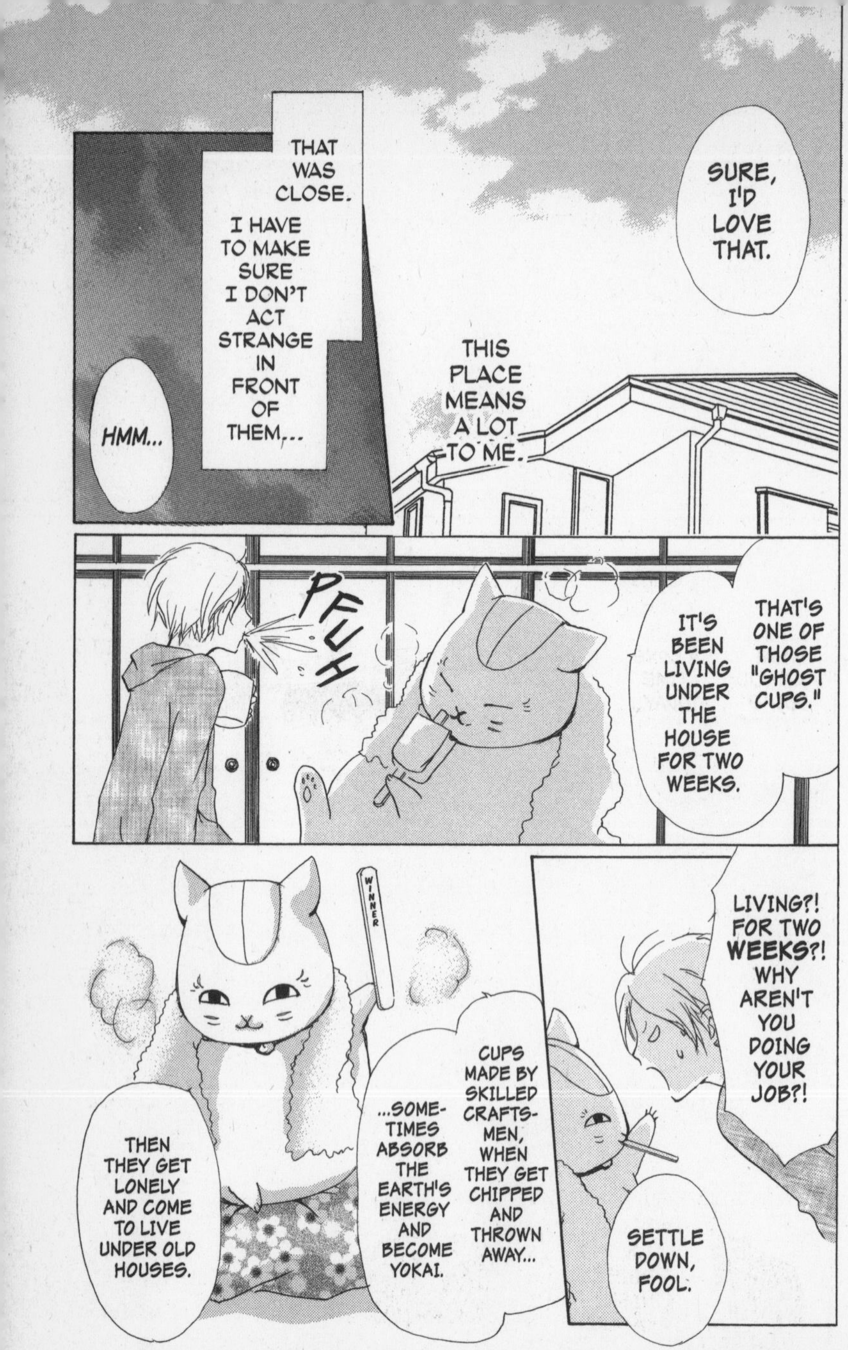
SURE, I'D LOVE THAT.
THIS PLACE MEANS A LOT TO ME.
THAT WAS CLOSE.
I HAVE TO MAKE SURE I DON'T ACT STRANGE IN FRONT OF THEM,...
HMM...
THAT'S ONE OF THOSE "GHOST CUPS."
IT'S BEEN LIVING UNDER THE HOUSE FOR TWO WEEKS.
PFUH
LIVING?! FOR TWO **WEEKS**?! WHY AREN'T YOU DOING YOUR JOB?!
SETTLE DOWN, FOOL.
WINNER
CUPS MADE BY SKILLED CRAFTS-MEN, WHEN THEY GET CHIPPED AND THROWN AWAY...
...SOME-TIMES ABSORB THE EARTH'S ENERGY AND BECOME YOKAI.
THEN THEY GET LONELY AND COME TO LIVE UNDER OLD HOUSES.

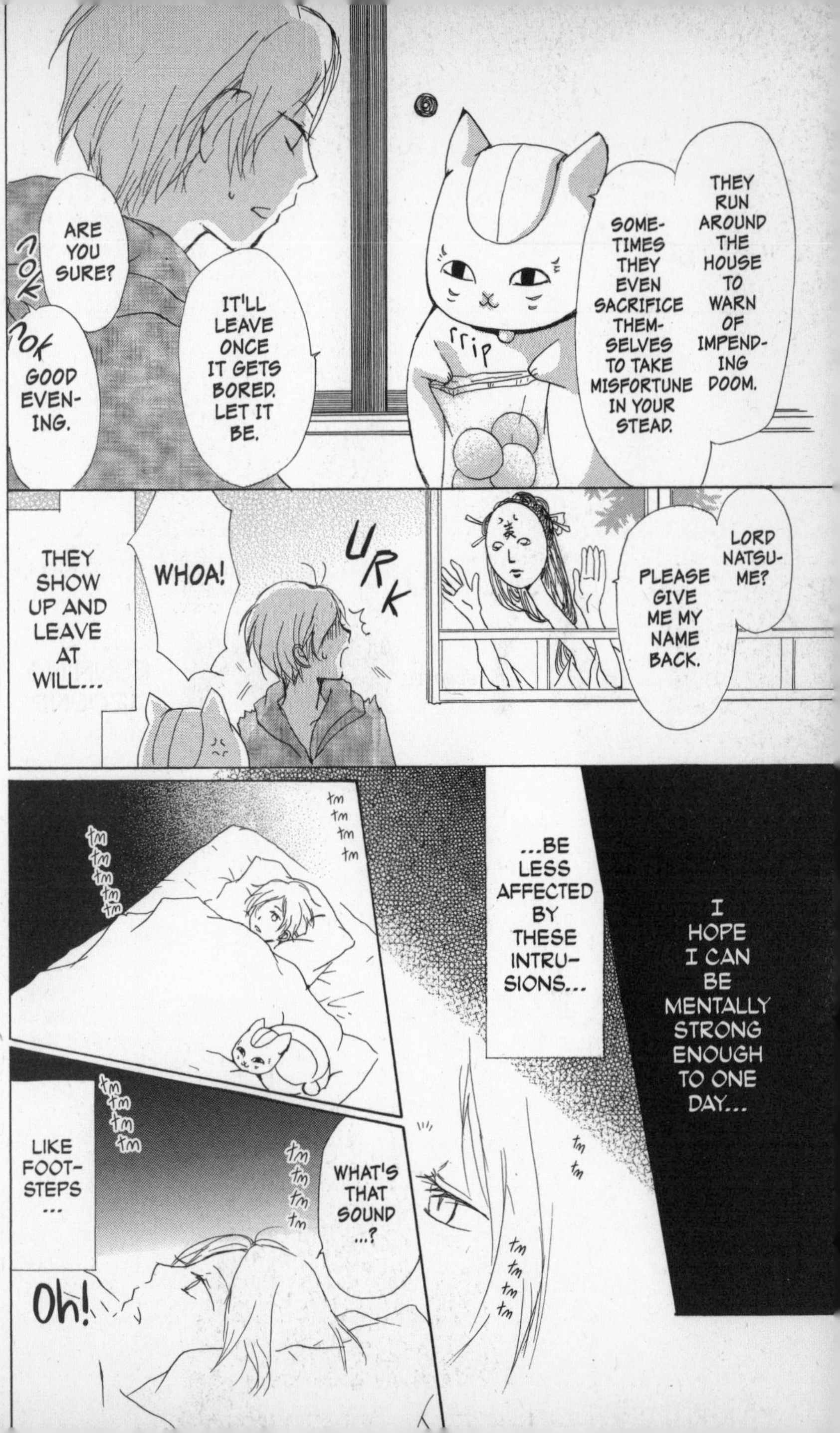
THEY RUN AROUND THE HOUSE TO WARN OF IMPENDING DOOM.
SOMETIMES THEY EVEN SACRIFICE THEMSELVES TO TAKE MISFORTUNE IN YOUR STEAD.
rrip
IT'LL LEAVE ONCE IT GETS BORED. LET IT BE.
ARE YOU SURE?
GOOD EVENING.
LORD NATSUME?
PLEASE GIVE ME MY NAME BACK.
URK
WHOA!
THEY SHOW UP AND LEAVE AT WILL...
I HOPE I CAN BE MENTALLY STRONG ENOUGH TO ONE DAY...
...BE LESS AFFECTED BY THESE INTRUSIONS...
tm tm tm tm
tm tm tm tm tm
tm tm
tm tm tm tm tm
WHAT'S THAT SOUND ...?
tm tm tm tm
tm tm tm tm
LIKE FOOTSTEPS ...
Oh!

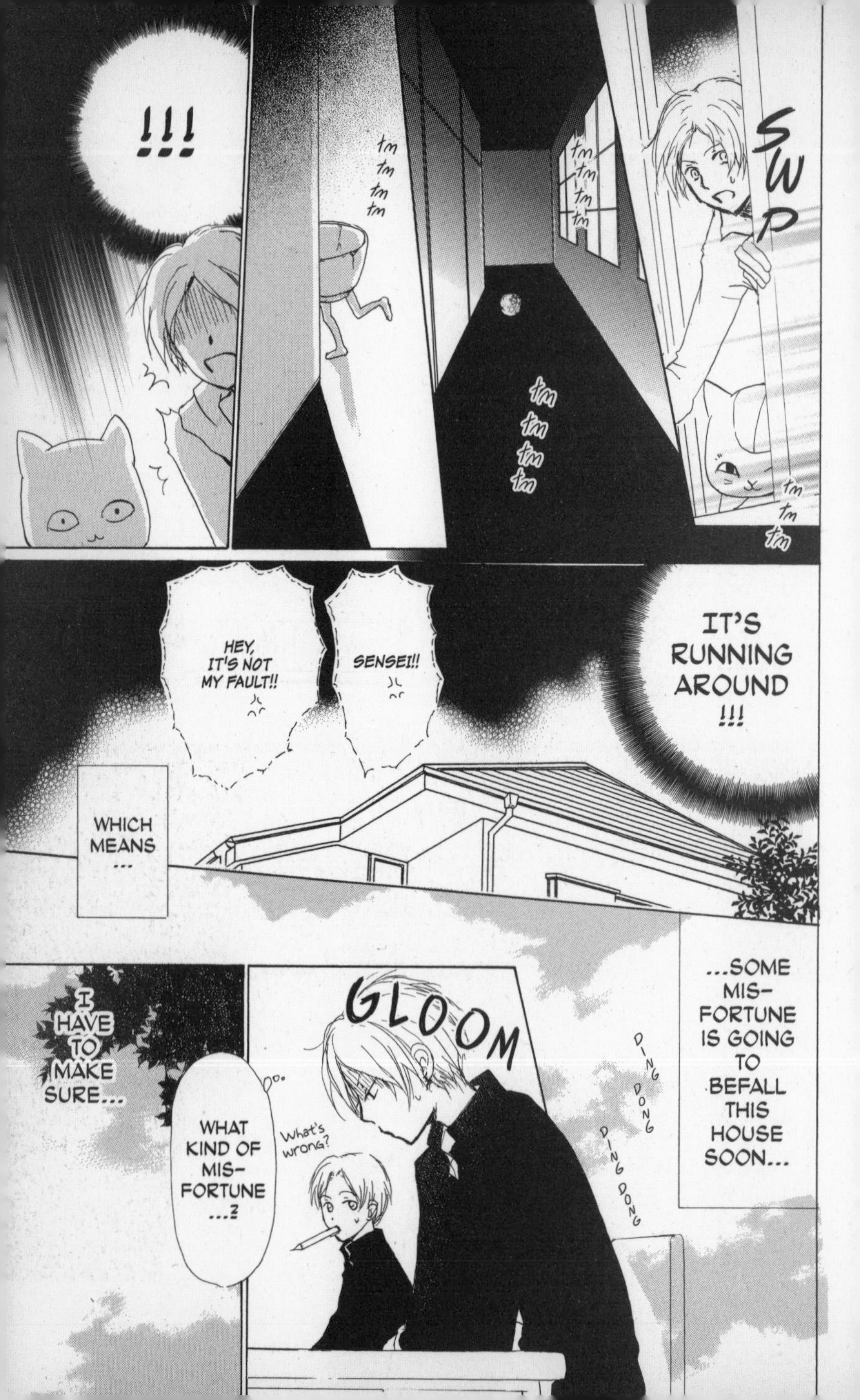
SWP
tm tm tm tm
tm tm tm
tm tm tm tm
tm tm tm tm
!!!
IT'S RUNNING AROUND !!!
SENSEI!!
HEY, IT'S NOT MY FAULT!!
WHICH MEANS ...
...SOME MIS-FORTUNE IS GOING TO BEFALL THIS HOUSE SOON...
DING DONG DING DONG
GLOOM
What's wrong?
WHAT KIND OF MIS-FORTUNE ...?
I HAVE TO MAKE SURE...

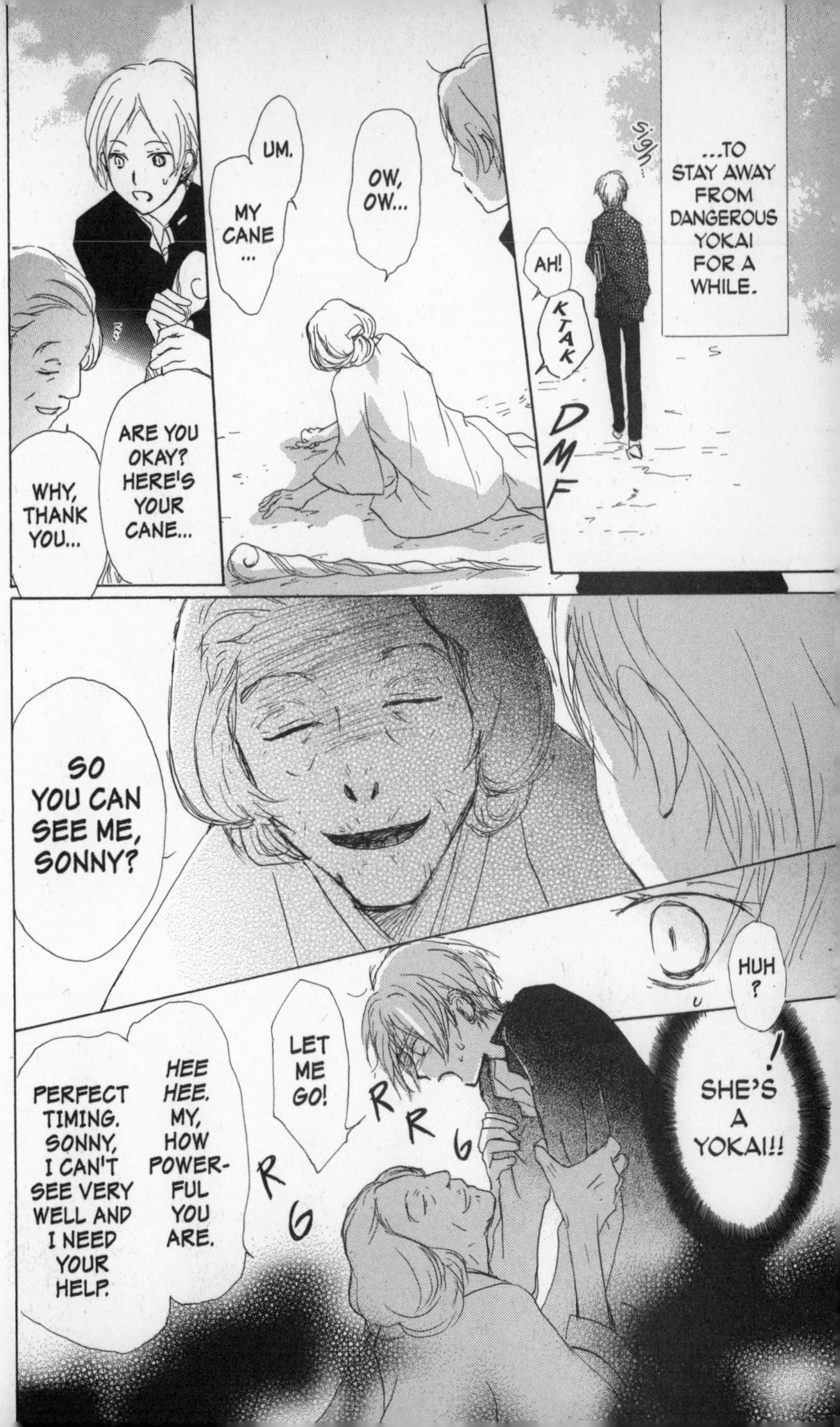
...TO STAY AWAY FROM DANGEROUS YOKAI FOR A WHILE.
sigh...
AH!
KTAK
DMF
OW, OW...
UM. MY CANE ...
ARE YOU OKAY? HERE'S YOUR CANE...
WHY, THANK YOU...
SO YOU CAN SEE ME, SONNY?
HUH?
!
SHE'S A YOKAI!!
LET ME GO!
RRG
RRG
HEE HEE. MY, HOW POWERFUL YOU ARE.
PERFECT TIMING. SONNY, I CAN'T SEE VERY WELL AND I NEED YOUR HELP.

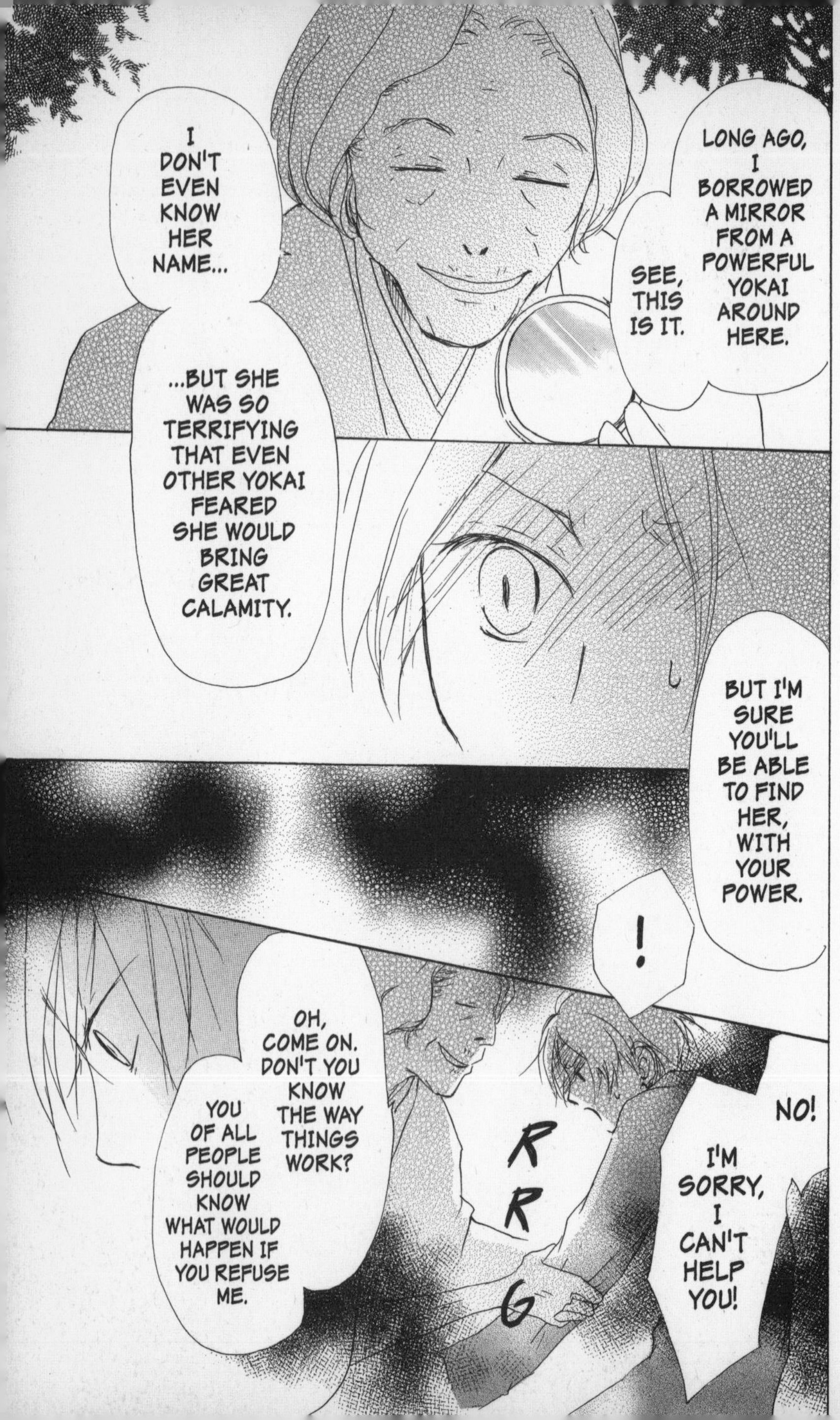
LONG AGO, I BORROWED A MIRROR FROM A POWERFUL YOKAI AROUND HERE.
SEE, THIS IS IT.
I DON'T EVEN KNOW HER NAME...
...BUT SHE WAS SO TERRIFYING THAT EVEN OTHER YOKAI FEARED SHE WOULD BRING GREAT CALAMITY.
BUT I'M SURE YOU'LL BE ABLE TO FIND HER, WITH YOUR POWER.
!
NO!
I'M SORRY, I CAN'T HELP YOU!
RRG
OH, COME ON. DON'T YOU KNOW THE WAY THINGS WORK?
YOU OF ALL PEOPLE SHOULD KNOW WHAT WOULD HAPPEN IF YOU REFUSE ME.

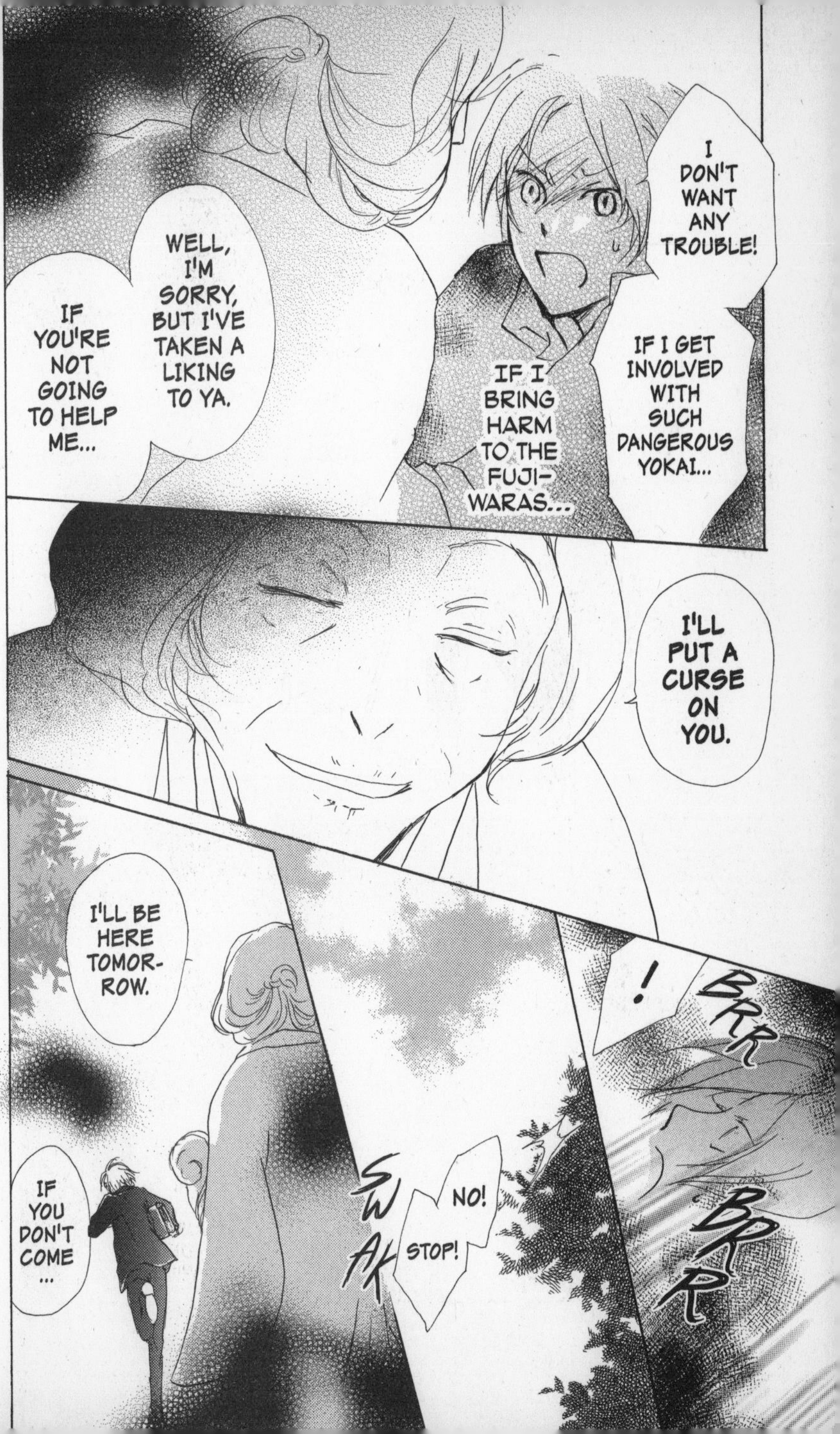
I DON'T WANT ANY TROUBLE!
IF I GET INVOLVED WITH SUCH DANGEROUS YOKAI...
IF I BRING HARM TO THE FUJI-WARAS...
WELL, I'M SORRY, BUT I'VE TAKEN A LIKING TO YA.
IF YOU'RE NOT GOING TO HELP ME...
I'LL PUT A CURSE ON YOU.
!
BRRR
BRRR
NO!
STOP!
SWAK
I'LL BE HERE TOMORROW.
IF YOU DON'T COME ...

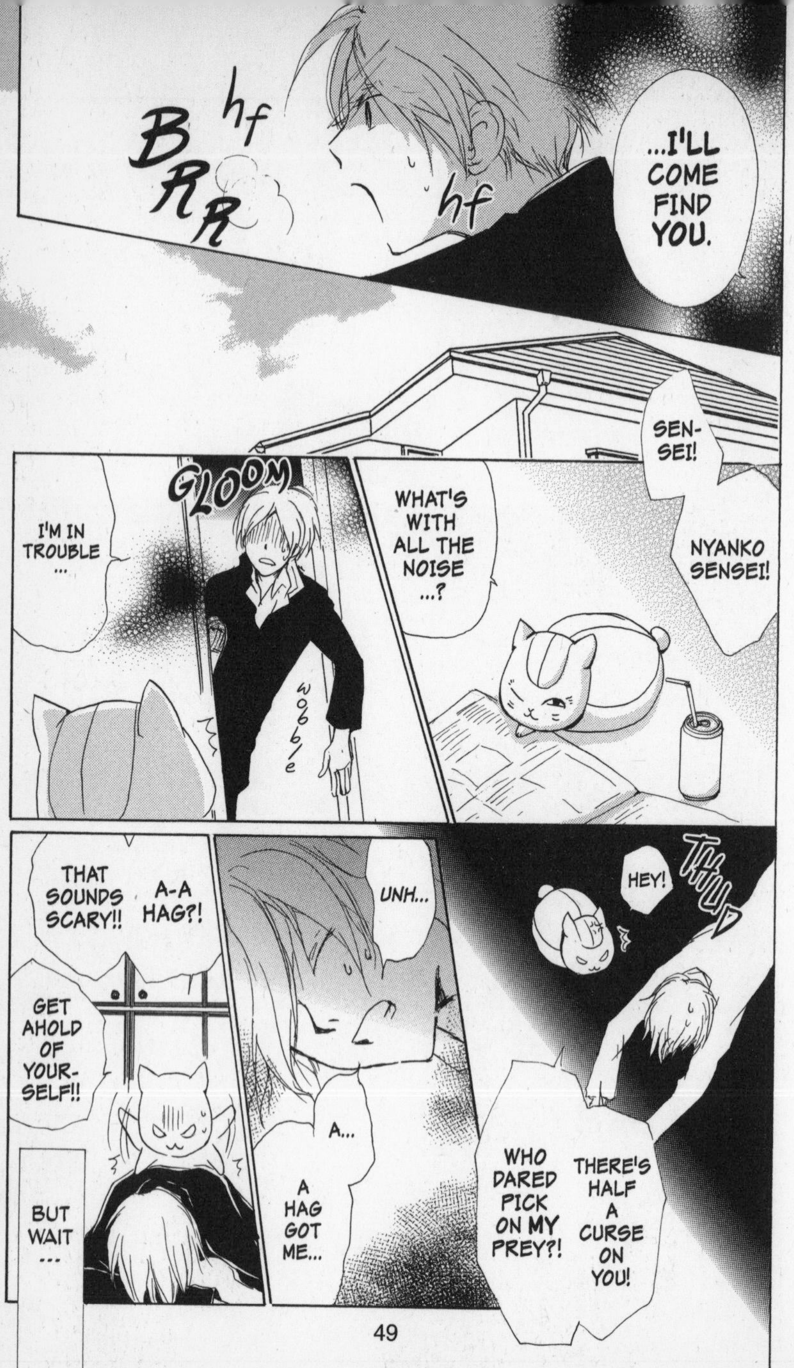
...I'LL COME FIND YOU.
hf
hf
BRRR
SEN-SEI!
NYANKO SENSEI!
WHAT'S WITH ALL THE NOISE ...?
GLOOM
I'M IN TROUBLE ...
wobble
THUD
HEY!
THERE'S HALF A CURSE ON YOU!
WHO DARED PICK ON MY PREY?!
UNH...
A...
A HAG GOT ME...
A-A HAG?!
THAT SOUNDS SCARY!!
GET AHOLD OF YOURSELF!!
BUT WAIT ...

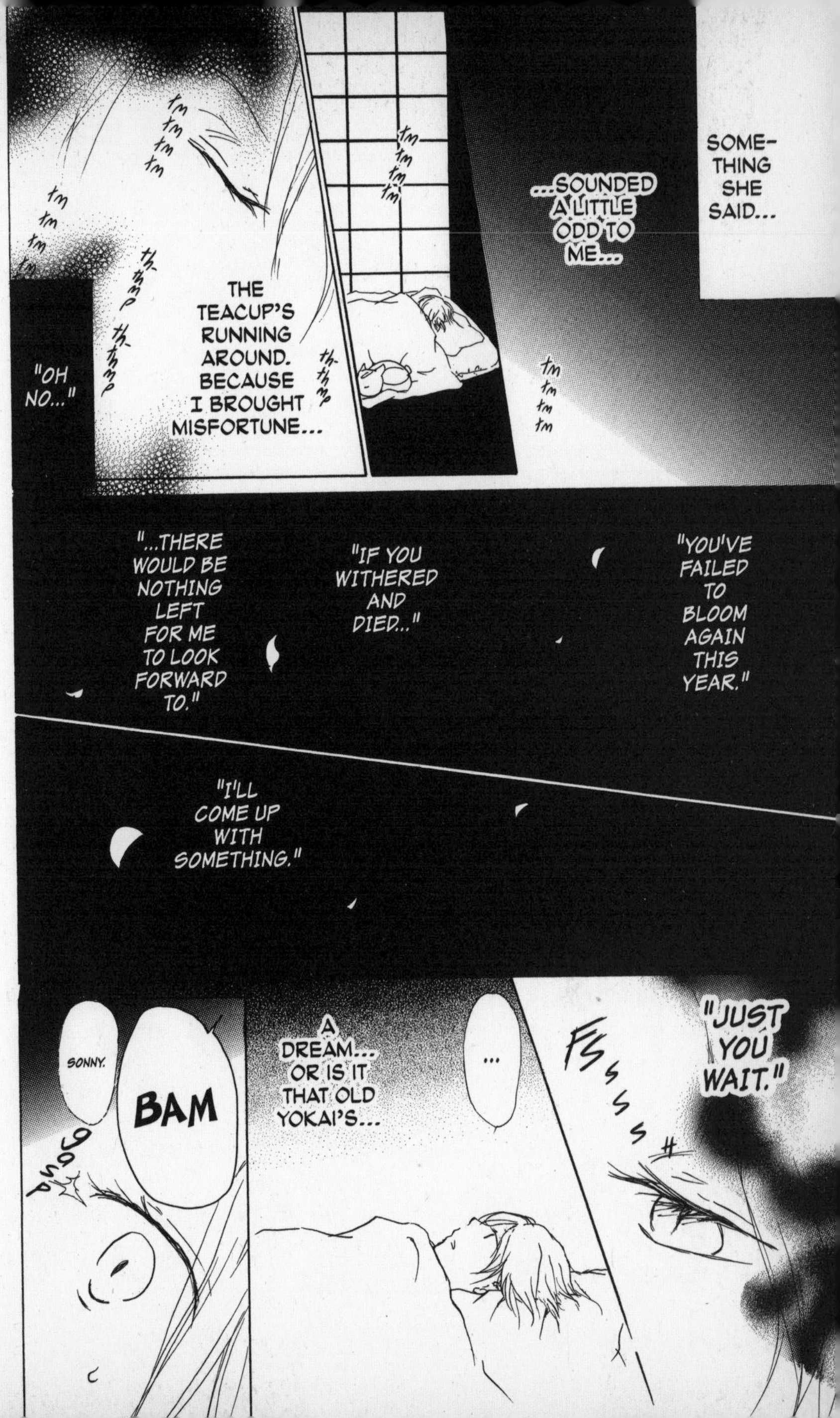
SOME-THING SHE SAID...
...SOUNDED A LITTLE ODD TO ME...
tm tm tm tm
tm tm tm tm
THE TEACUP'S RUNNING AROUND. BECAUSE I BROUGHT MISFORTUNE...
th-thmp
tm tm tm tm
tm tm tm tm
th-thmp th-thmp
"OH NO..."
"YOU'VE FAILED TO BLOOM AGAIN THIS YEAR."
"IF YOU WITHERED AND DIED..."
"...THERE WOULD BE NOTHING LEFT FOR ME TO LOOK FORWARD TO."
"I'LL COME UP WITH SOMETHING."
"JUST YOU WAIT."
FSSSSH
...
A DREAM... OR IS IT THAT OLD YOKAI'S...
BAM
SONNY.

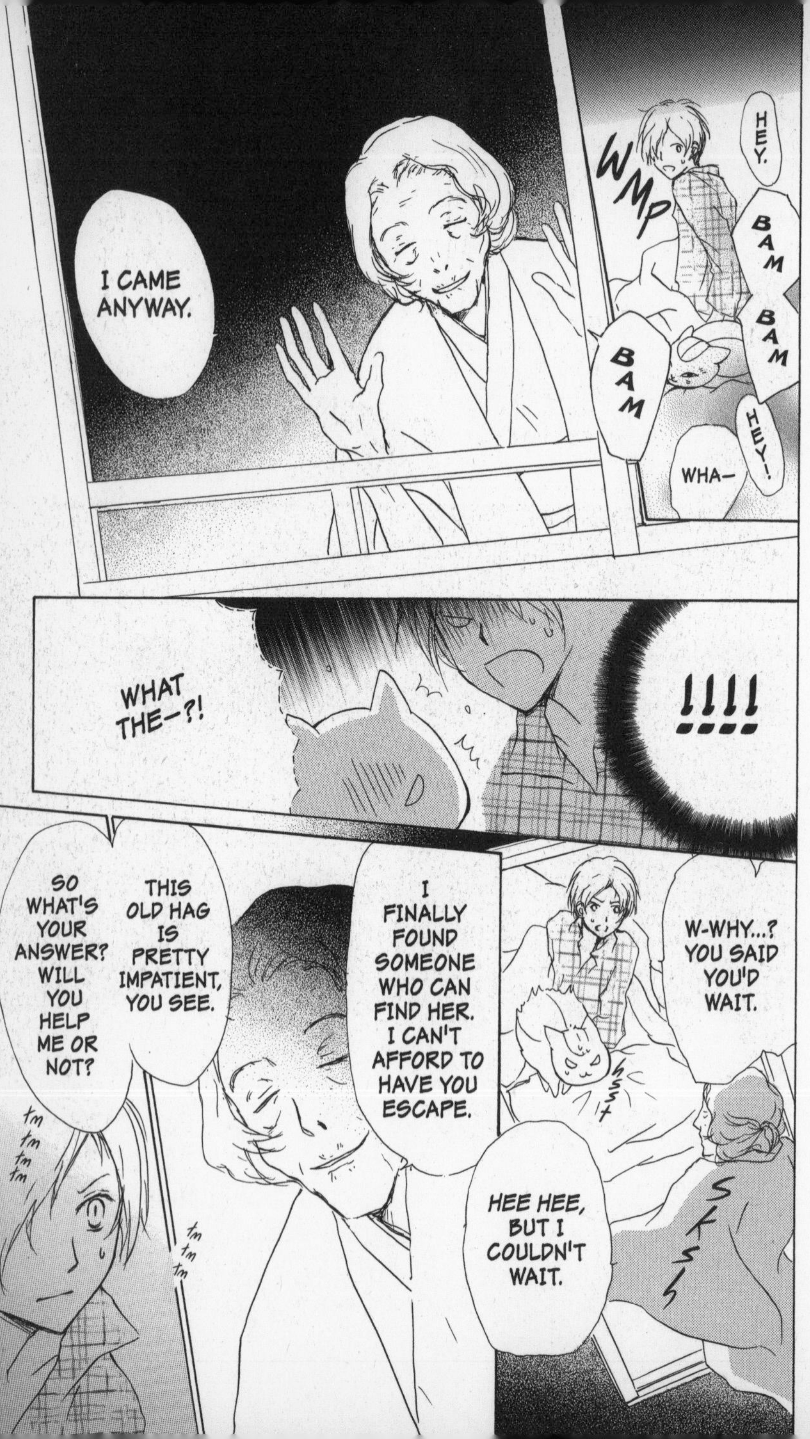
HEY.
WMP
BAM BAM
BAM
HEY!
WHA—
I CAME ANYWAY.
!!!!
WHAT THE—?!
W-WHY...? YOU SAID YOU'D WAIT.
hssst
SKSH
HEE HEE, BUT I COULDN'T WAIT.
I FINALLY FOUND SOMEONE WHO CAN FIND HER. I CAN'T AFFORD TO HAVE YOU ESCAPE.
THIS OLD HAG IS PRETTY IMPATIENT, YOU SEE.
SO WHAT'S YOUR ANSWER? WILL YOU HELP ME OR NOT?
tm tm tm tm
tm tm tm

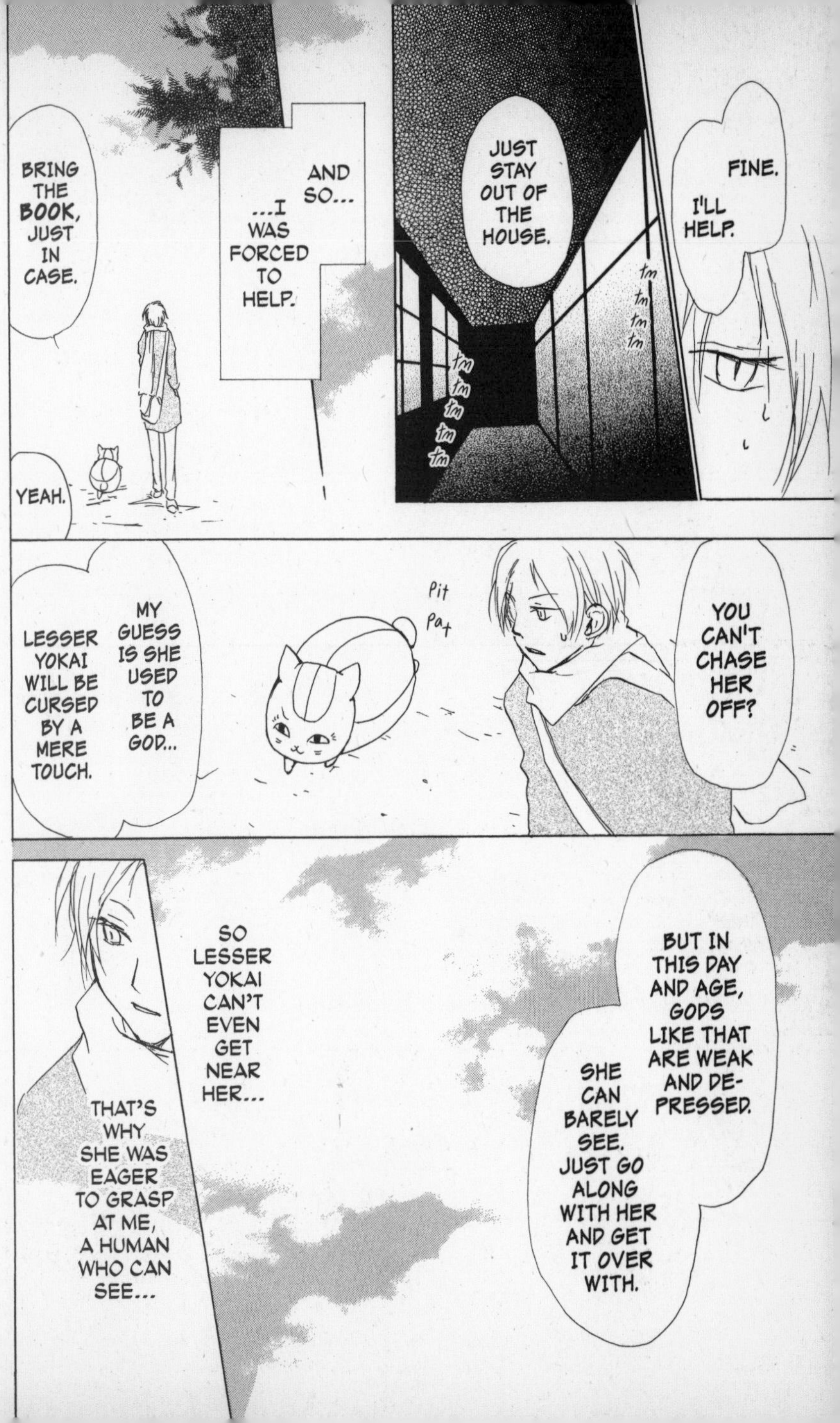
FINE. I'LL HELP.
JUST STAY OUT OF THE HOUSE.
tm tm tm tm
tm tm tm tm tm
AND SO...
...I WAS FORCED TO HELP.
BRING THE BOOK, JUST IN CASE.
YEAH.
YOU CAN'T CHASE HER OFF?
Pit Pat
MY GUESS IS SHE USED TO BE A GOD...
LESSER YOKAI WILL BE CURSED BY A MERE TOUCH.
BUT IN THIS DAY AND AGE, GODS LIKE THAT ARE WEAK AND DE-PRESSED.
SHE CAN BARELY SEE. JUST GO ALONG WITH HER AND GET IT OVER WITH.
SO LESSER YOKAI CAN'T EVEN GET NEAR HER...
THAT'S WHY SHE WAS EAGER TO GRASP AT ME, A HUMAN WHO CAN SEE...

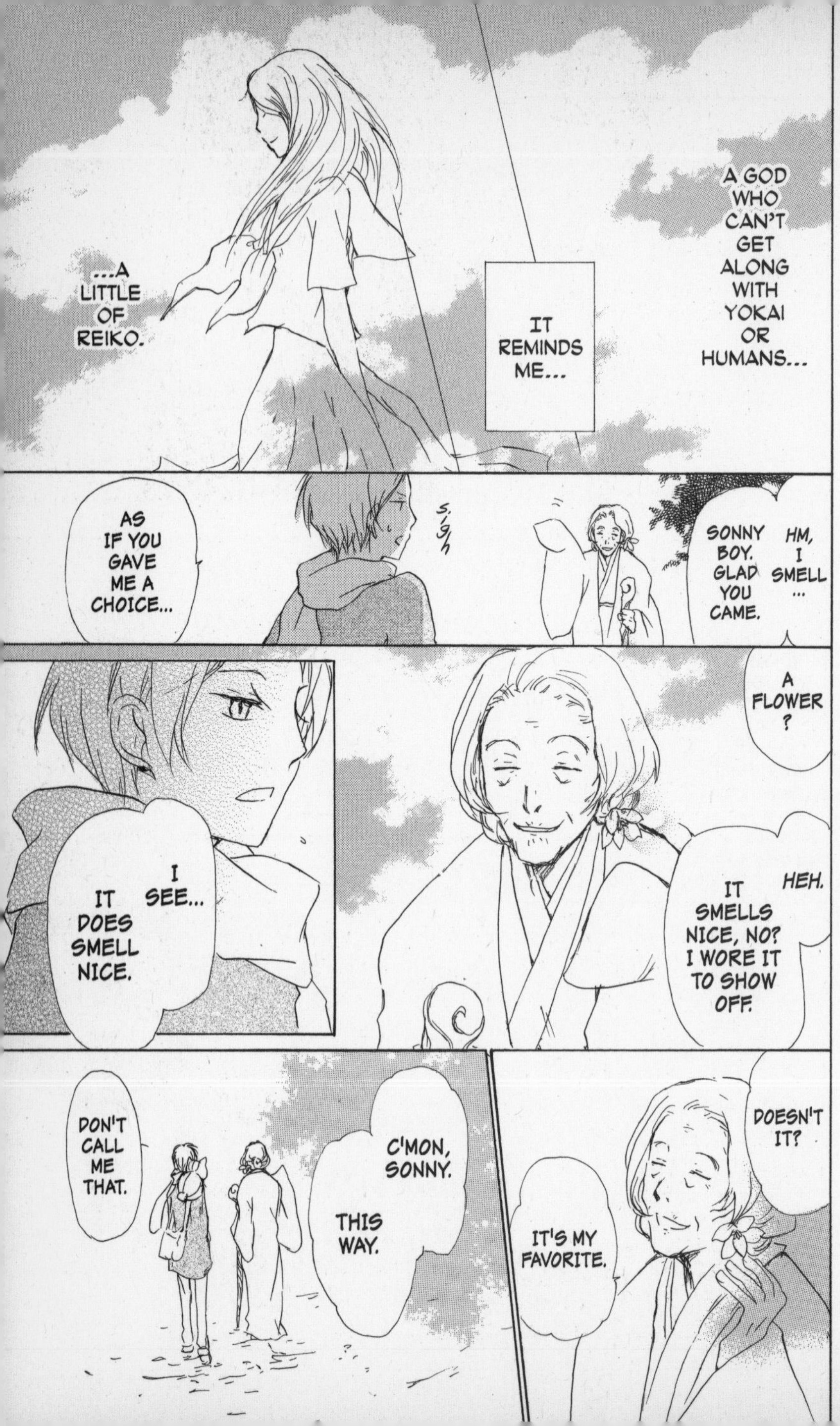
A GOD WHO CAN'T GET ALONG WITH YOKAI OR HUMANS...
IT REMINDS ME...
...A LITTLE OF REIKO.
HM, I SMELL ...
SONNY BOY. GLAD YOU CAME.
sigh
AS IF YOU GAVE ME A CHOICE...
A FLOWER?
HEH.
IT SMELLS NICE, NO? I WORE IT TO SHOW OFF.
I SEE...
IT DOES SMELL NICE.
DOESN'T IT?
IT'S MY FAVORITE.
C'MON, SONNY.
THIS WAY.
DON'T CALL ME THAT.

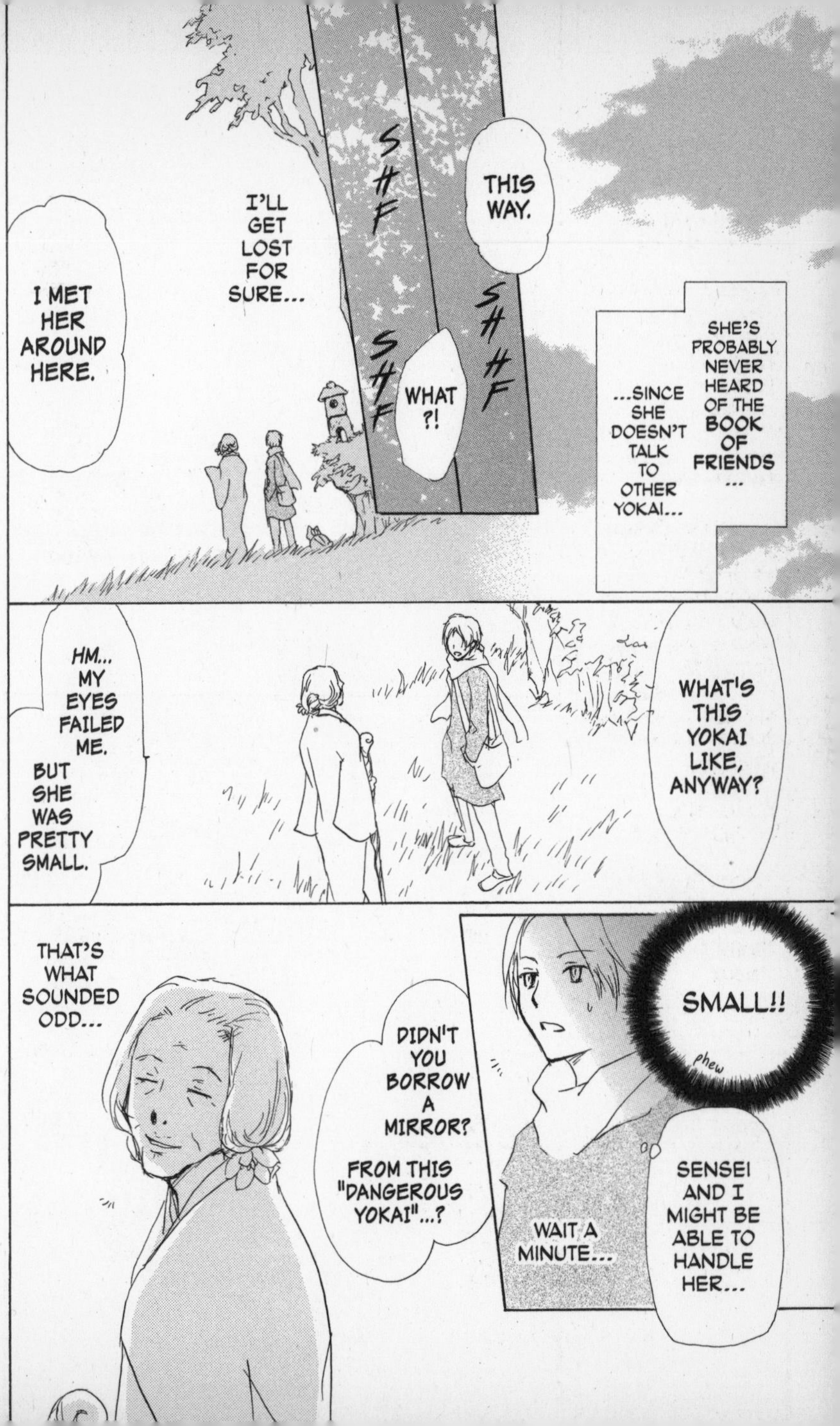
SHE'S PROBABLY NEVER HEARD OF THE BOOK OF FRIENDS ...
...SINCE SHE DOESN'T TALK TO OTHER YOKAI...
THIS WAY.
SHHF
WHAT?!
SHF
SHF
I'LL GET LOST FOR SURE...
I MET HER AROUND HERE.
WHAT'S THIS YOKAI LIKE, ANYWAY?
HM... MY EYES FAILED ME.
BUT SHE WAS PRETTY SMALL.
SMALL!!
phew
SENSEI AND I MIGHT BE ABLE TO HANDLE HER...
WAIT A MINUTE...
DIDN'T YOU BORROW A MIRROR?
FROM THIS "DANGEROUS YOKAI"...?
THAT'S WHAT SOUNDED ODD...

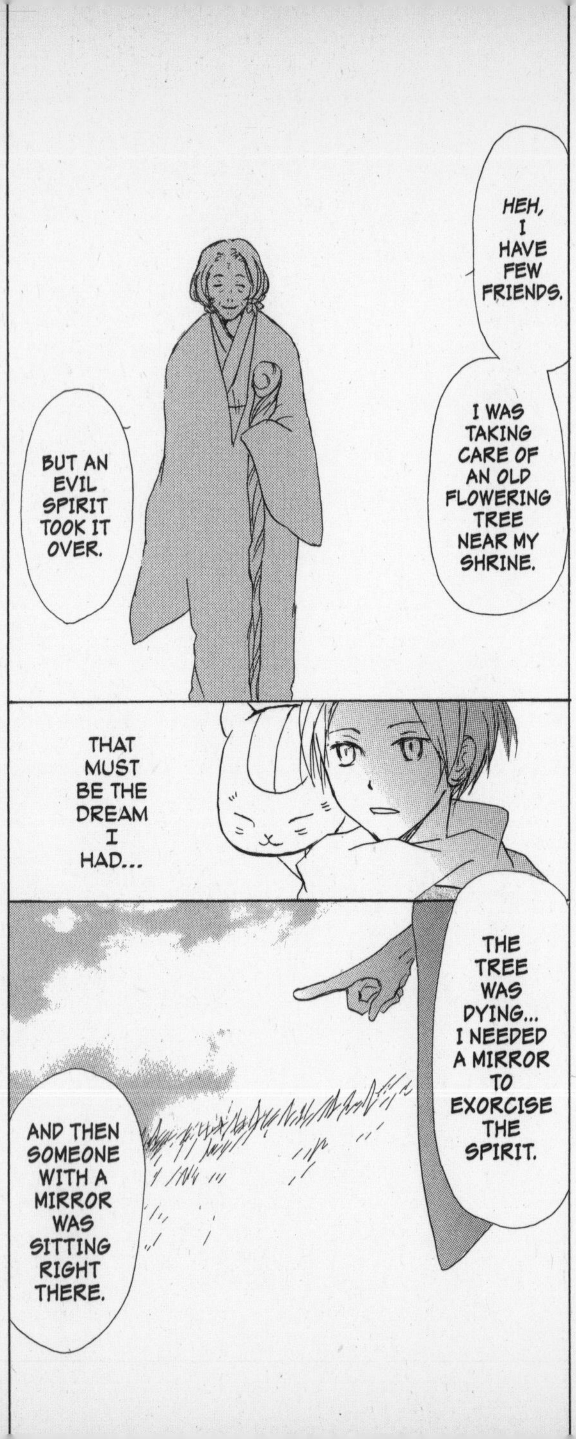
HEH, I HAVE FEW FRIENDS.
I WAS TAKING CARE OF AN OLD FLOWERING TREE NEAR MY SHRINE.
BUT AN EVIL SPIRIT TOOK IT OVER.
THAT MUST BE THE DREAM I HAD...
THE TREE WAS DYING... I NEEDED A MIRROR TO EXORCISE THE SPIRIT.
AND THEN SOMEONE WITH A MIRROR WAS SITTING RIGHT THERE.

02

❋"Hotarubi no Mori e"

I wrote a short story called "Hotarubi no Mori e" a while back, and Director Ohmori and the staff for the Natsume anime made it into a 40-minute anime.

It was also blessed with talented voice actors, who gave life to an innocent, sweet yet strong Hotaru, and a mysterious Gin, who isn't human but grows to face his confusing human emotions.

It's scheduled to air on Sept. 17, 2011

Tokyo: Cine Libre Ikebukuro

Osaka: Theater Umeda

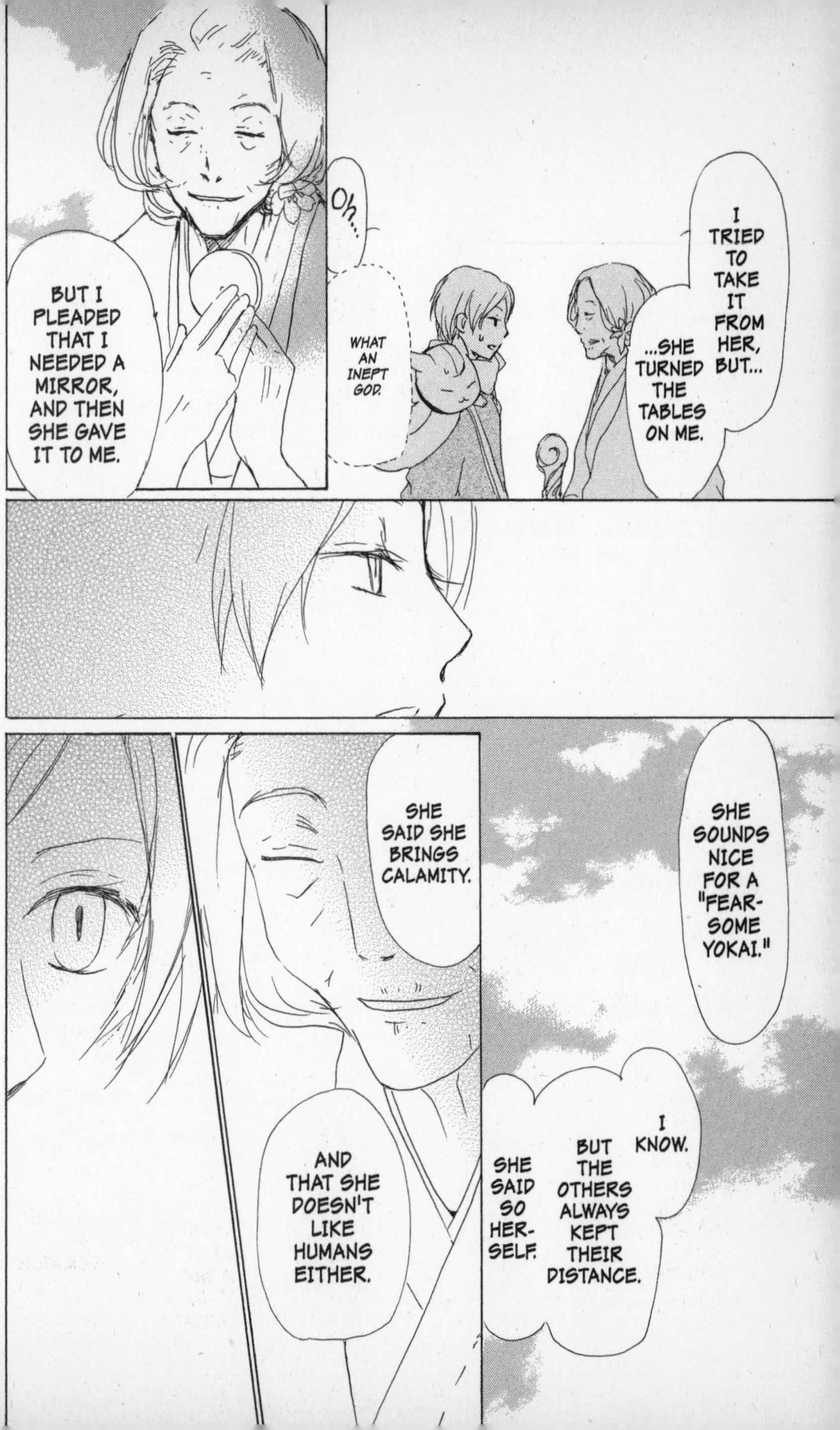
I TRIED TO TAKE IT FROM HER, BUT...
...SHE TURNED THE TABLES ON ME.
Oh...
WHAT AN INEPT GOD.
BUT I PLEADED THAT I NEEDED A MIRROR, AND THEN SHE GAVE IT TO ME.
SHE SOUNDS NICE FOR A "FEAR-SOME YOKAI."
I KNOW.
BUT THE OTHERS ALWAYS KEPT THEIR DISTANCE.
SHE SAID SO HER-SELF.
SHE SAID SHE BRINGS CALAMITY.
AND THAT SHE DOESN'T LIKE HUMANS EITHER.

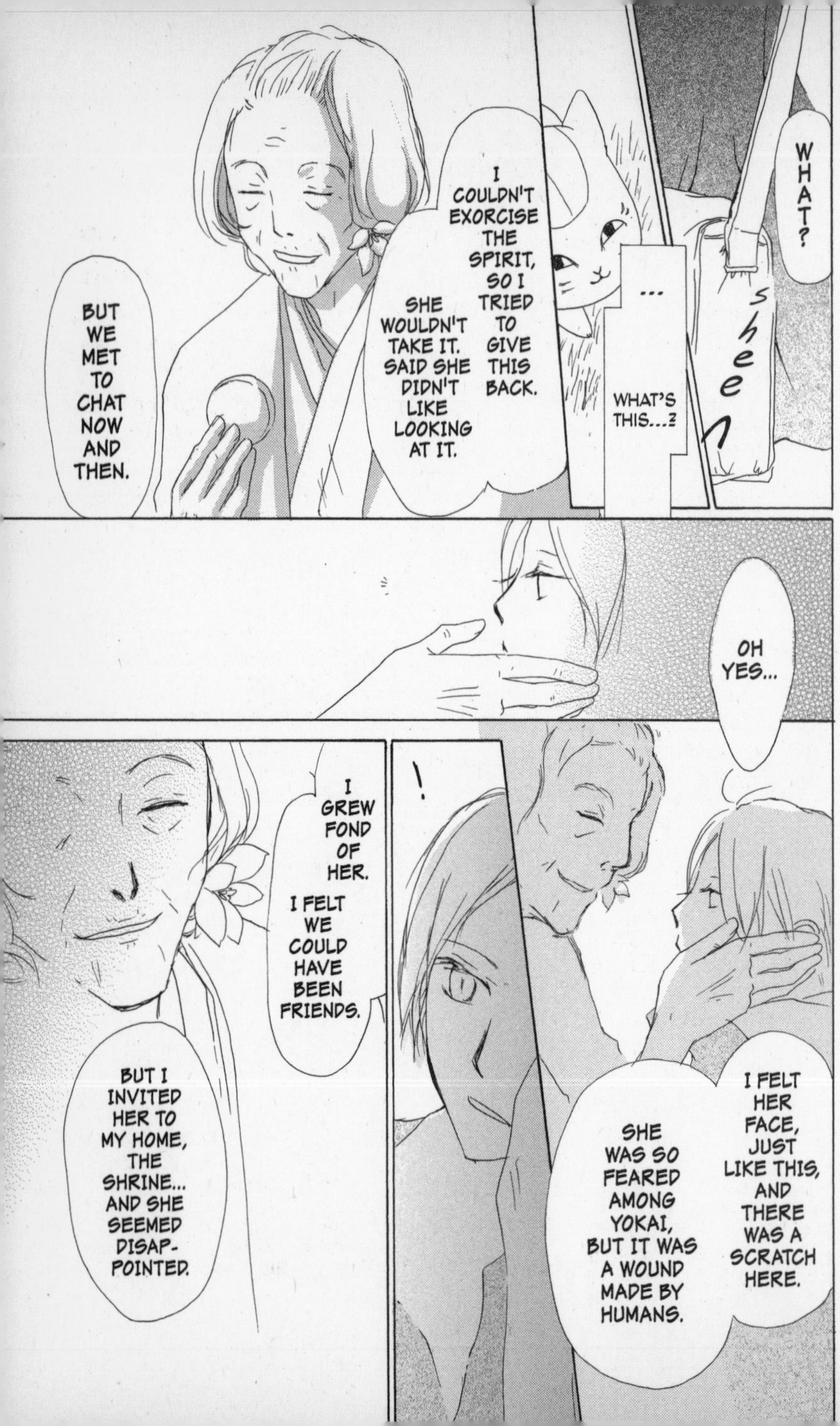
WHAT?
sheen
...
WHAT'S THIS...?
I COULDN'T EXORCISE THE SPIRIT, SO I TRIED TO GIVE THIS BACK.
SHE WOULDN'T TAKE IT. SAID SHE DIDN'T LIKE LOOKING AT IT.
BUT WE MET TO CHAT NOW AND THEN.
OH YES...
I FELT HER FACE, JUST LIKE THIS, AND THERE WAS A SCRATCH HERE.
SHE WAS SO FEARED AMONG YOKAI, BUT IT WAS A WOUND MADE BY HUMANS.
!
I GREW FOND OF HER.
I FELT WE COULD HAVE BEEN FRIENDS.
BUT I INVITED HER TO MY HOME, THE SHRINE... AND SHE SEEMED DISAPPOINTED.

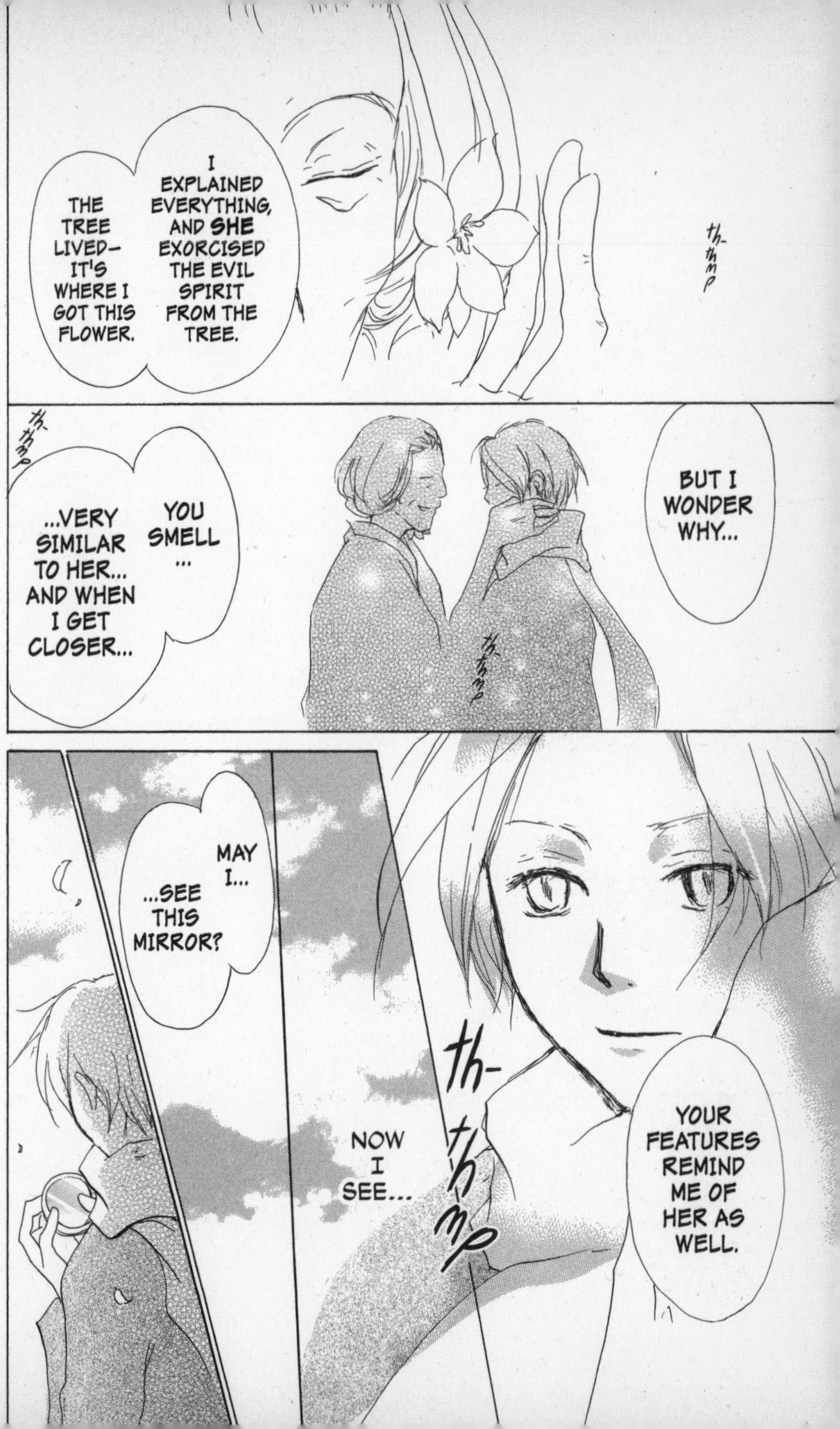
I EXPLAINED EVERYTHING, AND SHE EXORCISED THE EVIL SPIRIT FROM THE TREE.
THE TREE LIVED— IT'S WHERE I GOT THIS FLOWER.
th-thmp
BUT I WONDER WHY...
th-thmp
YOU SMELL ...
...VERY SIMILAR TO HER... AND WHEN I GET CLOSER...
th-thmp
YOUR FEATURES REMIND ME OF HER AS WELL.
th-thmp
NOW I SEE...
MAY I...
...SEE THIS MIRROR?

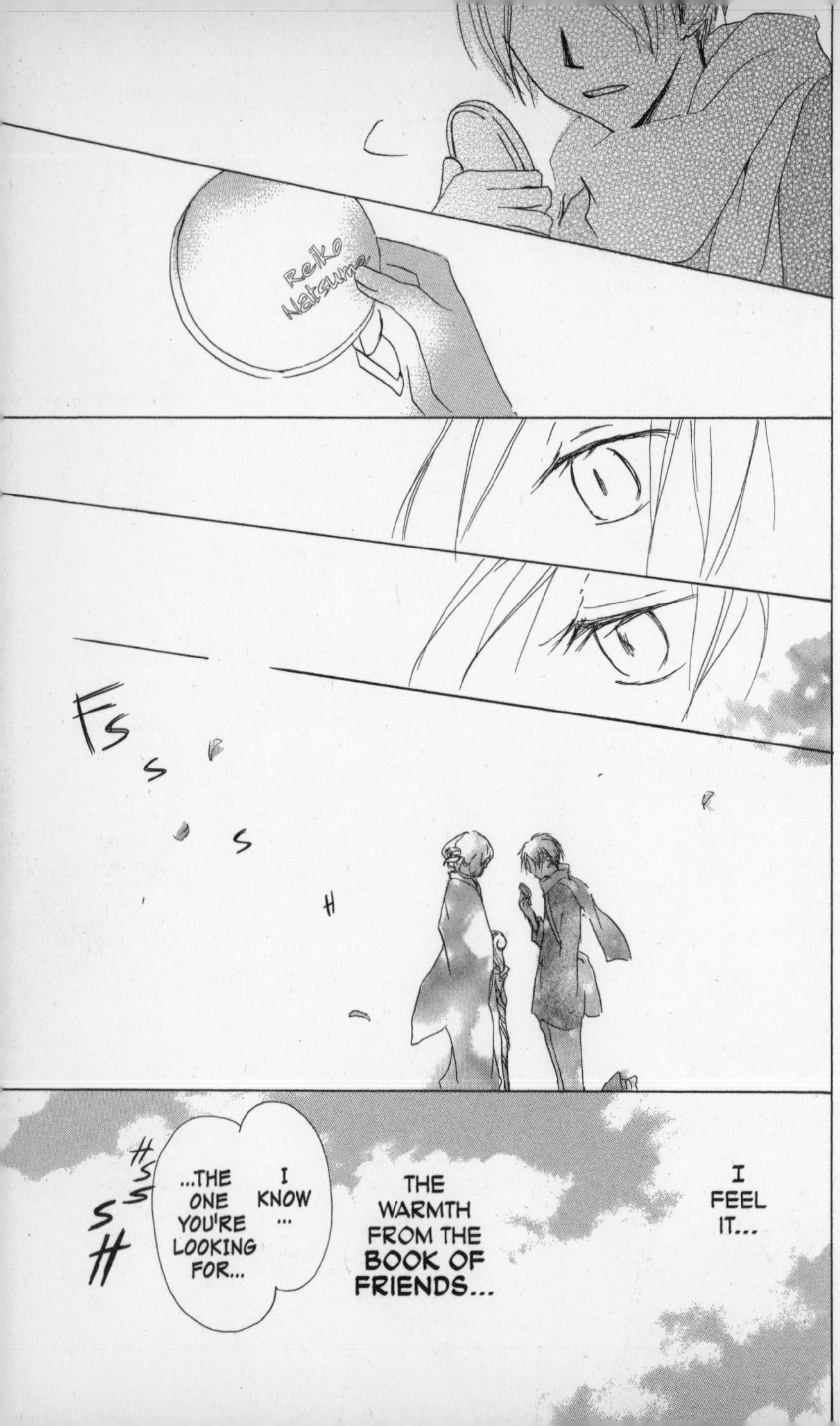
Reiko Natsume
FSSSH
I FEEL IT...
THE WARMTH FROM THE BOOK OF FRIENDS...
I KNOW...
...THE ONE YOU'RE LOOKING FOR...
HSSSH

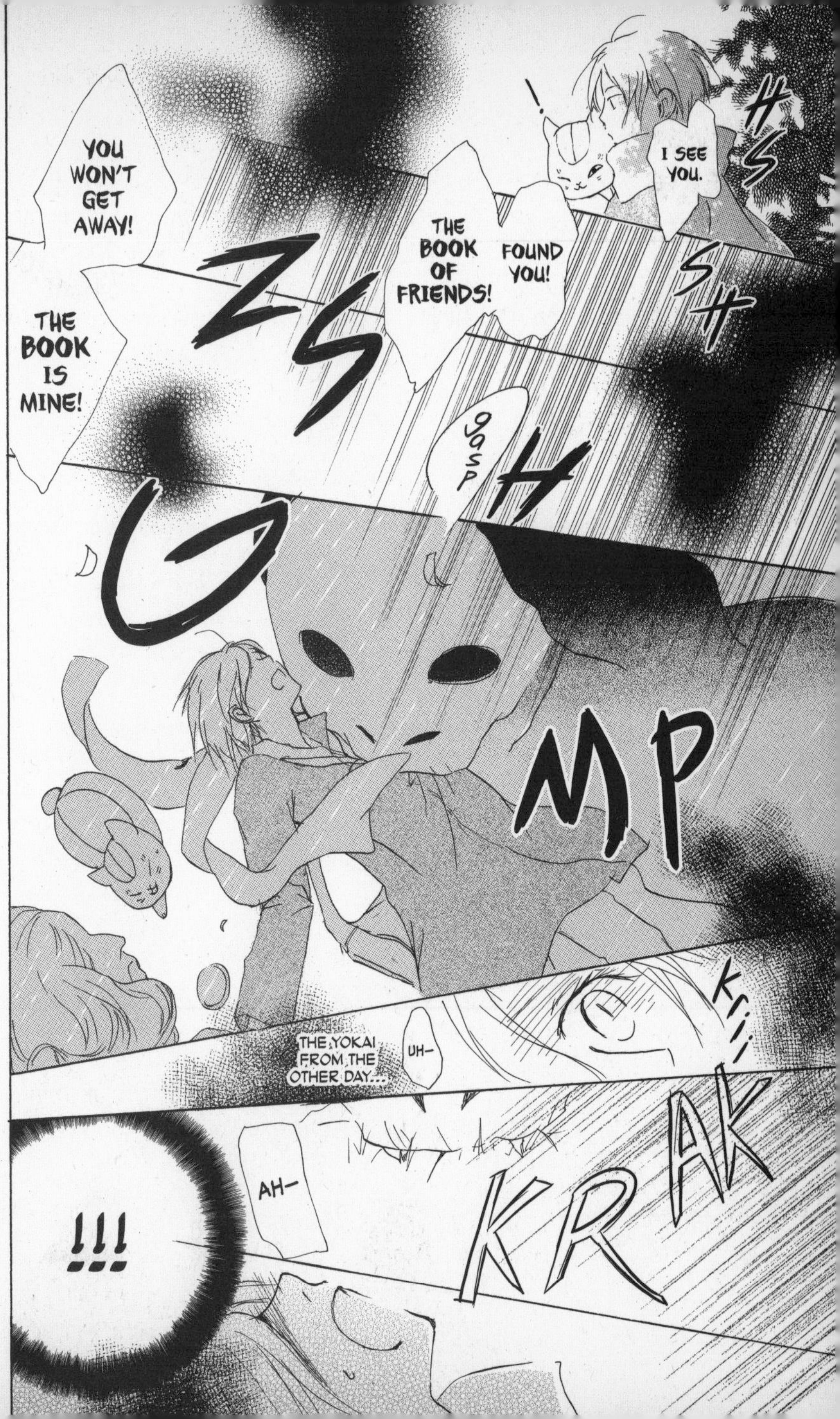

HS
I SEE YOU.
SH
!
FOUND YOU!
THE BOOK OF FRIENDS!
ZS
YOU WON'T GET AWAY!
THE BOOK IS MINE!
gasp
H
U
MP
kri
UH-
THE YOKAI FROM THE OTHER DAY...
KRAK
AH-
!!!

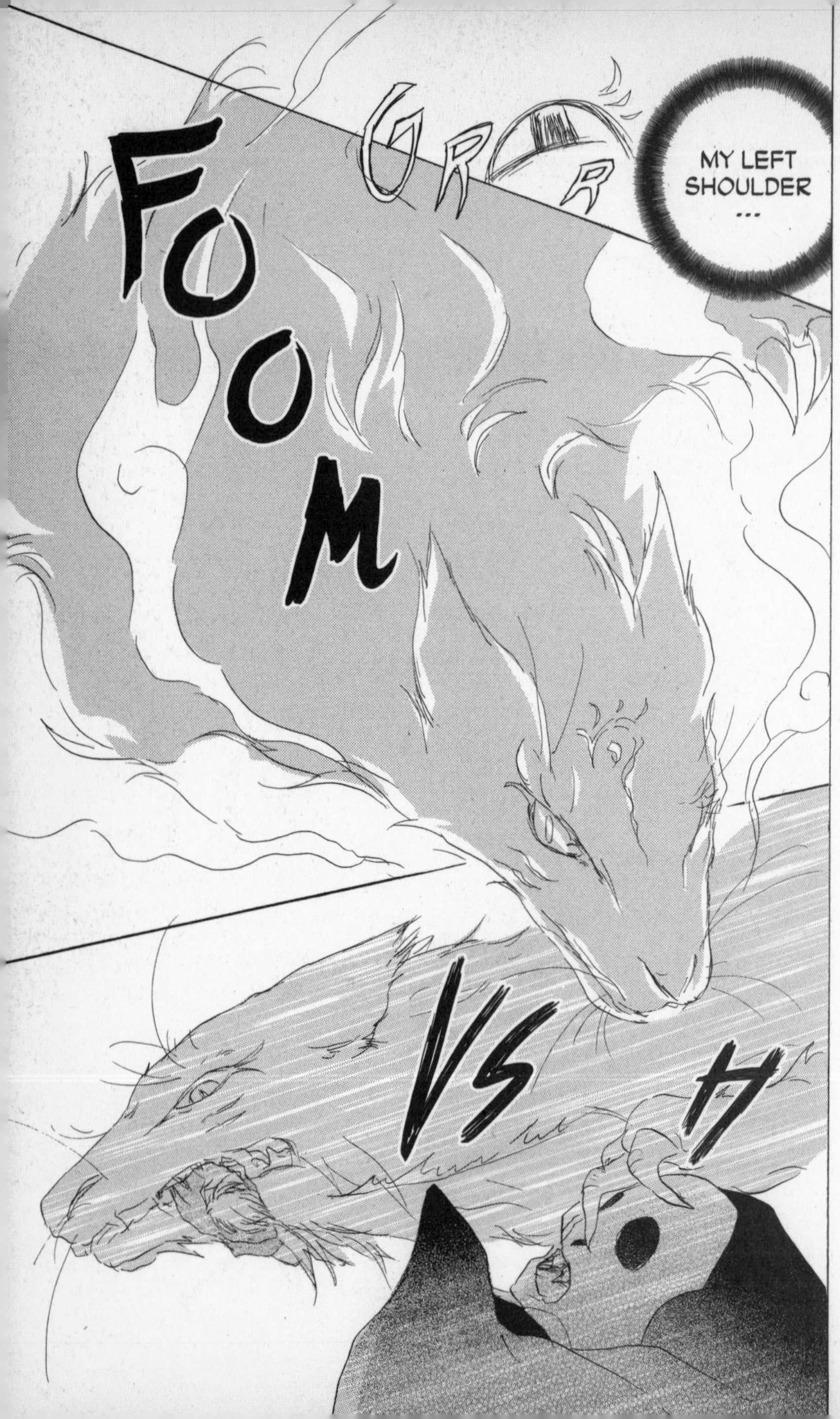
MY LEFT SHOULDER ...
GRRR
FOOM
VSH

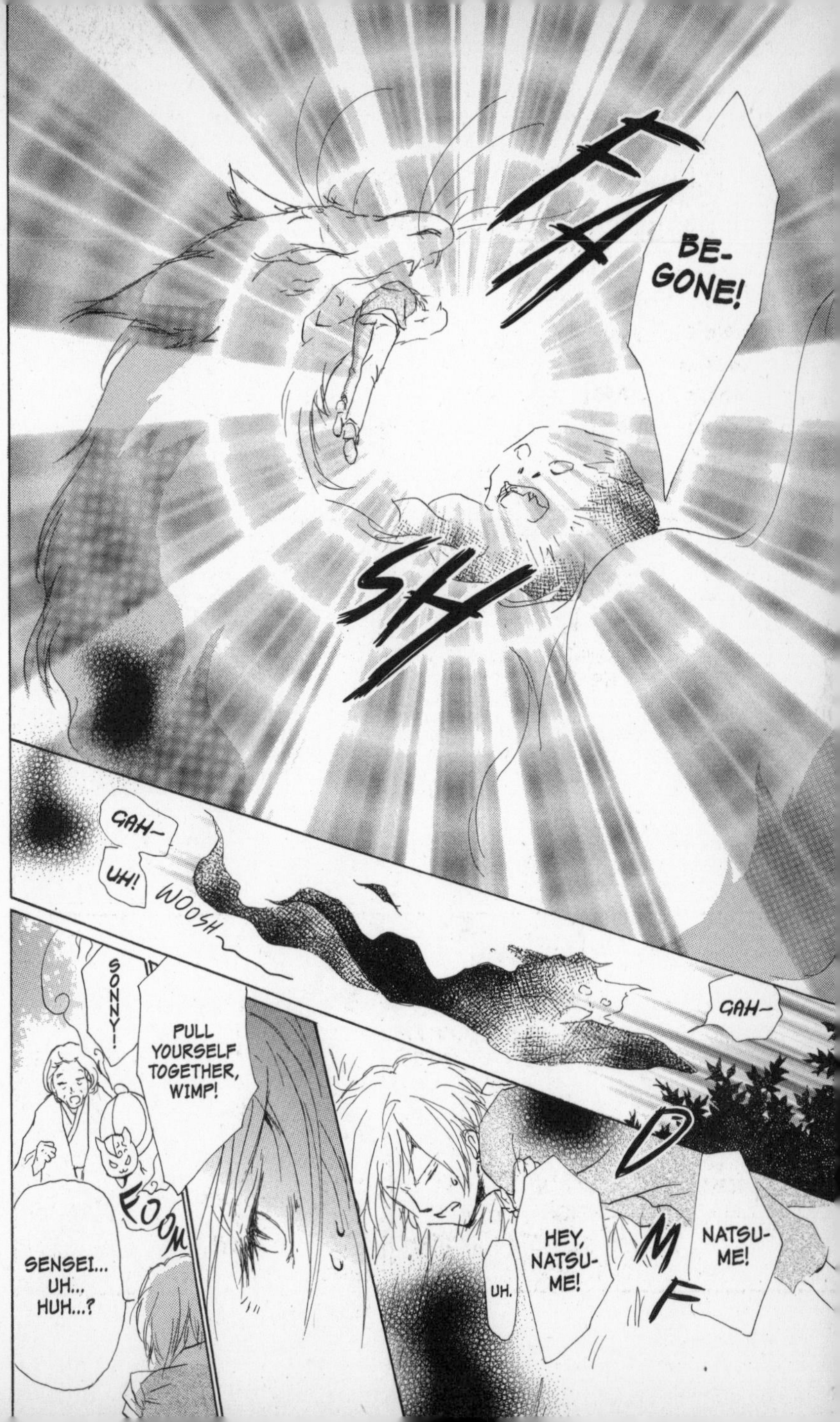
BE-GONE!
FA
SH
GAH-
WOOSH
GAH-UH!
NATSU-ME!
DOMF
HEY, NATSU-ME!
UH.
PULL YOURSELF TOGETHER, WIMP!
SONNY!
FOOM
SENSEI... UH... HUH...?

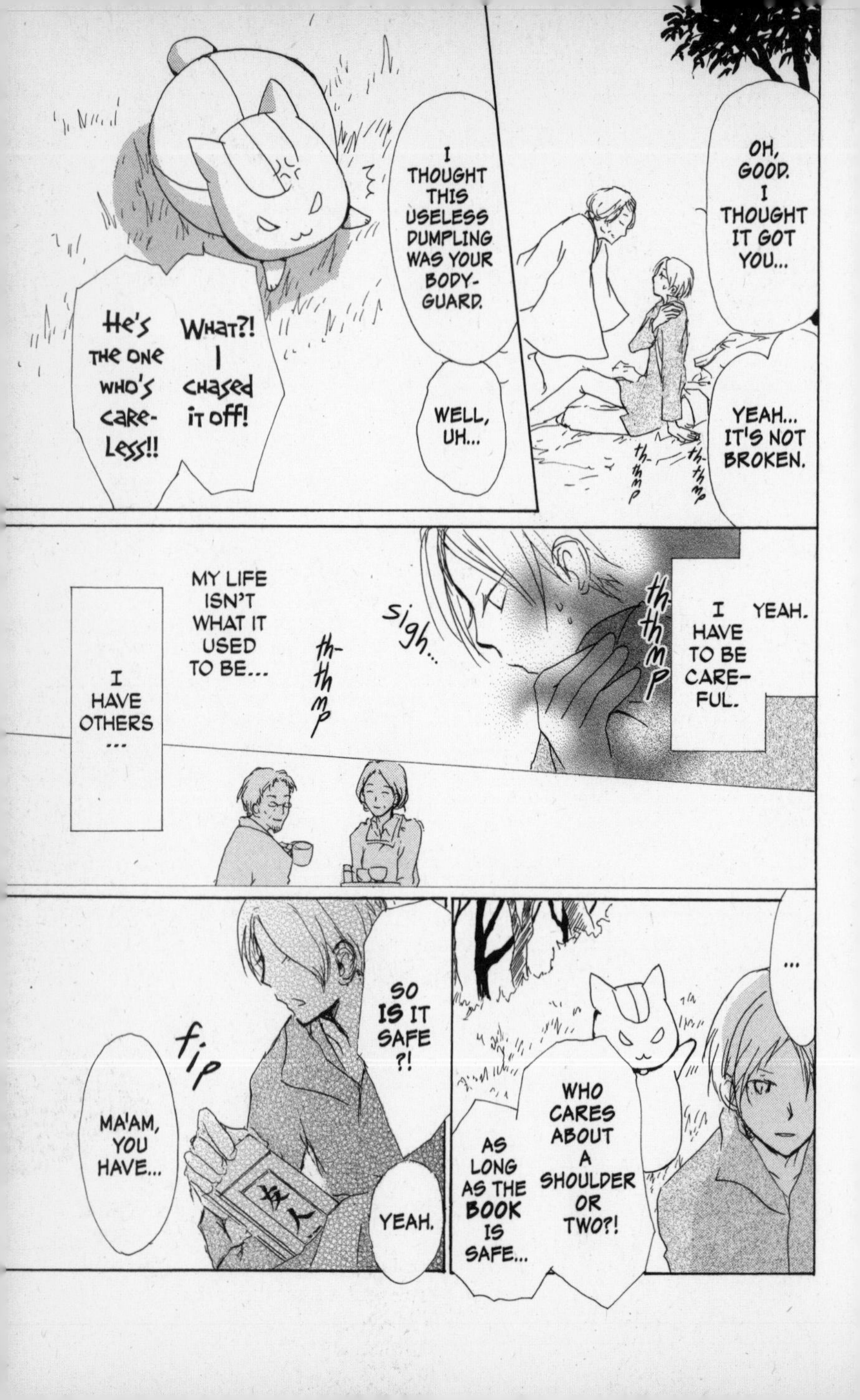
OH, GOOD. I THOUGHT IT GOT YOU...
YEAH... IT'S NOT BROKEN.
th-thmp
th-thmp
I THOUGHT THIS USELESS DUMPLING WAS YOUR BODY-GUARD.
WELL, UH...
WHAT?! I chased it off!
He's the one who's care-Less!!
th-thmp
YEAH.
I HAVE TO BE CARE-FUL.
sigh...
th-thmp
MY LIFE ISN'T WHAT IT USED TO BE...
I HAVE OTHERS...
...
WHO CARES ABOUT A SHOULDER OR TWO?!
AS LONG AS THE BOOK IS SAFE...
SO IS IT SAFE?!
YEAH.
fip
MA'AM, YOU HAVE...

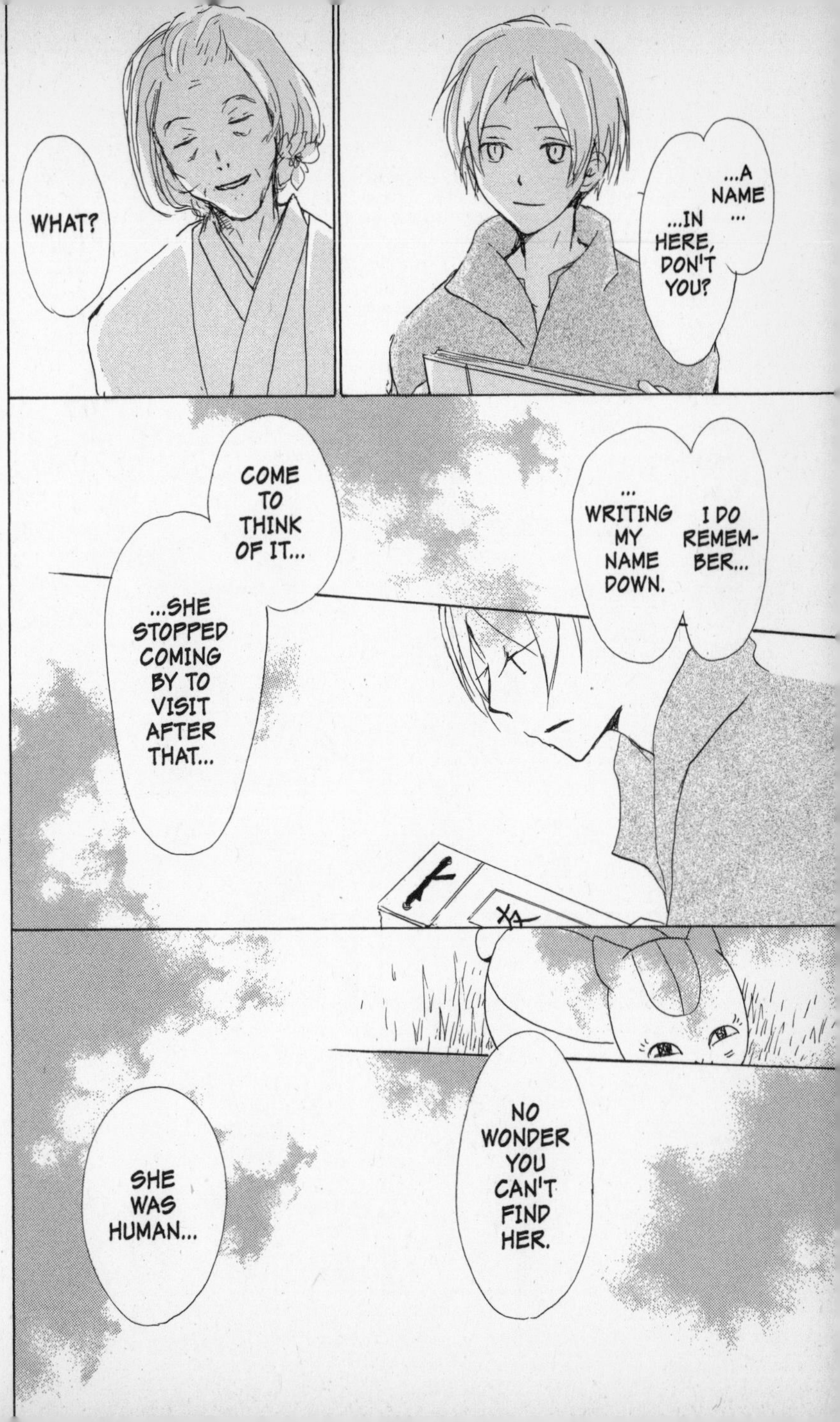
...A NAME ...
...IN HERE, DON'T YOU?
WHAT?
I DO REMEMBER...
...WRITING MY NAME DOWN.
COME TO THINK OF IT...
...SHE STOPPED COMING BY TO VISIT AFTER THAT...
NO WONDER YOU CAN'T FIND HER.
SHE WAS HUMAN...

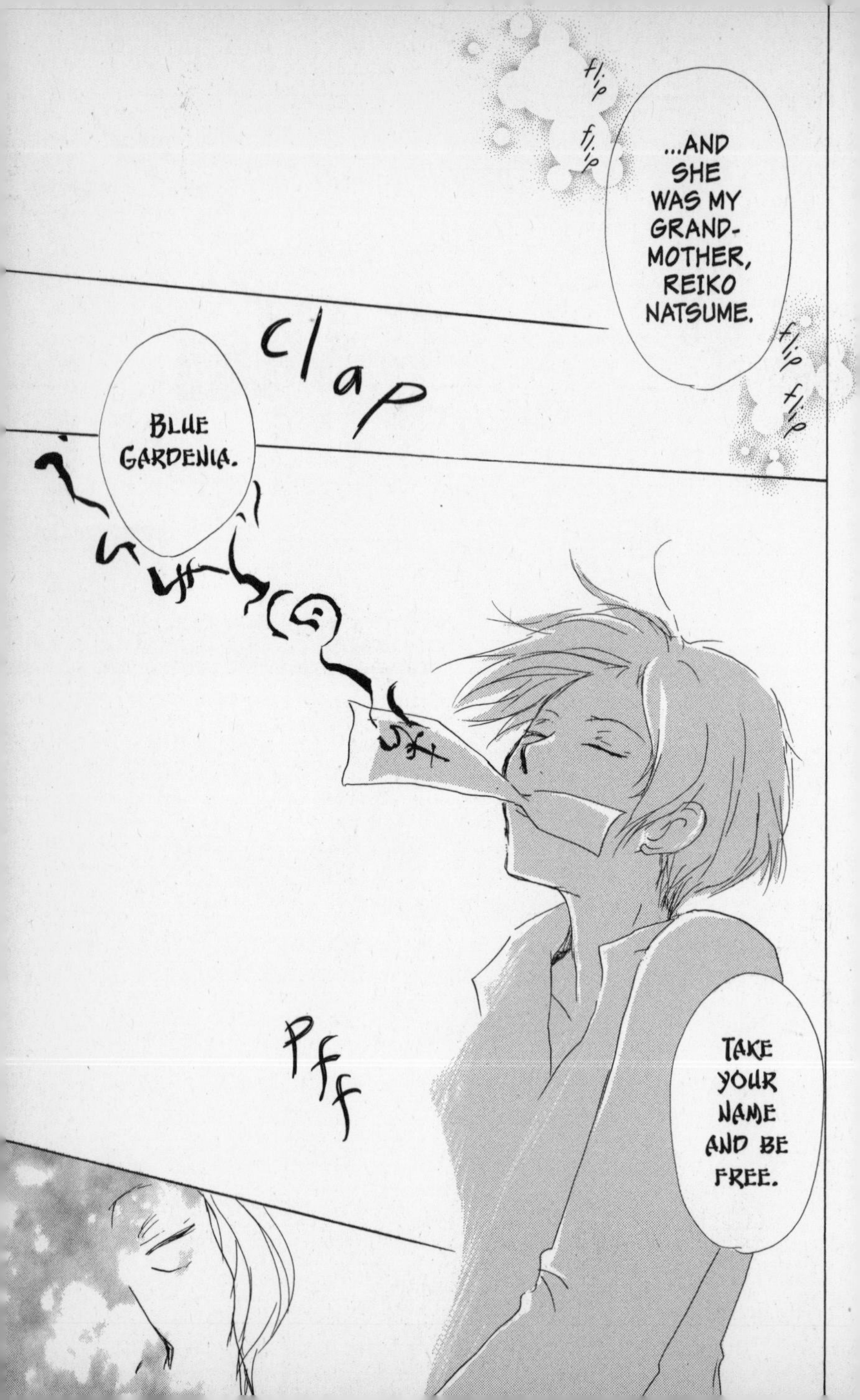
flip flip
...AND SHE WAS MY GRANDMOTHER, REIKO NATSUME.
flip flip
clap
BLUE GARDENIA.
TAKE YOUR NAME AND BE FREE.
Pff

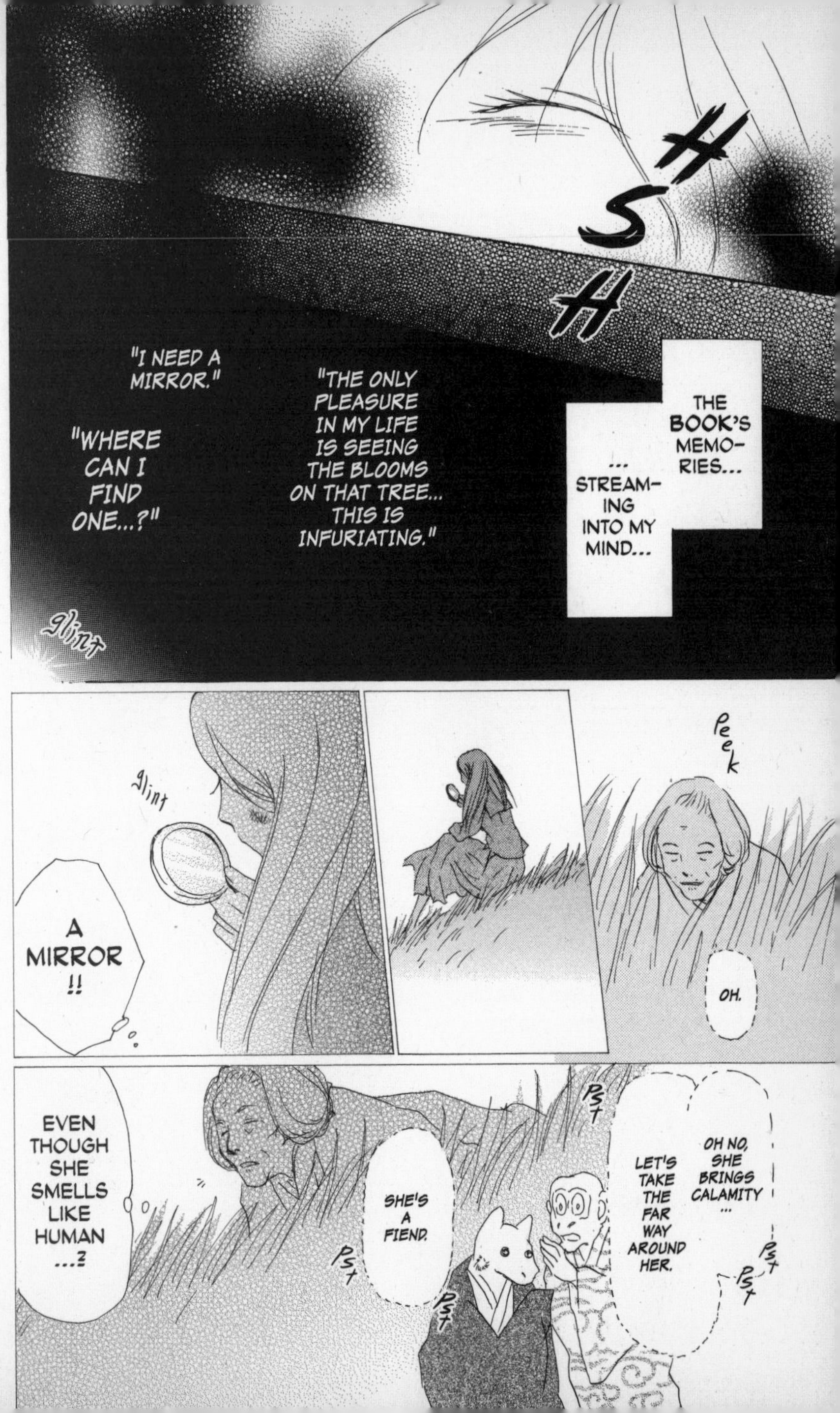
HSH
THE BOOK'S MEMO-RIES...
...STREAM-ING INTO MY MIND...
"THE ONLY PLEASURE IN MY LIFE IS SEEING THE BLOOMS ON THAT TREE... THIS IS INFURIATING."
"I NEED A MIRROR."
"WHERE CAN I FIND ONE...?"
glint
Peek
OH.
glint
A MIRROR !!
PST
OH NO, SHE BRINGS CALAMITY...
LET'S TAKE THE FAR WAY AROUND HER.
PST
PST
SHE'S A FIEND.
PST
PST
EVEN THOUGH SHE SMELLS LIKE HUMAN...?

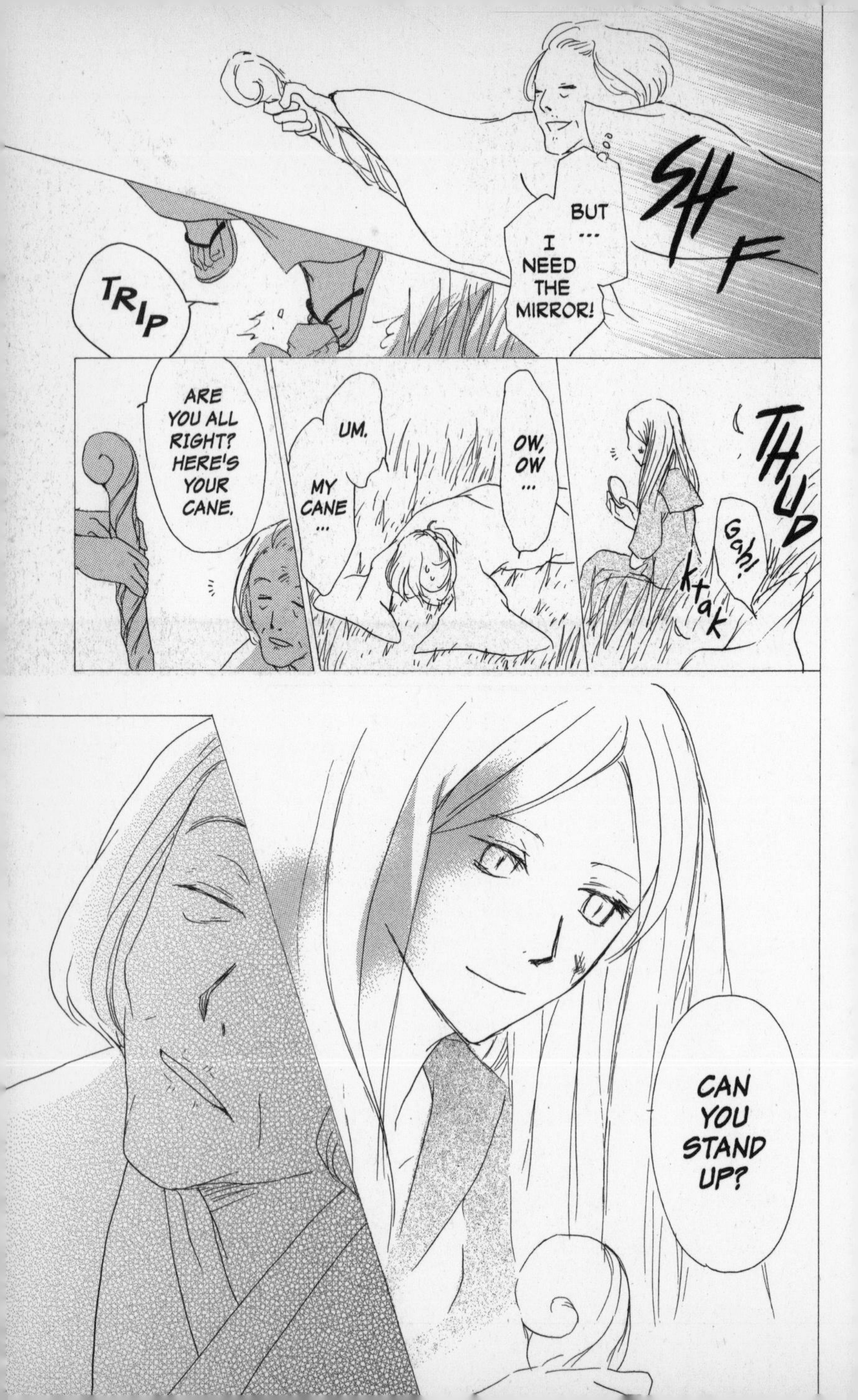
SHF
BUT ... I NEED THE MIRROR!
TRIP
THUD
Gah!
ktak
OW, OW ...
UM.
MY CANE ...
ARE YOU ALL RIGHT? HERE'S YOUR CANE.
CAN YOU STAND UP?

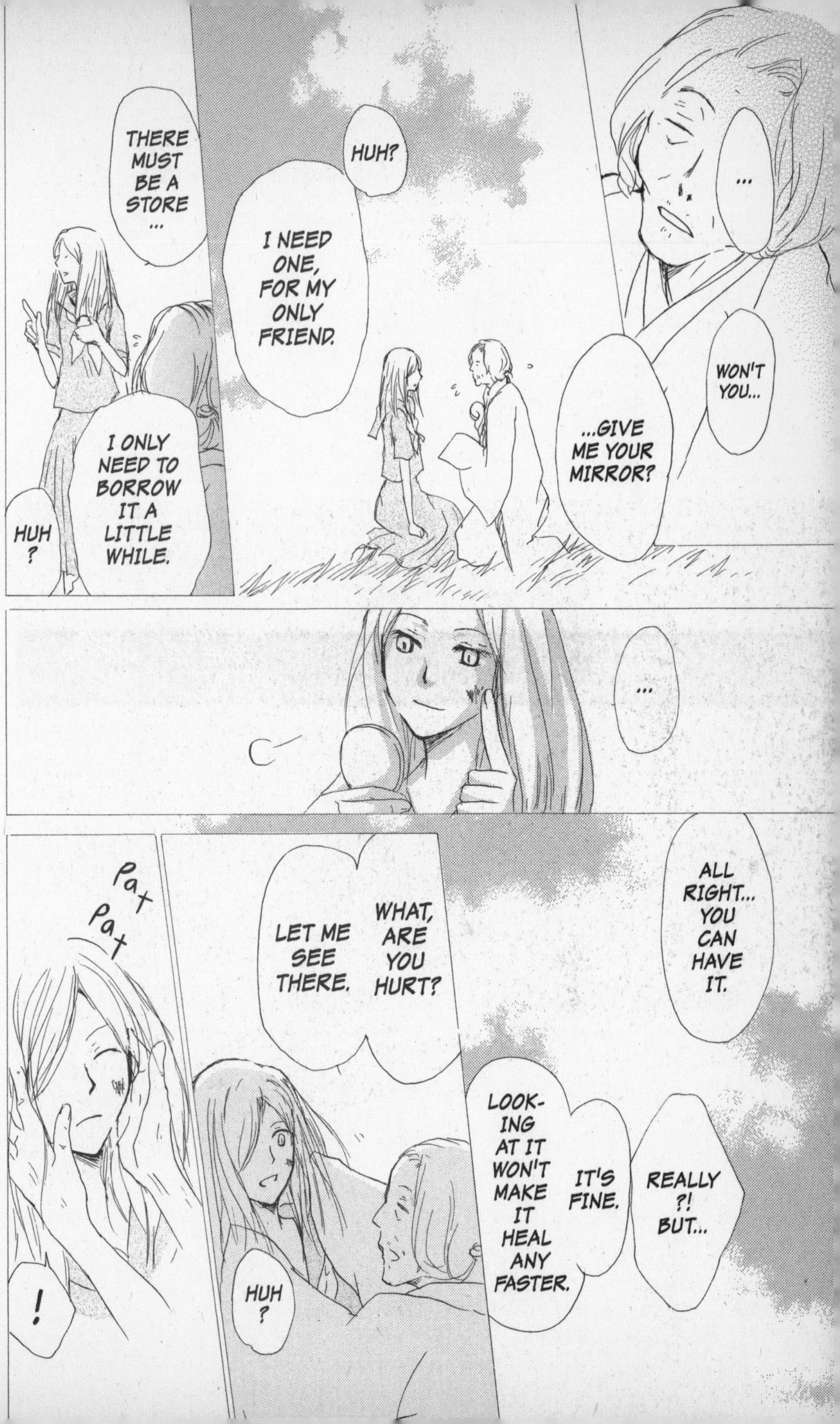
...
WON'T YOU...
...GIVE ME YOUR MIRROR?
HUH?
I NEED ONE, FOR MY ONLY FRIEND.
THERE MUST BE A STORE ...
I ONLY NEED TO BORROW IT A LITTLE WHILE.
HUH ?
...
ALL RIGHT... YOU CAN HAVE IT.
REALLY ?! BUT...
IT'S FINE.
LOOK-ING AT IT WON'T MAKE IT HEAL ANY FASTER.
WHAT, ARE YOU HURT?
LET ME SEE THERE.
HUH ?
Pat Pat
!

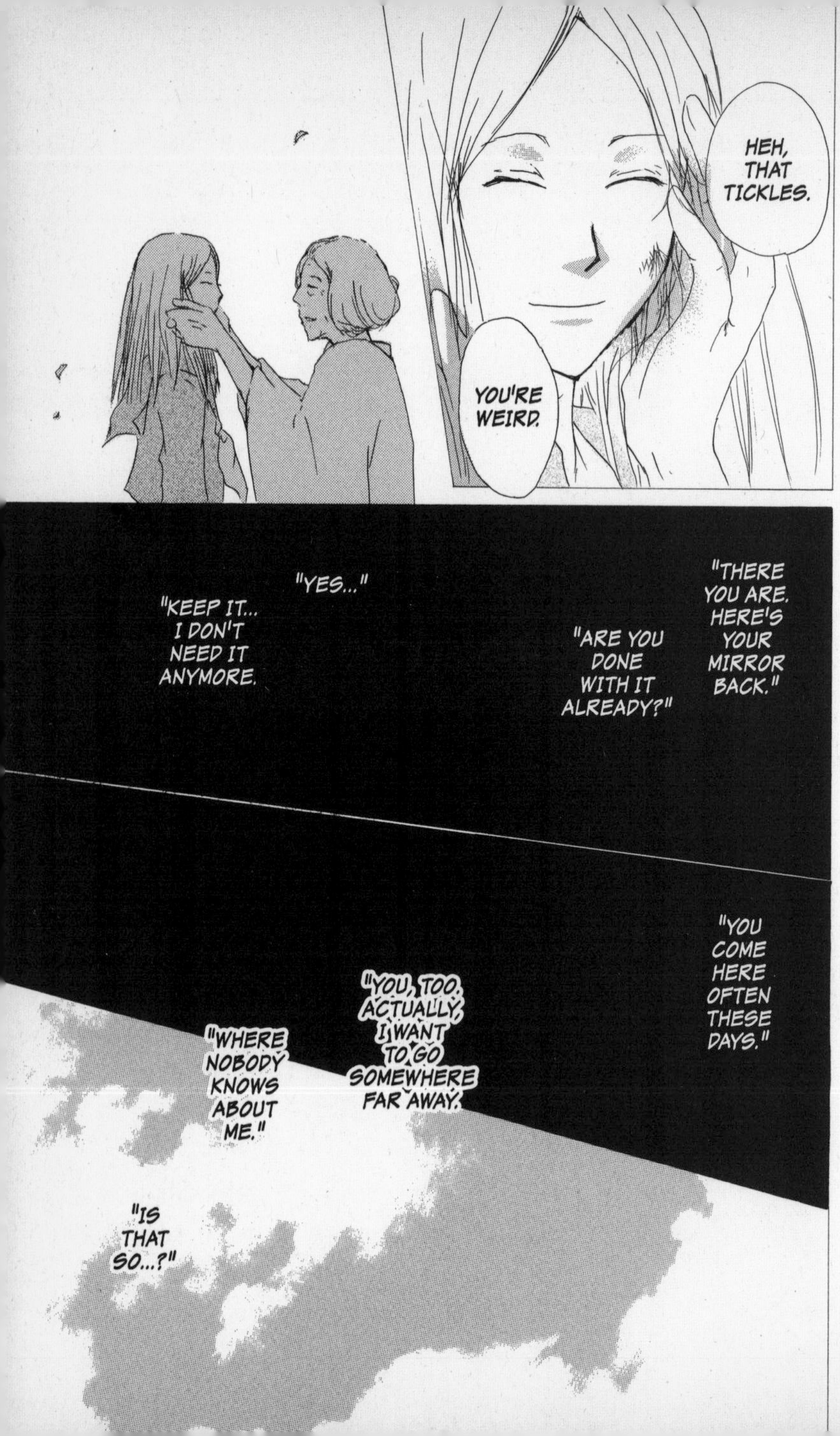
HEH, THAT TICKLES.
YOU'RE WEIRD.
"THERE YOU ARE. HERE'S YOUR MIRROR BACK."
"ARE YOU DONE WITH IT ALREADY?"
"YES..."
"KEEP IT... I DON'T NEED IT ANYMORE.
"YOU COME HERE OFTEN THESE DAYS."
"YOU, TOO. ACTUALLY, I WANT TO GO SOMEWHERE FAR AWAY.
"WHERE NOBODY KNOWS ABOUT ME."
"IS THAT SO...?"

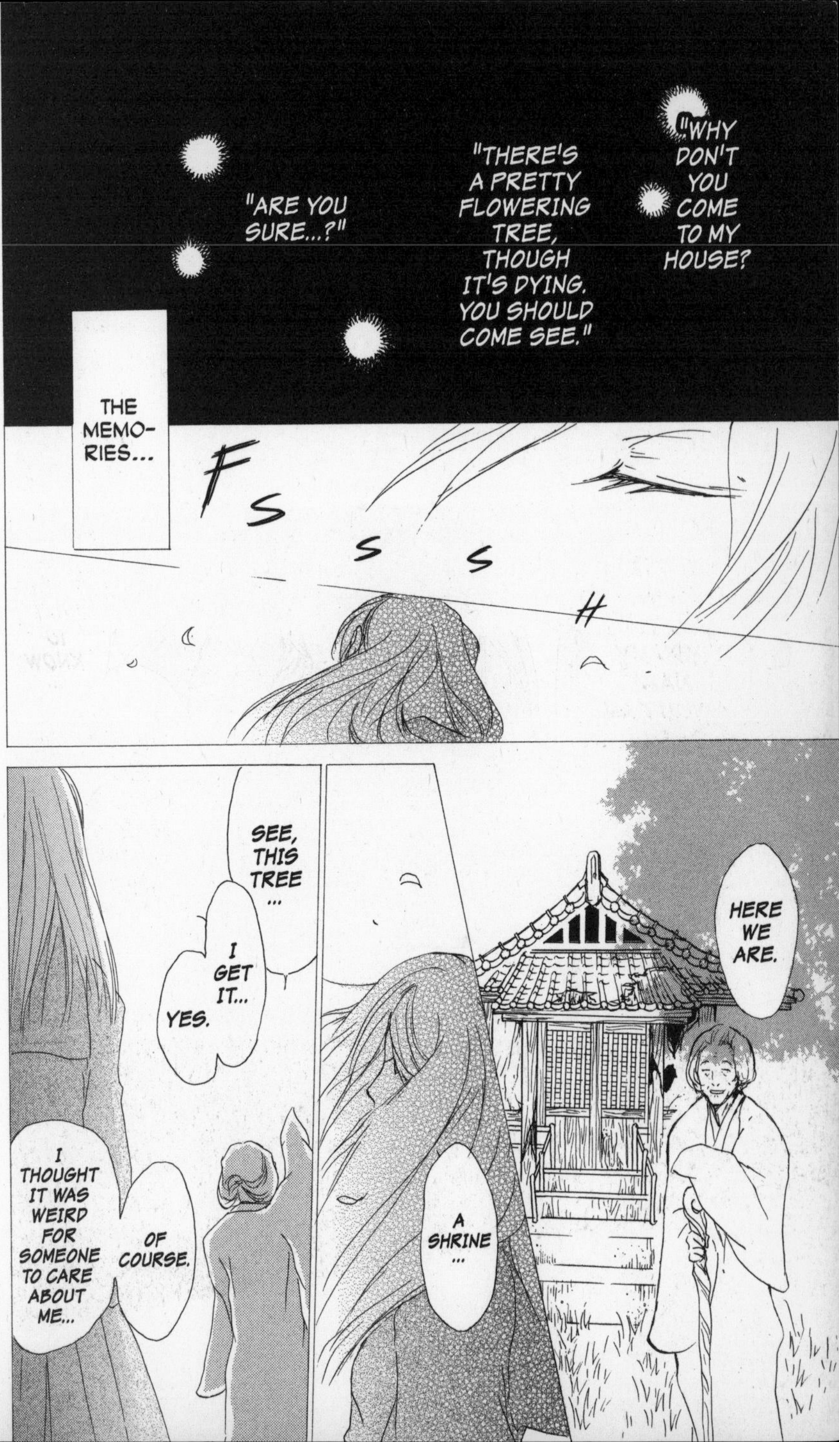
"WHY DON'T YOU COME TO MY HOUSE?
"THERE'S A PRETTY FLOWERING TREE, THOUGH IT'S DYING. YOU SHOULD COME SEE."
"ARE YOU SURE...?"
THE MEMO-RIES...
FSSSH
HERE WE ARE.
A SHRINE ...
SEE, THIS TREE ...
I GET IT... YES.
OF COURSE.
I THOUGHT IT WAS WEIRD FOR SOMEONE TO CARE ABOUT ME...

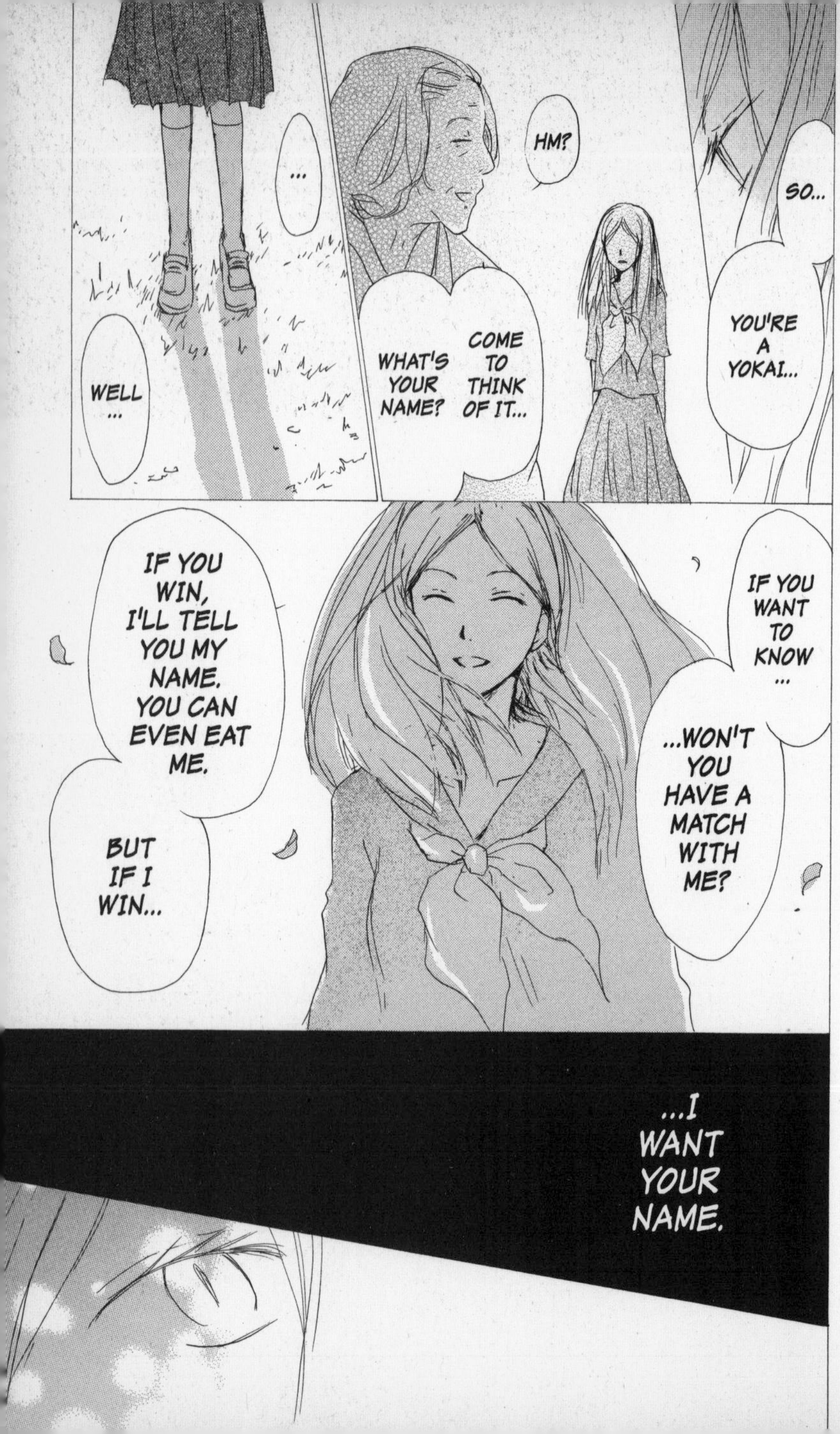
SO...
YOU'RE A YOKAI...
HM?
COME TO THINK OF IT...
WHAT'S YOUR NAME?
...
WELL...
IF YOU WANT TO KNOW...
...WON'T YOU HAVE A MATCH WITH ME?
IF YOU WIN, I'LL TELL YOU MY NAME. YOU CAN EVEN EAT ME.
BUT IF I WIN...
...I WANT YOUR NAME.

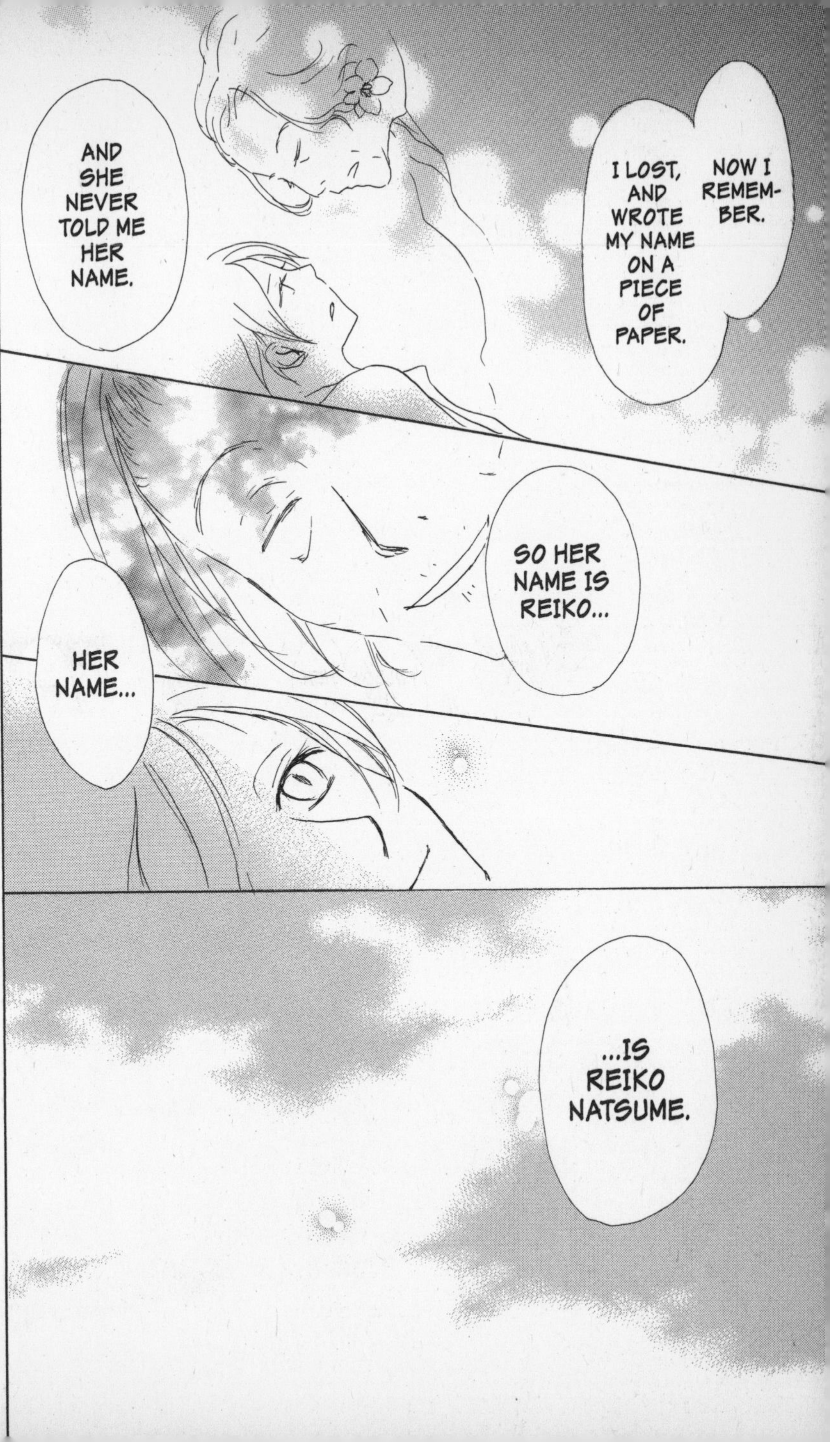
NOW I REMEMBER.
I LOST, AND WROTE MY NAME ON A PIECE OF PAPER.
AND SHE NEVER TOLD ME HER NAME.
SO HER NAME IS REIKO...
HER NAME...
...IS REIKO NATSUME.

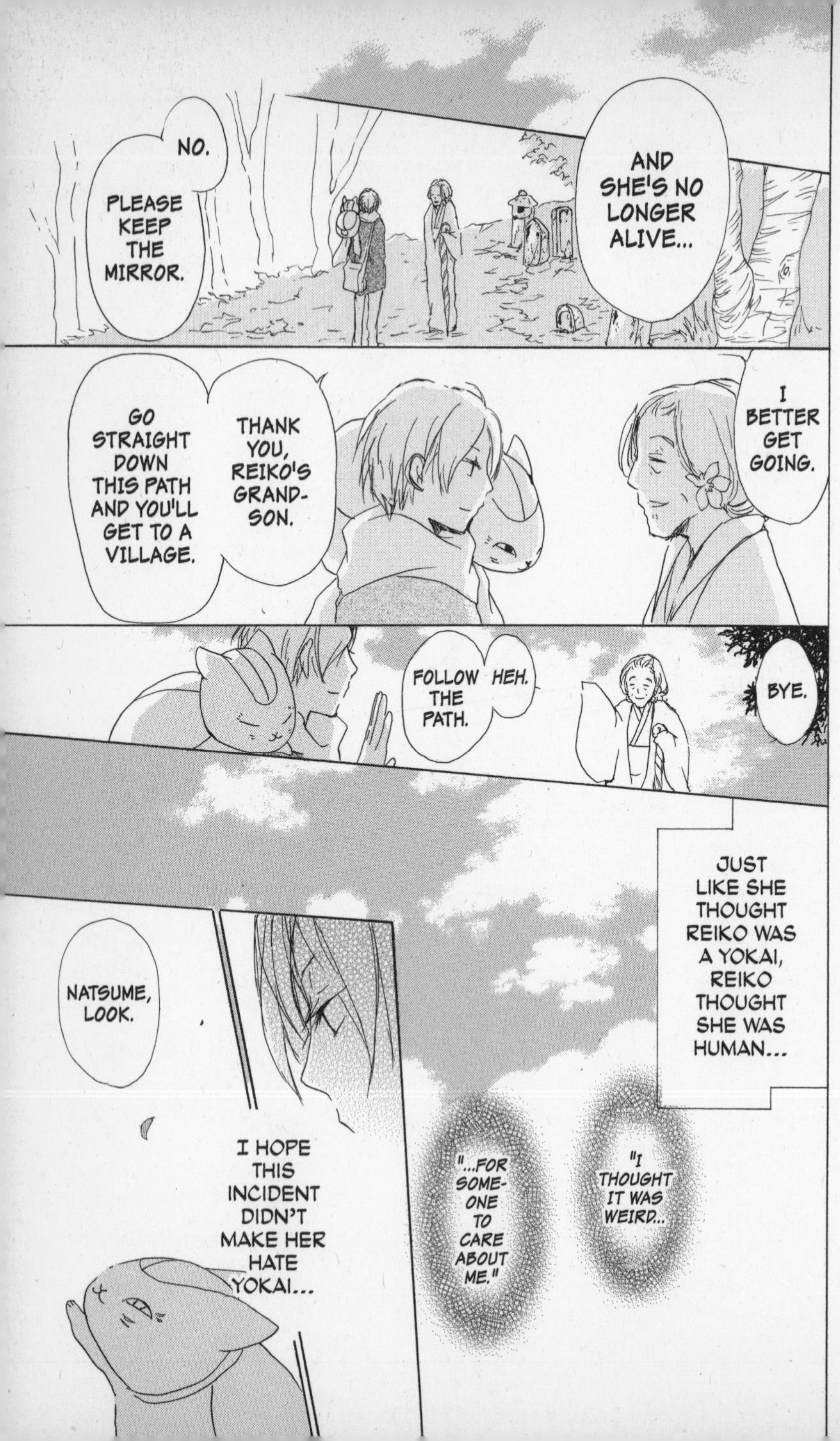
AND SHE'S NO LONGER ALIVE...
NO.
PLEASE KEEP THE MIRROR.
I BETTER GET GOING.
THANK YOU, REIKO'S GRAND-SON.
GO STRAIGHT DOWN THIS PATH AND YOU'LL GET TO A VILLAGE.
BYE.
HEH.
FOLLOW THE PATH.
JUST LIKE SHE THOUGHT REIKO WAS A YOKAI, REIKO THOUGHT SHE WAS HUMAN...
"I THOUGHT IT WAS WEIRD...
"...FOR SOME-ONE TO CARE ABOUT ME."
NATSUME, LOOK.
I HOPE THIS INCIDENT DIDN'T MAKE HER HATE YOKAI...

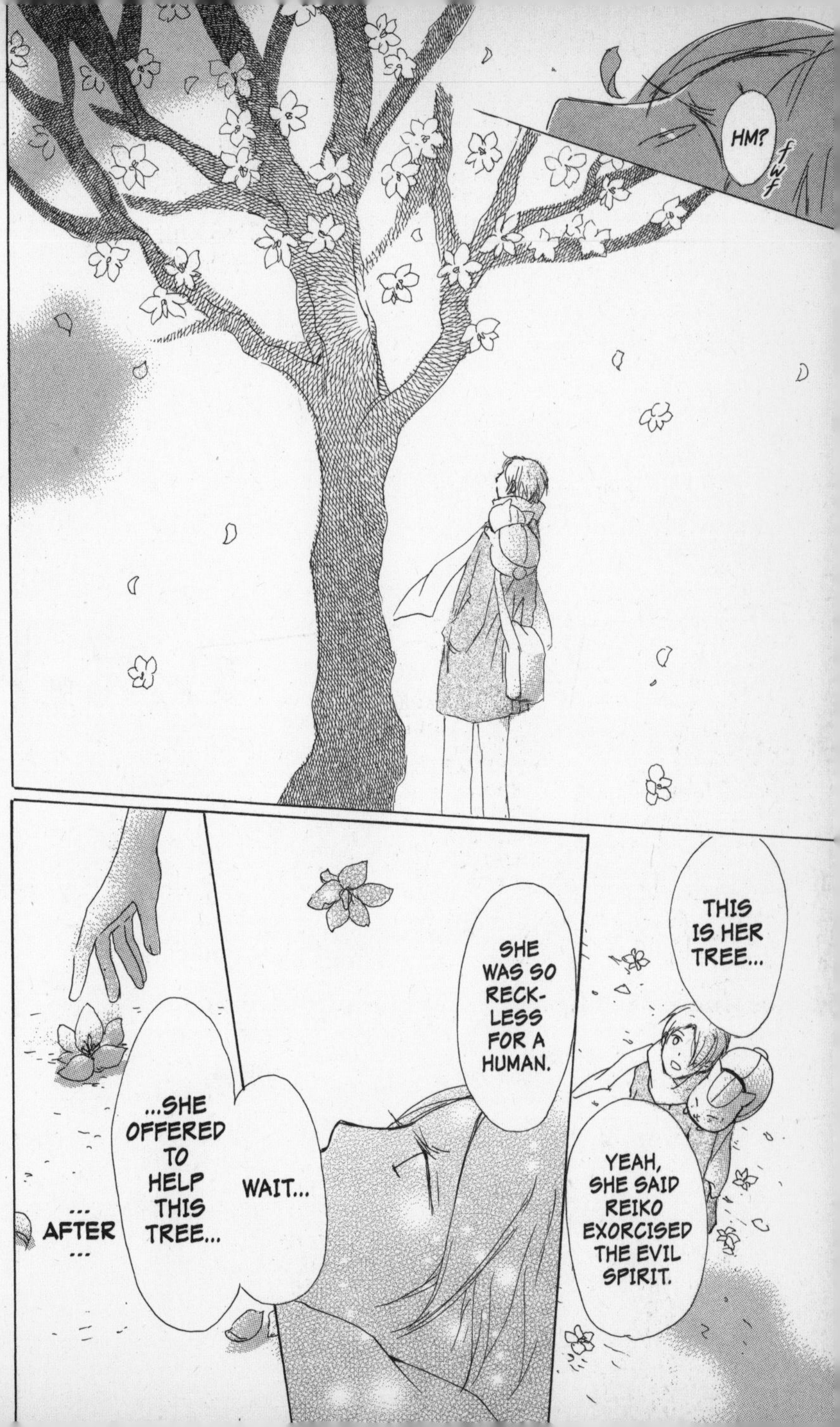
HM?
fwf
THIS IS HER TREE...
YEAH, SHE SAID REIKO EXORCISED THE EVIL SPIRIT.
SHE WAS SO RECKLESS FOR A HUMAN.
WAIT...
...SHE OFFERED TO HELP THIS TREE...
...AFTER...

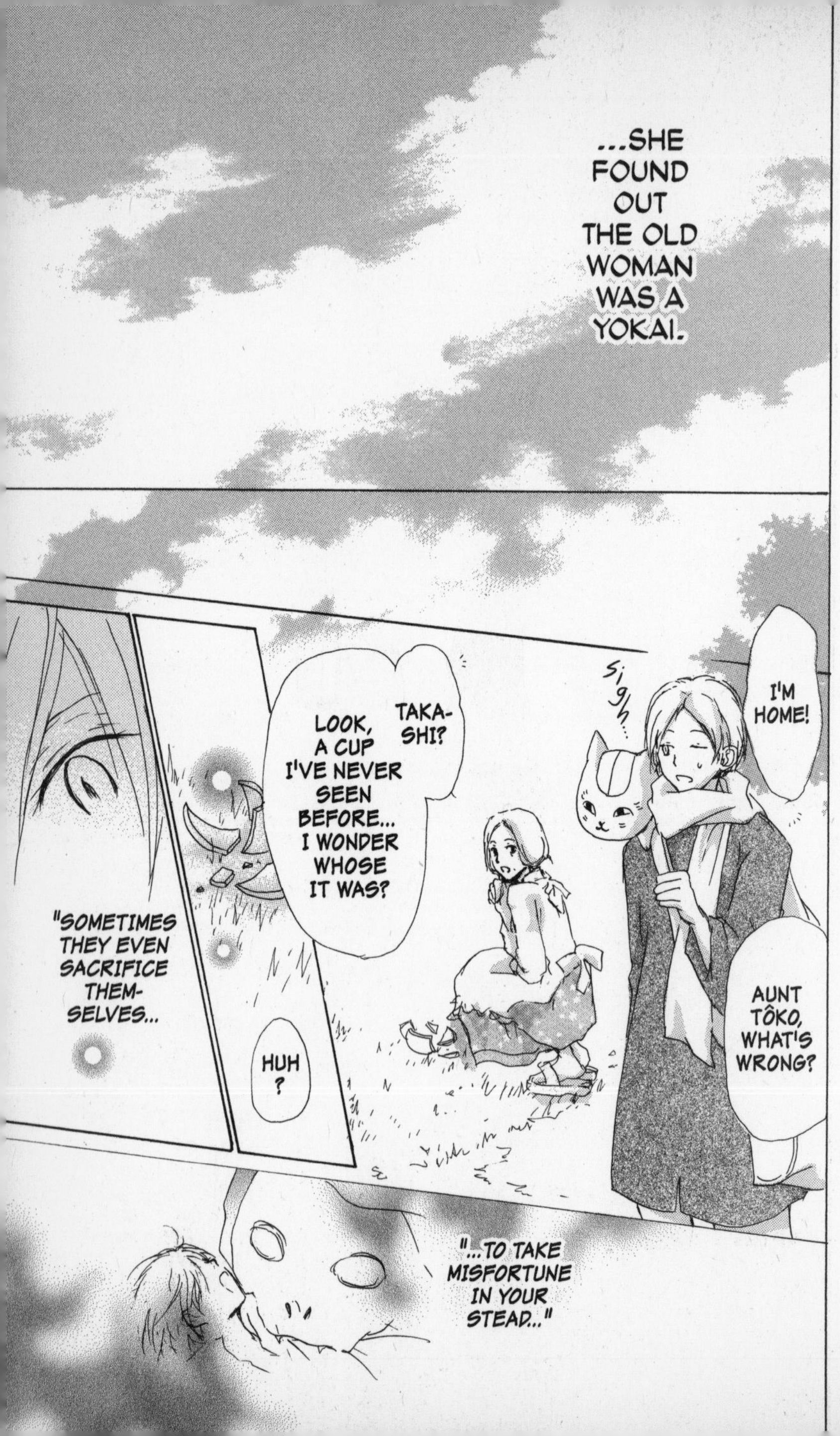
...SHE FOUND OUT THE OLD WOMAN WAS A YOKAI.
I'M HOME!
sigh...
AUNT TÔKO, WHAT'S WRONG?
TAKA-SHI?
LOOK, A CUP I'VE NEVER SEEN BEFORE... I WONDER WHOSE IT WAS?
HUH?
"SOMETIMES THEY EVEN SACRIFICE THEM-SELVES...
"...TO TAKE MISFORTUNE IN YOUR STEAD..."

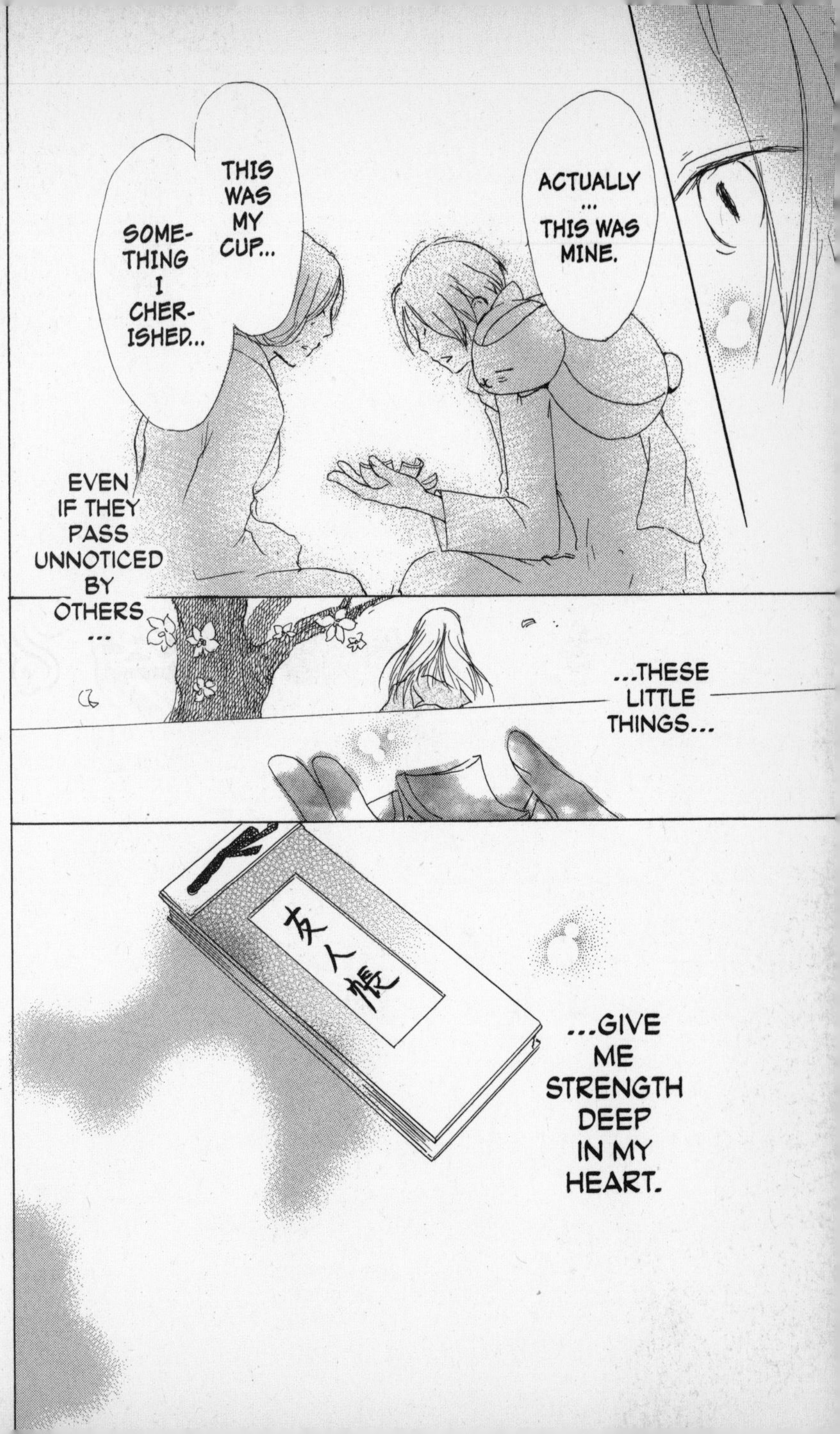
ACTUALLY ... THIS WAS MINE.
THIS WAS MY CUP...
SOMETHING I CHERISHED...
EVEN IF THEY PASS UNNOTICED BY OTHERS ...
...THESE LITTLE THINGS...
友人帳
...GIVE ME STRENGTH DEEP IN MY HEART.

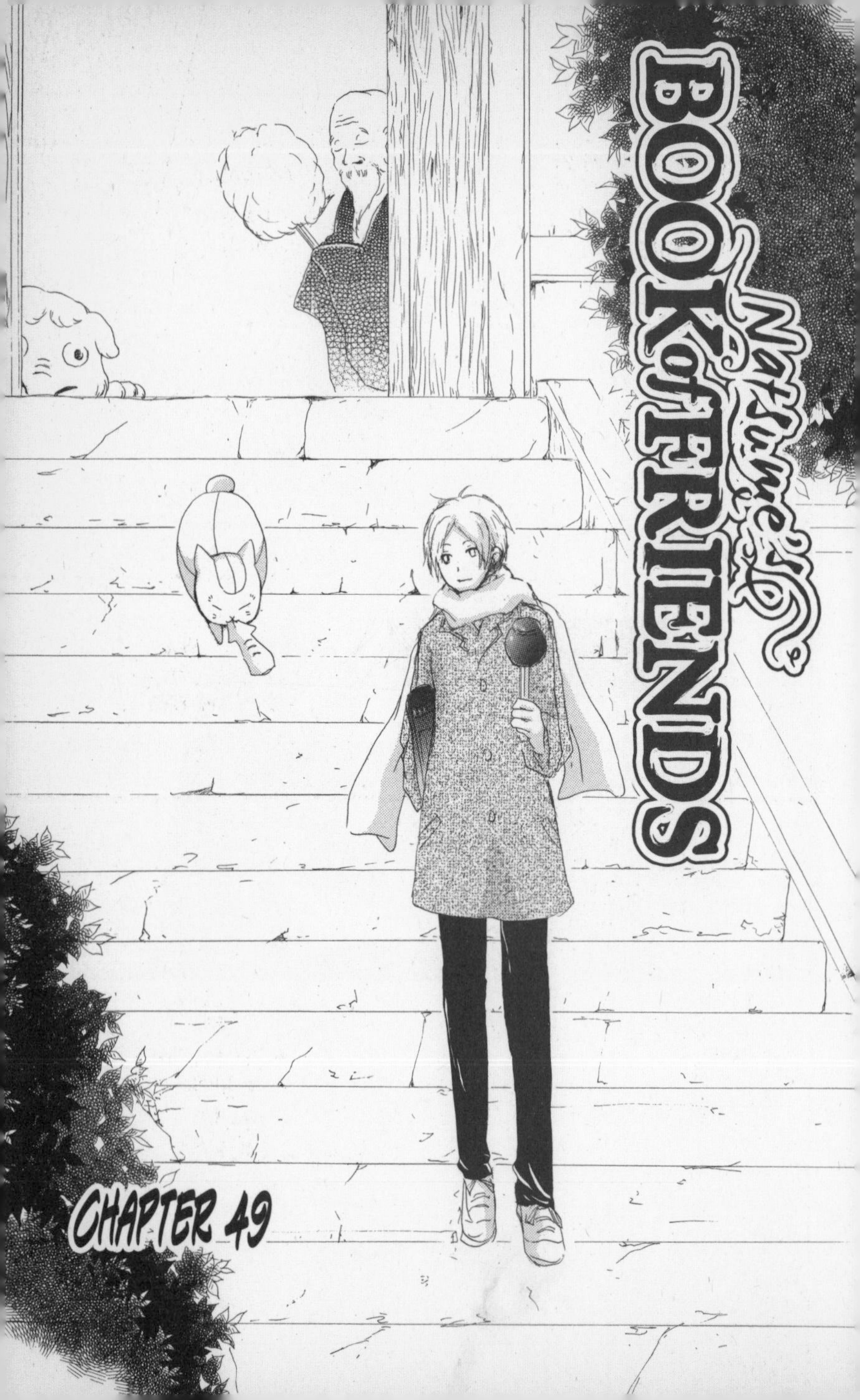
Natsume's
BOOK of FRIENDS
CHAPTER 49

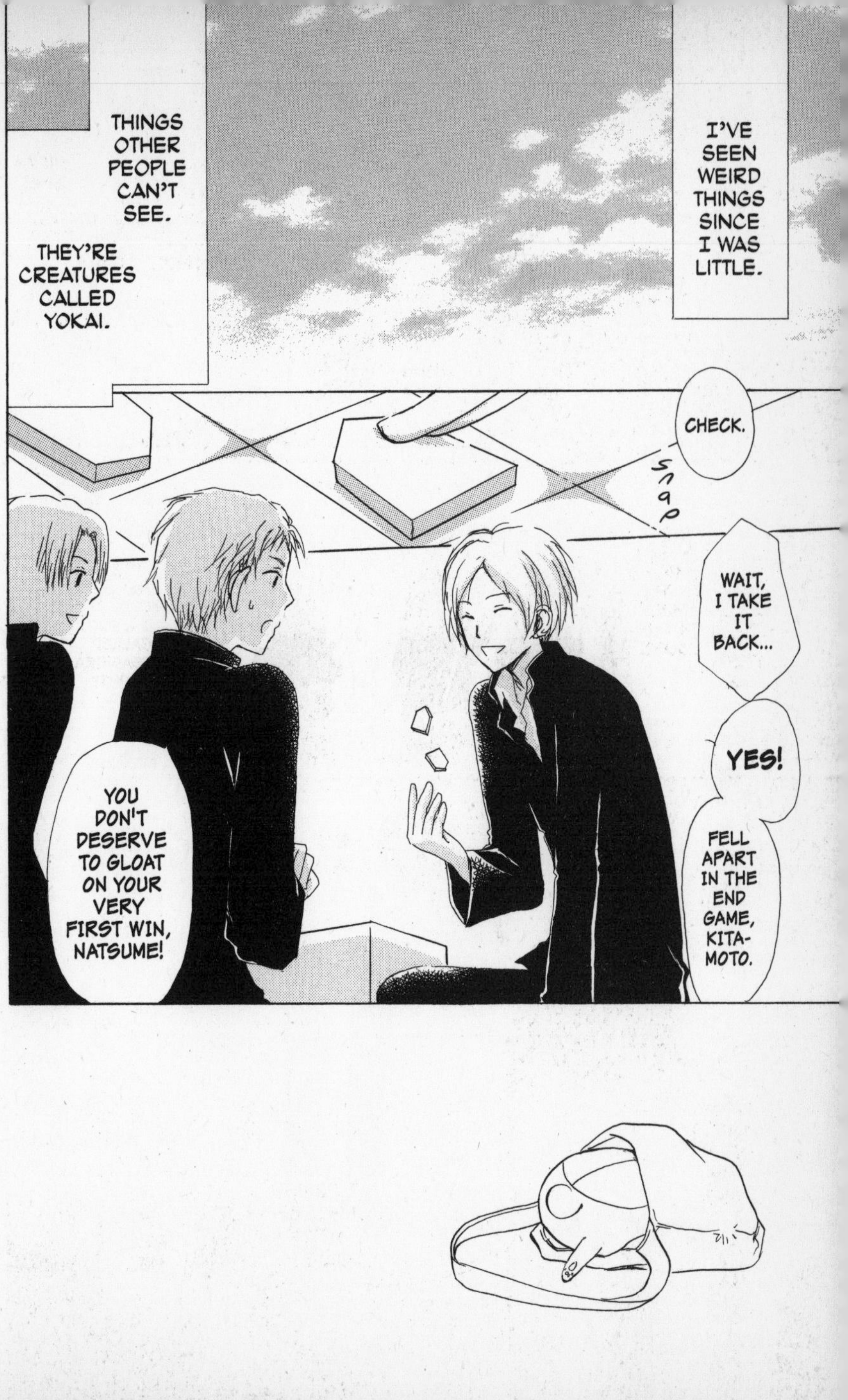
I'VE SEEN WEIRD THINGS SINCE I WAS LITTLE.
THINGS OTHER PEOPLE CAN'T SEE.
THEY'RE CREATURES CALLED YOKAI.
CHECK.
snap
WAIT, I TAKE IT BACK...
YES!
FELL APART IN THE END GAME, KITA-MOTO.
YOU DON'T DESERVE TO GLOAT ON YOUR VERY FIRST WIN, NATSUME!

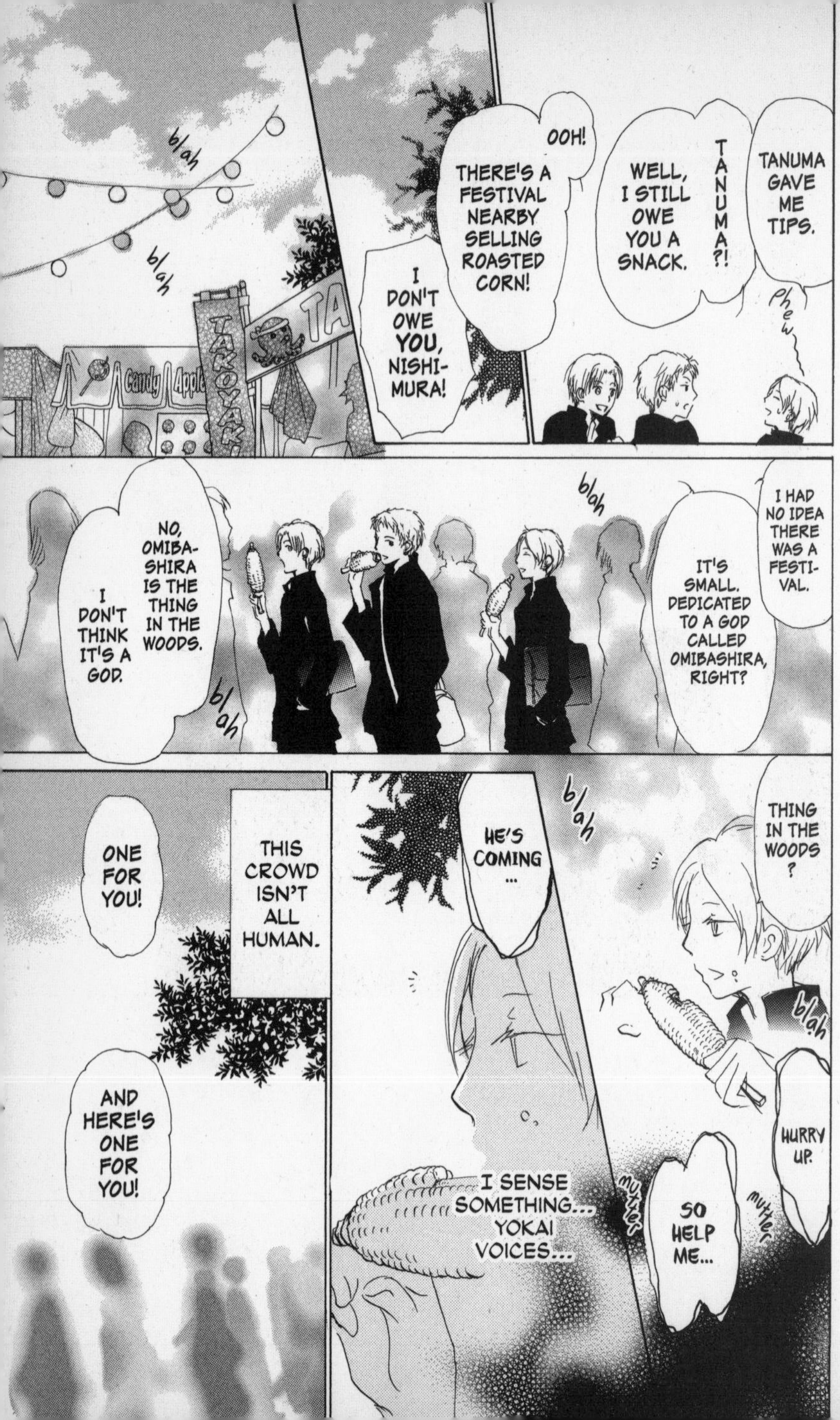
TANUMA GAVE ME TIPS.
Phew
TANUMA?!
WELL, I STILL OWE YOU A SNACK.
OOH!
THERE'S A FESTIVAL NEARBY SELLING ROASTED CORN!
I DON'T OWE YOU, NISHIMURA!
blah
blah
TAKOYAKI
Candy Apple
I HAD NO IDEA THERE WAS A FESTIVAL.
IT'S SMALL. DEDICATED TO A GOD CALLED OMIBASHIRA, RIGHT?
blah
NO, OMIBASHIRA IS THE THING IN THE WOODS.
I DON'T THINK IT'S A GOD.
blah
THING IN THE WOODS?
blah
HE'S COMING...
blah
HURRY UP.
mutter
SO HELP ME...
mutter
I SENSE SOMETHING... YOKAI VOICES...
THIS CROWD ISN'T ALL HUMAN.
ONE FOR YOU!
AND HERE'S ONE FOR YOU!

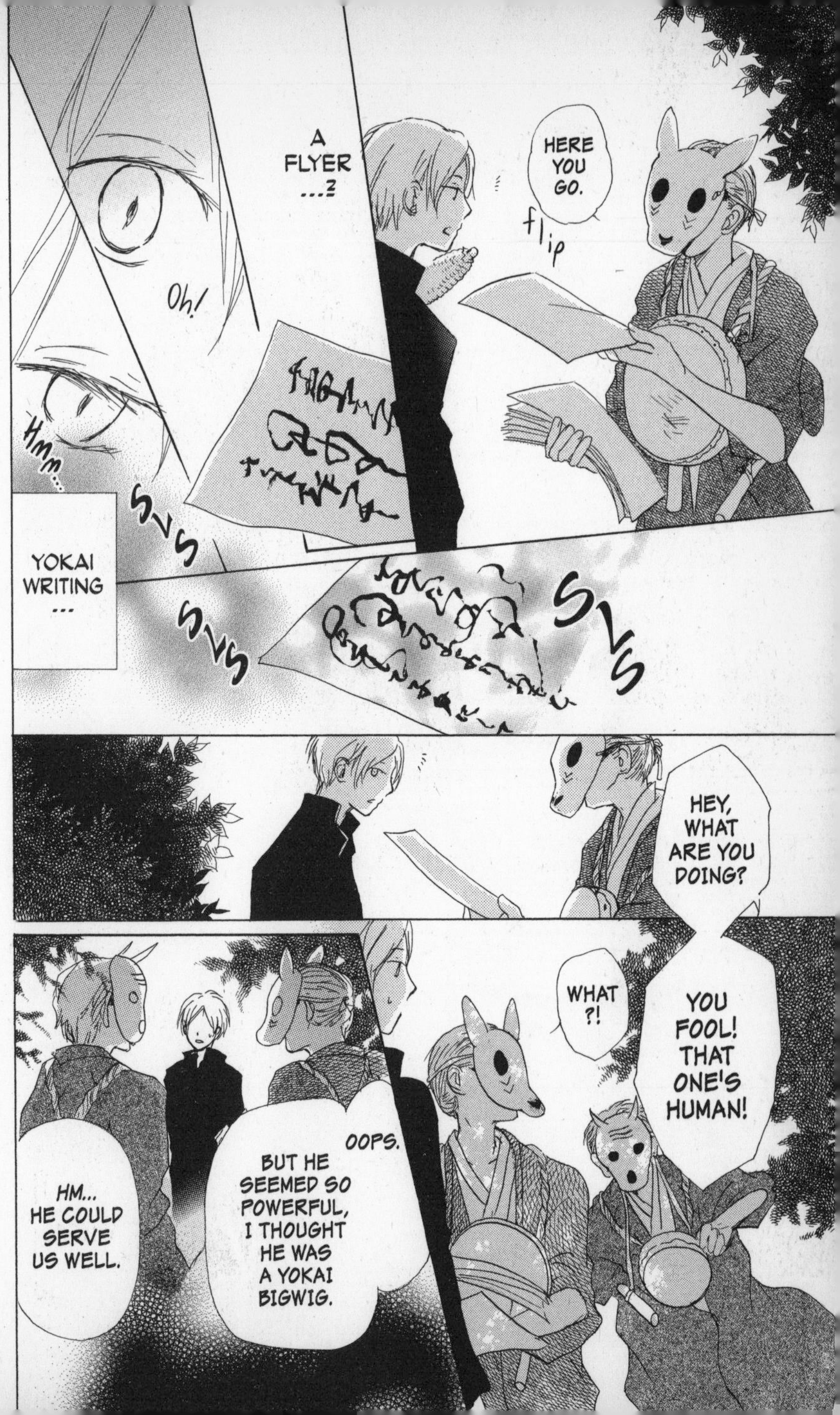
HERE YOU GO.
flip
A FLYER ...?
Oh!
Hmm...
YOKAI WRITING ...
HEY, WHAT ARE YOU DOING?
YOU FOOL! THAT ONE'S HUMAN!
WHAT ?!
OOPS.
BUT HE SEEMED SO POWERFUL, I THOUGHT HE WAS A YOKAI BIGWIG.
HM... HE COULD SERVE US WELL.

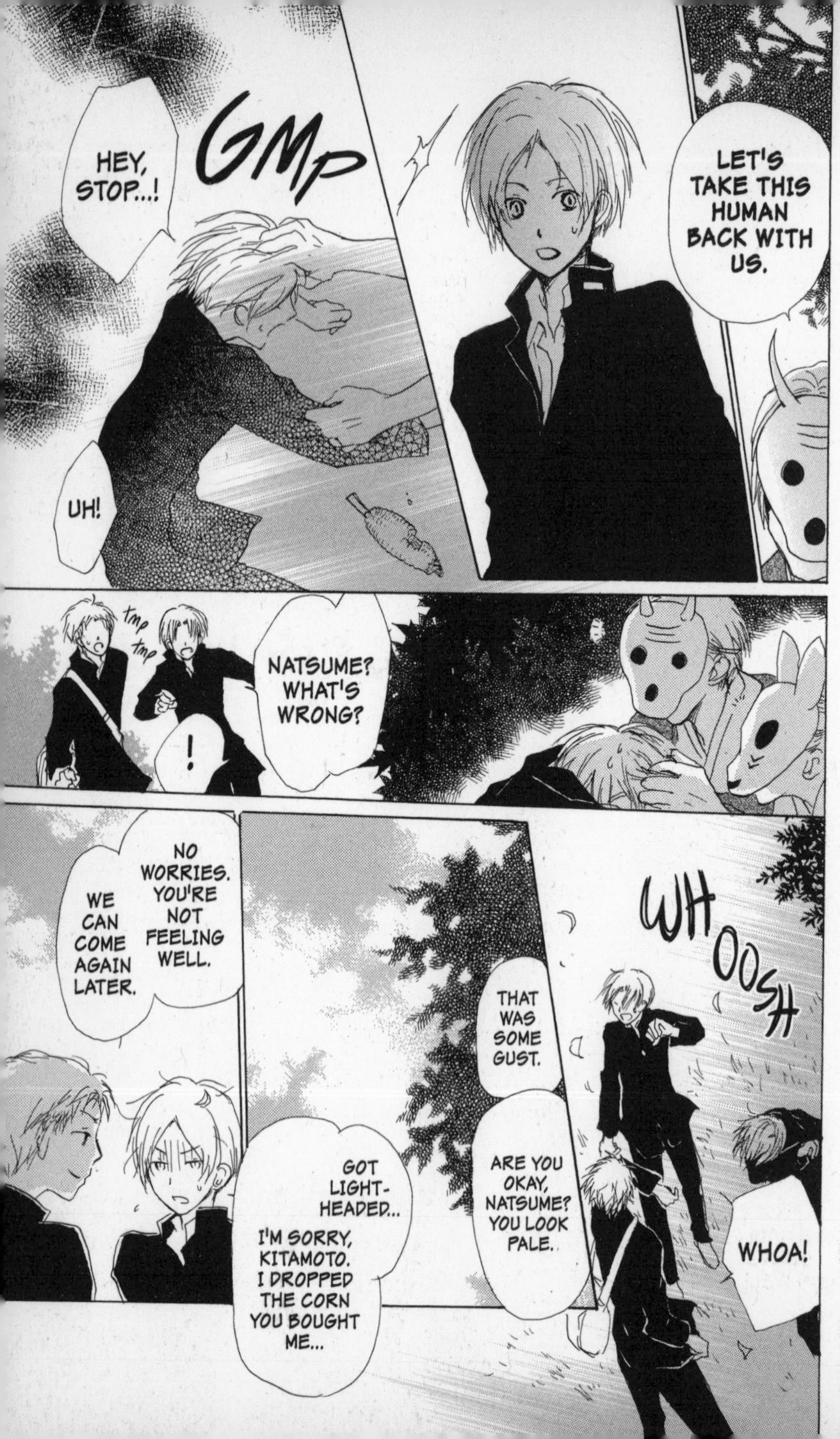
LET'S TAKE THIS HUMAN BACK WITH US.
GMP
HEY, STOP...!
UH!
NATSUME? WHAT'S WRONG?
!
tmp tmp
WHOOSH
WHOA!
THAT WAS SOME GUST.
ARE YOU OKAY, NATSUME? YOU LOOK PALE.
GOT LIGHT-HEADED...
I'M SORRY, KITAMOTO. I DROPPED THE CORN YOU BOUGHT ME...
NO WORRIES. YOU'RE NOT FEELING WELL.
WE CAN COME AGAIN LATER.

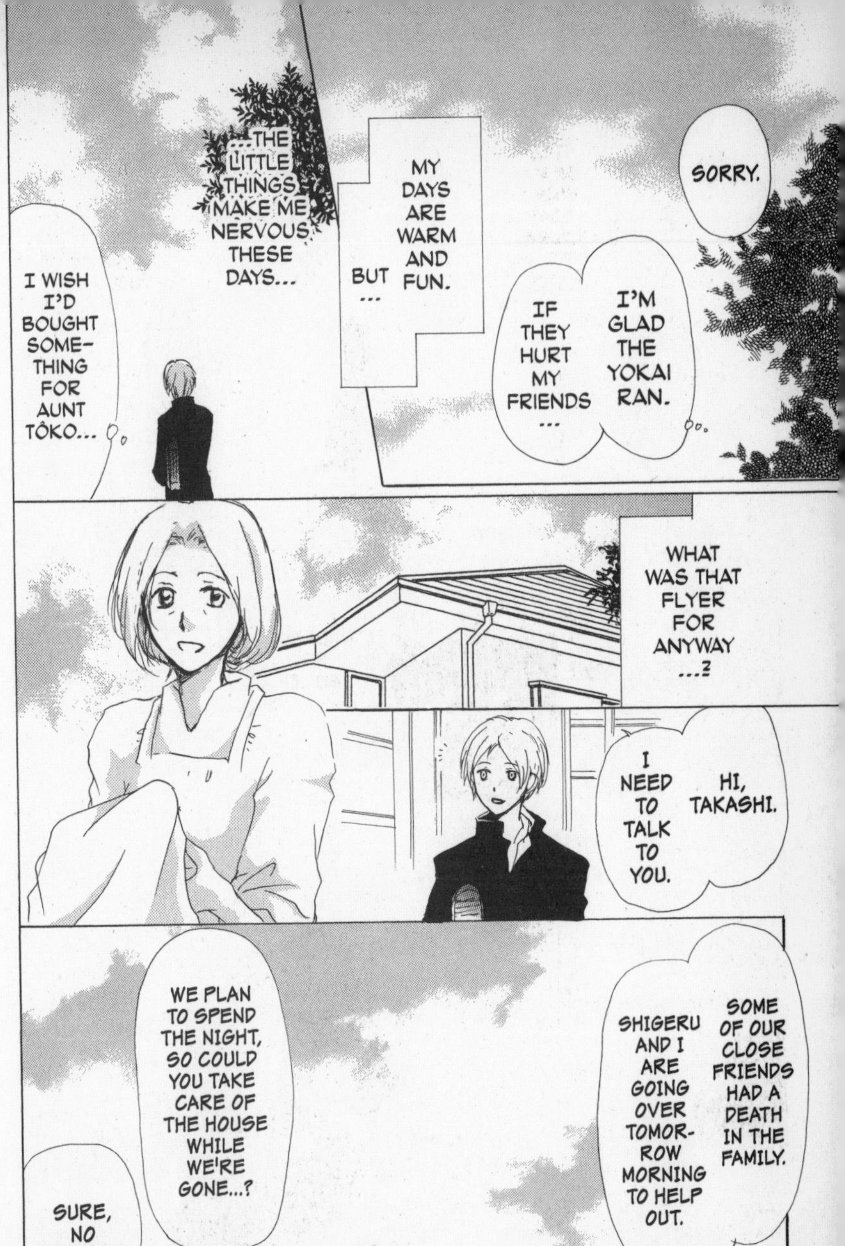
SORRY.
I'M GLAD THE YOKAI RAN.
IF THEY HURT MY FRIENDS...
MY DAYS ARE WARM AND FUN.
BUT...
...THE LITTLE THINGS MAKE ME NERVOUS THESE DAYS...
I WISH I'D BOUGHT SOME-THING FOR AUNT TÔKO...
WHAT WAS THAT FLYER FOR ANYWAY...?
HI, TAKASHI.
I NEED TO TALK TO YOU.
SOME OF OUR CLOSE FRIENDS HAD A DEATH IN THE FAMILY.
SHIGERU AND I ARE GOING OVER TOMOR-ROW MORNING TO HELP OUT.
WE PLAN TO SPEND THE NIGHT, SO COULD YOU TAKE CARE OF THE HOUSE WHILE WE'RE GONE...?
SURE, NO PROBLEM.

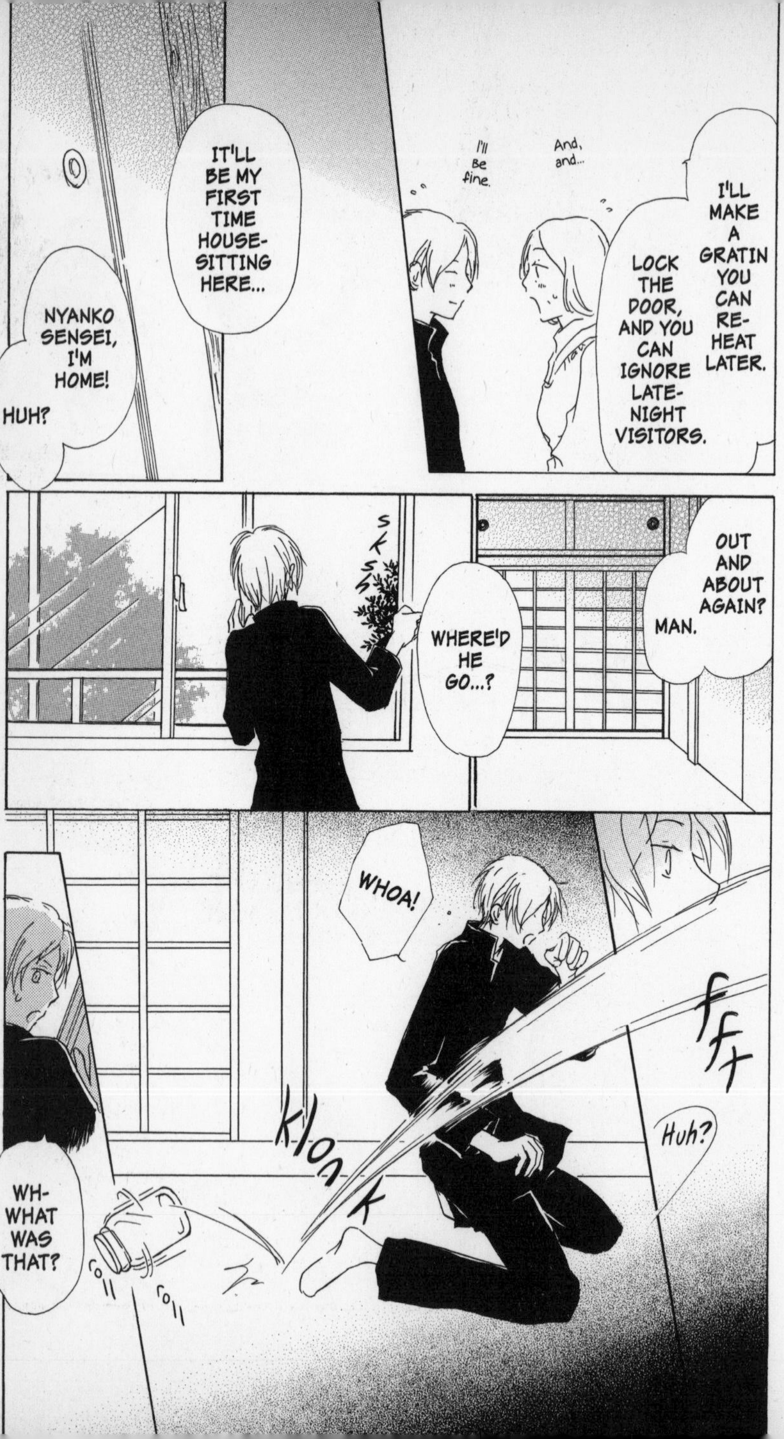
I'LL MAKE A GRATIN YOU CAN RE-HEAT LATER.
LOCK THE DOOR, AND YOU CAN IGNORE LATE-NIGHT VISITORS.
And, and...
I'll Be fine.
IT'LL BE MY FIRST TIME HOUSE-SITTING HERE...
NYANKO SENSEI, I'M HOME!
HUH?
OUT AND ABOUT AGAIN?
MAN.
WHERE'D HE GO...?
sksh
Huh?
fft
WHOA!
klonk
WH-WHAT WAS THAT?
coll
coll

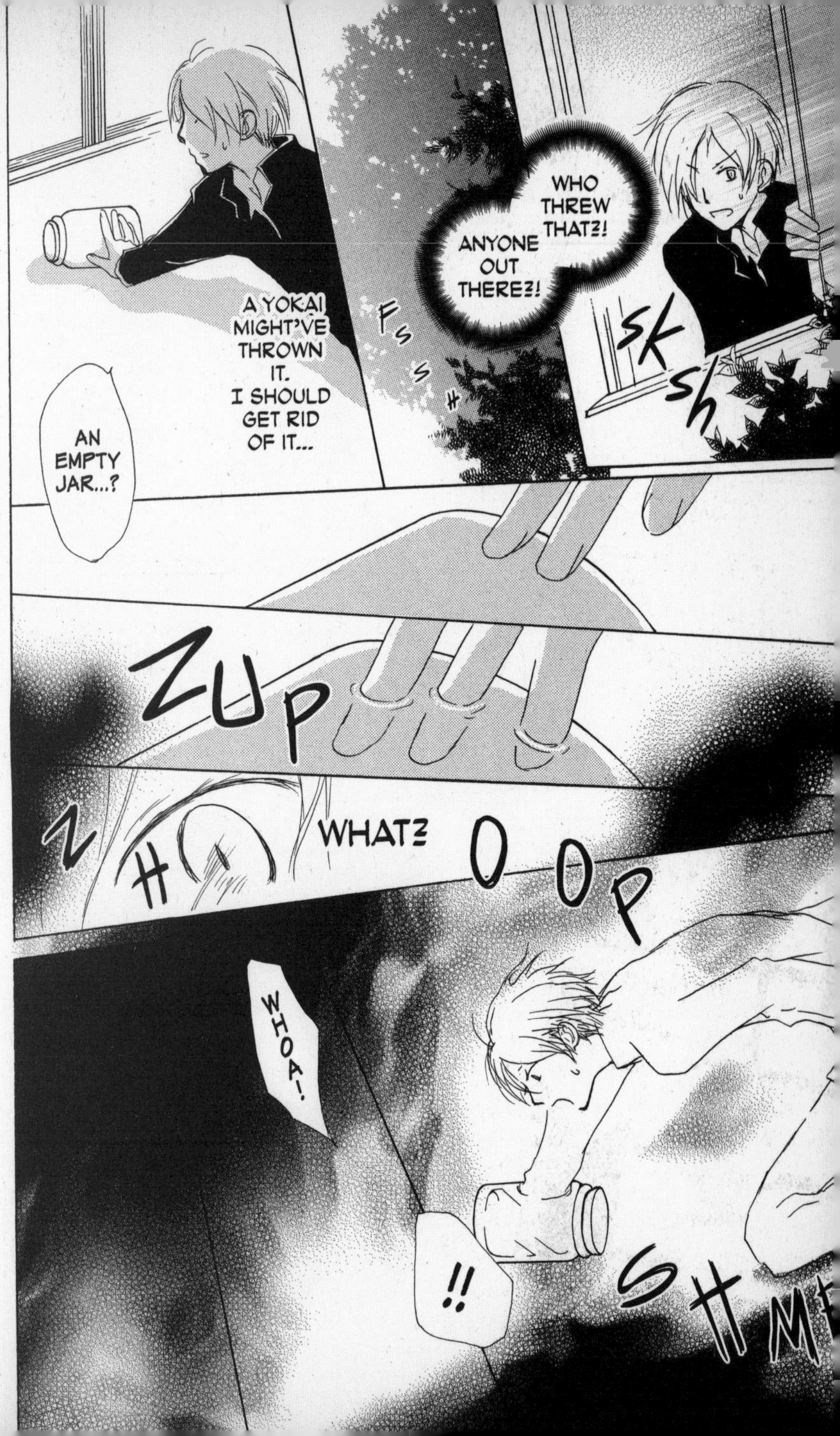

WHO THREW THAT?!
ANYONE OUT THERE?!
SKSH
FSSH
A YOKAI MIGHT'VE THROWN IT. I SHOULD GET RID OF IT...
AN EMPTY JAR...?
ZUP
OOP
WHAT?
ZH
WHOA!
!!
SHM

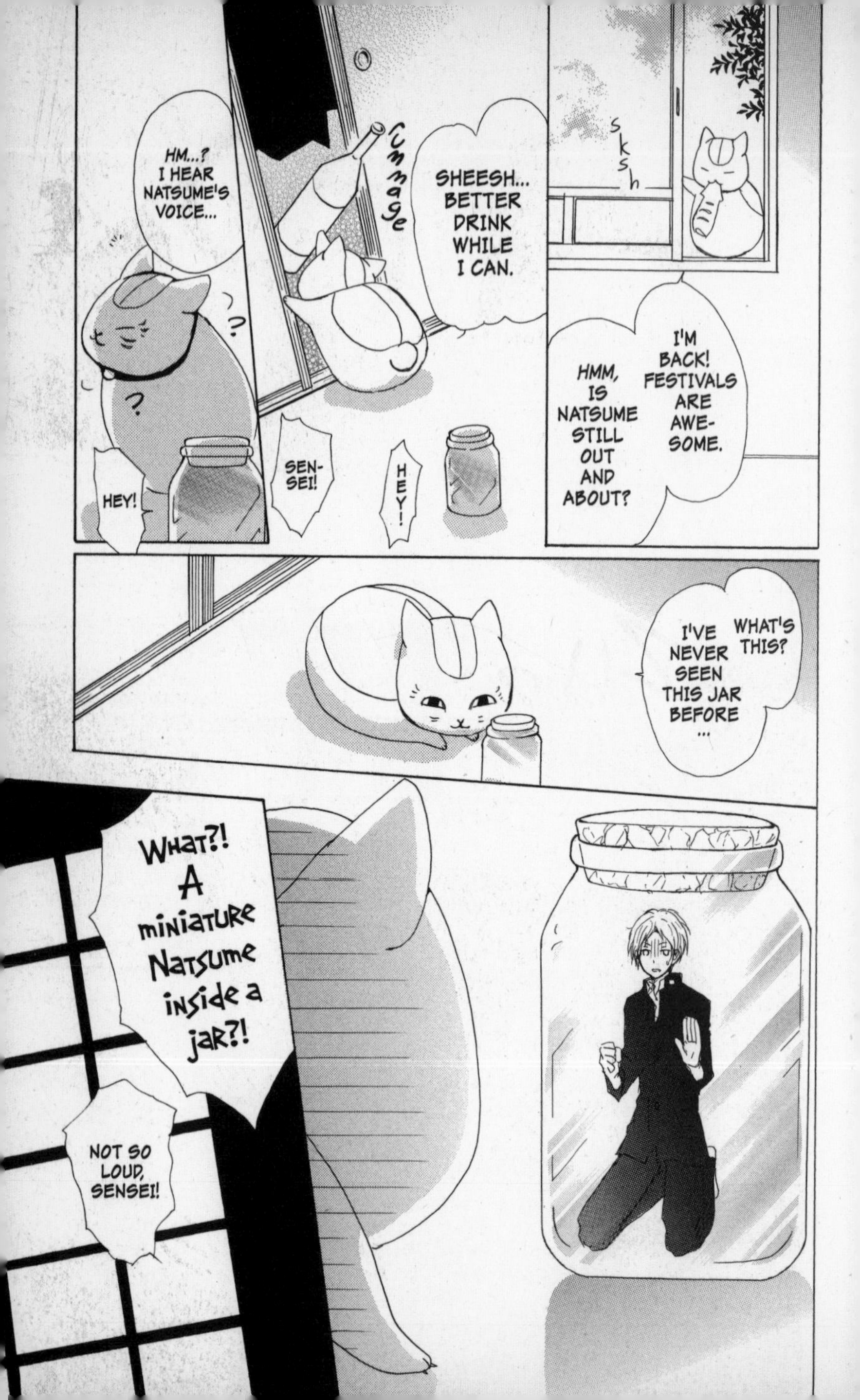

sksh
I'M BACK! FESTIVALS ARE AWESOME.
HMM, IS NATSUME STILL OUT AND ABOUT?
SHEESH... BETTER DRINK WHILE I CAN.
rummage
HEY!
SEN-SEI!
HM...? I HEAR NATSUME'S VOICE...
HEY!
WHAT'S THIS?
I'VE NEVER SEEN THIS JAR BEFORE...
WHAT?! A miniature Natsume inside a jar?!
NOT SO LOUD, SENSEI!

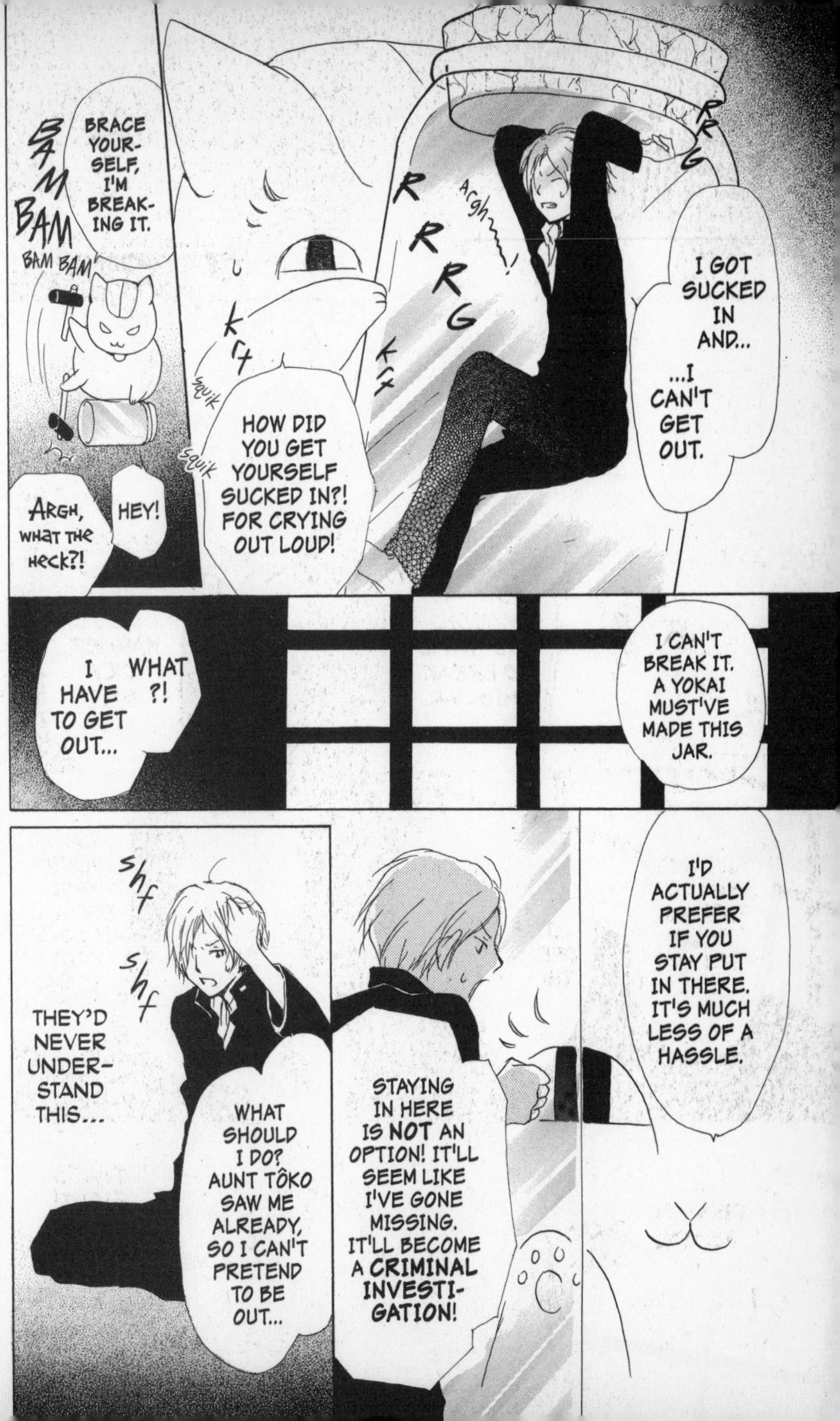

RRRG
I GOT SUCKED IN AND...
...I CAN'T GET OUT.
Argh!
RRRG
krt
krt
squik
squik
HOW DID YOU GET YOURSELF SUCKED IN?! FOR CRYING OUT LOUD!
BAM BAM
BRACE YOURSELF, I'M BREAKING IT.
BAM BAM
HEY!
ARGH, WHAT THE HECK?!
I CAN'T BREAK IT. A YOKAI MUST'VE MADE THIS JAR.
WHAT?!
I HAVE TO GET OUT...
I'D ACTUALLY PREFER IF YOU STAY PUT IN THERE. IT'S MUCH LESS OF A HASSLE.
STAYING IN HERE IS NOT AN OPTION! IT'LL SEEM LIKE I'VE GONE MISSING. IT'LL BECOME A CRIMINAL INVESTIGATION!
WHAT SHOULD I DO? AUNT TÔKO SAW ME ALREADY, SO I CAN'T PRETEND TO BE OUT...
shf
shf
THEY'D NEVER UNDERSTAND THIS...

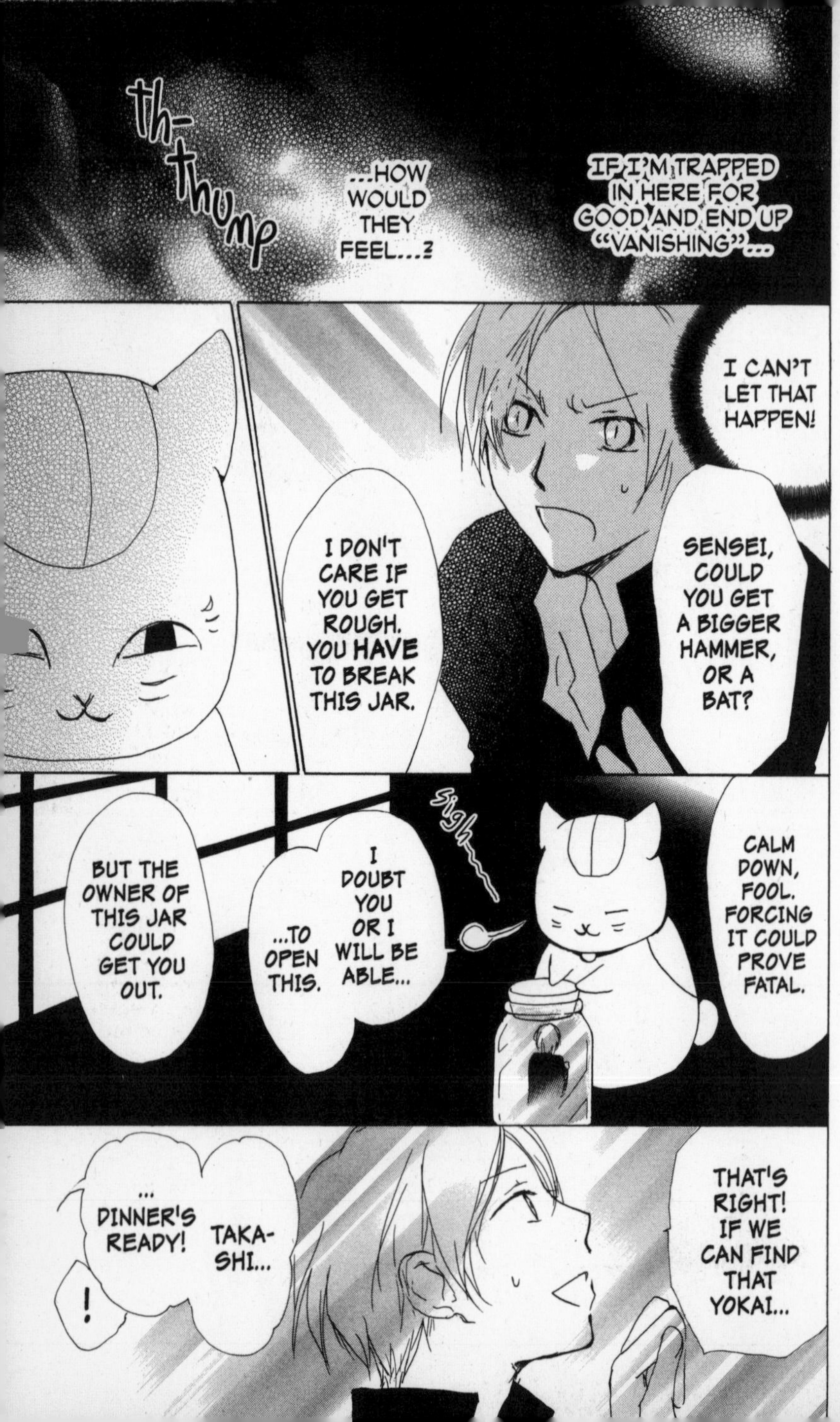
IF I'M TRAPPED IN HERE FOR GOOD AND END UP "VANISHING"...
...HOW WOULD THEY FEEL...?
th-thump
I CAN'T LET THAT HAPPEN!
SENSEI, COULD YOU GET A BIGGER HAMMER, OR A BAT?
I DON'T CARE IF YOU GET ROUGH. YOU HAVE TO BREAK THIS JAR.
CALM DOWN, FOOL. FORCING IT COULD PROVE FATAL.
Sigh~
I DOUBT YOU OR I WILL BE ABLE...
...TO OPEN THIS.
BUT THE OWNER OF THIS JAR COULD GET YOU OUT.
THAT'S RIGHT! IF WE CAN FIND THAT YOKAI...
TAKASHI...
...DINNER'S READY!
!

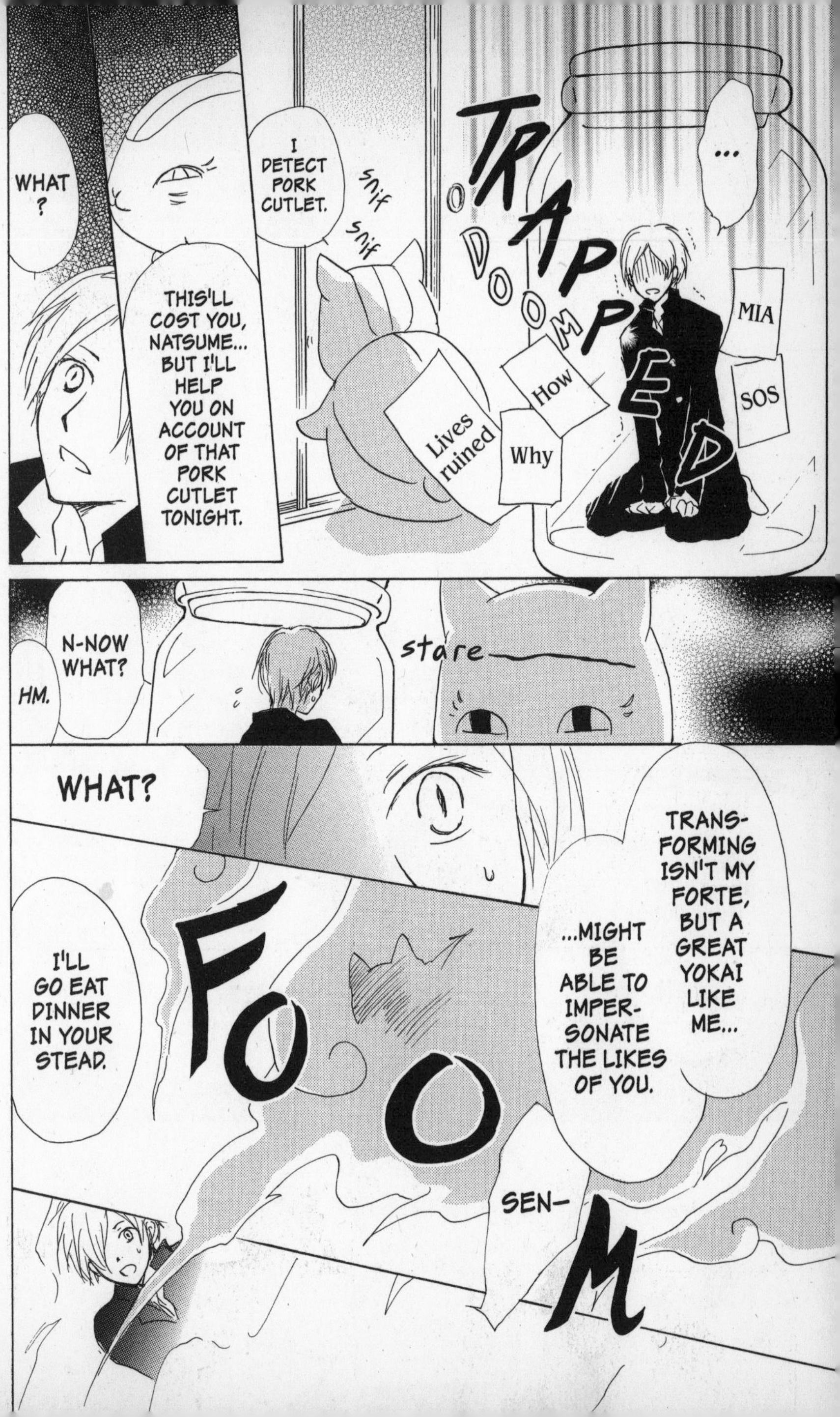
...
TRAPPED
DOOMED
MIA
SOS
How
Why
Lives ruined
I DETECT PORK CUTLET.
snif
snif
WHAT?
THIS'LL COST YOU, NATSUME... BUT I'LL HELP YOU ON ACCOUNT OF THAT PORK CUTLET TONIGHT.
stare
N-NOW WHAT?
HM.
TRANS-FORMING ISN'T MY FORTE, BUT A GREAT YOKAI LIKE ME...
...MIGHT BE ABLE TO IMPER-SONATE THE LIKES OF YOU.
WHAT?
I'LL GO EAT DINNER IN YOUR STEAD.
FOOOM
SEN-

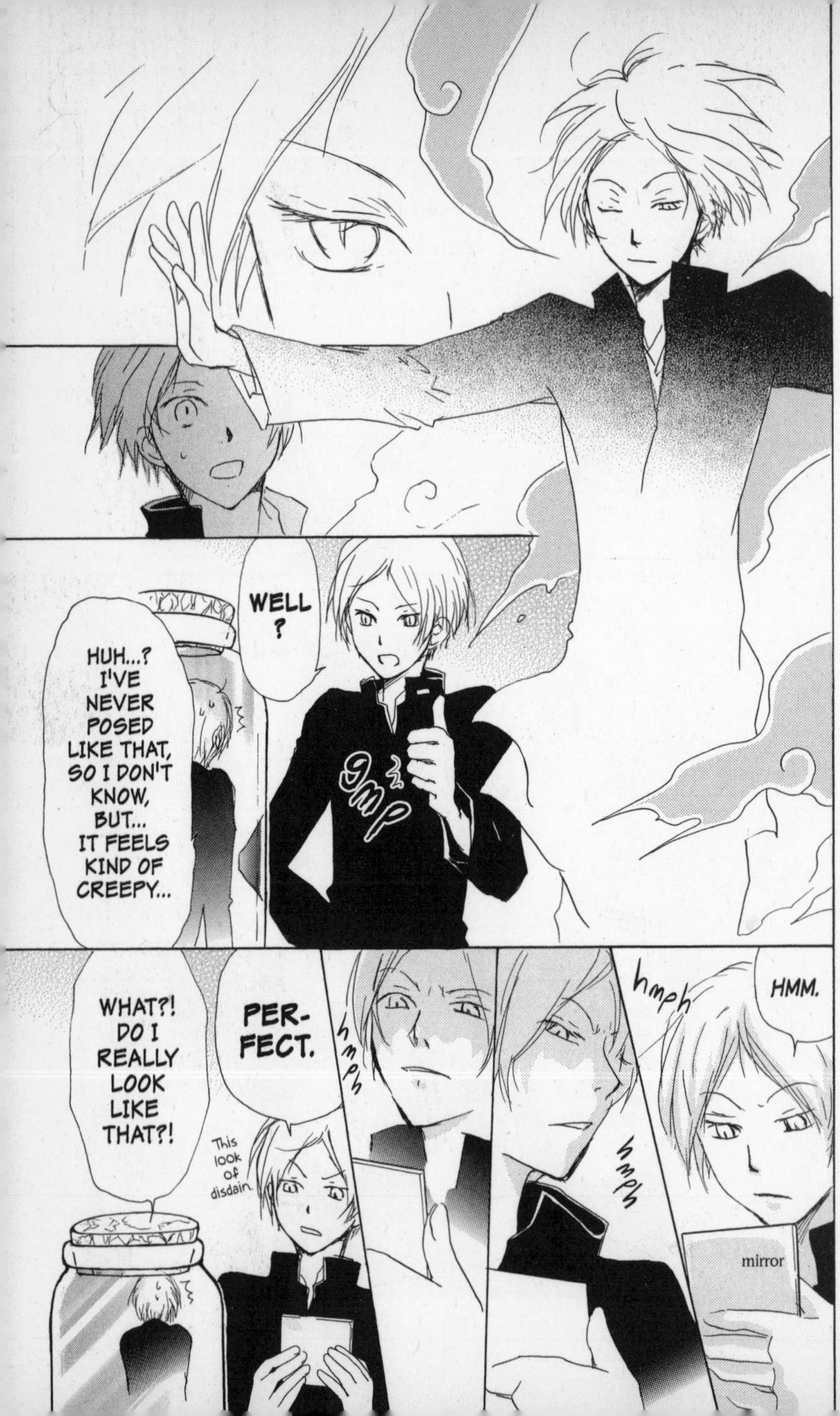
WELL?
gmp
HUH...? I'VE NEVER POSED LIKE THAT, SO I DON'T KNOW, BUT... IT FEELS KIND OF CREEPY...
HMM.
hmph
mirror
hmph
hmph
PER-FECT.
WHAT?! DO I REALLY LOOK LIKE THAT?!
This look of disdain.

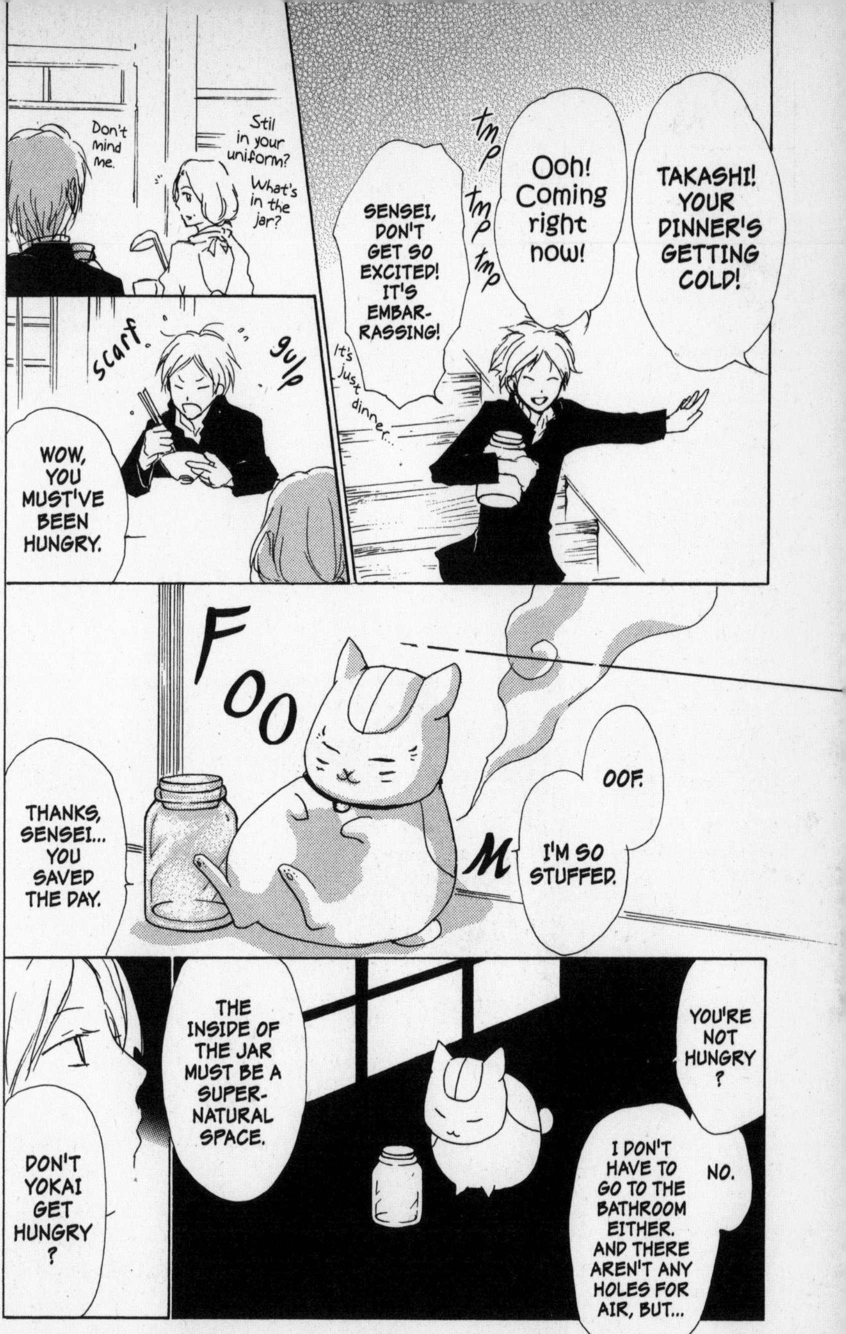
TAKASHI! YOUR DINNER'S GETTING COLD!
Ooh! Coming right now!
tmp tmp tmp tmp
SENSEI, DON'T GET SO EXCITED! IT'S EMBARRASSING!
It's just dinner...
Stil in your uniform?
What's in the jar?
Don't mind me.
gulp
scarf
WOW, YOU MUST'VE BEEN HUNGRY.
OOF.
I'M SO STUFFED.
M
FOO
THANKS, SENSEI... YOU SAVED THE DAY.
YOU'RE NOT HUNGRY?
NO.
I DON'T HAVE TO GO TO THE BATHROOM EITHER. AND THERE AREN'T ANY HOLES FOR AIR, BUT...
THE INSIDE OF THE JAR MUST BE A SUPERNATURAL SPACE.
DON'T YOKAI GET HUNGRY?

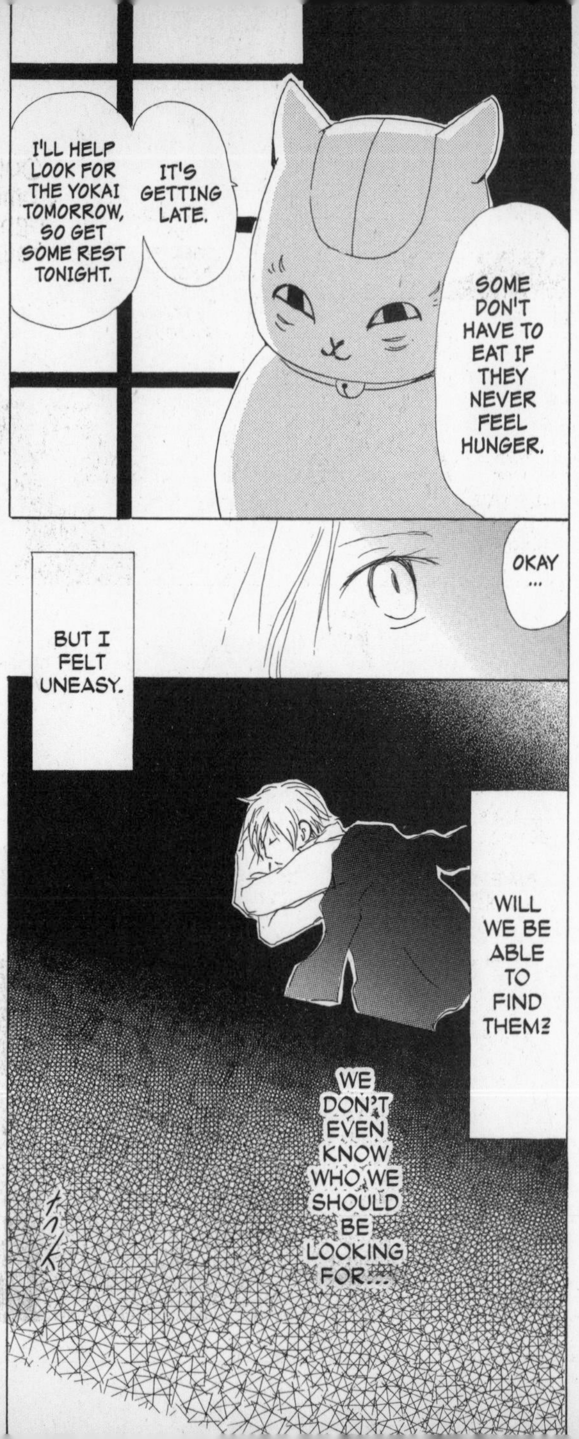
SOME DON'T HAVE TO EAT IF THEY NEVER FEEL HUNGER.
IT'S GETTING LATE.
I'LL HELP LOOK FOR THE YOKAI TOMORROW, SO GET SOME REST TONIGHT.
OKAY ...
BUT I FELT UNEASY.
WILL WE BE ABLE TO FIND THEM?
WE DON'T EVEN KNOW WHO WE SHOULD BE LOOKING FOR...

03

❋Colors

I was never fond of using the color blue for some reason, but after they made Natsume into an anime, and I saw its vivid world in full color, I think my perception of color has changed a little. It's almost like what I first assumed was blue was actually gray, and what I had assumed was light purple turned out to be pink. It was a very small difference, but it feels very strange. So now, deep blues and purples seem so beautiful that I'm obsessed with them these days.

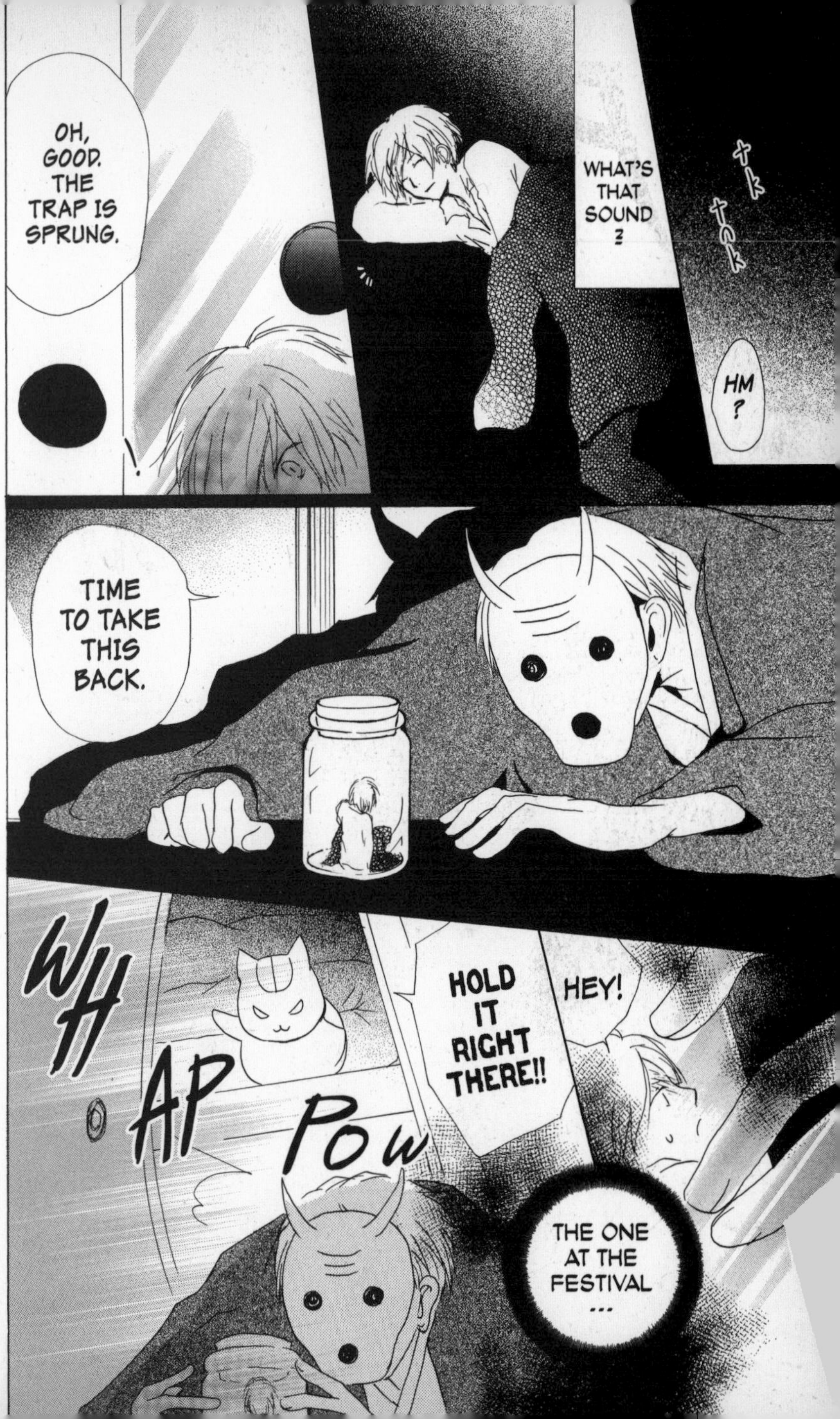
tk
tck
WHAT'S THAT SOUND?
HM?
OH, GOOD. THE TRAP IS SPRUNG.
!
TIME TO TAKE THIS BACK.
HEY!
HOLD IT RIGHT THERE!!
THE ONE AT THE FESTIVAL...
POW
WHAP

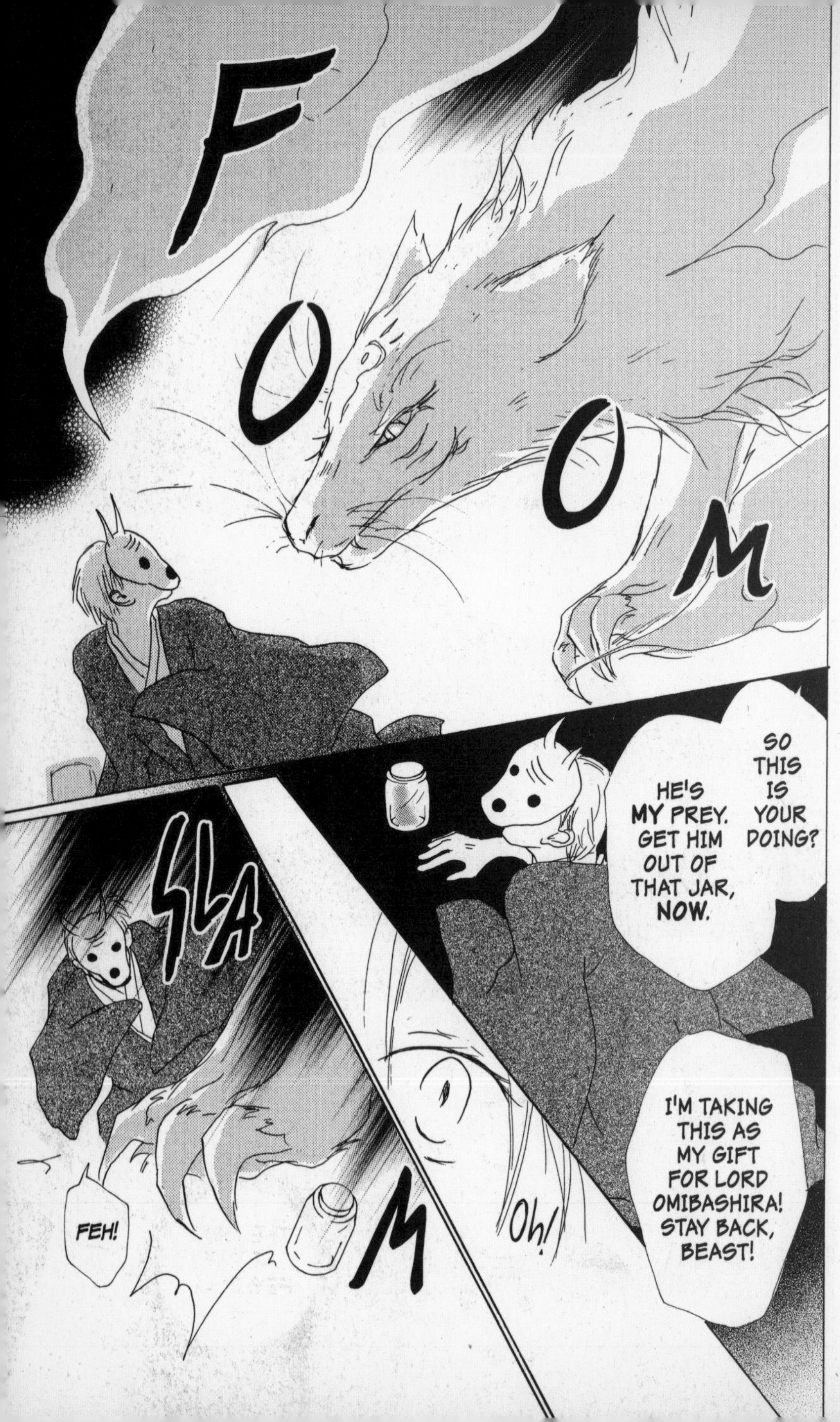
FOOM
SO THIS IS YOUR DOING?
HE'S MY PREY. GET HIM OUT OF THAT JAR, NOW.
I'M TAKING THIS AS MY GIFT FOR LORD OMIBASHIRA! STAY BACK, BEAST!
Oh!
SLAM
FEH!

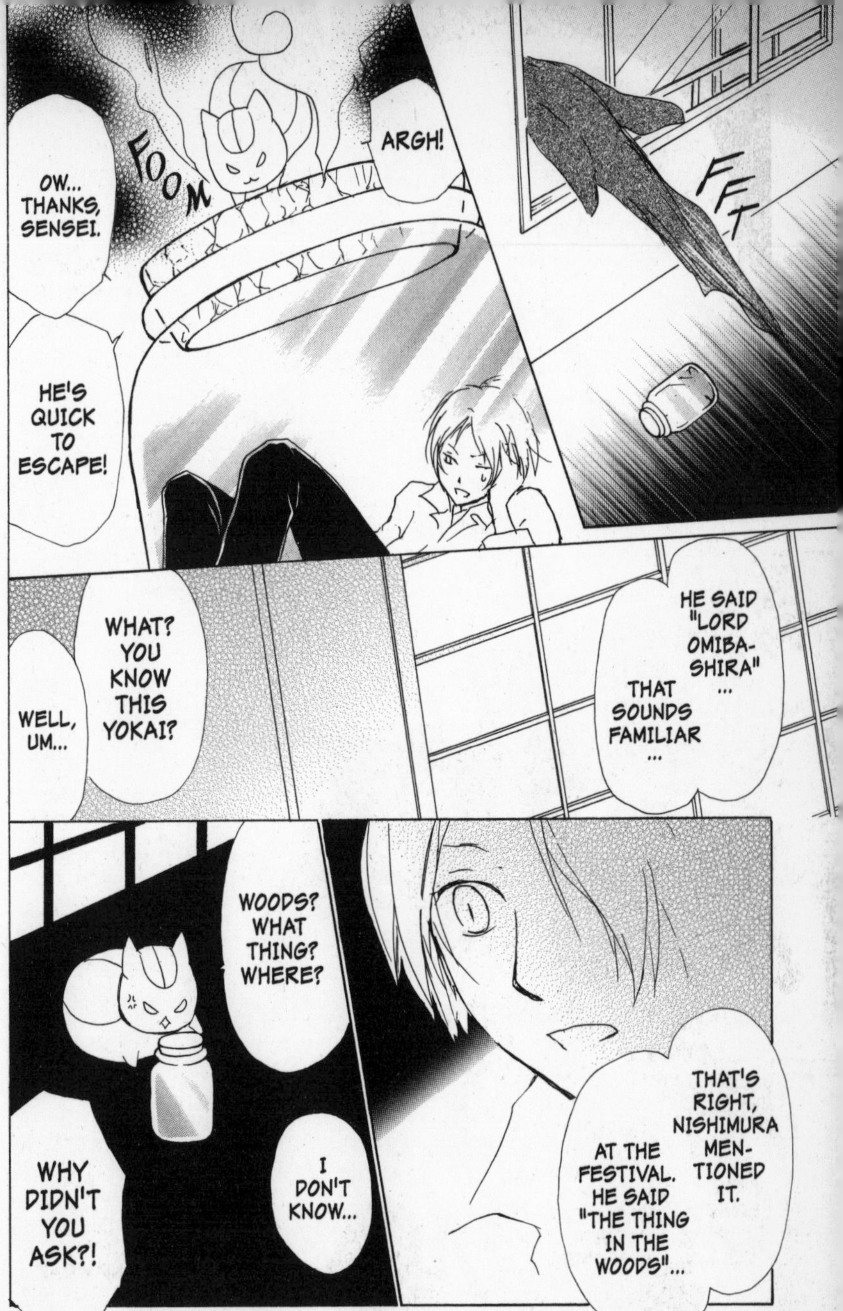
FFT
ARGH!
FOOM
OW... THANKS, SENSEI.
HE'S QUICK TO ESCAPE!
HE SAID "LORD OMIBA-SHIRA"...
THAT SOUNDS FAMILIAR...
WHAT? YOU KNOW THIS YOKAI?
WELL, UM...
THAT'S RIGHT, NISHIMURA MEN-TIONED IT.
AT THE FESTIVAL. HE SAID "THE THING IN THE WOODS"...
WOODS? WHAT THING? WHERE?
I DON'T KNOW...
WHY DIDN'T YOU ASK?!

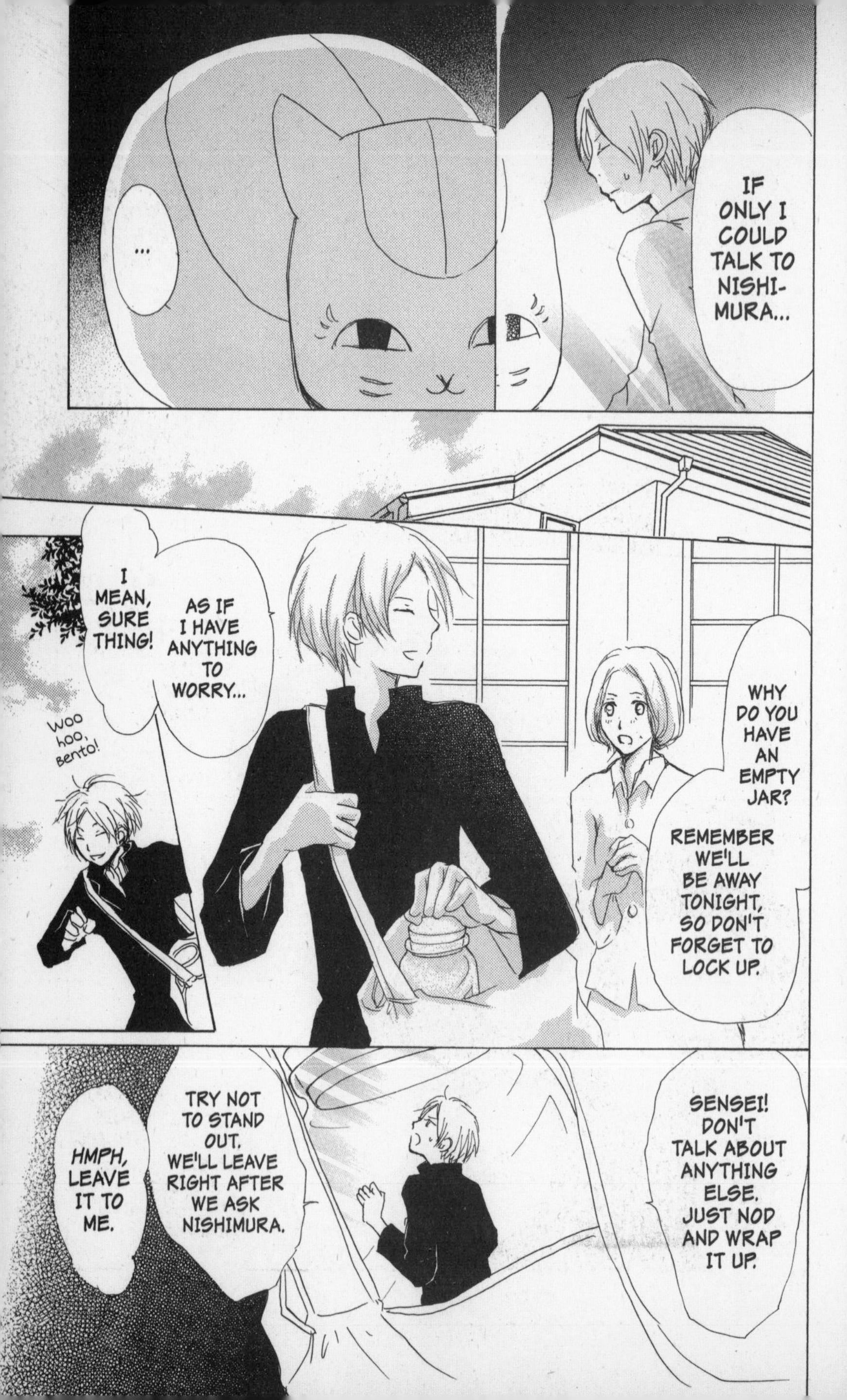
IF ONLY I COULD TALK TO NISHIMURA...
...
WHY DO YOU HAVE AN EMPTY JAR?
REMEMBER WE'LL BE AWAY TONIGHT, SO DON'T FORGET TO LOCK UP.
AS IF I HAVE ANYTHING TO WORRY...
I MEAN, SURE THING!
Woo hoo, Bento!
SENSEI! DON'T TALK ABOUT ANYTHING ELSE. JUST NOD AND WRAP IT UP.
TRY NOT TO STAND OUT. WE'LL LEAVE RIGHT AFTER WE ASK NISHIMURA.
HMPH, LEAVE IT TO ME.

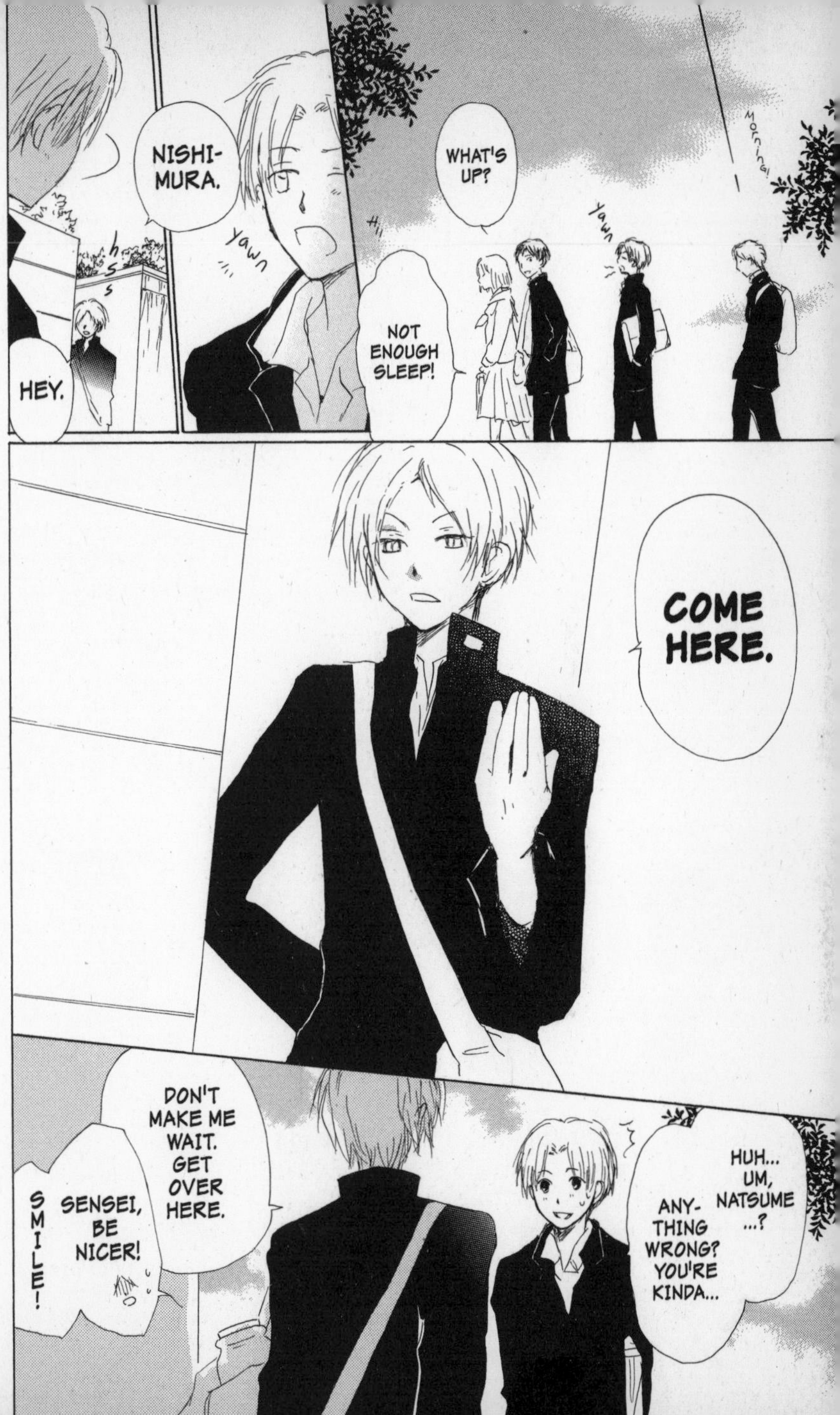
Morning!
Yawn
WHAT'S UP?
NOT ENOUGH SLEEP!
NISHI-MURA.
yawn
HEY.
COME HERE.
HUH... UM, NATSUME ...?
ANY-THING WRONG? YOU'RE KINDA...
DON'T MAKE ME WAIT. GET OVER HERE.
SENSEI, BE NICER!
SMILE!

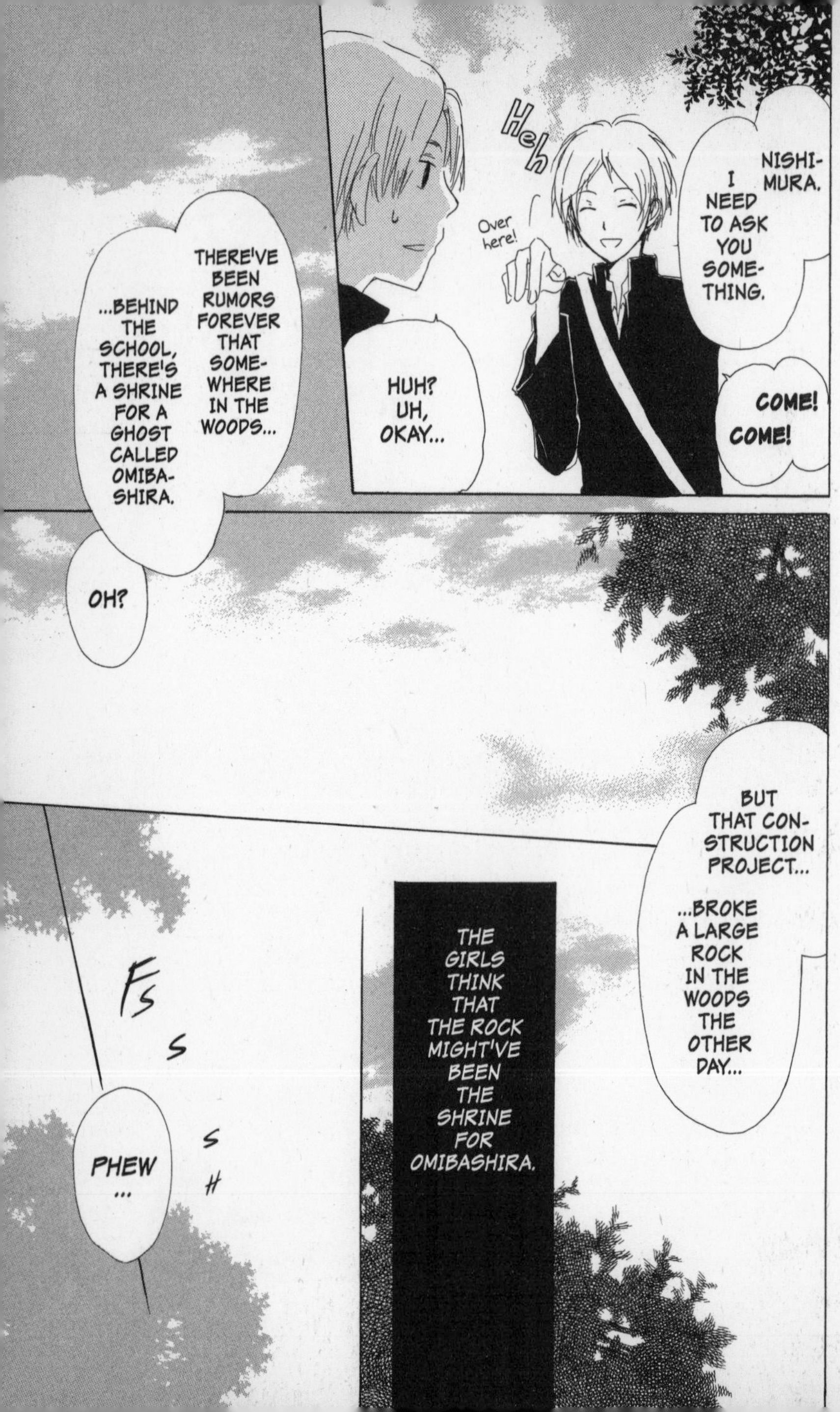

NISHIMURA. I NEED TO ASK YOU SOMETHING.
Heh
Over here!
COME! COME!
HUH? UH, OKAY...
THERE'VE BEEN RUMORS FOREVER THAT SOMEWHERE IN THE WOODS...
...BEHIND THE SCHOOL, THERE'S A SHRINE FOR A GHOST CALLED OMIBASHIRA.
OH?
BUT THAT CONSTRUCTION PROJECT...
...BROKE A LARGE ROCK IN THE WOODS THE OTHER DAY...
THE GIRLS THINK THAT THE ROCK MIGHT'VE BEEN THE SHRINE FOR OMIBASHIRA.
Fsssh
PHEW...

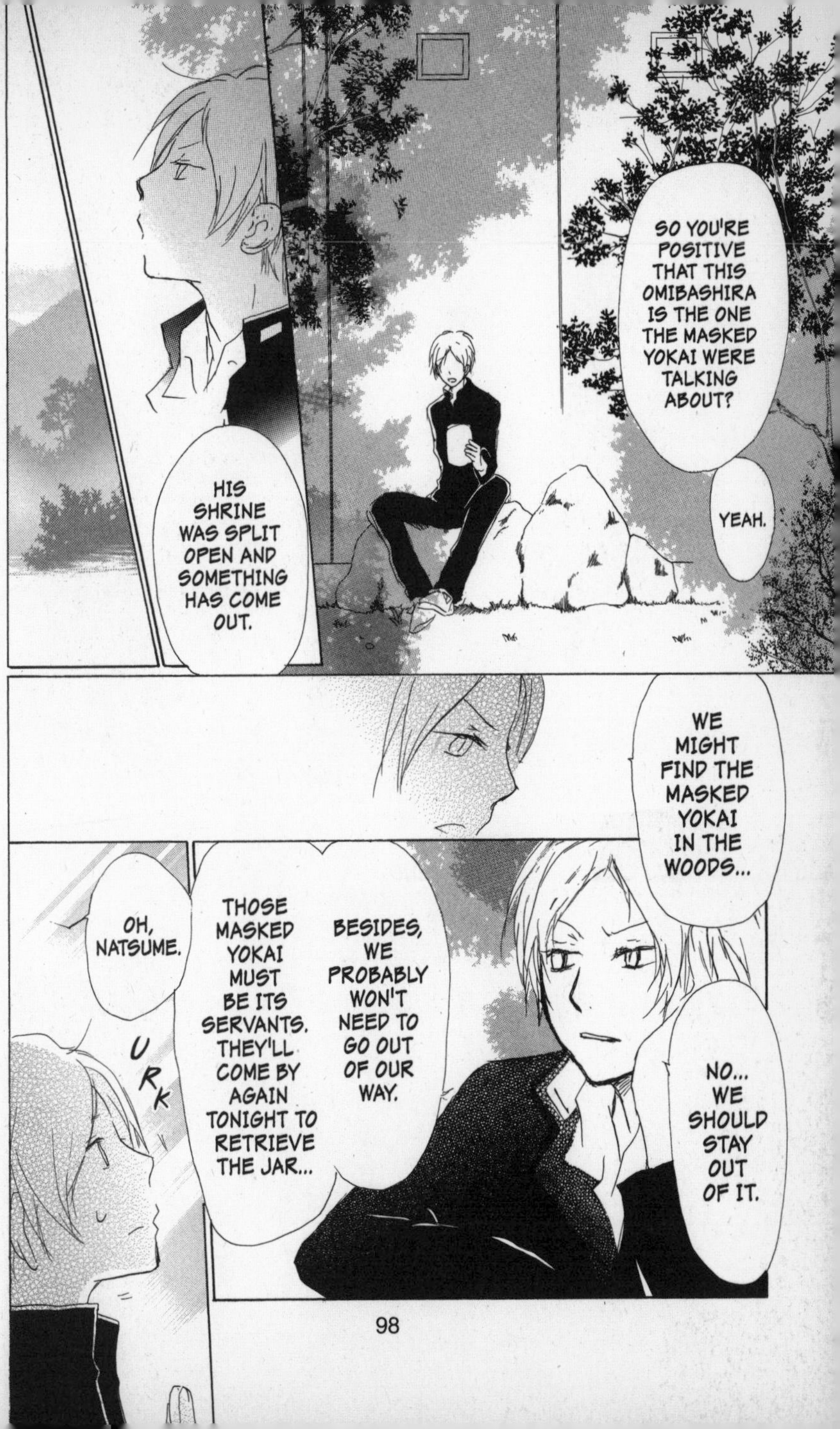
SO YOU'RE POSITIVE THAT THIS OMIBASHIRA IS THE ONE THE MASKED YOKAI WERE TALKING ABOUT?
YEAH.
HIS SHRINE WAS SPLIT OPEN AND SOMETHING HAS COME OUT.
WE MIGHT FIND THE MASKED YOKAI IN THE WOODS...
NO... WE SHOULD STAY OUT OF IT.
BESIDES, WE PROBABLY WON'T NEED TO GO OUT OF OUR WAY.
THOSE MASKED YOKAI MUST BE ITS SERVANTS. THEY'LL COME BY AGAIN TONIGHT TO RETRIEVE THE JAR...
OH, NATSUME.
URK

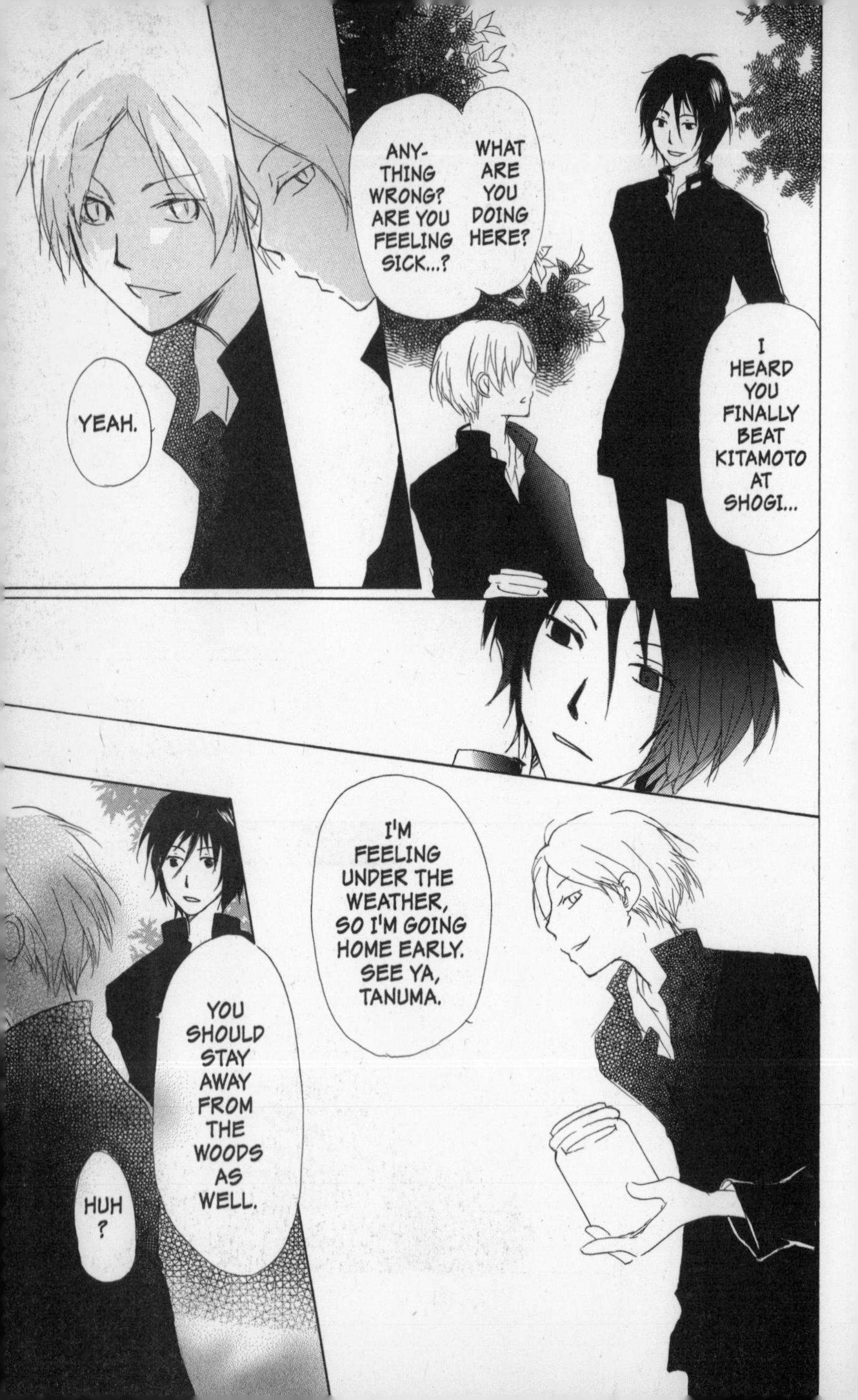
I HEARD YOU FINALLY BEAT KITAMOTO AT SHOGI...
WHAT ARE YOU DOING HERE?
ANY-THING WRONG? ARE YOU FEELING SICK...?
YEAH.
I'M FEELING UNDER THE WEATHER, SO I'M GOING HOME EARLY. SEE YA, TANUMA.
YOU SHOULD STAY AWAY FROM THE WOODS AS WELL.
HUH?

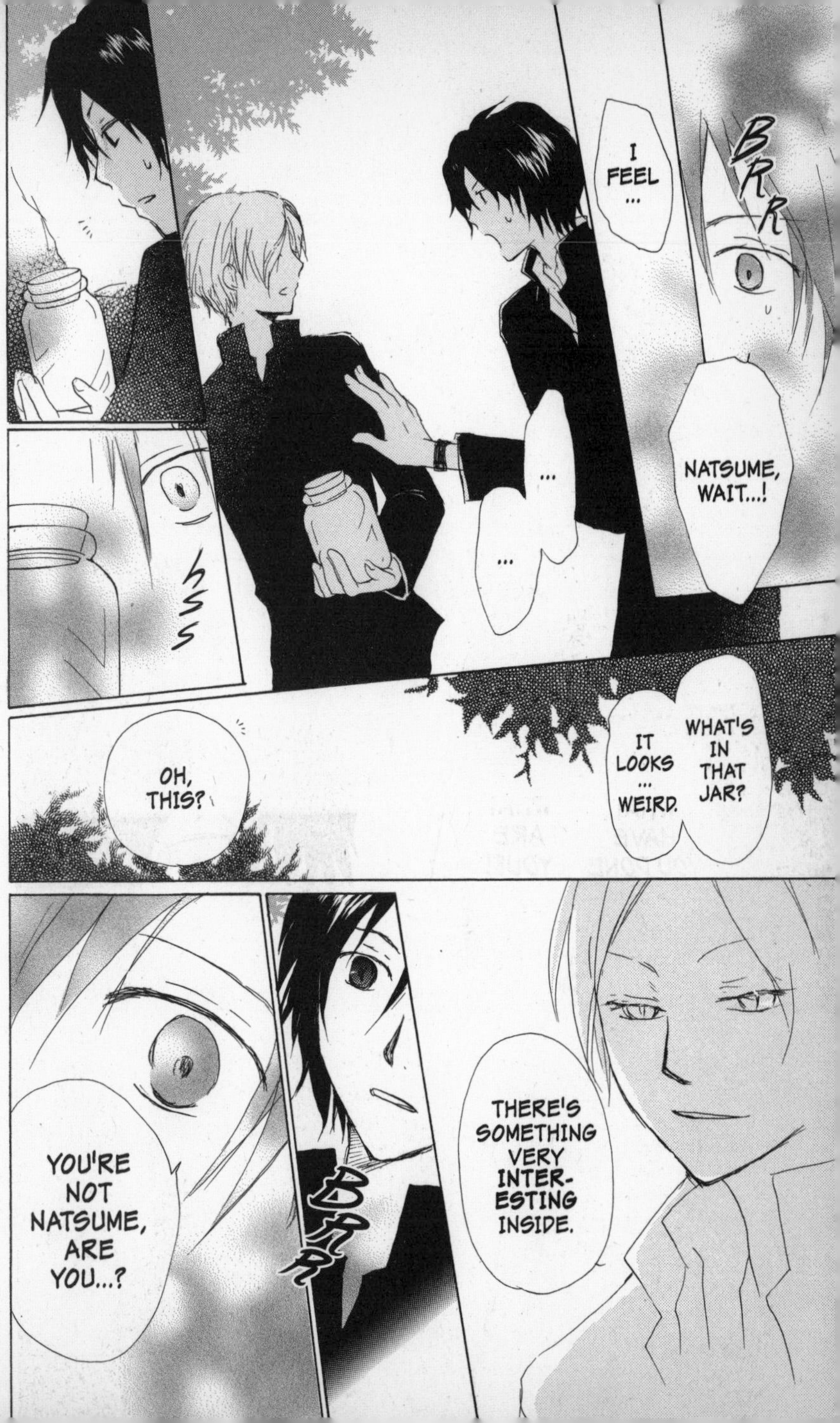
BRR
NATSUME, WAIT...!
I FEEL ...
...
...
SSS
WHAT'S IN THAT JAR?
IT LOOKS ... WEIRD.
OH, THIS?
THERE'S SOMETHING VERY INTER-ESTING INSIDE.
BRR
YOU'RE NOT NATSUME, ARE YOU...?

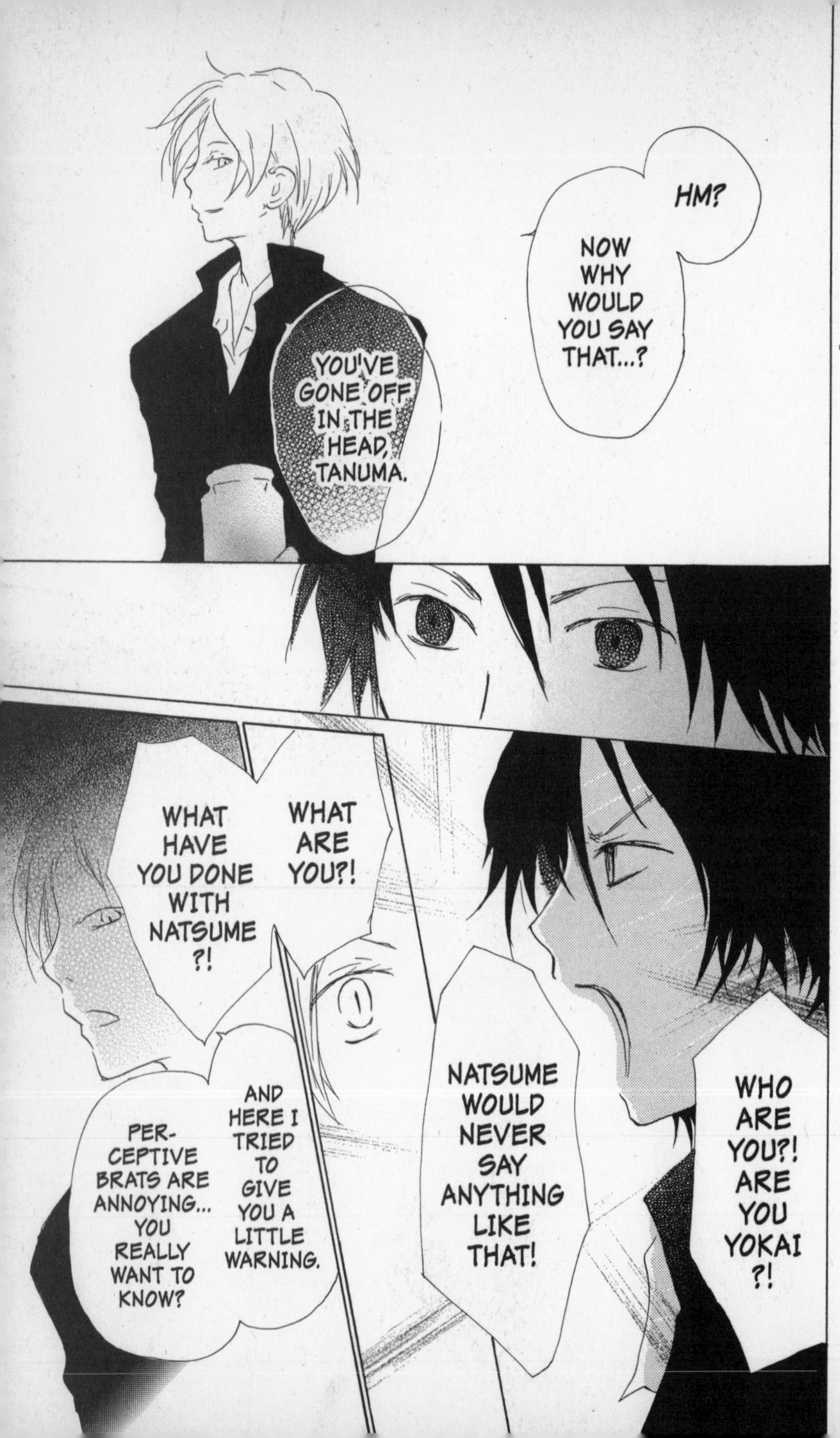
HM?
NOW WHY WOULD YOU SAY THAT...?
YOU'VE GONE OFF IN THE HEAD, TANUMA.
WHO ARE YOU?! ARE YOU YOKAI?!
NATSUME WOULD NEVER SAY ANYTHING LIKE THAT!
WHAT ARE YOU?!
WHAT HAVE YOU DONE WITH NATSUME?!
AND HERE I TRIED TO GIVE YOU A LITTLE WARNING.
PER-CEPTIVE BRATS ARE ANNOYING... YOU REALLY WANT TO KNOW?

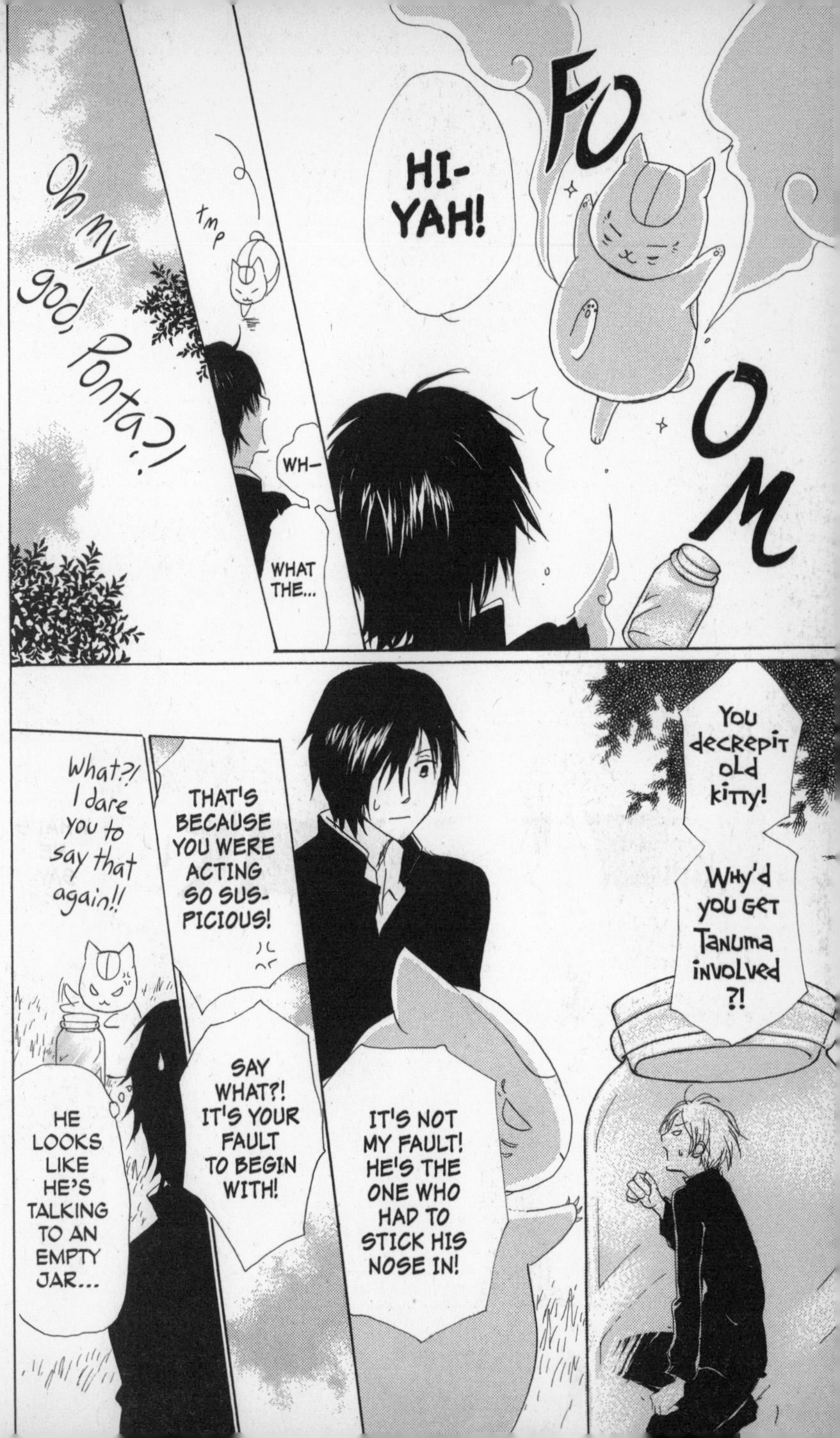
FOOM
HI-YAH!
WH-
WHAT THE...
tmp
Oh my god, Ponta?!
You decrepit old kitty!
Why'd you get Tanuma involved?!
IT'S NOT MY FAULT! HE'S THE ONE WHO HAD TO STICK HIS NOSE IN!
THAT'S BECAUSE YOU WERE ACTING SO SUS-PICIOUS!
SAY WHAT?! IT'S YOUR FAULT TO BEGIN WITH!
What?! I dare you to say that again!!
HE LOOKS LIKE HE'S TALKING TO AN EMPTY JAR...

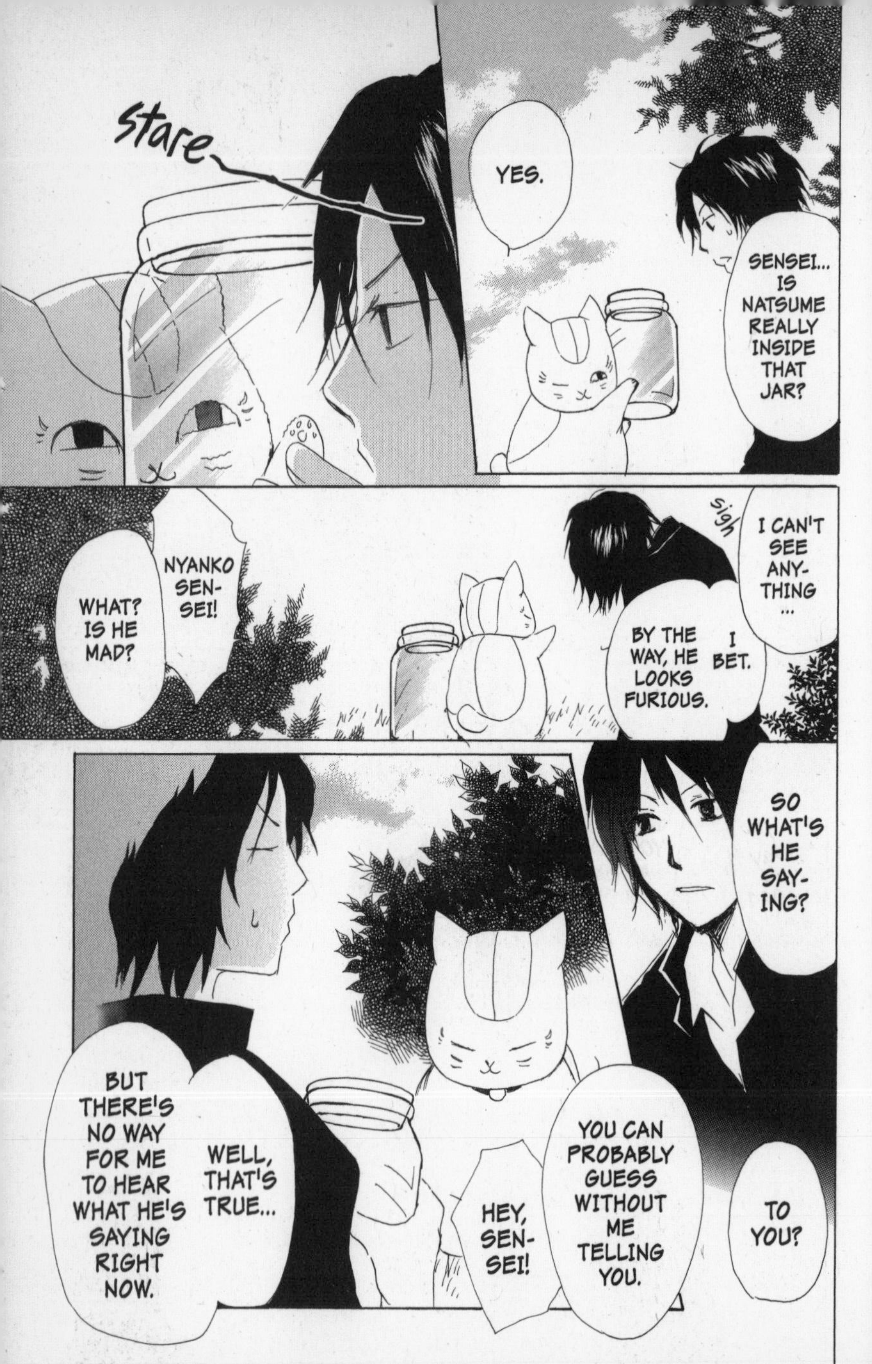
SENSEI... IS NATSUME REALLY INSIDE THAT JAR?
YES.
stare
I CAN'T SEE ANYTHING...
sigh
I BET.
BY THE WAY, HE LOOKS FURIOUS.
NYANKO SENSEI!
WHAT? IS HE MAD?
SO WHAT'S HE SAYING?
TO YOU?
YOU CAN PROBABLY GUESS WITHOUT ME TELLING YOU.
HEY, SENSEI!
WELL, THAT'S TRUE...
BUT THERE'S NO WAY FOR ME TO HEAR WHAT HE'S SAYING RIGHT NOW.

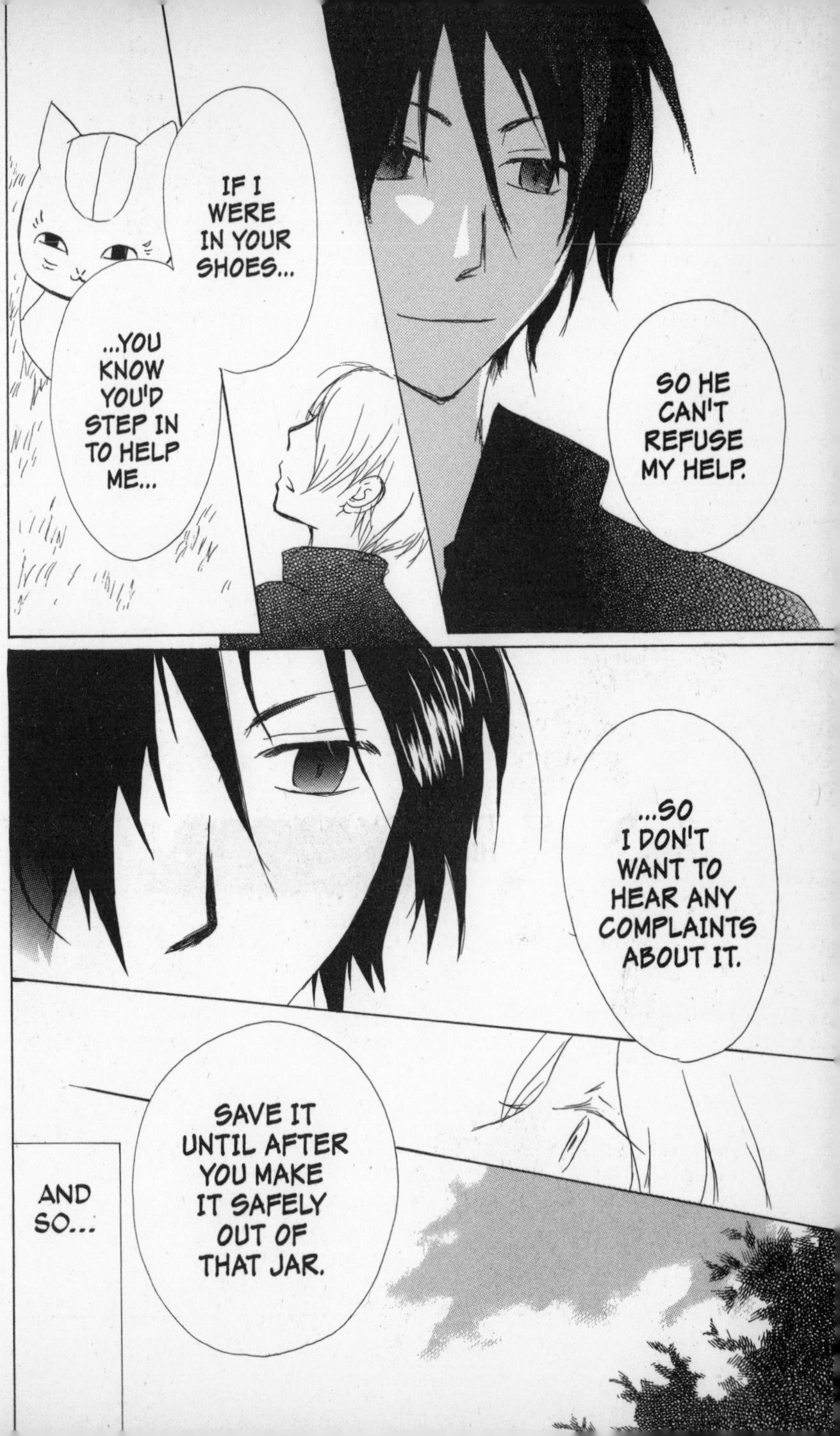
SO HE CAN'T REFUSE MY HELP.
IF I WERE IN YOUR SHOES...
...YOU KNOW YOU'D STEP IN TO HELP ME...
...SO I DON'T WANT TO HEAR ANY COMPLAINTS ABOUT IT.
SAVE IT UNTIL AFTER YOU MAKE IT SAFELY OUT OF THAT JAR.
AND SO...

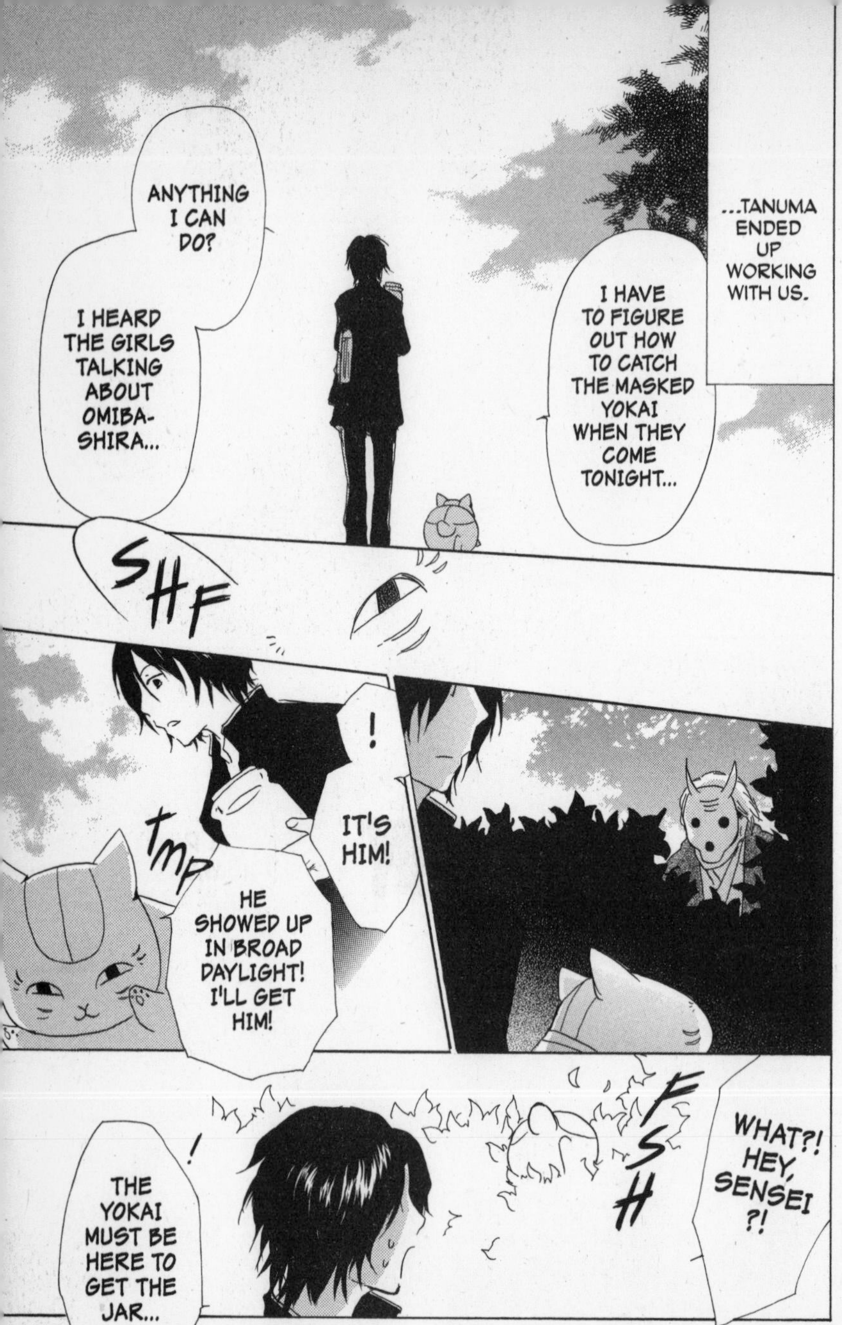
...TANUMA ENDED UP WORKING WITH US.
I HAVE TO FIGURE OUT HOW TO CATCH THE MASKED YOKAI WHEN THEY COME TONIGHT...
ANYTHING I CAN DO?
I HEARD THE GIRLS TALKING ABOUT OMIBA-SHIRA...
SHF
!
IT'S HIM!
tmp
HE SHOWED UP IN BROAD DAYLIGHT! I'LL GET HIM!
WHAT?! HEY, SENSEI?!
FSSH
!
THE YOKAI MUST BE HERE TO GET THE JAR...

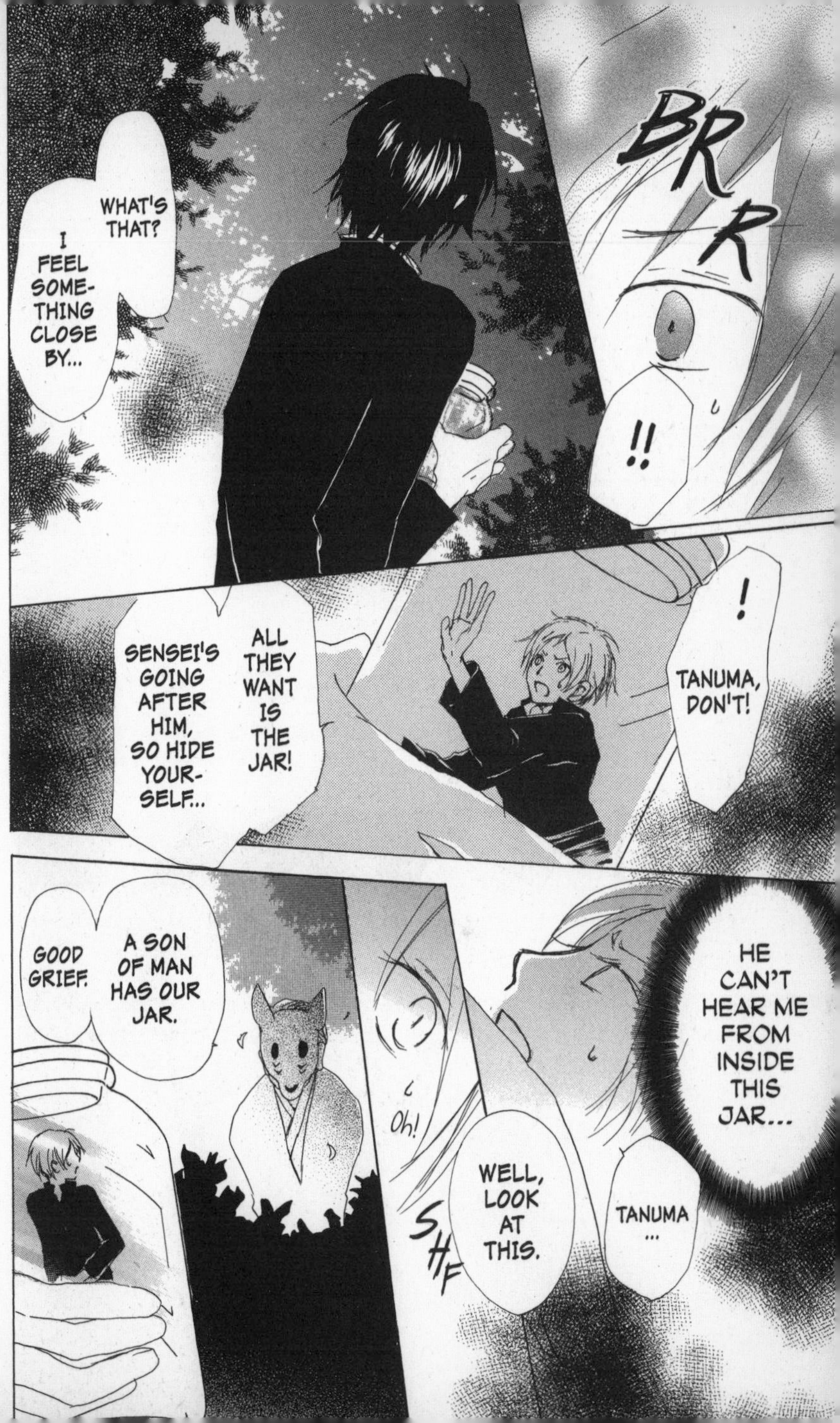
BRR
!!
WHAT'S THAT?
I FEEL SOME-THING CLOSE BY...
!
TANUMA, DON'T!
ALL THEY WANT IS THE JAR!
SENSEI'S GOING AFTER HIM, SO HIDE YOUR-SELF...
HE CAN'T HEAR ME FROM INSIDE THIS JAR...
Oh!
TANUMA...
WELL, LOOK AT THIS.
SHF
A SON OF MAN HAS OUR JAR.
GOOD GRIEF.

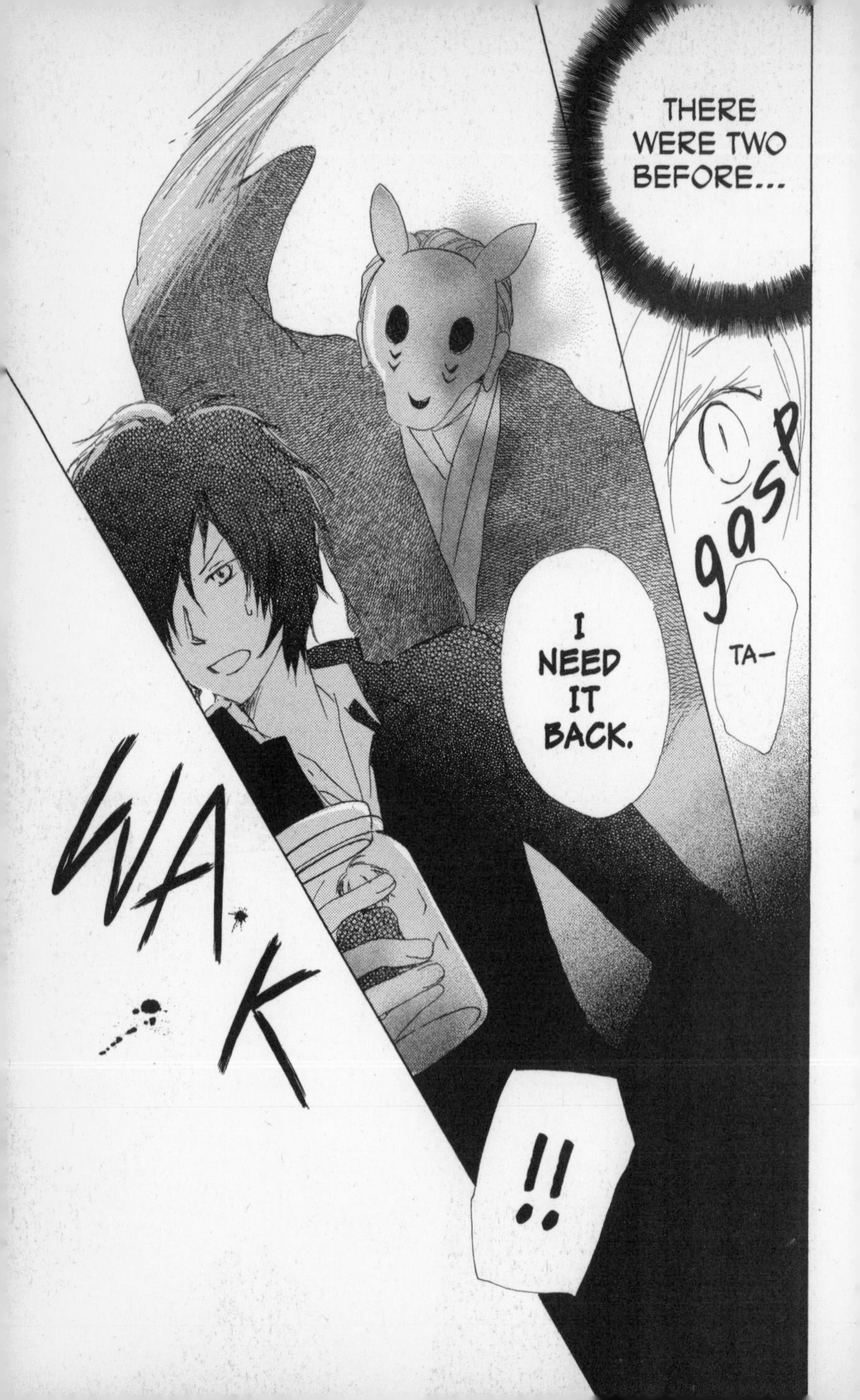
THERE WERE TWO BEFORE...
gasp
TA—
I NEED IT BACK.
WAK
!!

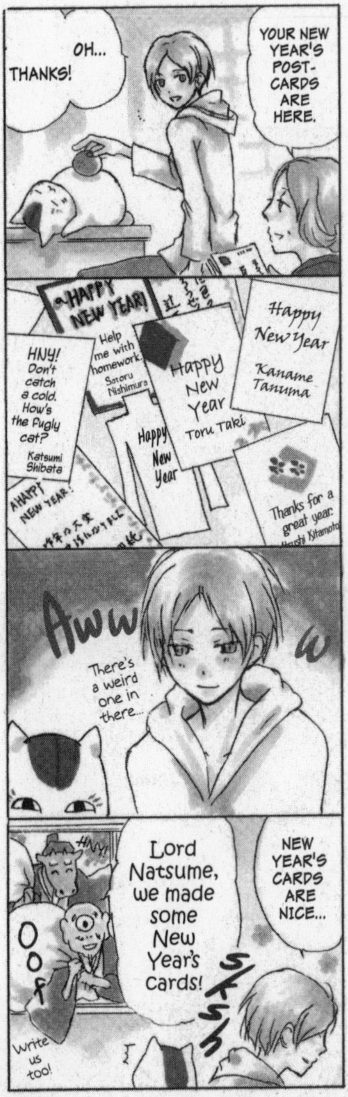
YOUR NEW YEAR'S POST-CARDS ARE HERE.
OH... THANKS!
Happy New Year Kaname Tanuma
Happy New Year Toru Taki
Thanks for a great year.
Help me with homework. Satoru Nishimura
HAPPY NEW YEAR!
HNY! Don't catch a cold. How's the fugly cat? Katsumi Shibata
Happy New Year
HAPPY NEW YEAR!
Awww
There's a weird one in there...
NEW YEAR'S CARDS ARE NICE...
Lord Natsume, we made some New Year's cards!
SKSH
HNY!
Oof
Write us too!

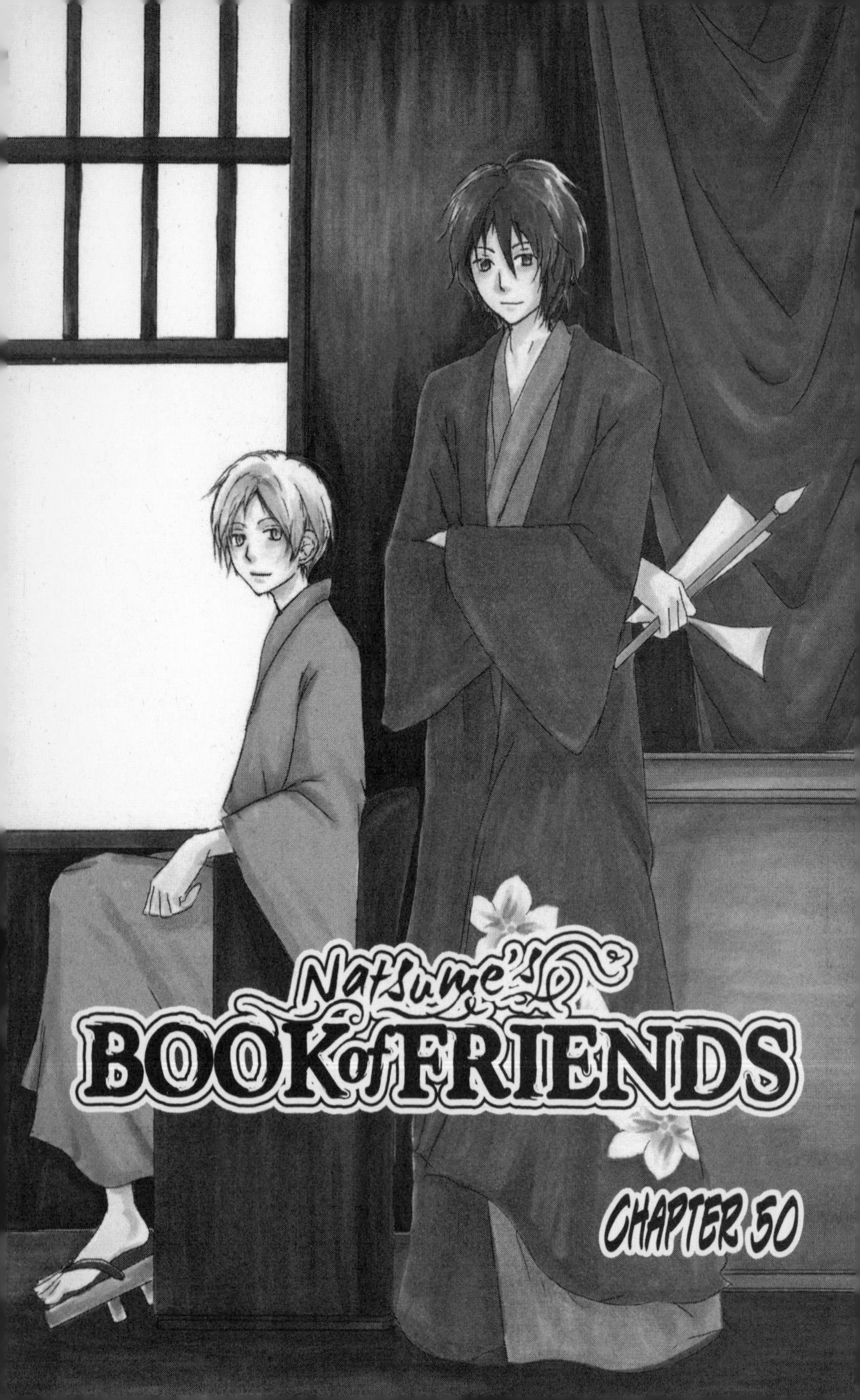
Natsume's
BOOK of FRIENDS
CHAPTER 50

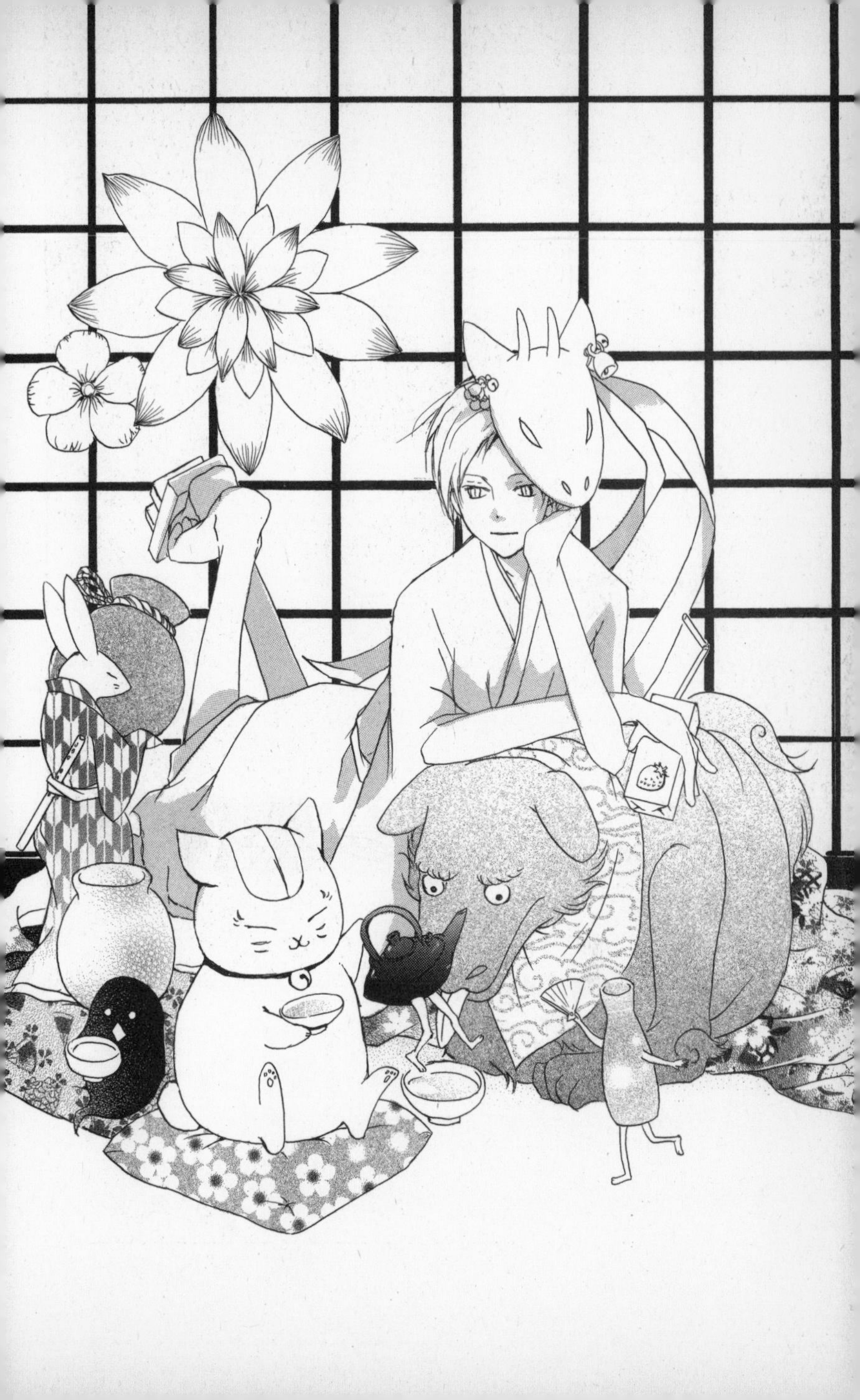

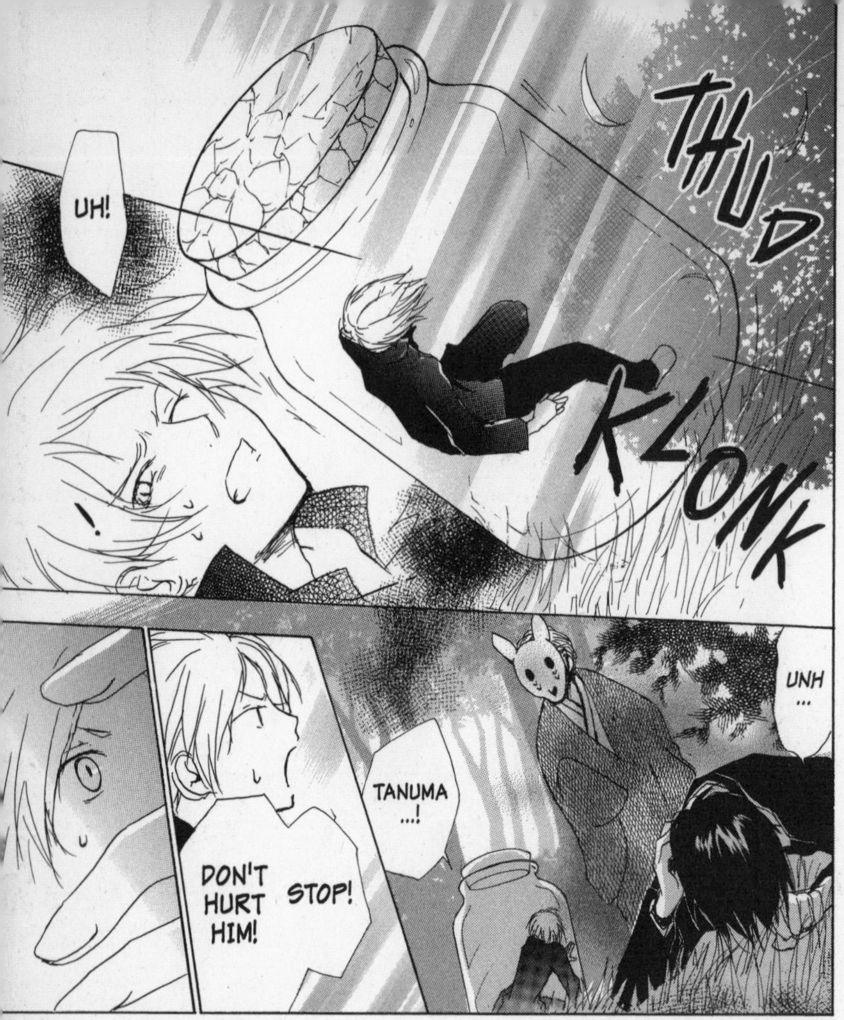
THUD
KLONK
UH!
UNH ...
TANUMA ...!
STOP!
DON'T HURT HIM!

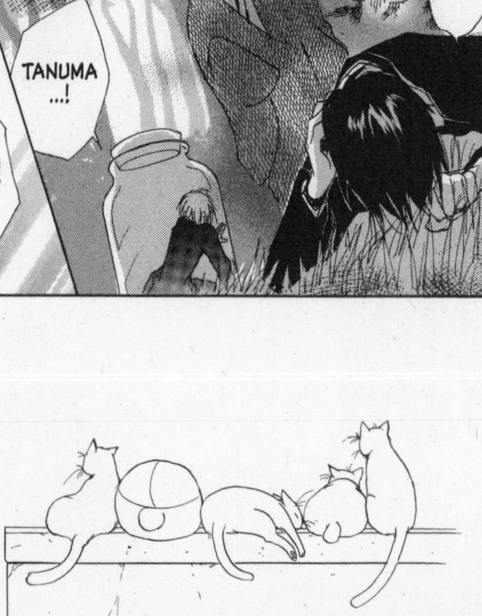

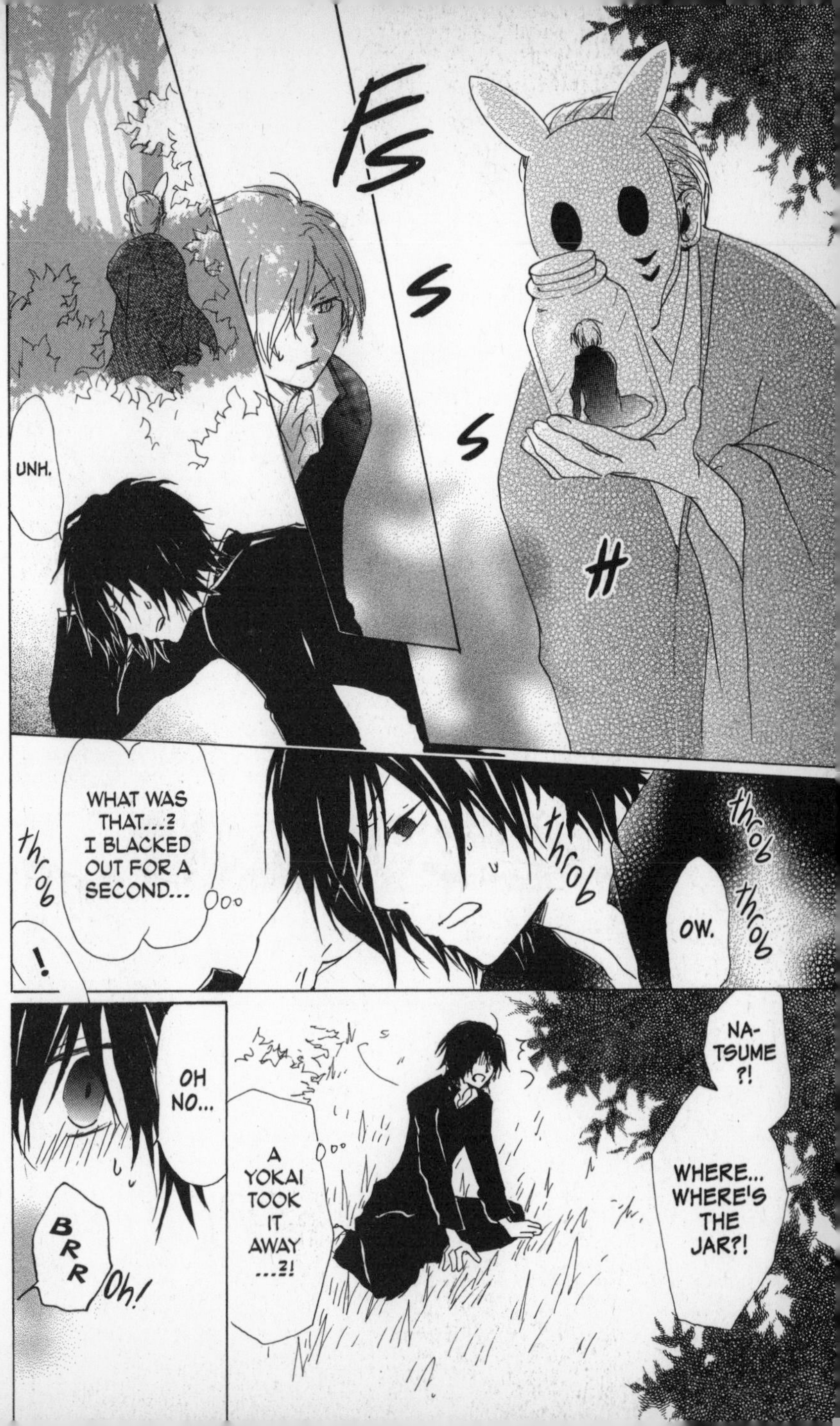
FS
S
S
H
UNH.
throb throb
OW.
throb
WHAT WAS THAT...? I BLACKED OUT FOR A SECOND...
throb
!
NA-TSUME?!
WHERE... WHERE'S THE JAR?!
A YOKAI TOOK IT AWAY...?!
OH NO...
BRR
Oh!

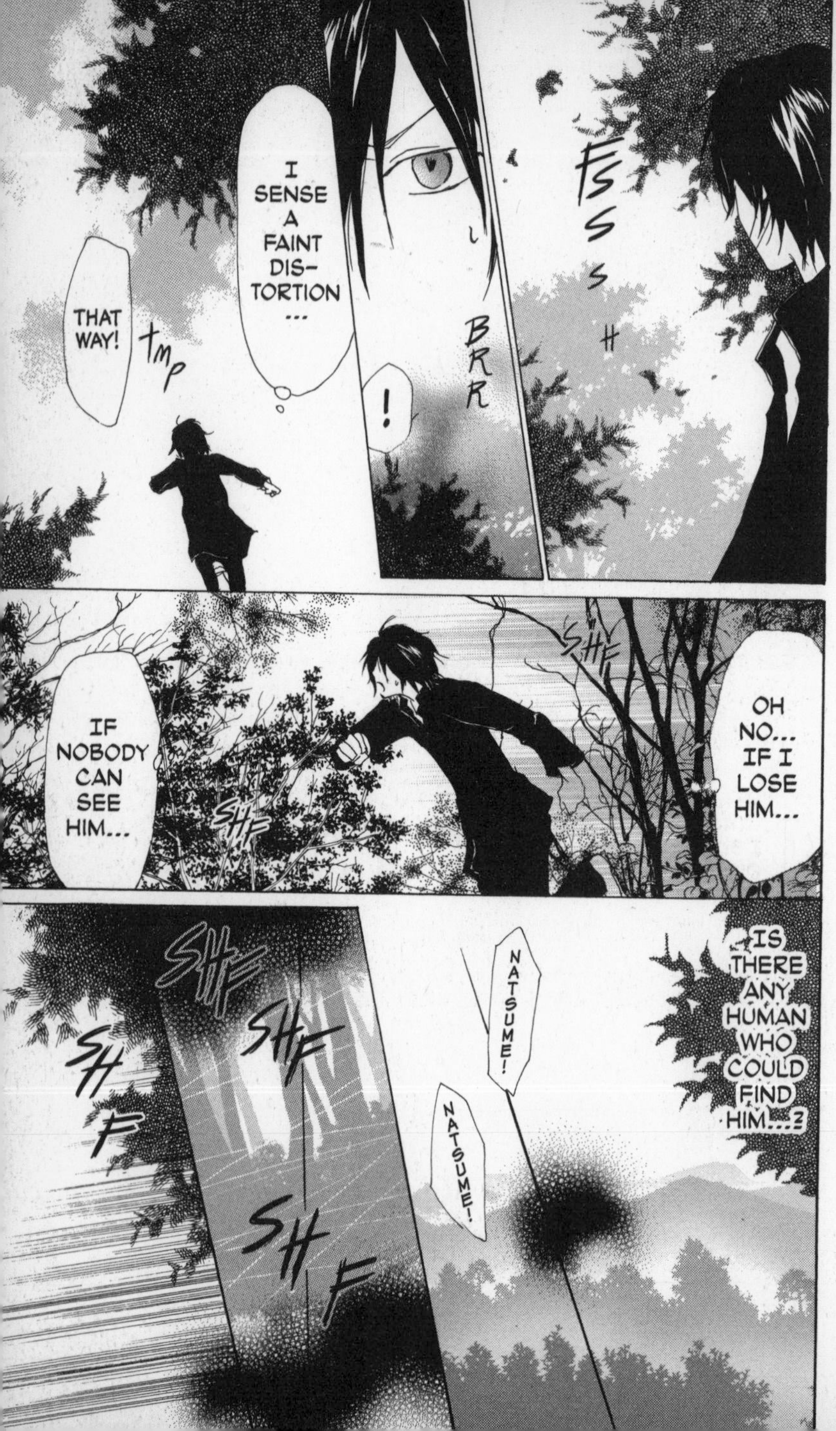
FSSSH
I SENSE A FAINT DISTORTION...
BRR
!
THAT WAY!
TMP
OH NO... IF I LOSE HIM...
SHF
IF NOBODY CAN SEE HIM...
SHF
IS THERE ANY HUMAN WHO COULD FIND HIM...?
NATSUME!
NATSUME!
SHF
SHF
SHF
SHF

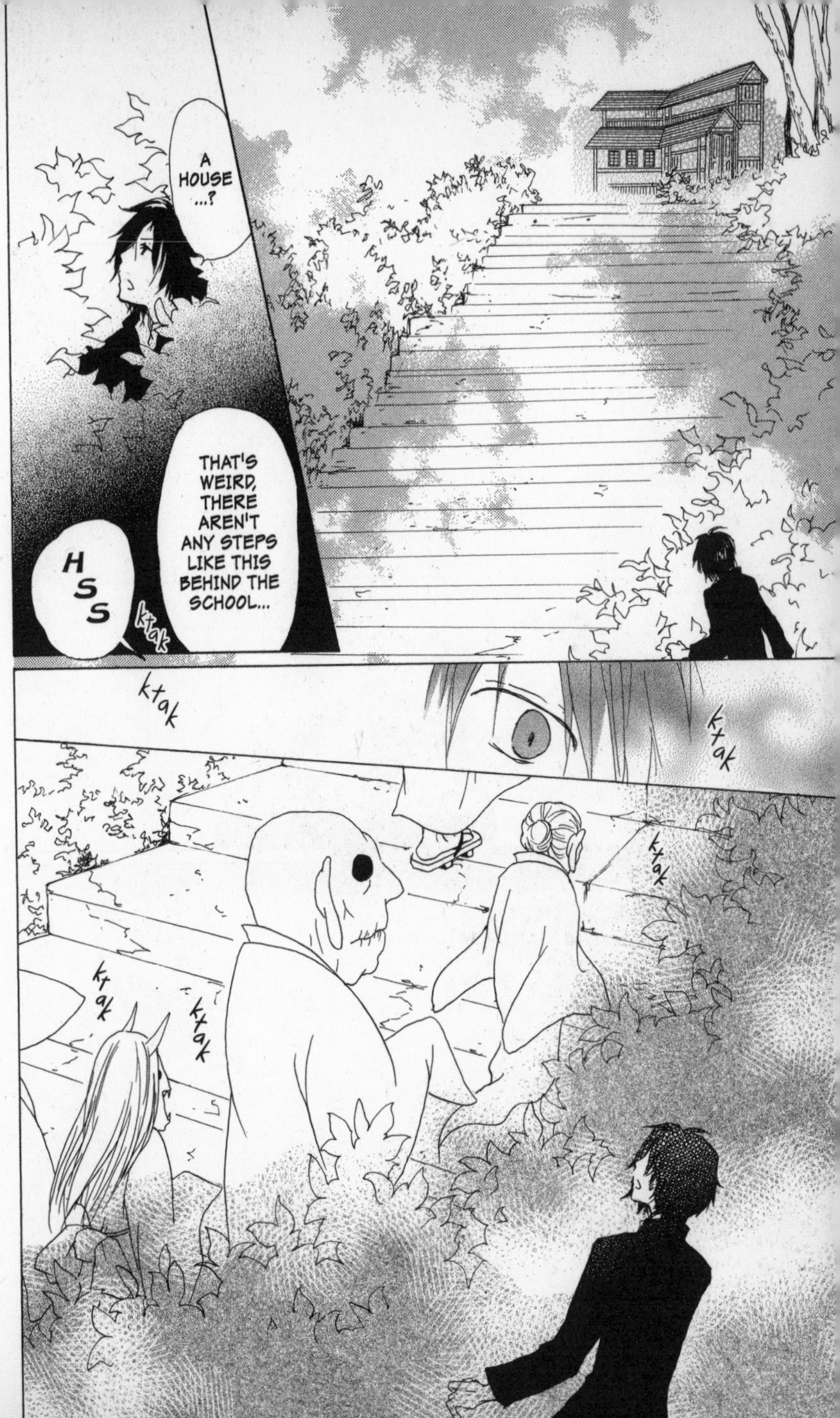
A HOUSE ...?
THAT'S WEIRD, THERE AREN'T ANY STEPS LIKE THIS BEHIND THE SCHOOL...
HSS
ktak
ktak
ktak
ktak
ktak
ktak

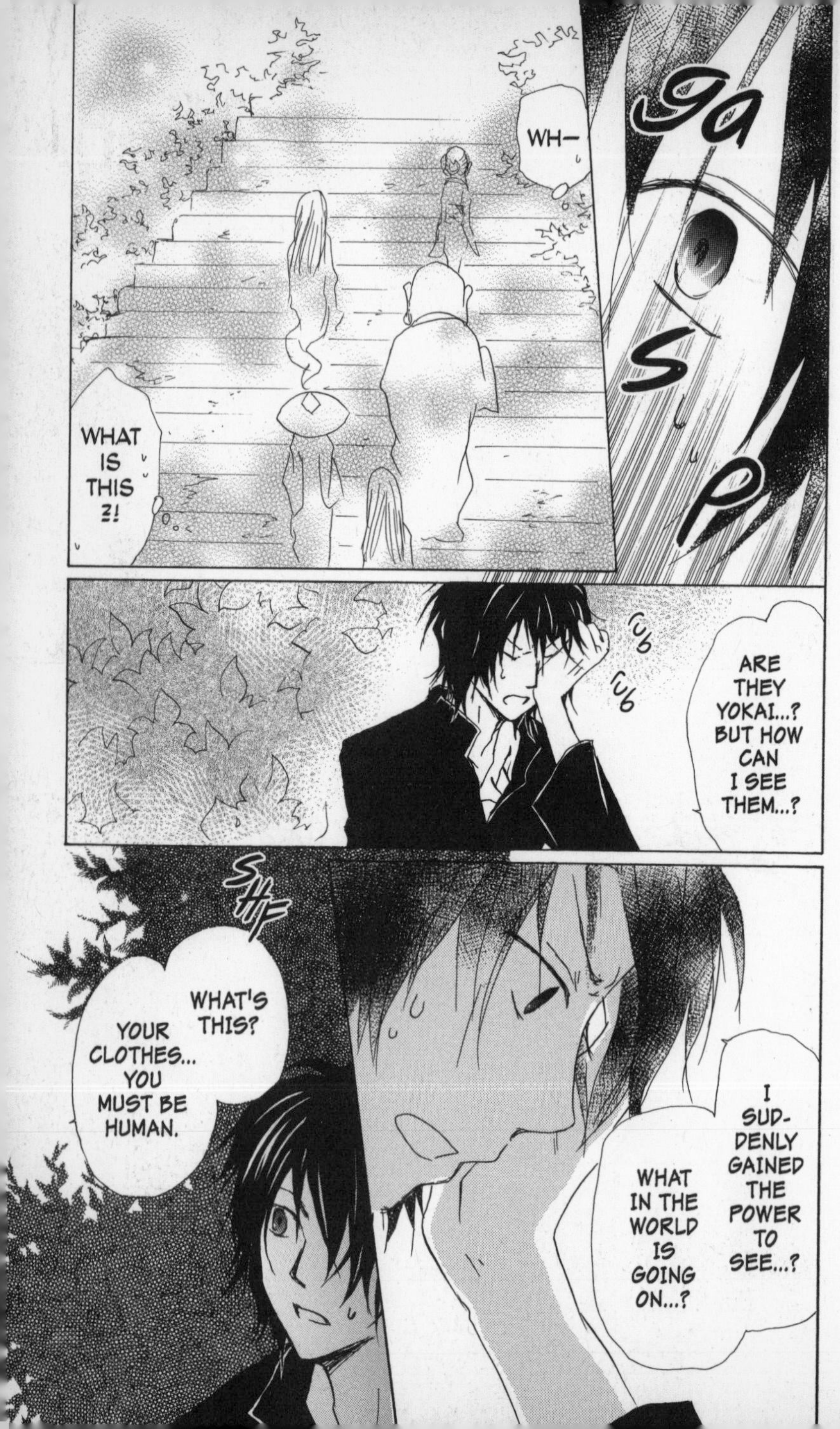
GASP
WH–
WHAT IS THIS?!
RUB RUB
ARE THEY YOKAI...? BUT HOW CAN I SEE THEM...?
SHF
I SUDDENLY GAINED THE POWER TO SEE...?
WHAT IN THE WORLD IS GOING ON...?
WHAT'S THIS?
YOUR CLOTHES... YOU MUST BE HUMAN.

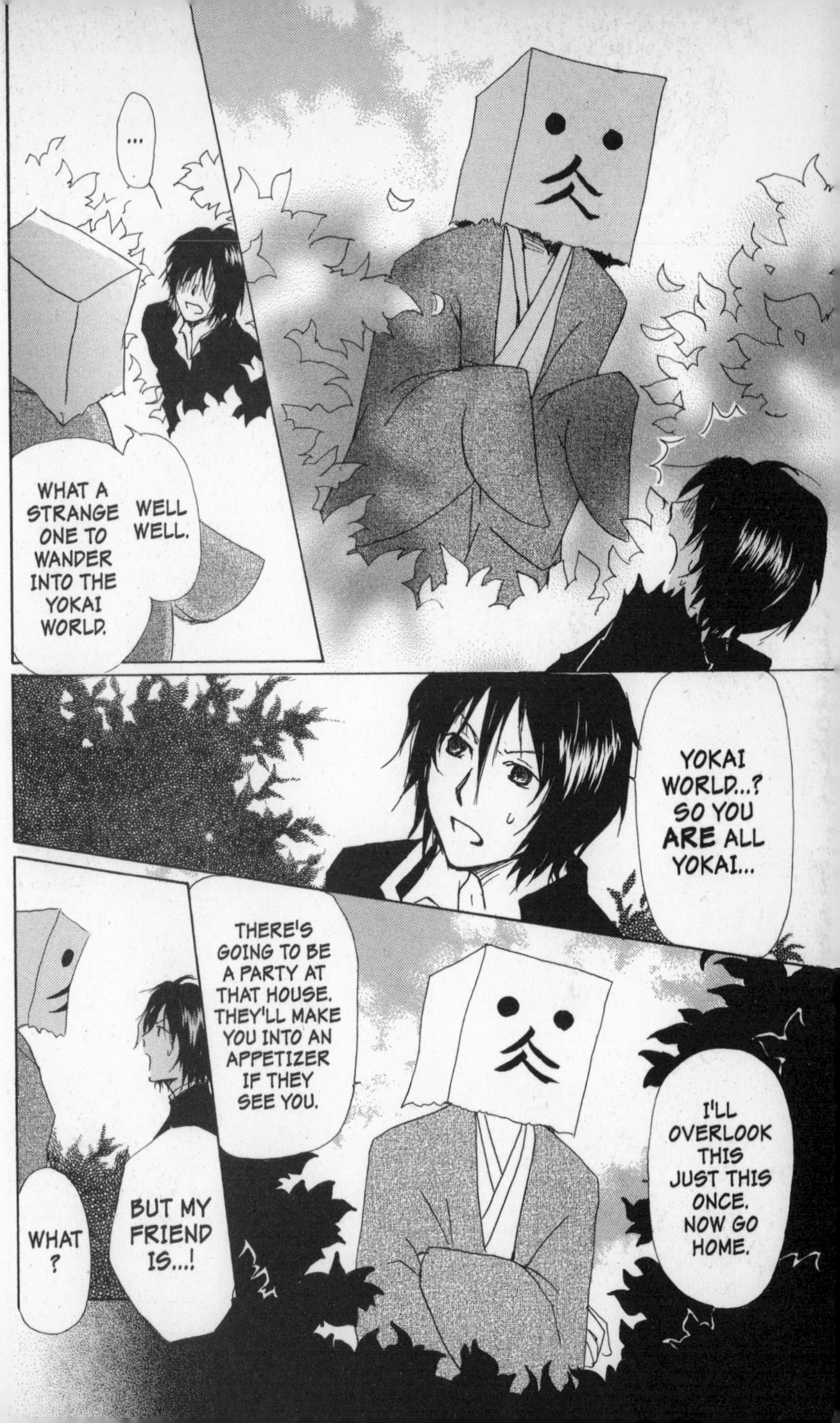
...
WELL WELL.
WHAT A STRANGE ONE TO WANDER INTO THE YOKAI WORLD.
YOKAI WORLD...? SO YOU **ARE** ALL YOKAI...
I'LL OVERLOOK THIS JUST THIS ONCE. NOW GO HOME.
THERE'S GOING TO BE A PARTY AT THAT HOUSE. THEY'LL MAKE YOU INTO AN APPETIZER IF THEY SEE YOU.
BUT MY FRIEND IS...!
WHAT?

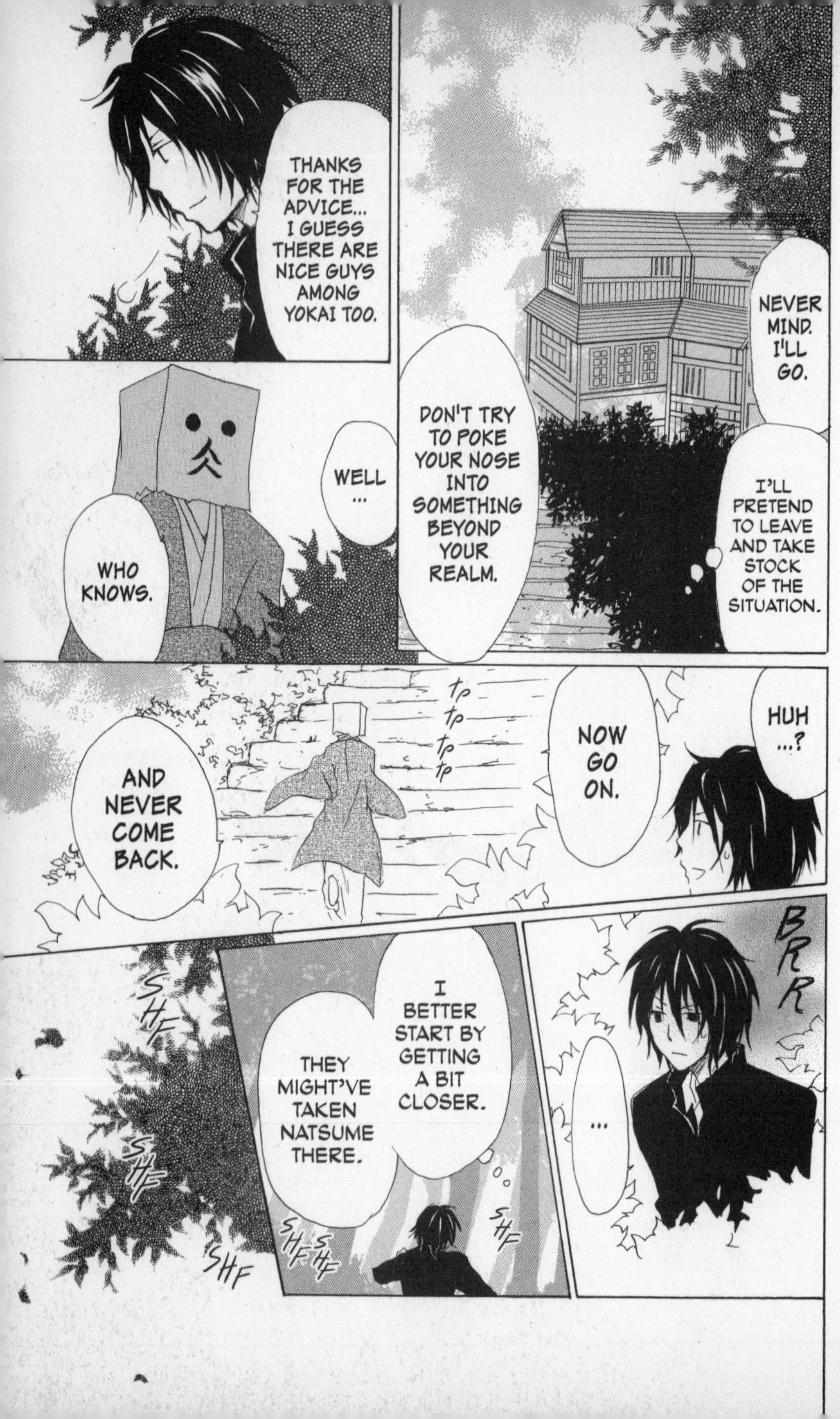
DON'T TRY TO POKE YOUR NOSE INTO SOMETHING BEYOND YOUR REALM.
NEVER MIND. I'LL GO.
I'LL PRETEND TO LEAVE AND TAKE STOCK OF THE SITUATION.
THANKS FOR THE ADVICE... I GUESS THERE ARE NICE GUYS AMONG YOKAI TOO.
WELL...
WHO KNOWS.
HUH...?
NOW GO ON.
tp tp tp tp
AND NEVER COME BACK.
BRR
...
I BETTER START BY GETTING A BIT CLOSER.
THEY MIGHT'VE TAKEN NATSUME THERE.
SHF
SHF
SHF
SHF SHF
SHF

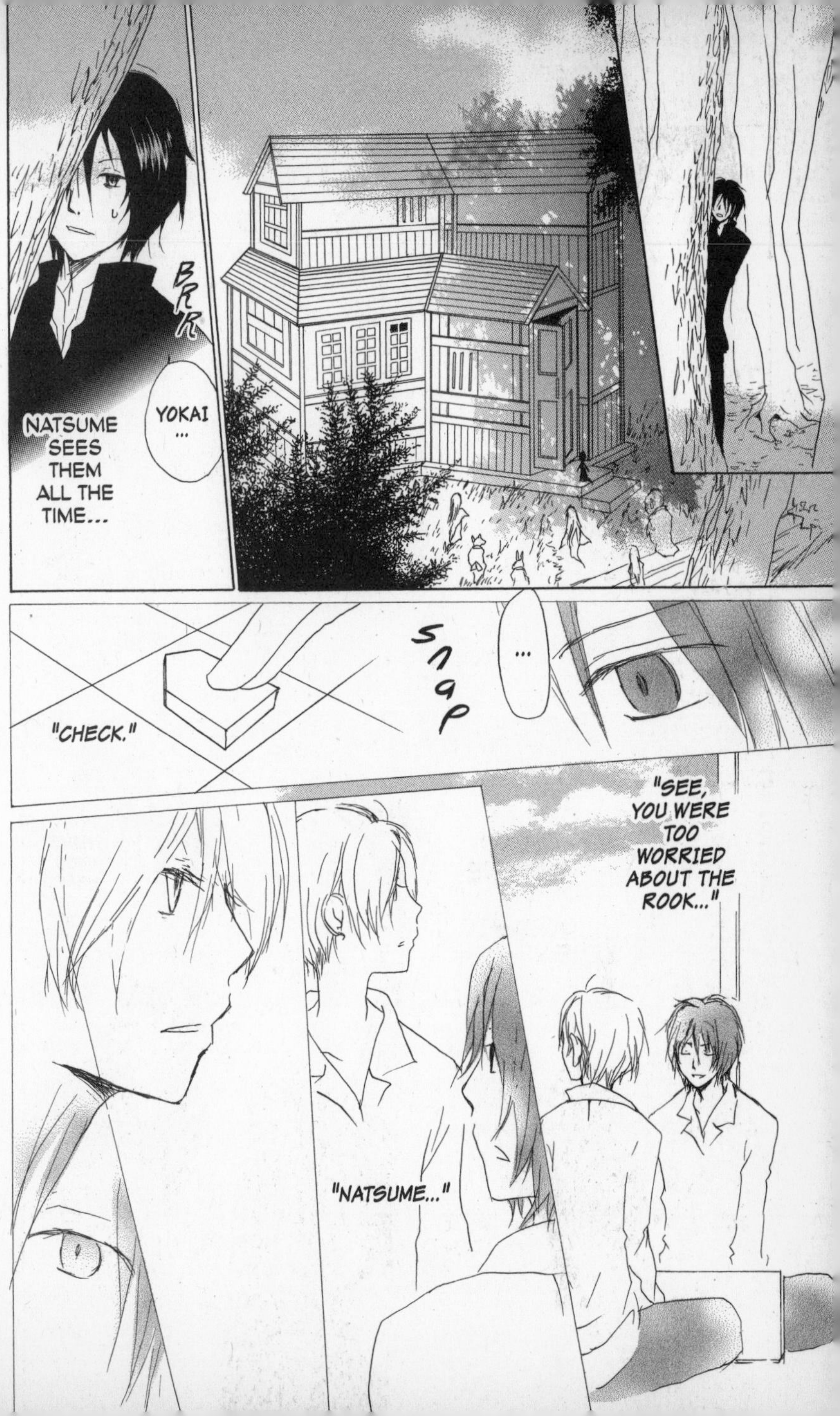
BRR
YOKAI ...
NATSUME SEES THEM ALL THE TIME...
...
SNAP
"CHECK."
"SEE, YOU WERE TOO WORRIED ABOUT THE ROOK..."
"NATSUME..."

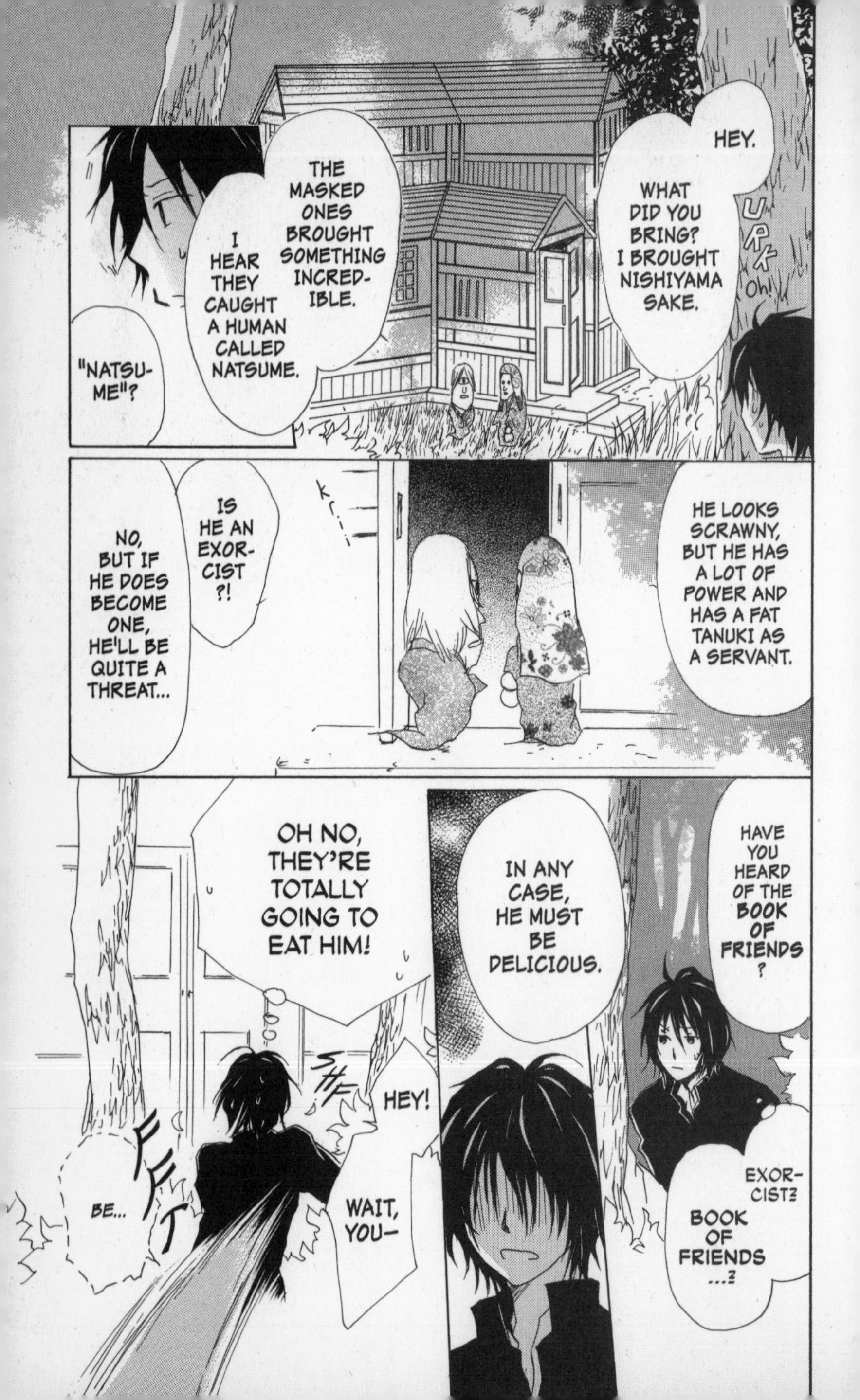
HEY.
WHAT DID YOU BRING? I BROUGHT NISHIYAMA SAKE.
URK
Oh!
THE MASKED ONES BROUGHT SOMETHING INCREDIBLE.
I HEAR THEY CAUGHT A HUMAN CALLED NATSUME.
"NATSUME"?
HE LOOKS SCRAWNY, BUT HE HAS A LOT OF POWER AND HAS A FAT TANUKI AS A SERVANT.
IS HE AN EXORCIST?!
NO, BUT IF HE DOES BECOME ONE, HE'LL BE QUITE A THREAT...
HAVE YOU HEARD OF THE BOOK OF FRIENDS?
IN ANY CASE, HE MUST BE DELICIOUS.
EXORCIST?
BOOK OF FRIENDS...?
OH NO, THEY'RE TOTALLY GOING TO EAT HIM!
SHF
HEY!
WAIT, YOU-
FFT
BE...

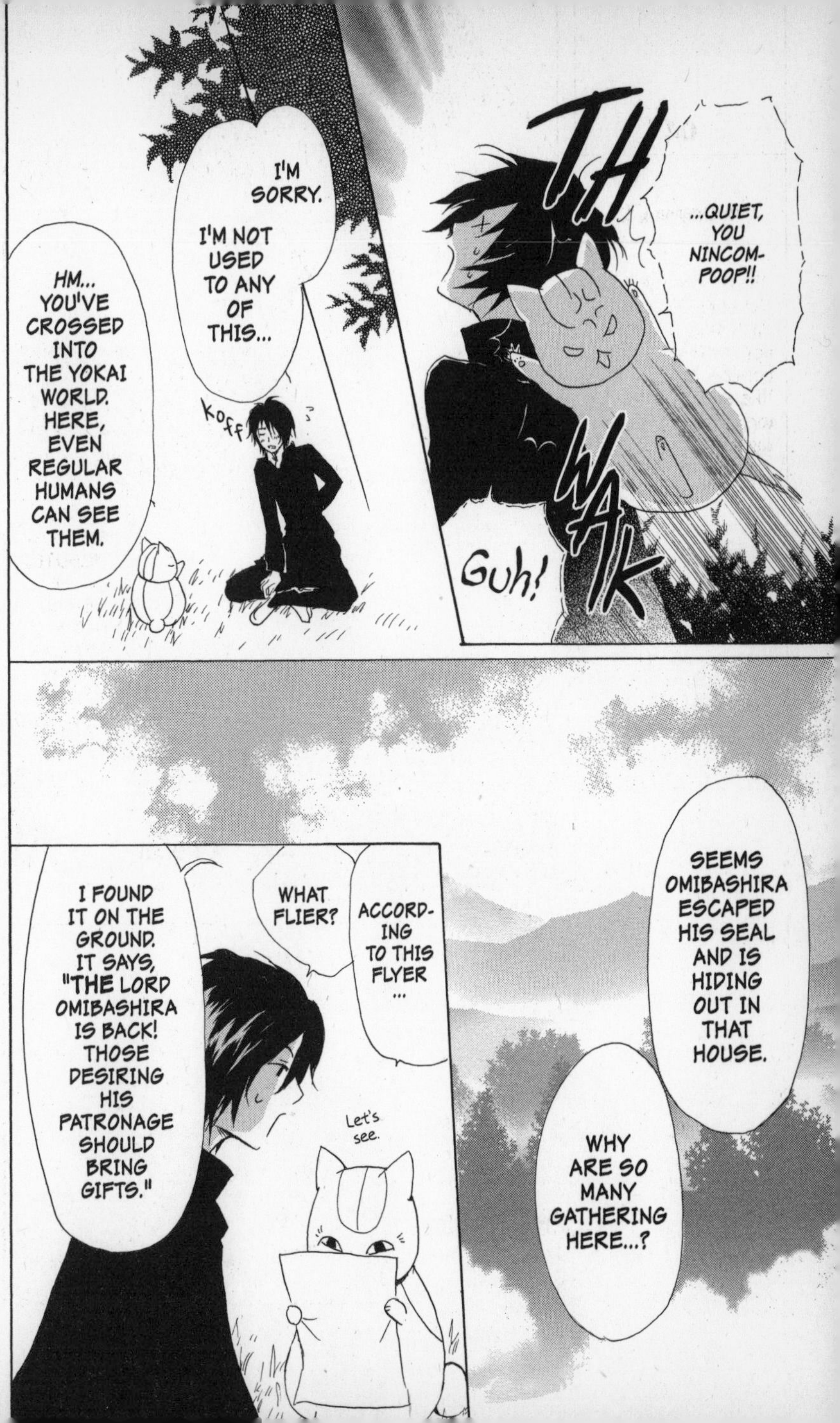

THWAK
...QUIET, YOU NINCOM-POOP!!
Guh!
I'M SORRY.
I'M NOT USED TO ANY OF THIS...
koff
HM... YOU'VE CROSSED INTO THE YOKAI WORLD. HERE, EVEN REGULAR HUMANS CAN SEE THEM.
SEEMS OMIBASHIRA ESCAPED HIS SEAL AND IS HIDING OUT IN THAT HOUSE.
WHY ARE SO MANY GATHERING HERE...?
ACCORD-ING TO THIS FLYER ...
WHAT FLIER?
I FOUND IT ON THE GROUND. IT SAYS, "THE LORD OMIBASHIRA IS BACK! THOSE DESIRING HIS PATRONAGE SHOULD BRING GIFTS."
Let's see.

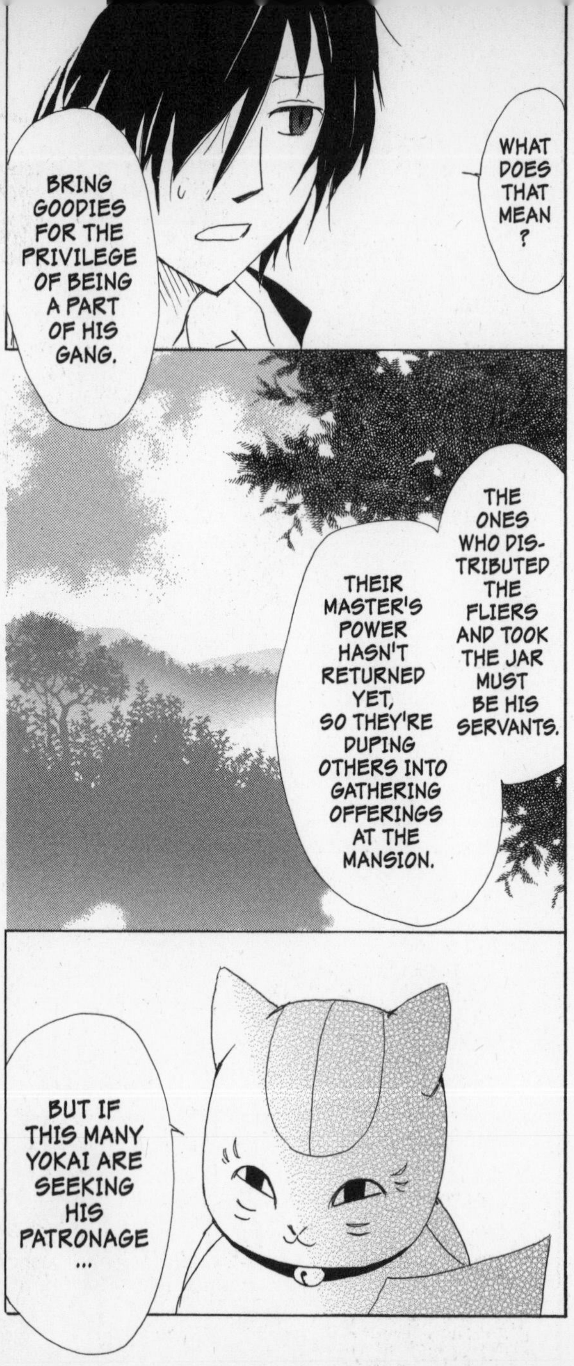
WHAT DOES THAT MEAN?
BRING GOODIES FOR THE PRIVILEGE OF BEING A PART OF HIS GANG.
THE ONES WHO DIS-TRIBUTED THE FLIERS AND TOOK THE JAR MUST BE HIS SERVANTS.
THEIR MASTER'S POWER HASN'T RETURNED YET, SO THEY'RE DUPING OTHERS INTO GATHERING OFFERINGS AT THE MANSION.
BUT IF THIS MANY YOKAI ARE SEEKING HIS PATRONAGE...

04

❋ Drama CD

They made a drama CD that comes with the Septem-ber issue of LaLa, coming out July 23. The anime script-writers wrote a wonderful original story. And the actors gave it life. Please check it out.

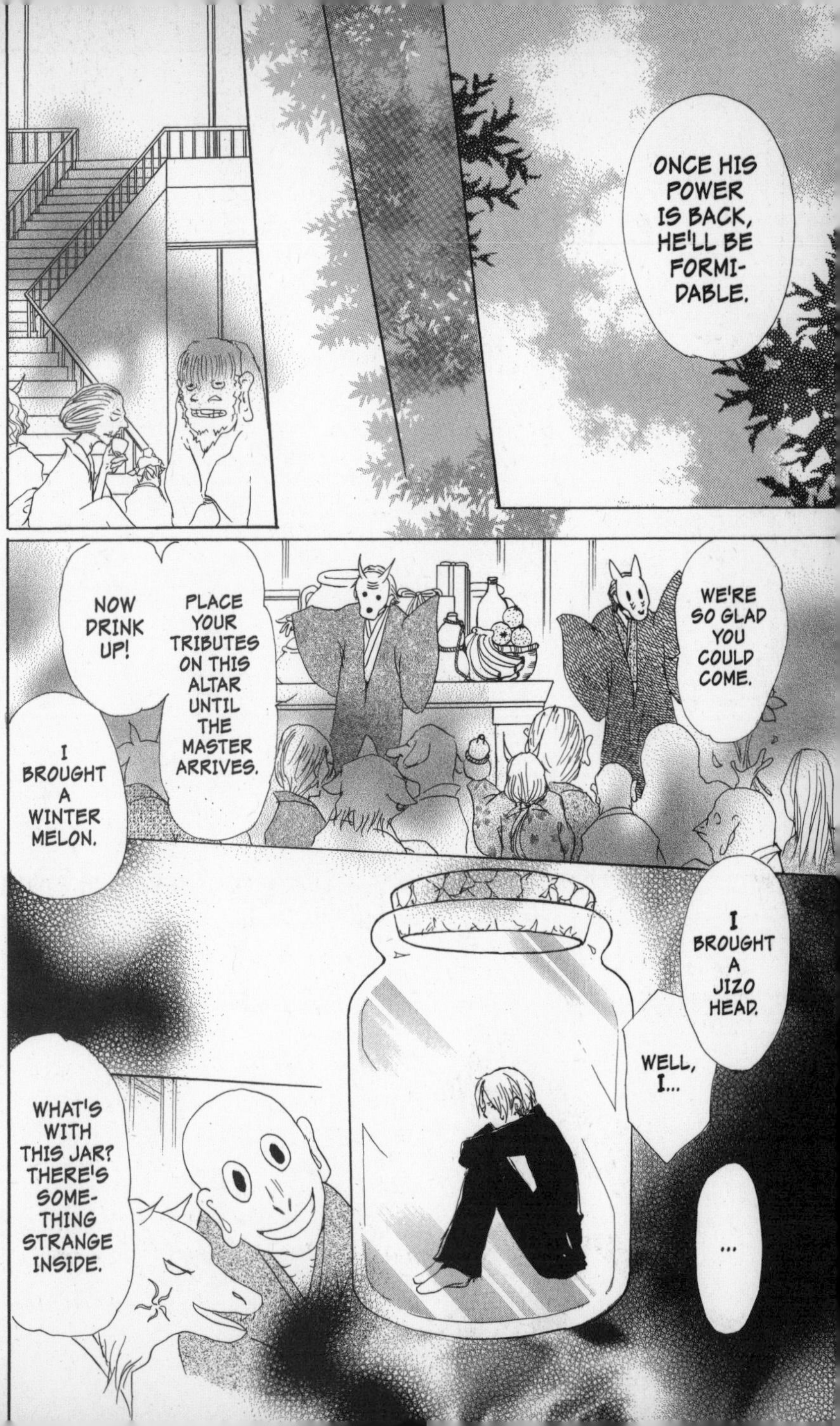
ONCE HIS POWER IS BACK, HE'LL BE FORMIDABLE.
WE'RE SO GLAD YOU COULD COME.
PLACE YOUR TRIBUTES ON THIS ALTAR UNTIL THE MASTER ARRIVES.
NOW DRINK UP!
I BROUGHT A WINTER MELON.
I BROUGHT A JIZO HEAD.
WELL, I...
...
WHAT'S WITH THIS JAR? THERE'S SOMETHING STRANGE INSIDE.

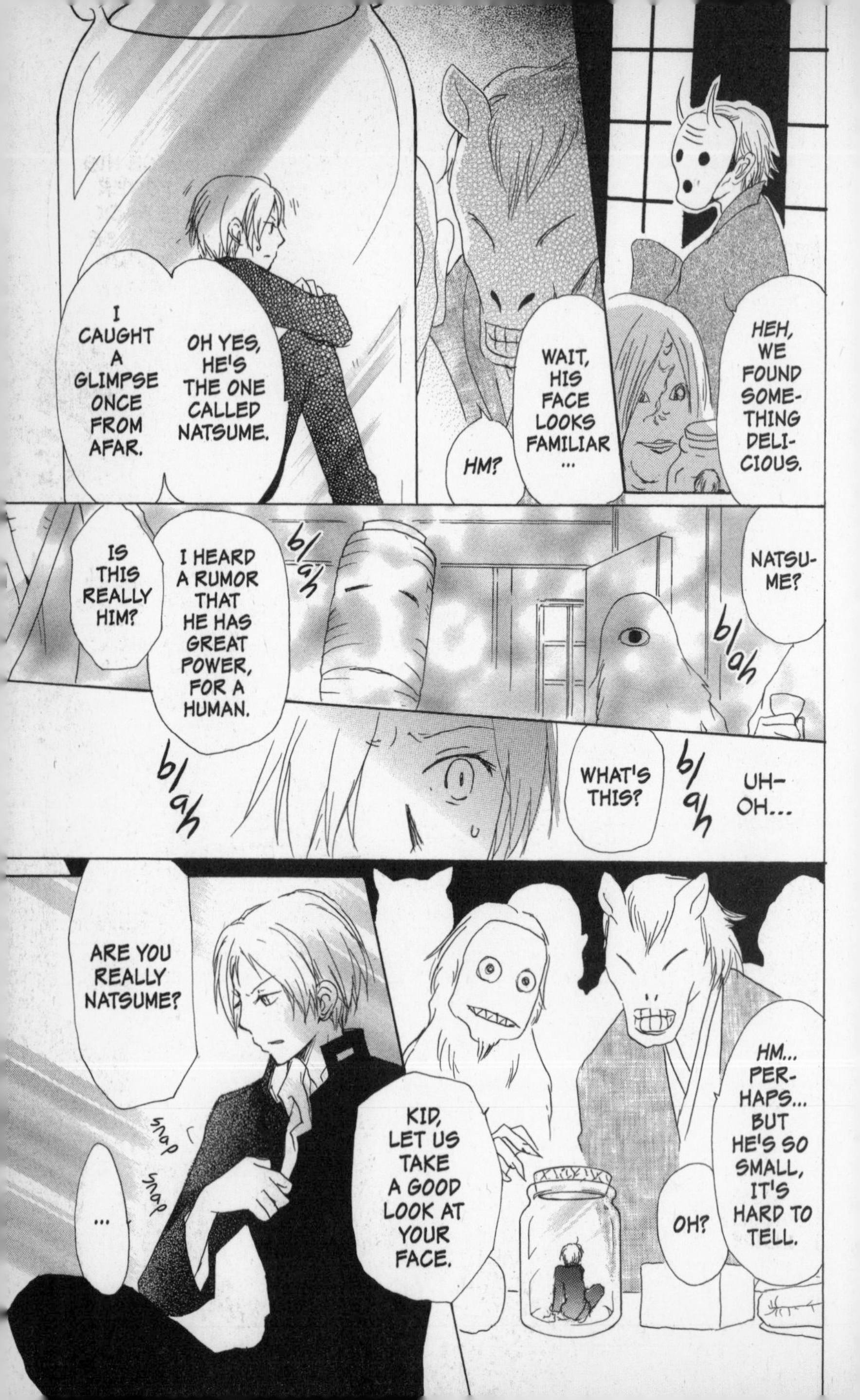
HEH, WE FOUND SOME-THING DELI-CIOUS.
WAIT, HIS FACE LOOKS FAMILIAR ...
HM?
OH YES, HE'S THE ONE CALLED NATSUME.
I CAUGHT A GLIMPSE ONCE FROM AFAR.
NATSU-ME?
blah
blah
I HEARD A RUMOR THAT HE HAS GREAT POWER, FOR A HUMAN.
IS THIS REALLY HIM?
UH-OH...
blah
WHAT'S THIS?
blah
HM... PER-HAPS... BUT HE'S SO SMALL, IT'S HARD TO TELL.
OH?
KID, LET US TAKE A GOOD LOOK AT YOUR FACE.
ARE YOU REALLY NATSUME?
snap
snap
...

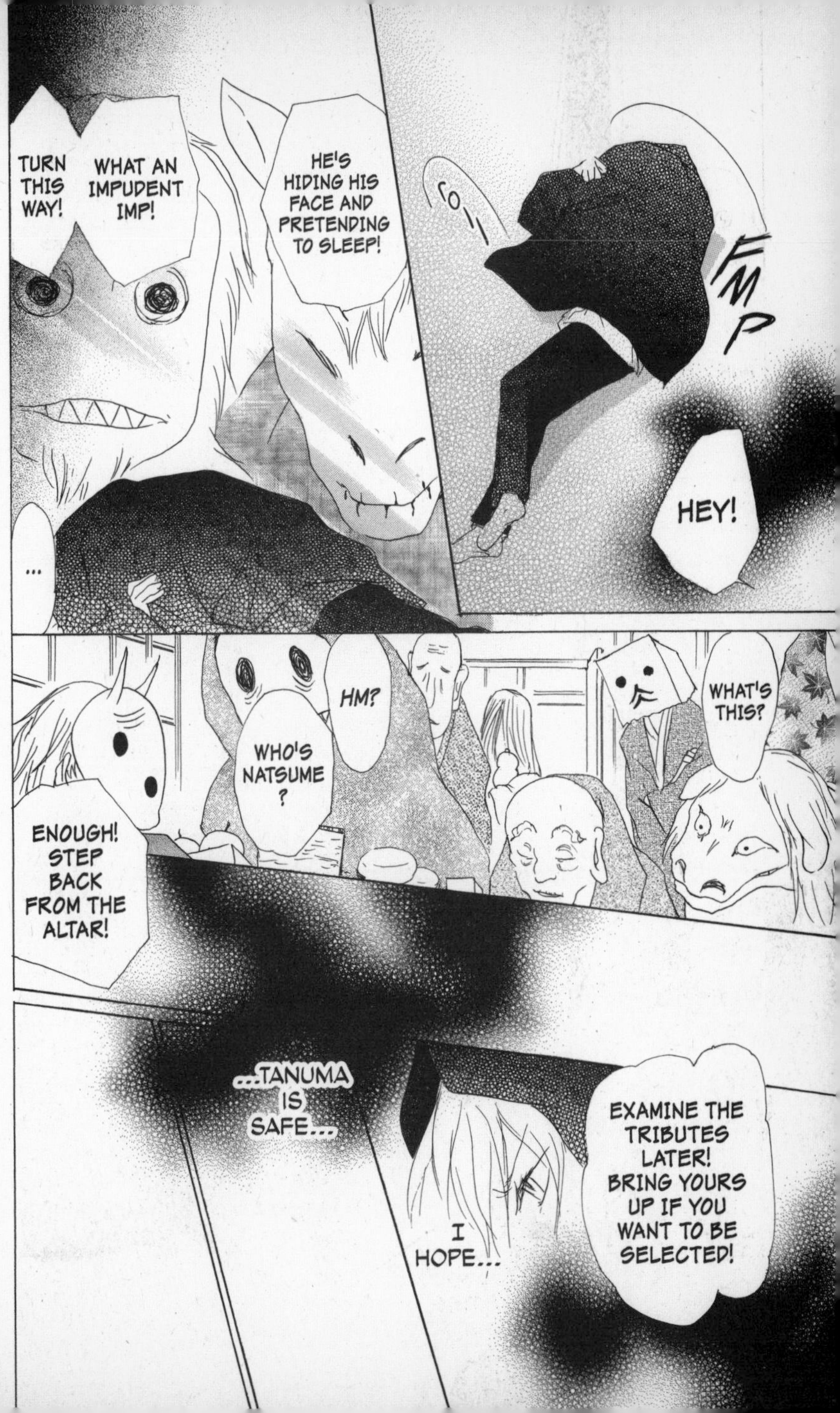
FMP
HEY!
HE'S HIDING HIS FACE AND PRETENDING TO SLEEP!
WHAT AN IMPUDENT IMP!
TURN THIS WAY!
...
WHAT'S THIS?
HM?
WHO'S NATSUME?
ENOUGH! STEP BACK FROM THE ALTAR!
EXAMINE THE TRIBUTES LATER! BRING YOURS UP IF YOU WANT TO BE SELECTED!
I HOPE...
...TANUMA IS SAFE...

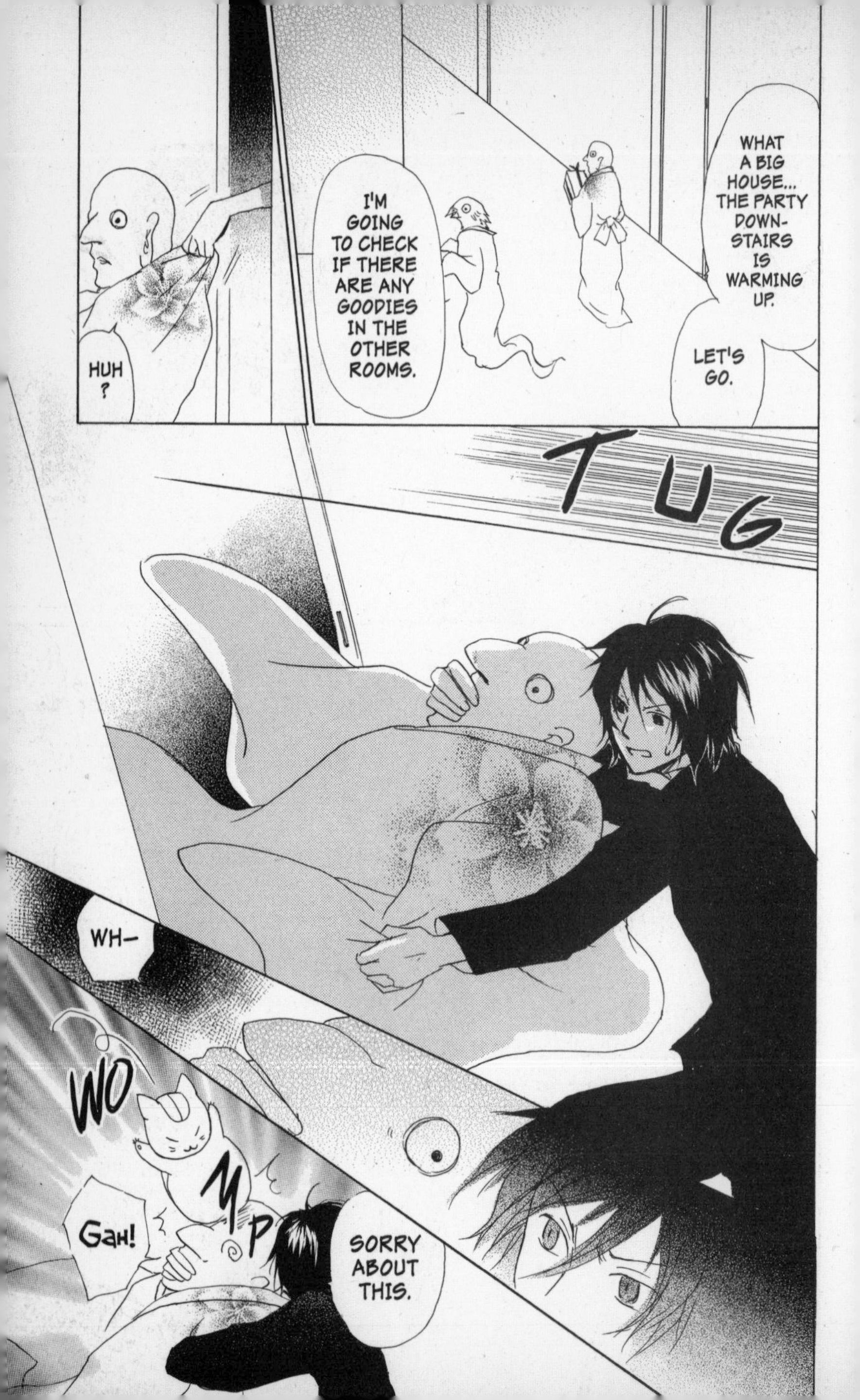
WHAT A BIG HOUSE... THE PARTY DOWN-STAIRS IS WARMING UP.
LET'S GO.
I'M GOING TO CHECK IF THERE ARE ANY GOODIES IN THE OTHER ROOMS.
HUH?
TUG
WH-
SORRY ABOUT THIS.
WOMP
Gah!

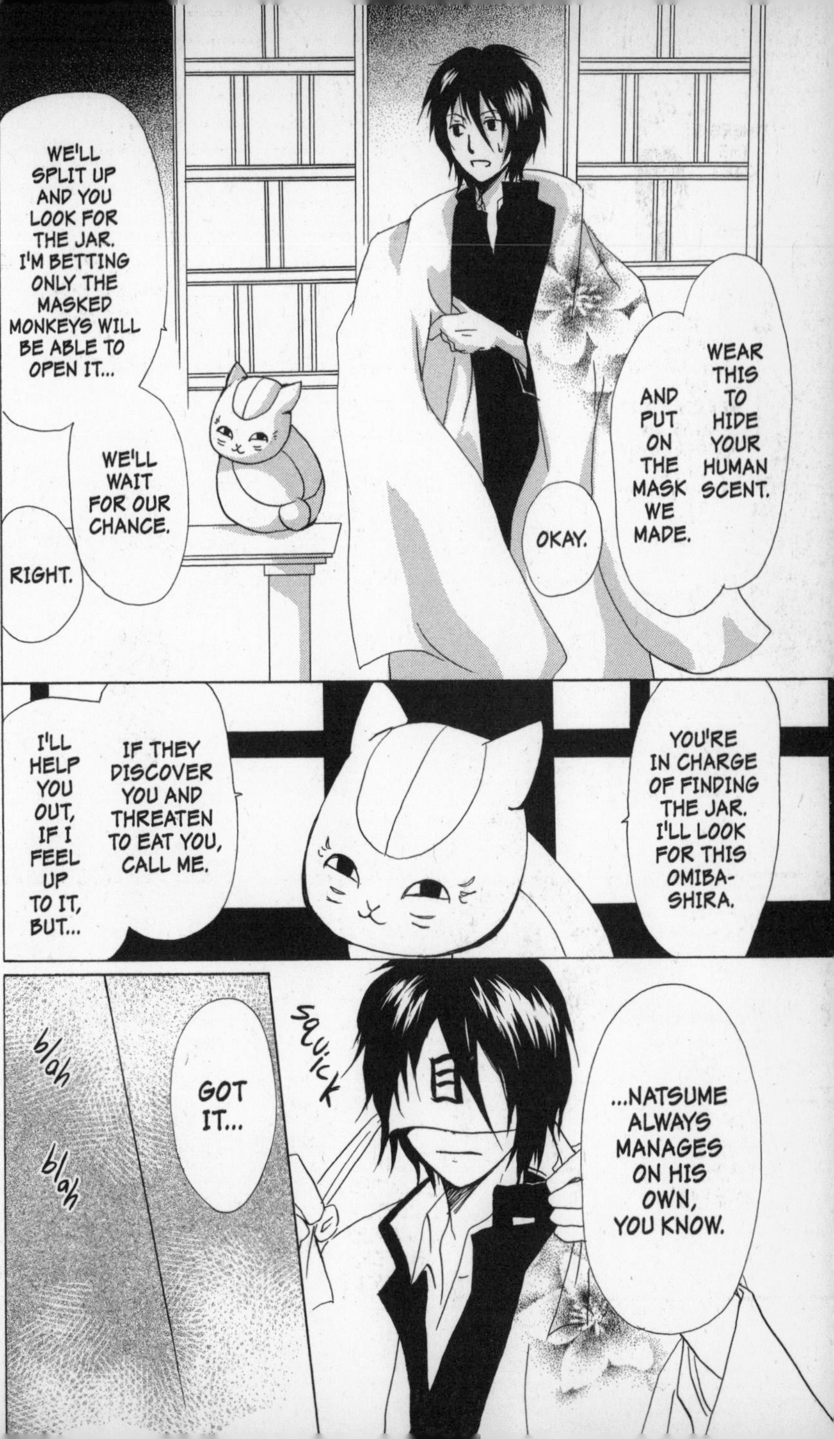
WEAR THIS TO HIDE YOUR HUMAN SCENT.
AND PUT ON THE MASK WE MADE.
OKAY.
WE'LL SPLIT UP AND YOU LOOK FOR THE JAR. I'M BETTING ONLY THE MASKED MONKEYS WILL BE ABLE TO OPEN IT...
WE'LL WAIT FOR OUR CHANCE.
RIGHT.
YOU'RE IN CHARGE OF FINDING THE JAR. I'LL LOOK FOR THIS OMIBA-SHIRA.
IF THEY DISCOVER YOU AND THREATEN TO EAT YOU, CALL ME.
I'LL HELP YOU OUT, IF I FEEL UP TO IT, BUT...
...NATSUME ALWAYS MANAGES ON HIS OWN, YOU KNOW.
SQUICK
GOT IT...
blah
blah

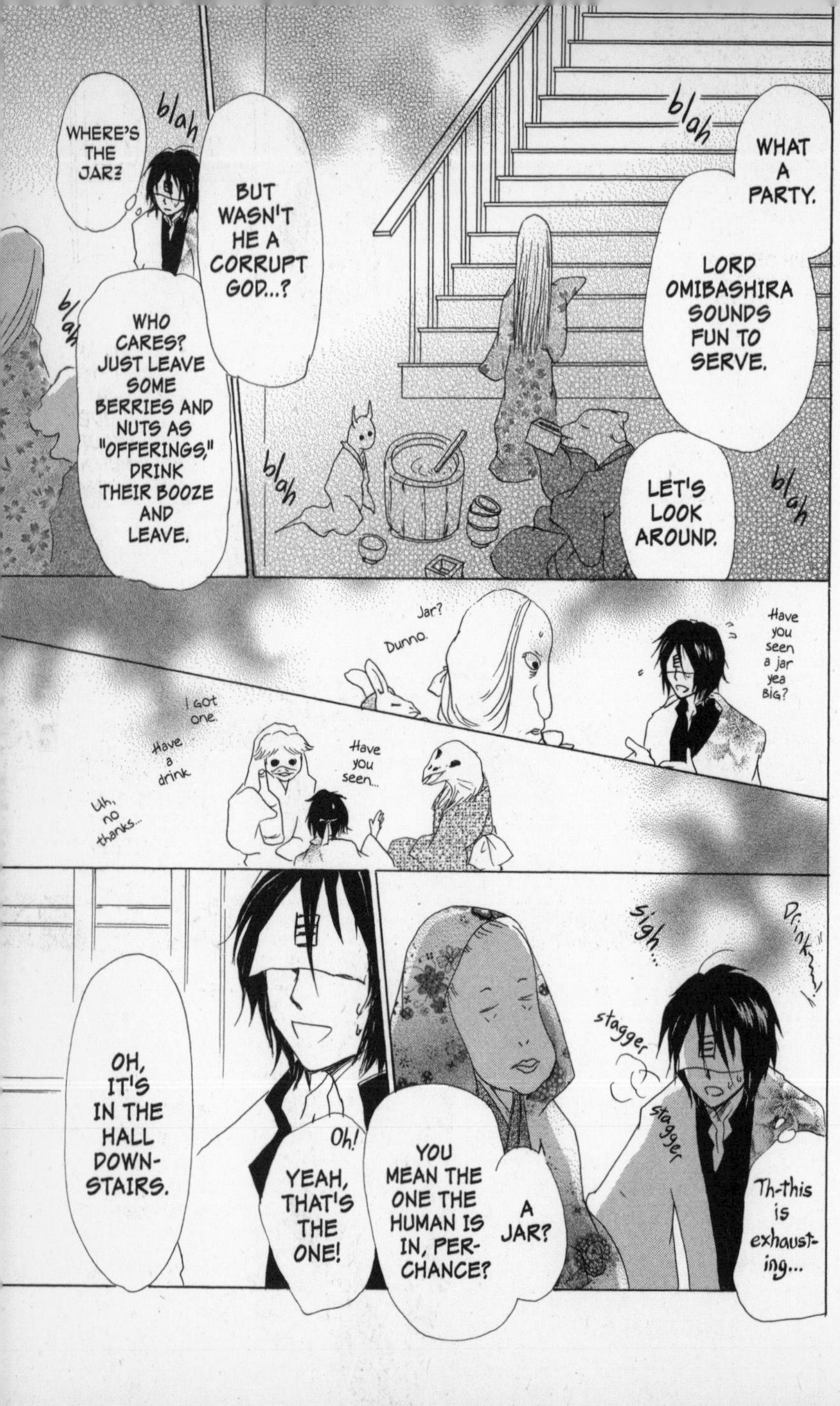
blah
WHAT A PARTY.
LORD OMIBASHIRA SOUNDS FUN TO SERVE.
blah
LET'S LOOK AROUND.
blah
WHERE'S THE JAR?
blah
BUT WASN'T HE A CORRUPT GOD...?
blah
WHO CARES? JUST LEAVE SOME BERRIES AND NUTS AS "OFFERINGS," DRINK THEIR BOOZE AND LEAVE.
Have you seen a jar yea BIG?
Jar?
Dunno.
Have you seen...
I got one.
Have a drink.
Uh, no thanks...
Drink!
sigh...
stagger
stagger
Th-this is exhaust-ing...
A JAR?
YOU MEAN THE ONE THE HUMAN IS IN, PER-CHANCE?
Oh!
YEAH, THAT'S THE ONE!
OH, IT'S IN THE HALL DOWN-STAIRS.

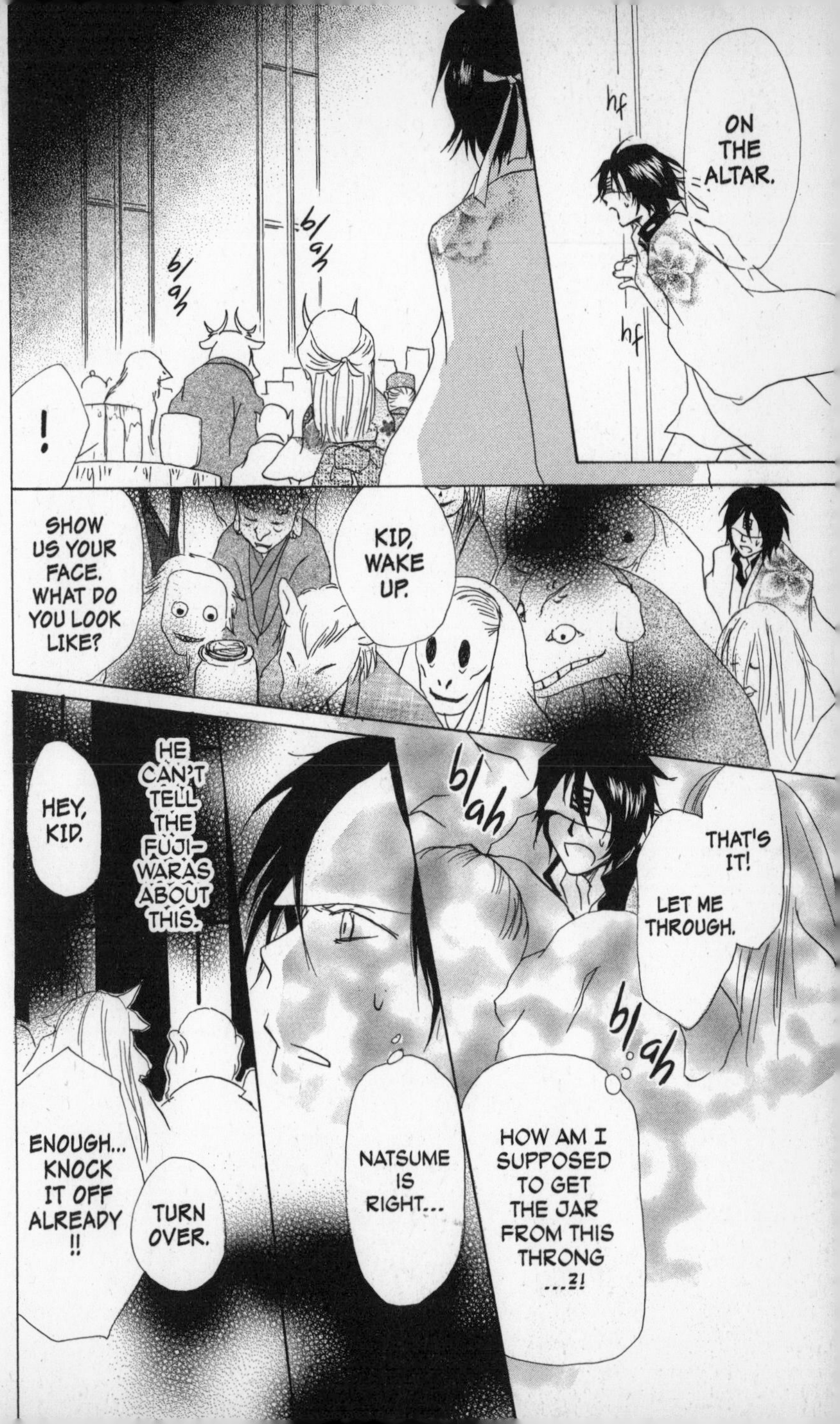
hf
ON THE ALTAR.
hf
blah
blah
!
KID, WAKE UP.
SHOW US YOUR FACE. WHAT DO YOU LOOK LIKE?
THAT'S IT!
LET ME THROUGH.
blah
HE CAN'T TELL THE FUJI-WARAS ABOUT THIS.
HEY, KID.
blah
HOW AM I SUPPOSED TO GET THE JAR FROM THIS THRONG ...?!
NATSUME IS RIGHT...
TURN OVER.
ENOUGH... KNOCK IT OFF ALREADY !!

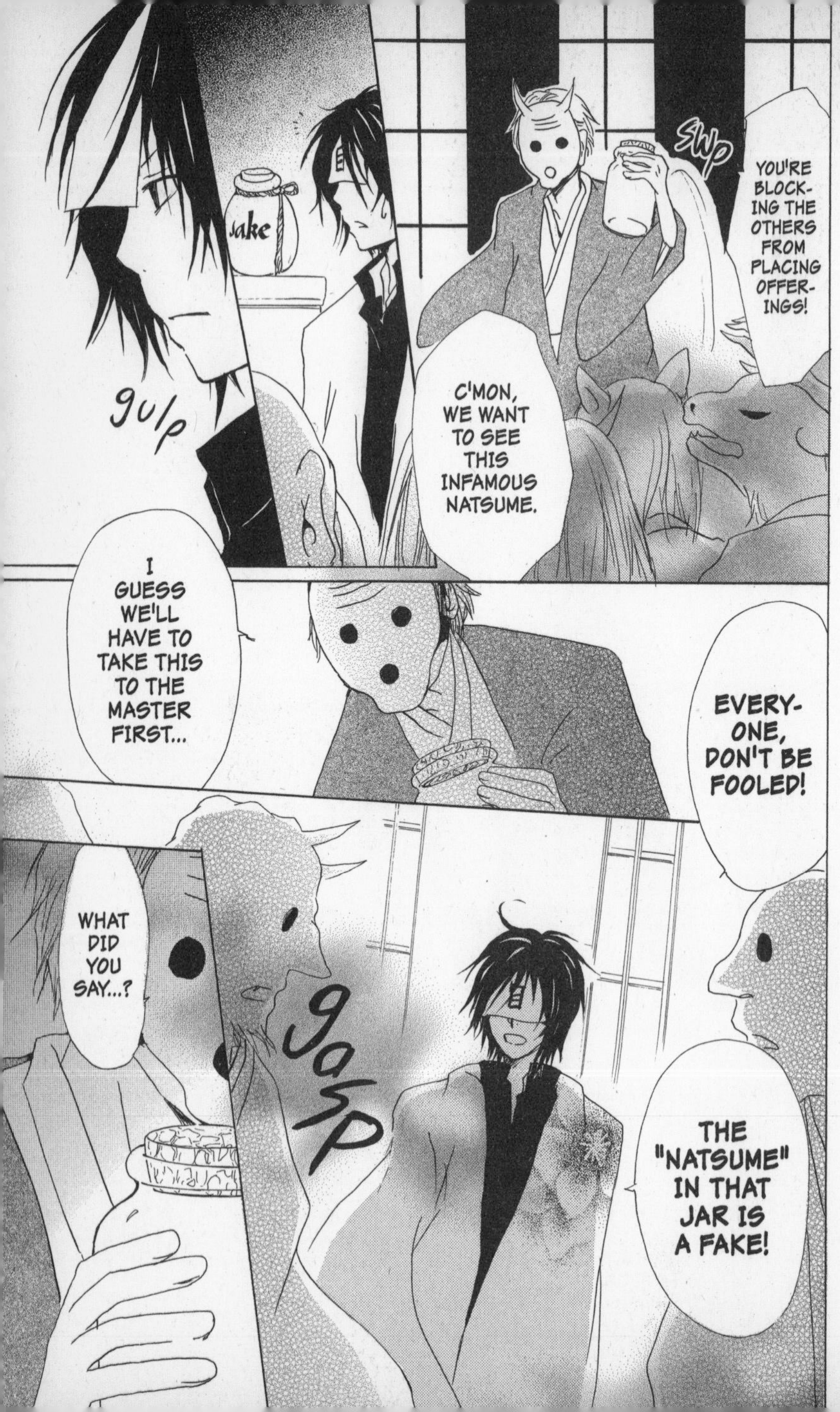
SWP
YOU'RE BLOCKING THE OTHERS FROM PLACING OFFERINGS!
C'MON, WE WANT TO SEE THIS INFAMOUS NATSUME.
sake
gulp
I GUESS WE'LL HAVE TO TAKE THIS TO THE MASTER FIRST...
EVERYONE, DON'T BE FOOLED!
THE "NATSUME" IN THAT JAR IS A FAKE!
WHAT DID YOU SAY...?
gasp

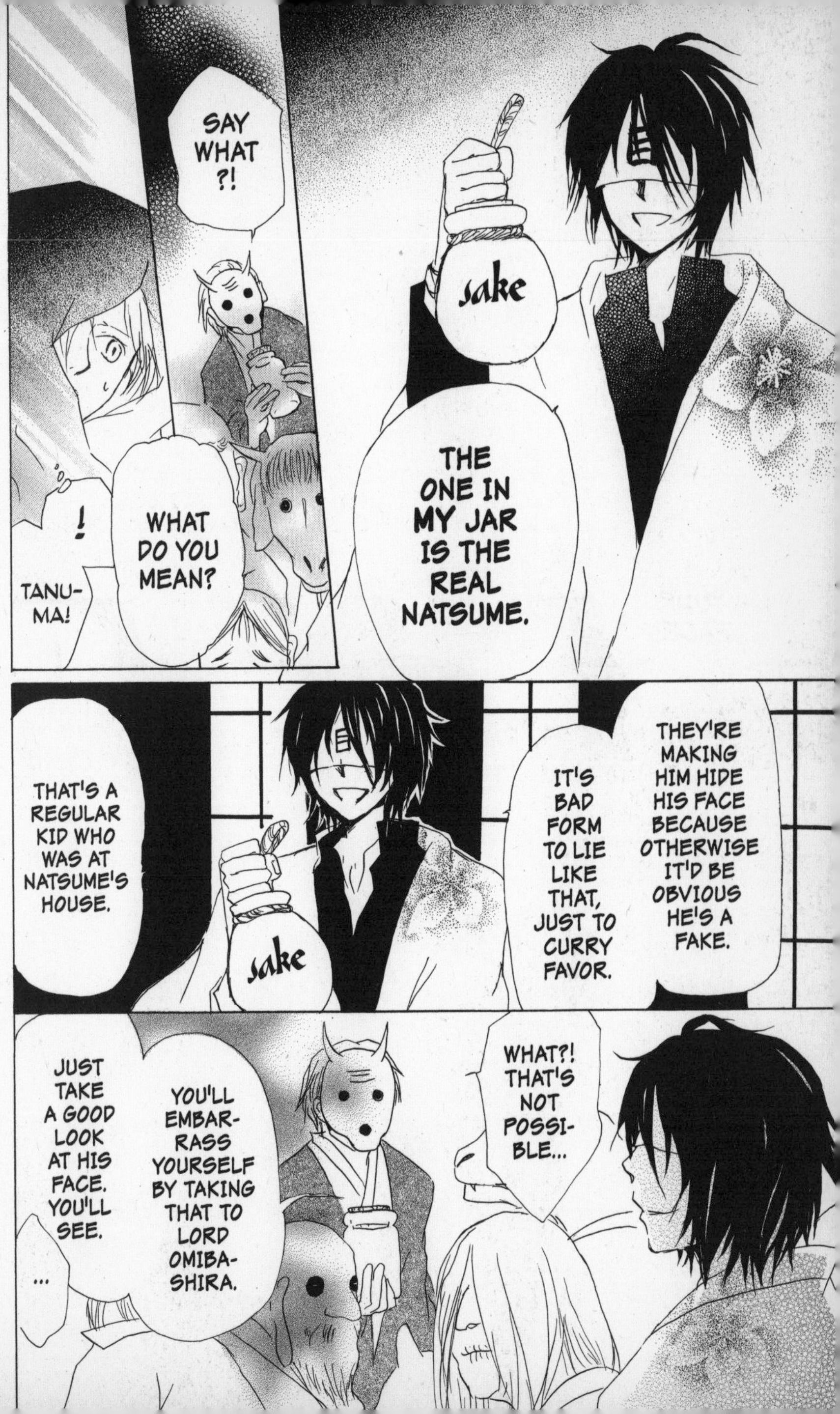
sake
THE ONE IN MY JAR IS THE REAL NATSUME.
SAY WHAT?!
WHAT DO YOU MEAN?
!
TANUMA!
THEY'RE MAKING HIM HIDE HIS FACE BECAUSE OTHERWISE IT'D BE OBVIOUS HE'S A FAKE.
IT'S BAD FORM TO LIE LIKE THAT, JUST TO CURRY FAVOR.
sake
THAT'S A REGULAR KID WHO WAS AT NATSUME'S HOUSE.
WHAT?! THAT'S NOT POSSIBLE...
YOU'LL EMBARRASS YOURSELF BY TAKING THAT TO LORD OMIBASHIRA.
JUST TAKE A GOOD LOOK AT HIS FACE. YOU'LL SEE.
...

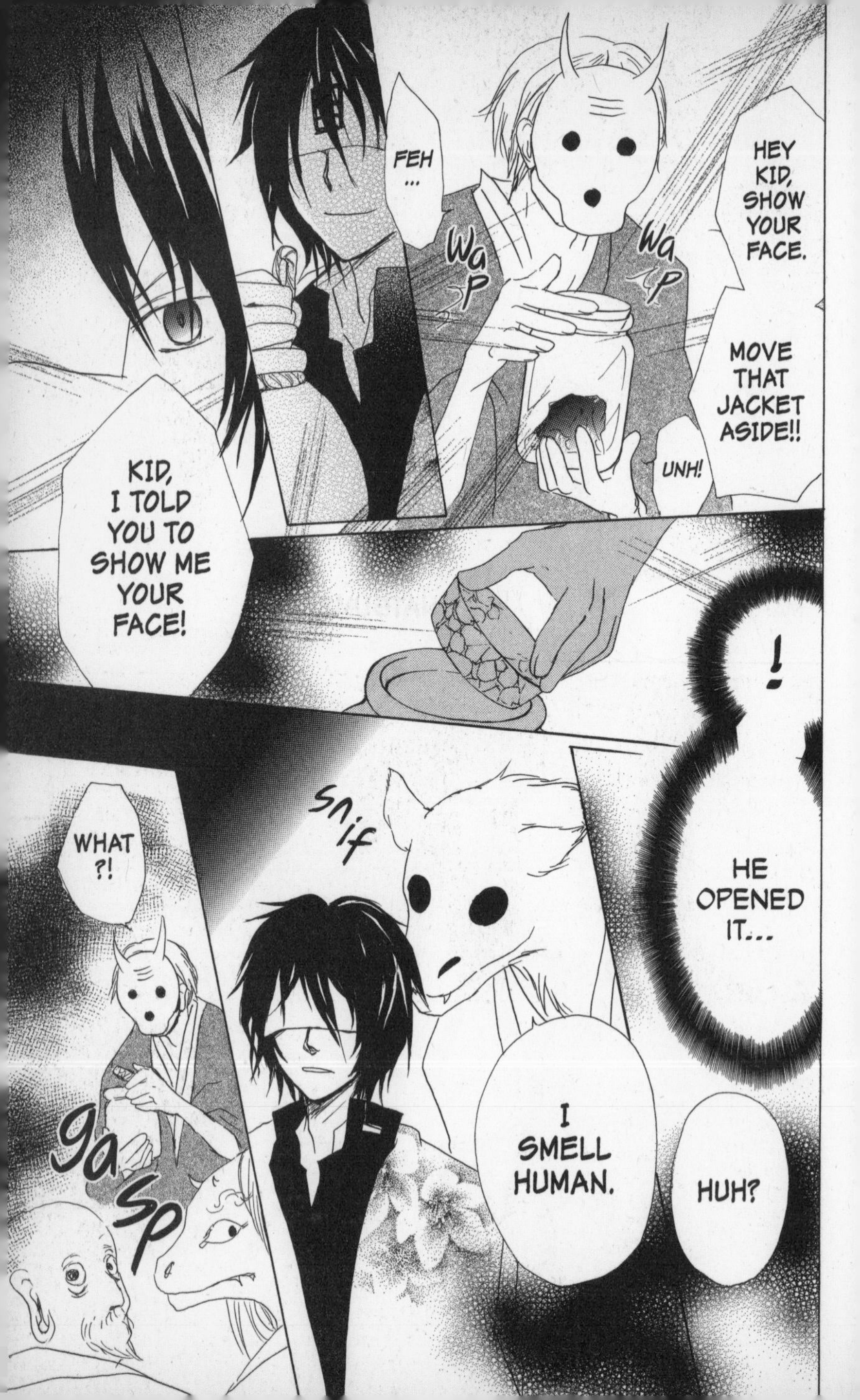
HEY KID, SHOW YOUR FACE.
MOVE THAT JACKET ASIDE!!
UNH!
Wap
Wap
FEH...
KID, I TOLD YOU TO SHOW ME YOUR FACE!
!
HE OPENED IT...
HUH?
I SMELL HUMAN.
snif
WHAT?!
gasp

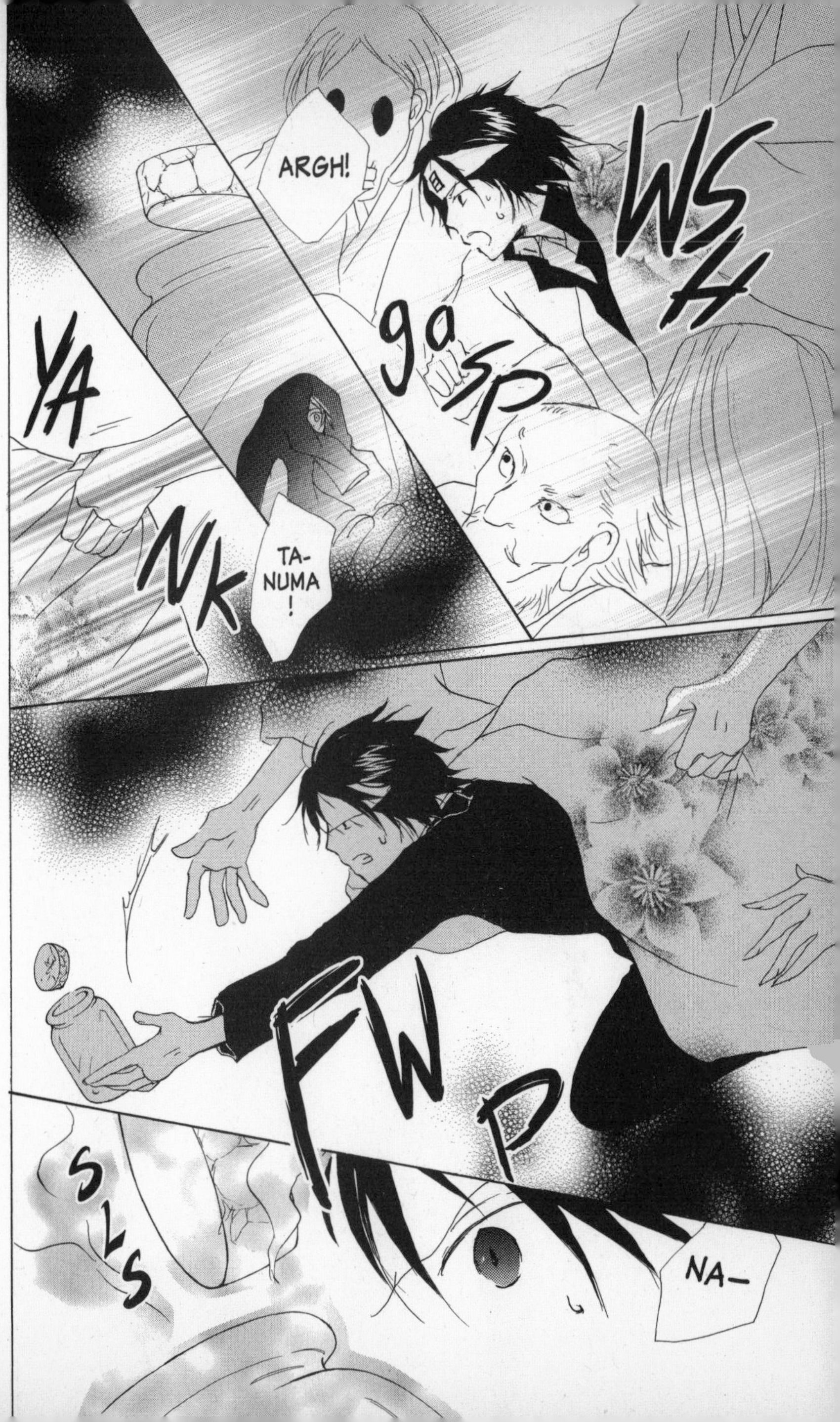
ARGH!
WSH
gasp
YANK
TA-NUMA!
FWP
NA-
SLS

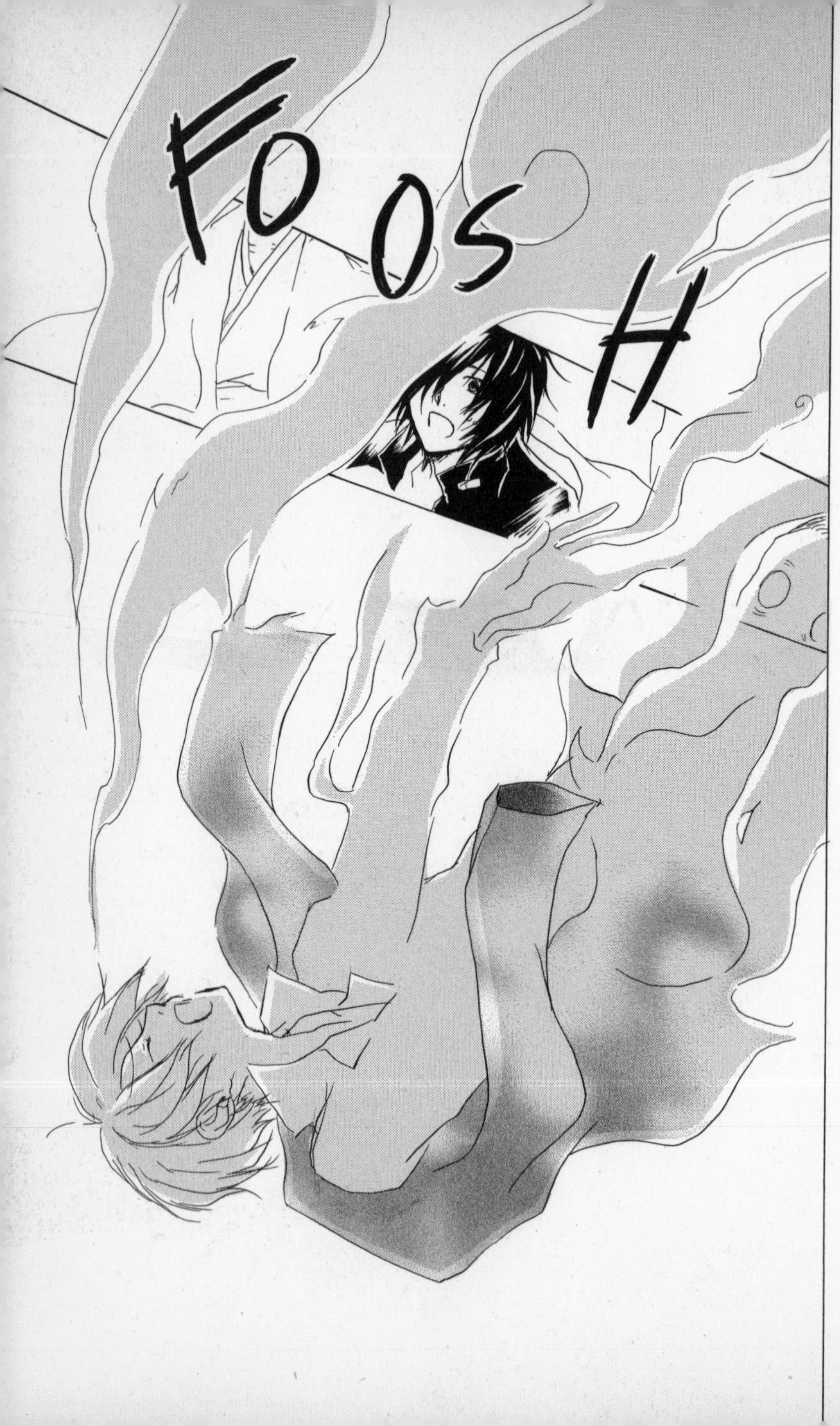
FOOSH

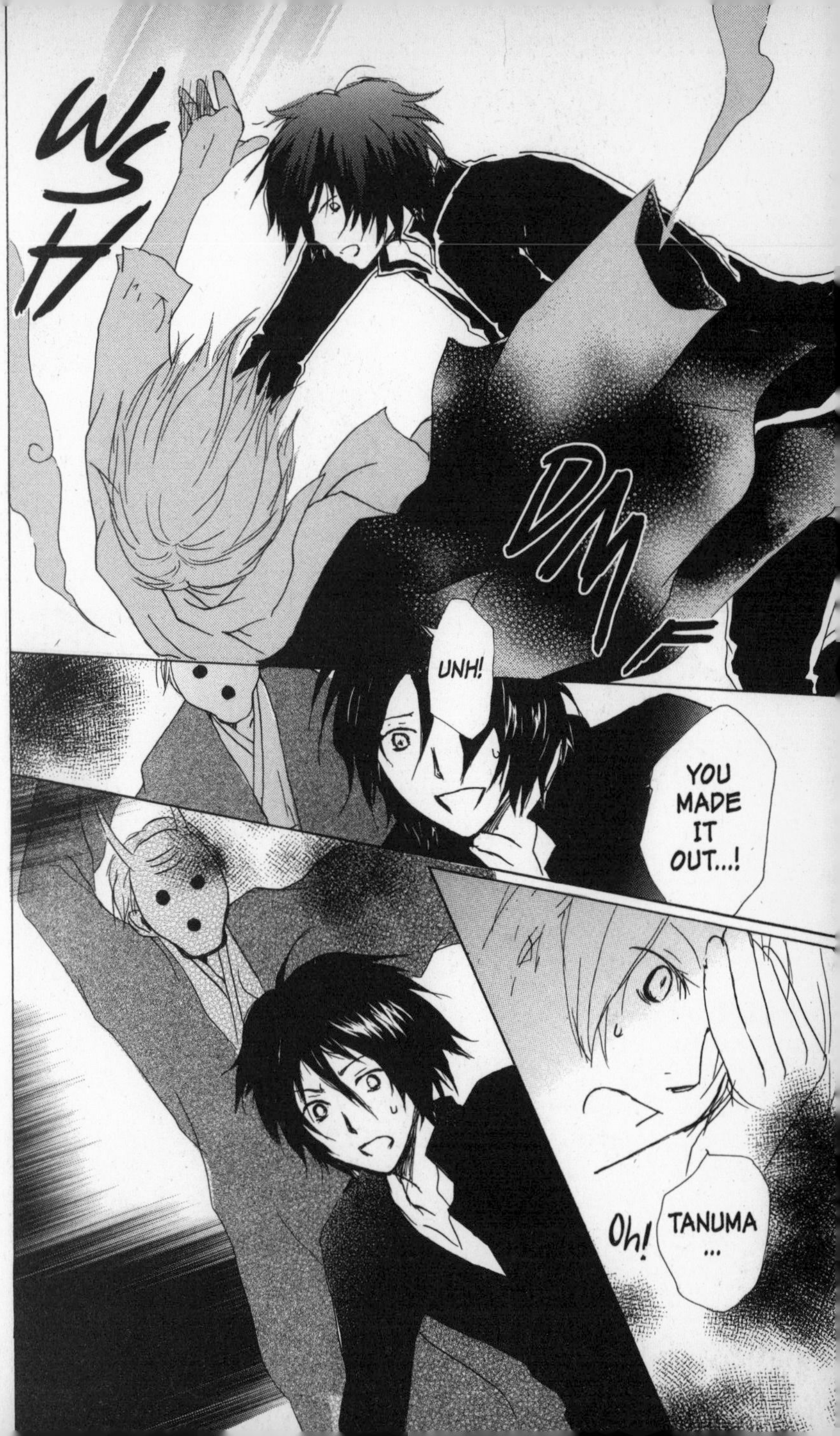
WSH
DMF
UNH!
YOU MADE IT OUT...!
TANUMA ...
Oh!

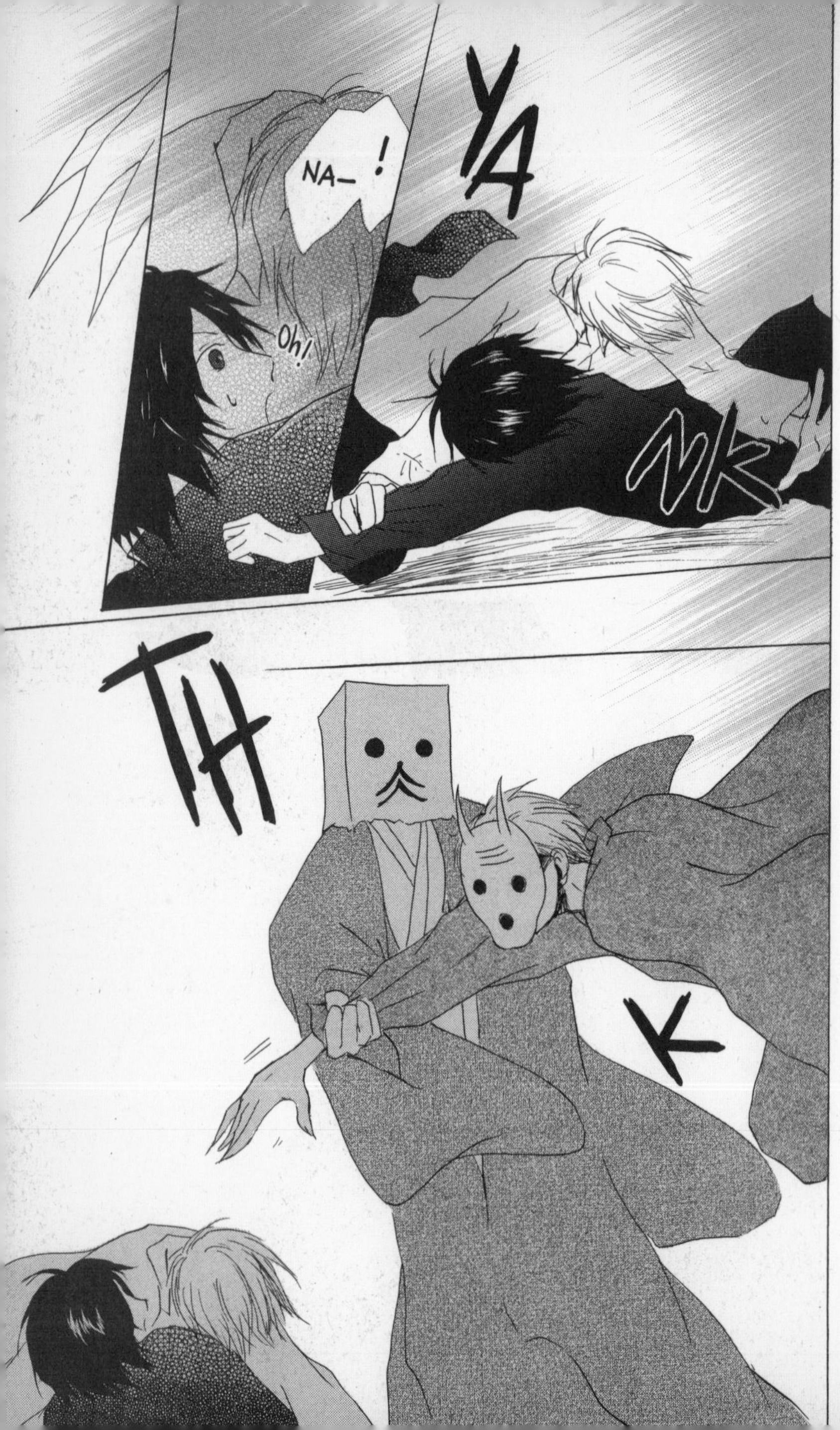
YA
NK
NA– !
Oh!
TH
K

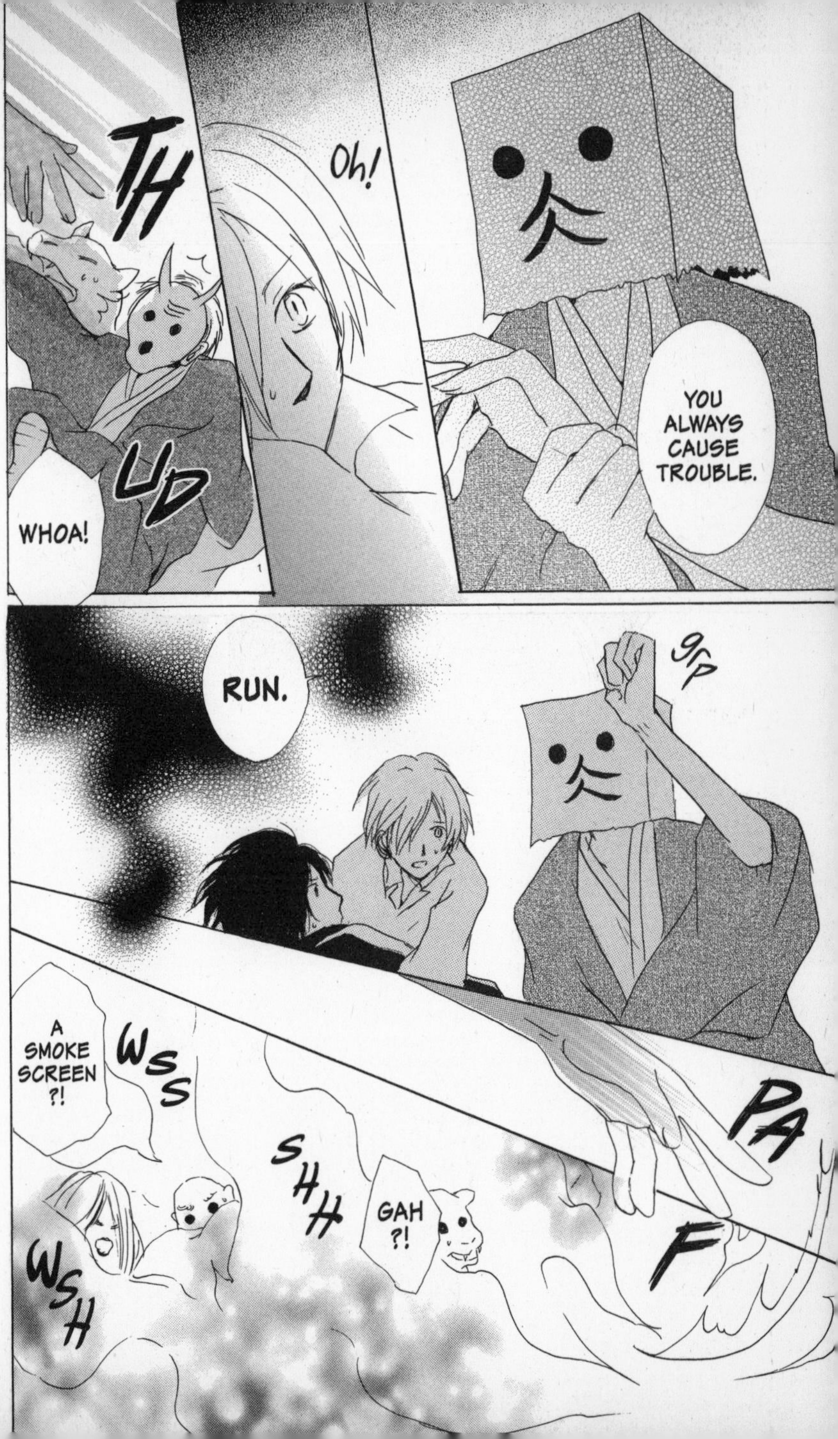
YOU ALWAYS CAUSE TROUBLE.
Oh!
THUD
WHOA!
grp
RUN.
PAF
GAH ?!
SHH
WSS
A SMOKE SCREEN ?!
WSH

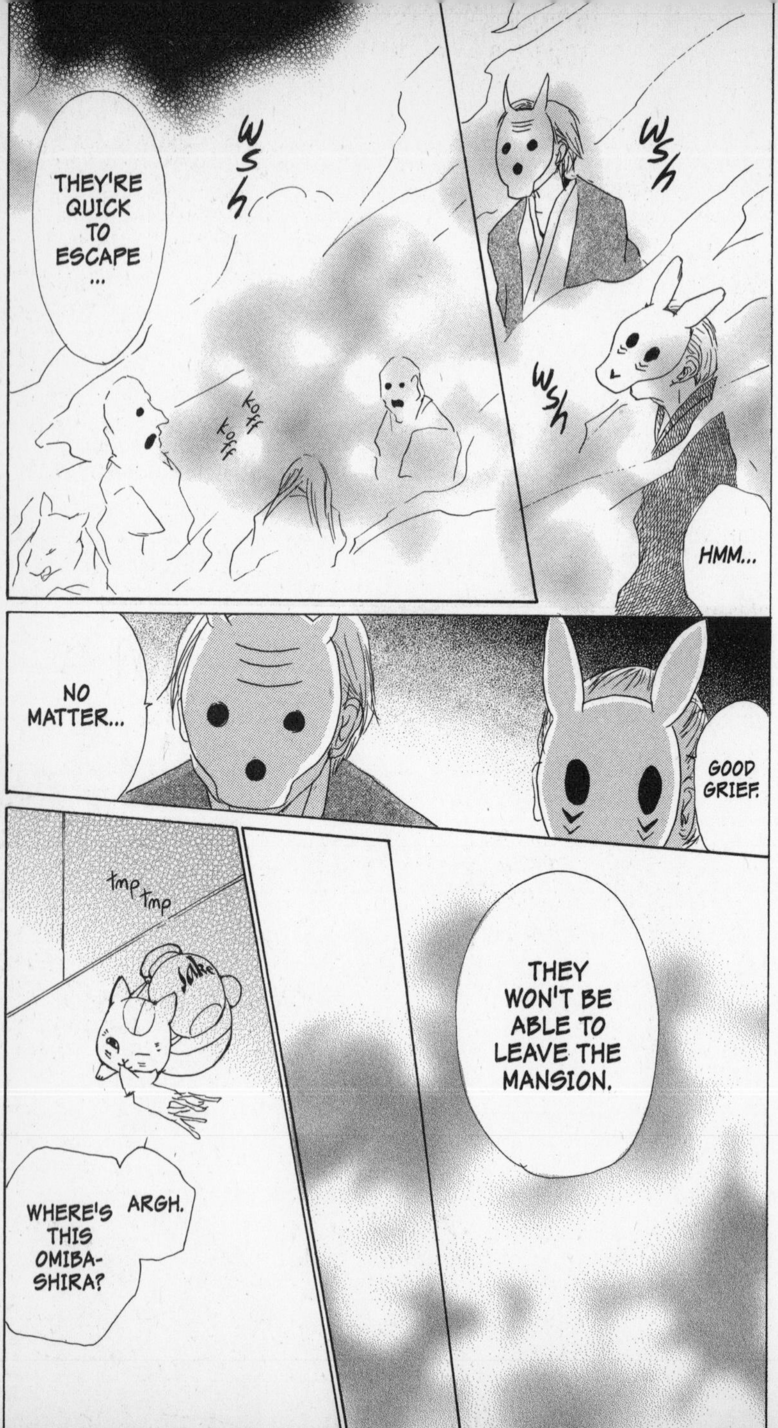
Wsh
Wsh
HMM...
Wsh
THEY'RE QUICK TO ESCAPE ...
koff koff
GOOD GRIEF.
NO MATTER...
THEY WON'T BE ABLE TO LEAVE THE MANSION.
tmp tmp
sake
ARGH.
WHERE'S THIS OMIBA-SHIRA?

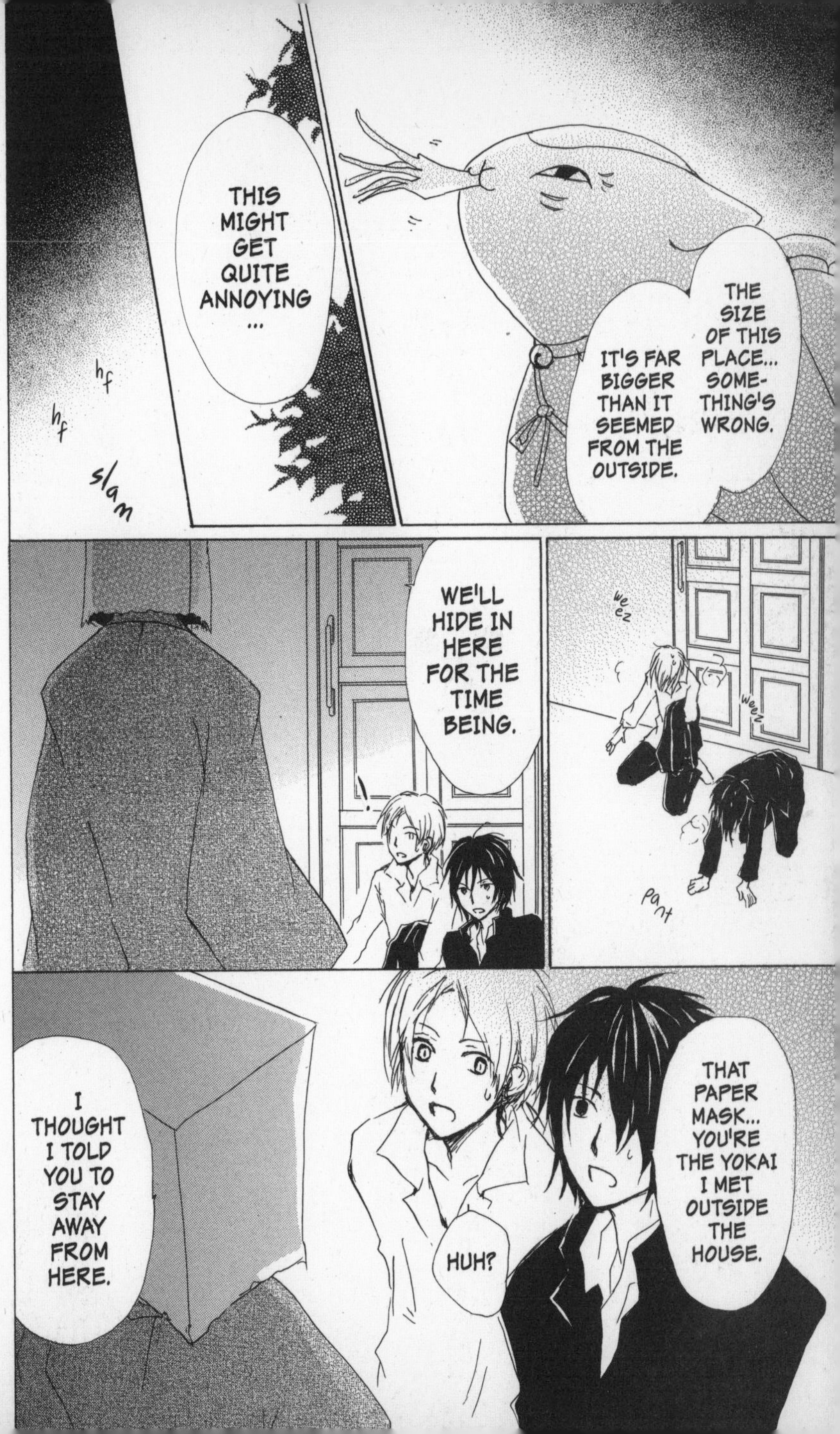
THE SIZE OF THIS PLACE... SOMETHING'S WRONG.
IT'S FAR BIGGER THAN IT SEEMED FROM THE OUTSIDE.
THIS MIGHT GET QUITE ANNOYING...
hf
hf
slam
weez
weez
pant
WE'LL HIDE IN HERE FOR THE TIME BEING.
!
THAT PAPER MASK... YOU'RE THE YOKAI I MET OUTSIDE THE HOUSE.
HUH?
I THOUGHT I TOLD YOU TO STAY AWAY FROM HERE.

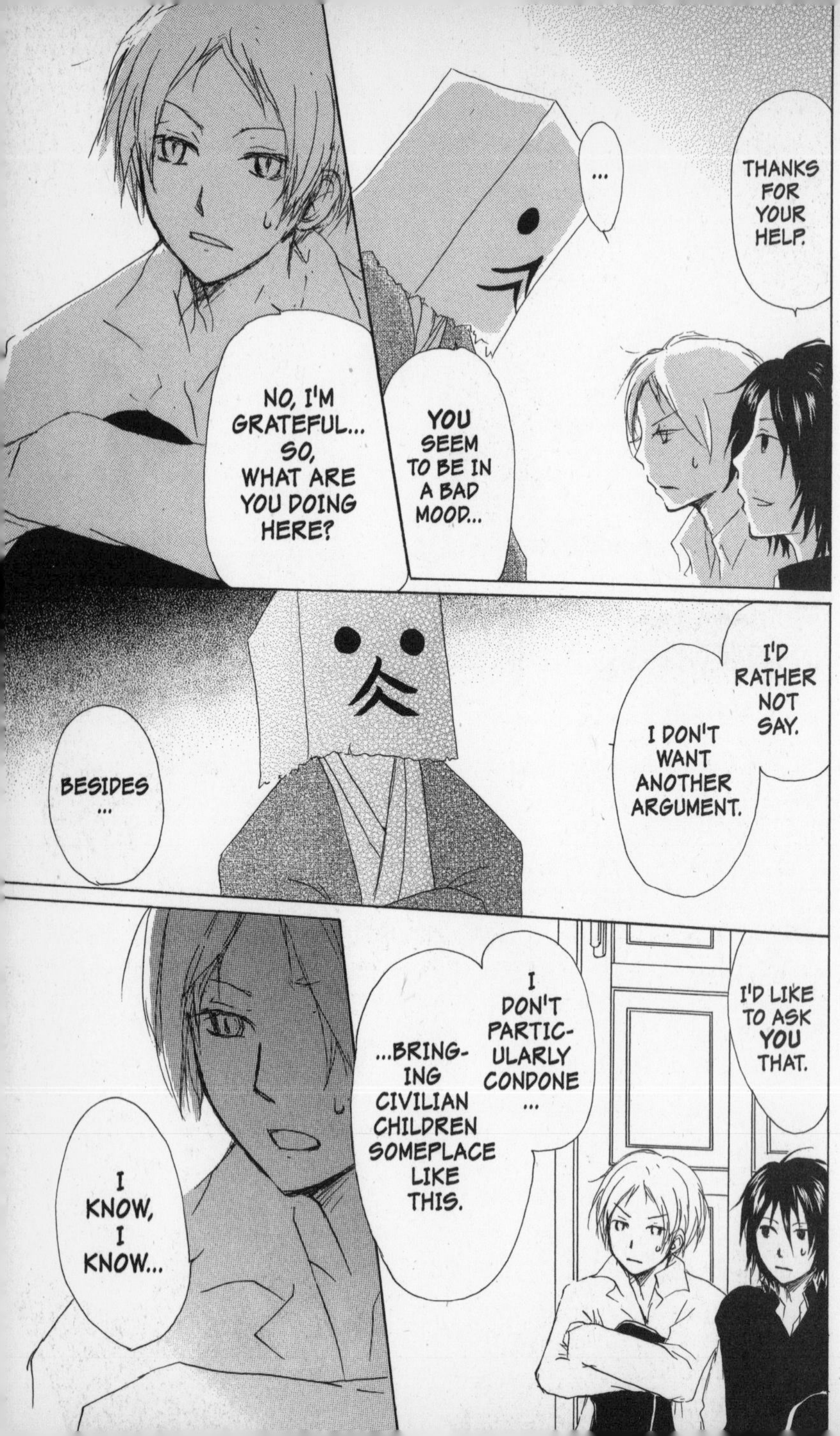
THANKS FOR YOUR HELP.
...
YOU SEEM TO BE IN A BAD MOOD...
NO, I'M GRATEFUL... SO, WHAT ARE YOU DOING HERE?
I'D RATHER NOT SAY.
I DON'T WANT ANOTHER ARGUMENT.
BESIDES...
I'D LIKE TO ASK YOU THAT.
I DON'T PARTICULARLY CONDONE...
...BRINGING CIVILIAN CHILDREN SOMEPLACE LIKE THIS.
I KNOW, I KNOW...

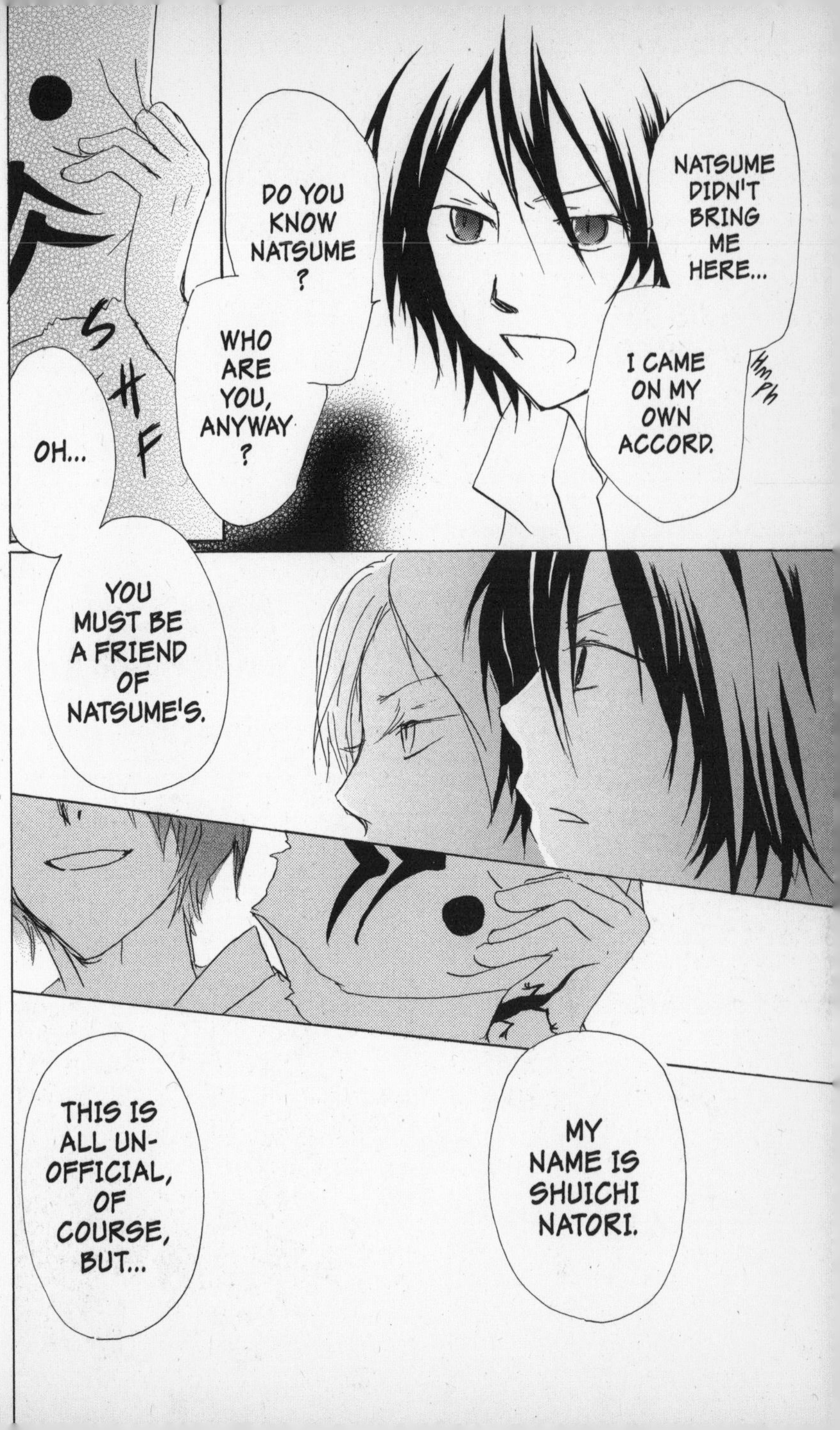
NATSUME DIDN'T BRING ME HERE...
I CAME ON MY OWN ACCORD.
Hmph
DO YOU KNOW NATSUME?
WHO ARE YOU, ANYWAY?
SHF
OH...
YOU MUST BE A FRIEND OF NATSUME'S.
MY NAME IS SHUICHI NATORI.
THIS IS ALL UN-OFFICIAL, OF COURSE, BUT...

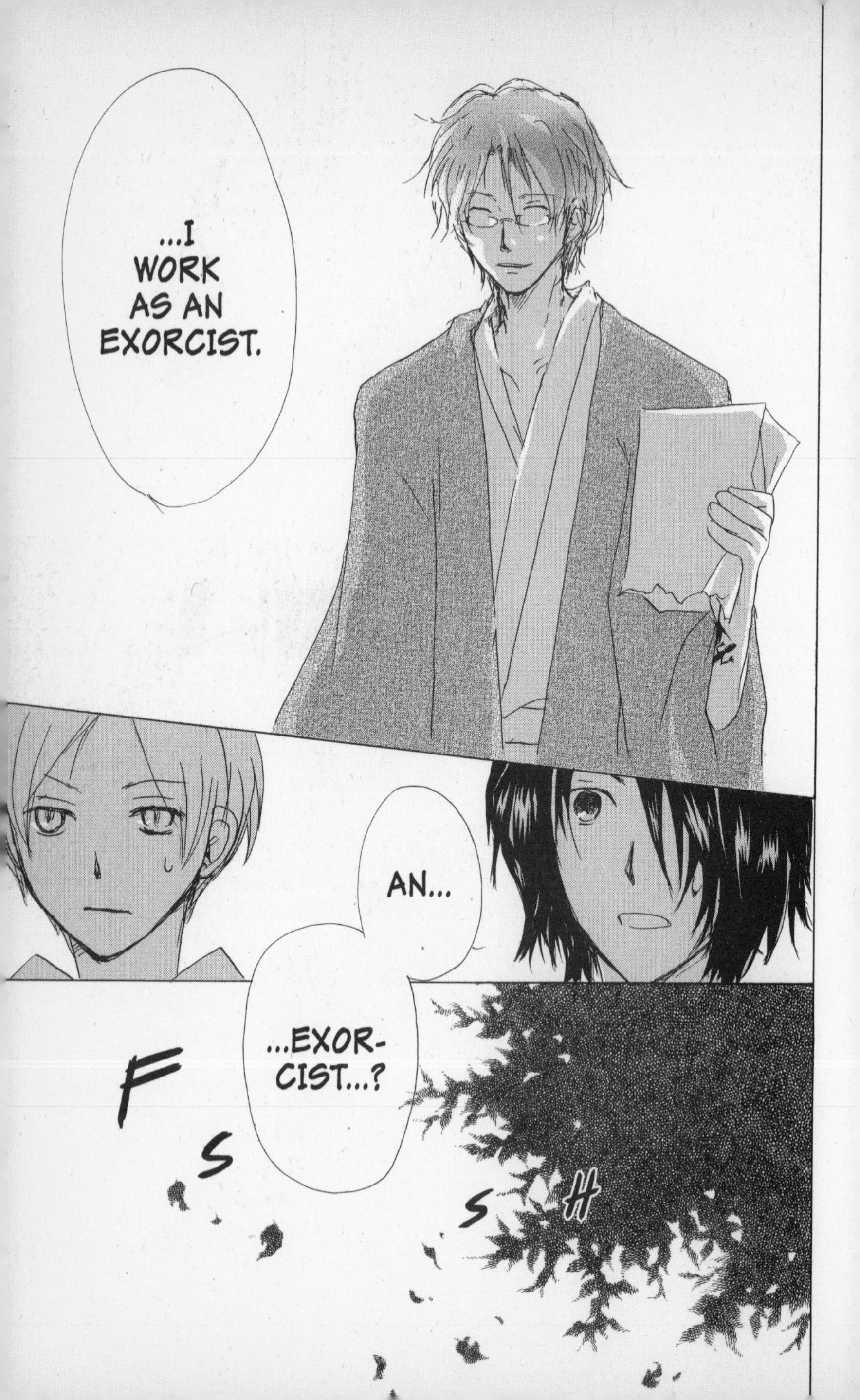
...I WORK AS AN EXORCIST.
AN...
...EXOR-CIST...?
FSSH

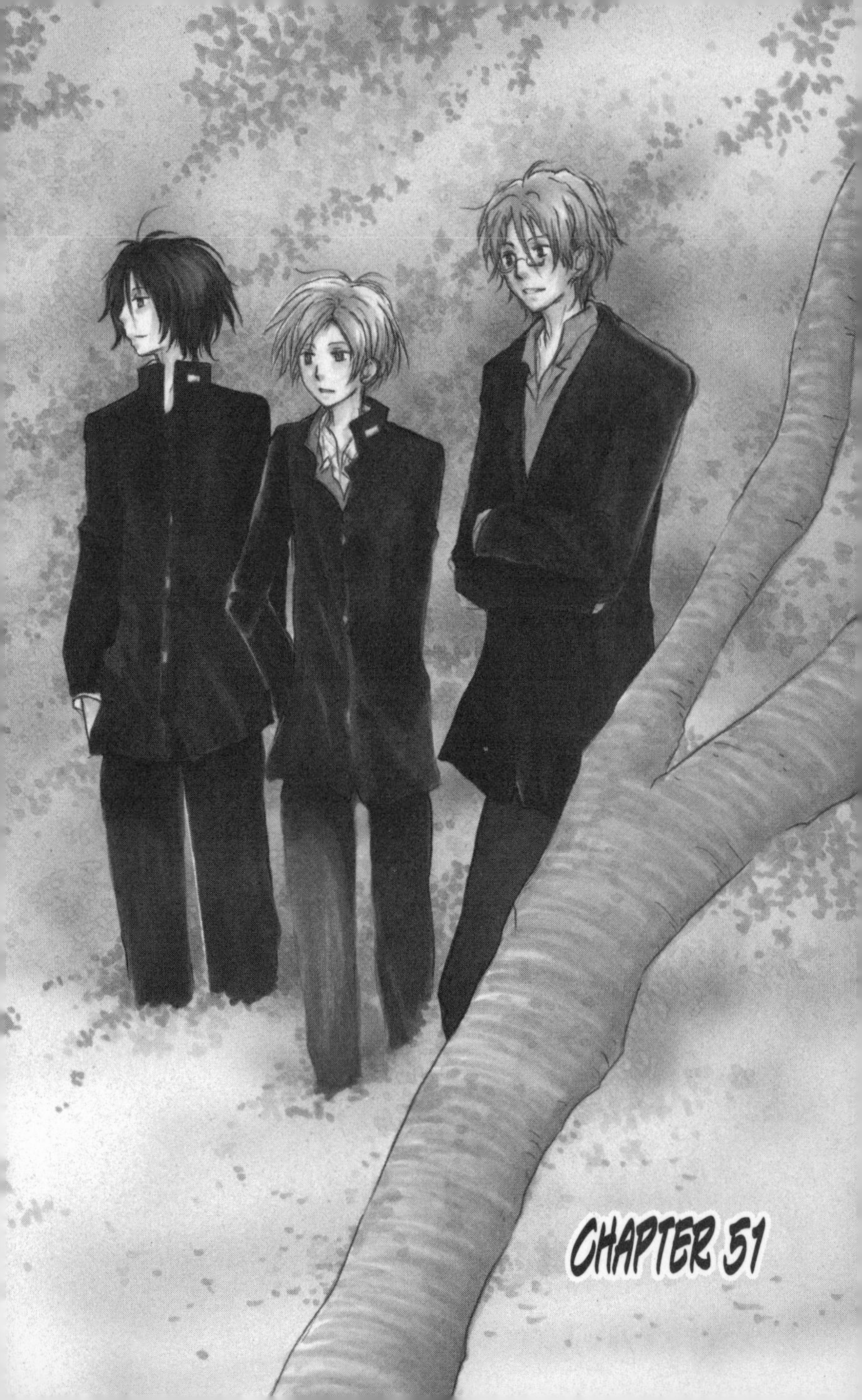
CHAPTER 51

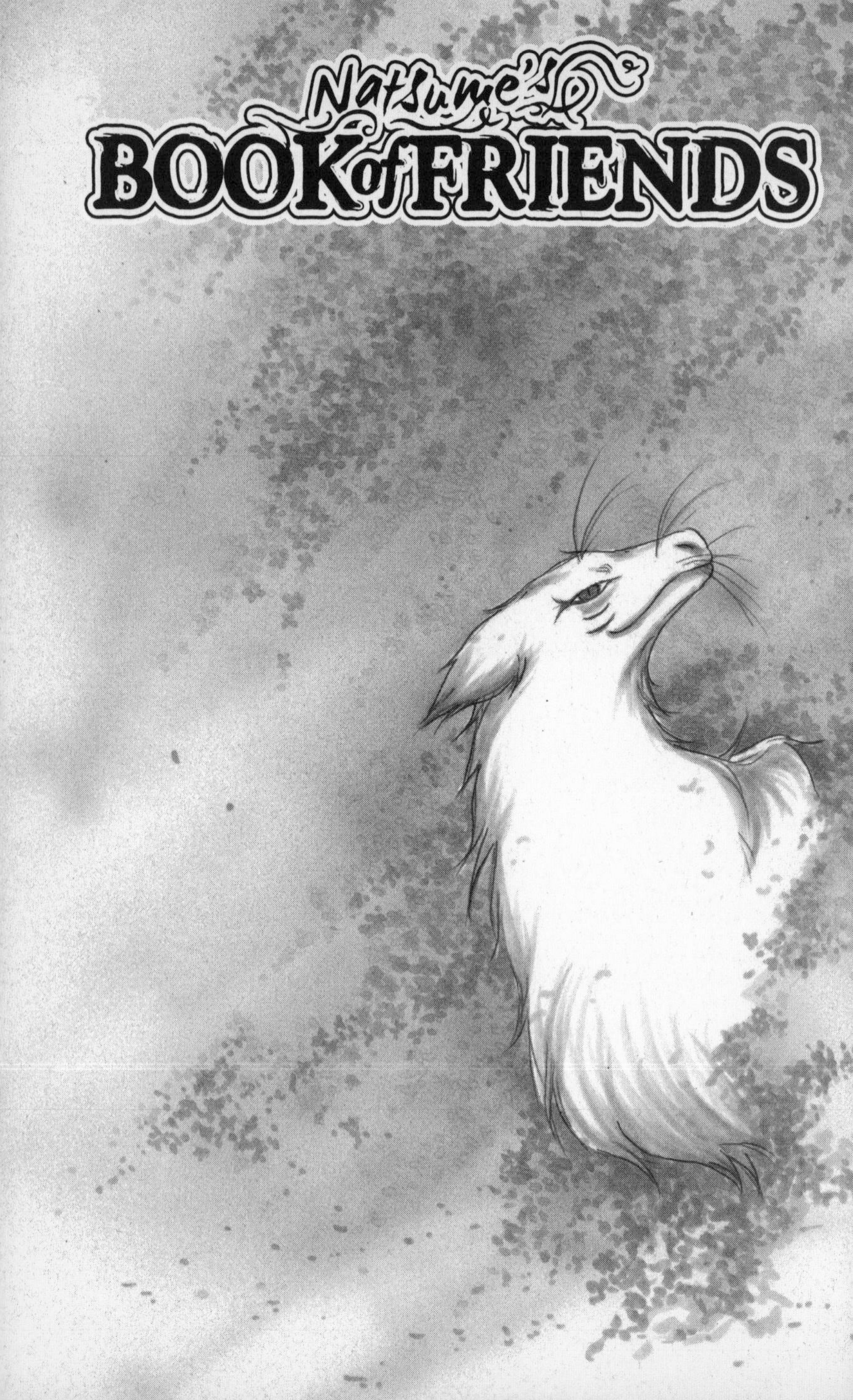
Natsume's
BOOK of FRIENDS

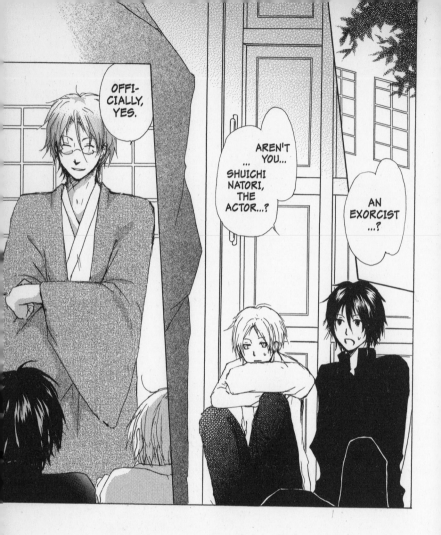

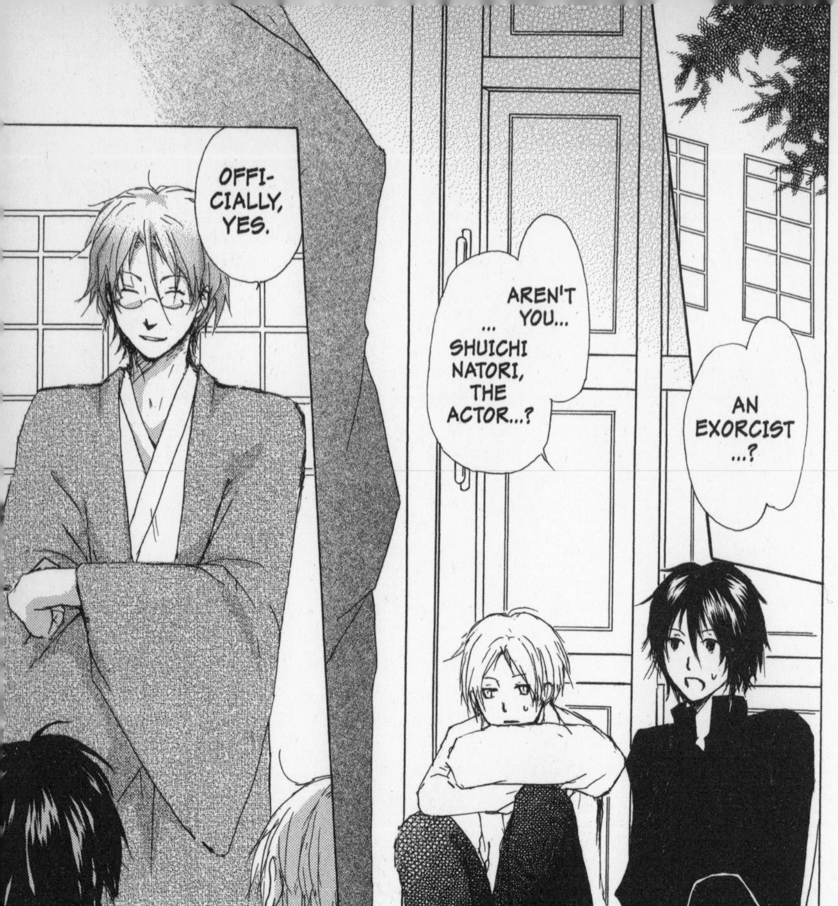
AN EXORCIST ...?
AREN'T YOU... ...SHUICHI NATORI, THE ACTOR...?
OFFI-CIALLY, YES.

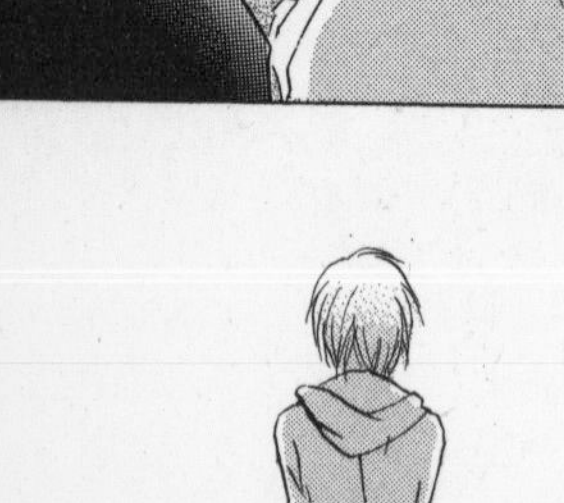

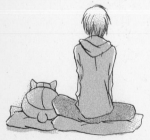

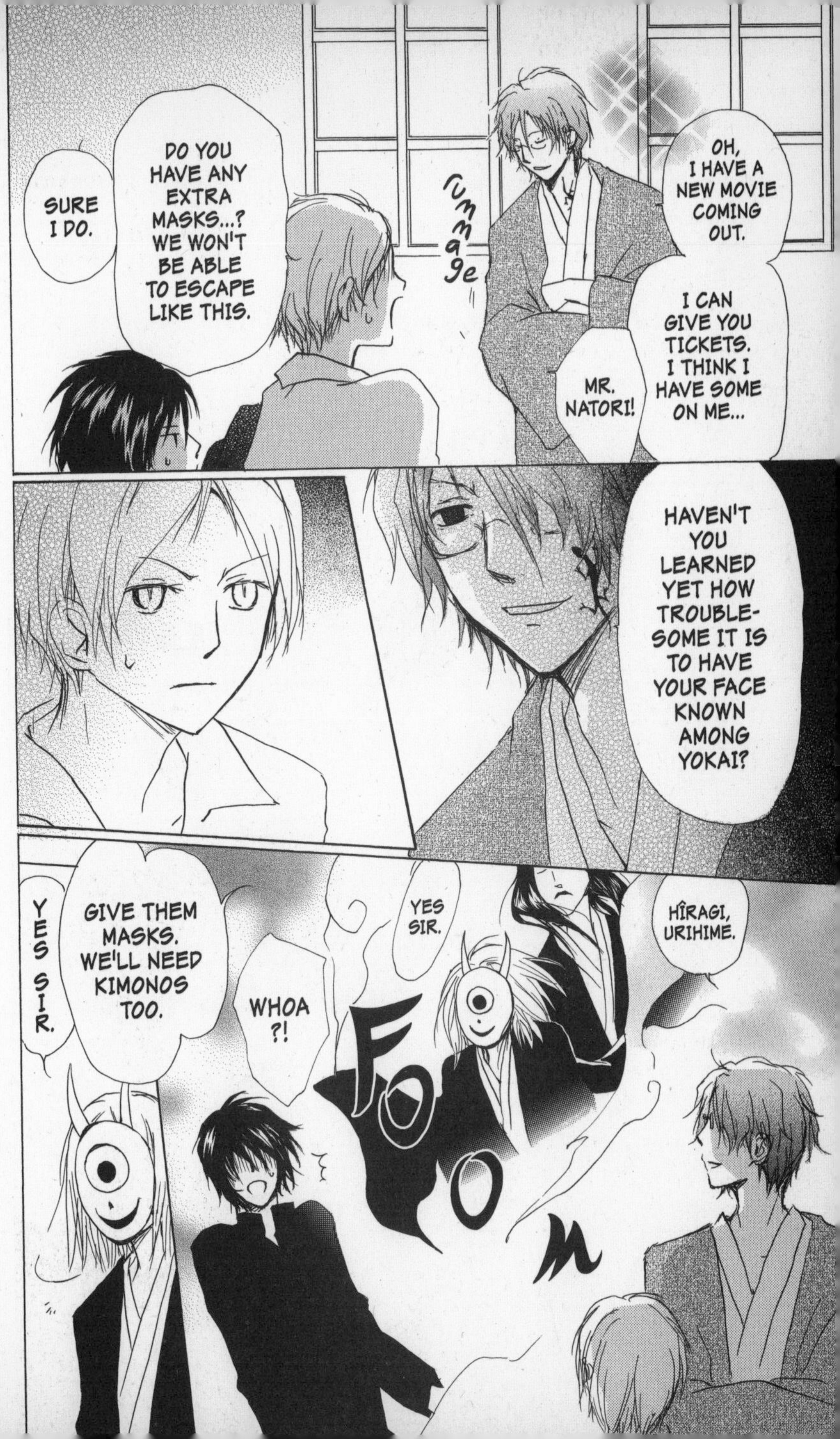
OH, I HAVE A NEW MOVIE COMING OUT.
I CAN GIVE YOU TICKETS. I THINK I HAVE SOME ON ME...
MR. NATORI!
rummage
DO YOU HAVE ANY EXTRA MASKS...? WE WON'T BE ABLE TO ESCAPE LIKE THIS.
SURE I DO.
HAVEN'T YOU LEARNED YET HOW TROUBLE-SOME IT IS TO HAVE YOUR FACE KNOWN AMONG YOKAI?
HÎRAGI, URIHIME.
YES SIR.
FOOM
WHOA?!
GIVE THEM MASKS. WE'LL NEED KIMONOS TOO.
YES SIR.

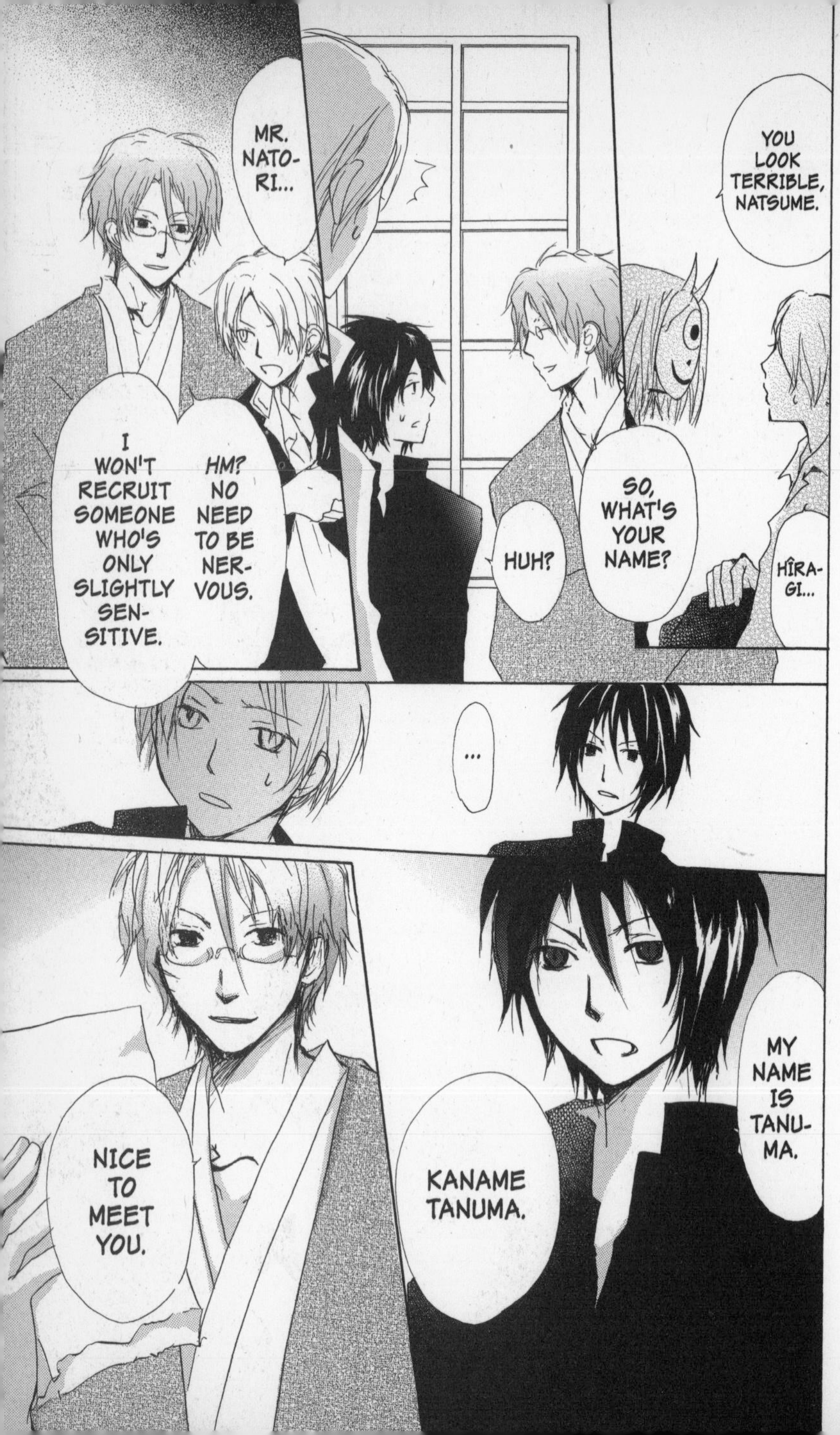
YOU LOOK TERRIBLE, NATSUME.
HÎRAGI...
SO, WHAT'S YOUR NAME?
HUH?
MR. NATO-RI...
HM? NO NEED TO BE NER-VOUS.
I WON'T RECRUIT SOMEONE WHO'S ONLY SLIGHTLY SEN-SITIVE.
...
MY NAME IS TANU-MA.
KANAME TANUMA.
NICE TO MEET YOU.

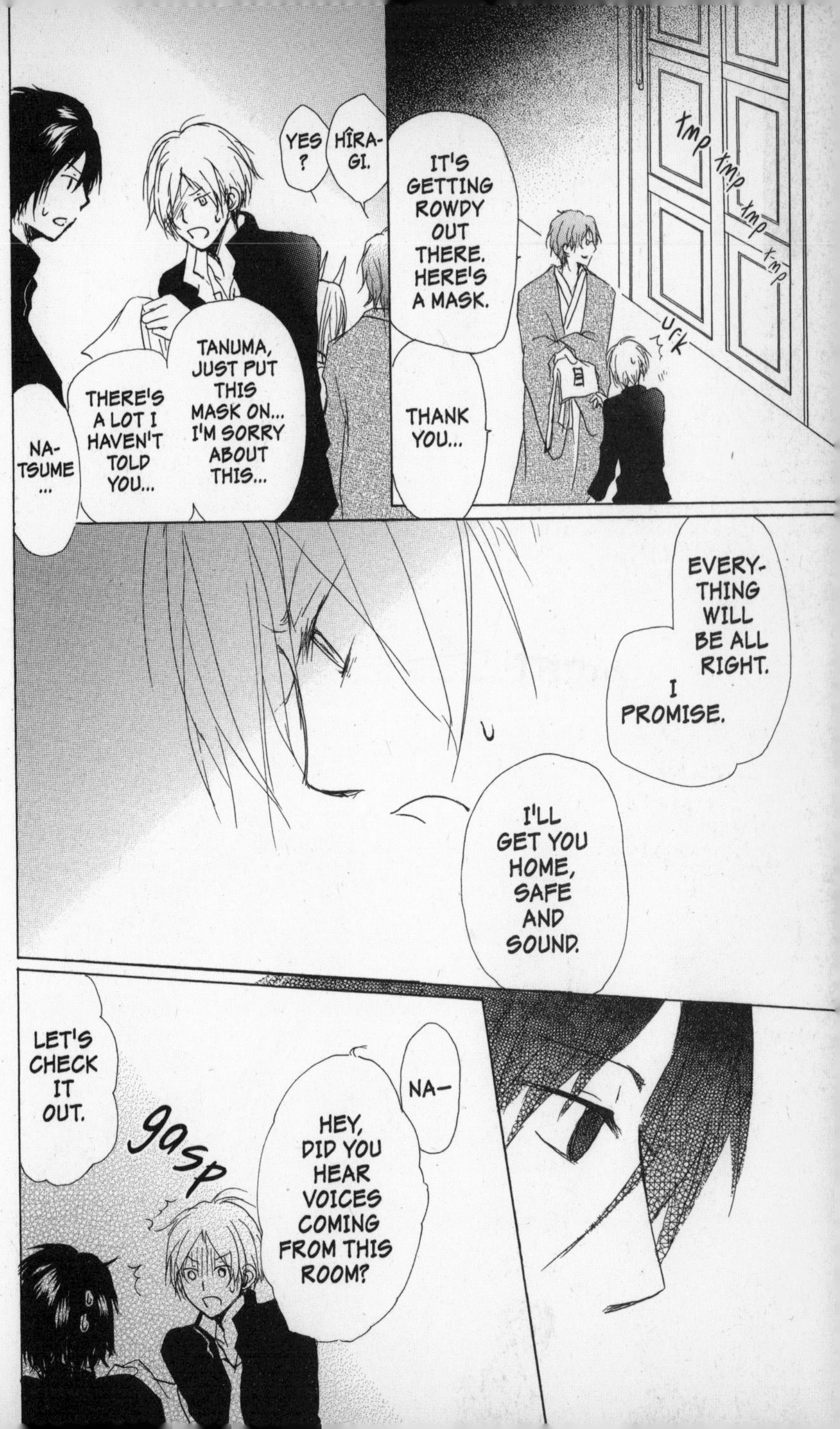
xmp xmp xmp xmp
IT'S GETTING ROWDY OUT THERE. HERE'S A MASK.
urk
THANK YOU...
HÎRA-GI.
YES?
TANUMA, JUST PUT THIS MASK ON... I'M SORRY ABOUT THIS...
THERE'S A LOT I HAVEN'T TOLD YOU...
NA-TSUME...
EVERY-THING WILL BE ALL RIGHT.
I PROMISE.
I'LL GET YOU HOME, SAFE AND SOUND.
NA-
HEY, DID YOU HEAR VOICES COMING FROM THIS ROOM?
gasp
LET'S CHECK IT OUT.

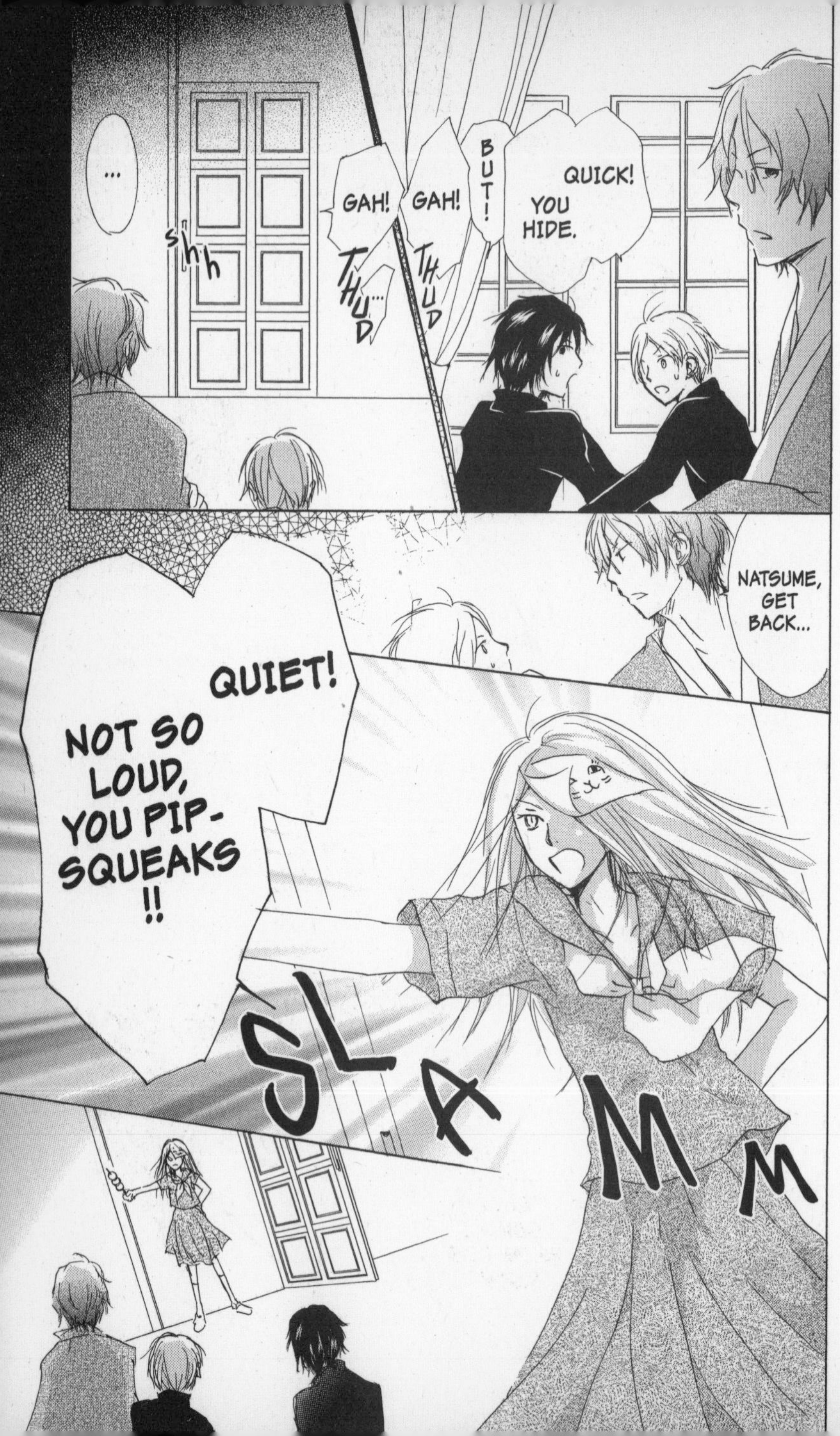
QUICK! YOU HIDE.
BUT!
GAH!
GAH!
THUD
THUD...
...
shhh
NATSUME, GET BACK...
QUIET! NOT SO LOUD, YOU PIP-SQUEAKS !!
SLAMM

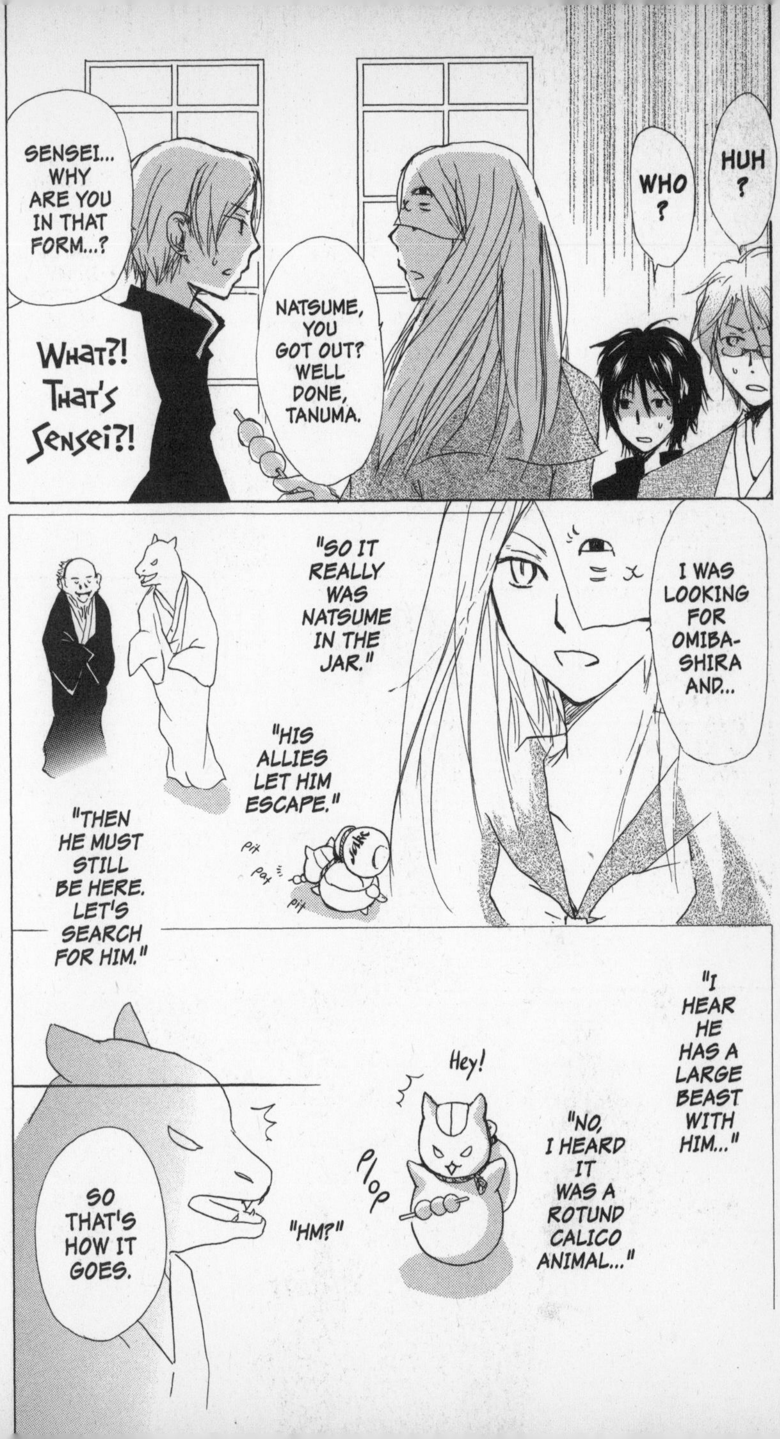
HUH?
WHO?
NATSUME, YOU GOT OUT? WELL DONE, TANUMA.
SENSEI... WHY ARE YOU IN THAT FORM...?
WHAT?! THAT'S SENSEI?!
I WAS LOOKING FOR OMIBA-SHIRA AND...
"SO IT REALLY WAS NATSUME IN THE JAR."
"HIS ALLIES LET HIM ESCAPE."
pit pat pit
"THEN HE MUST STILL BE HERE. LET'S SEARCH FOR HIM."
"I HEAR HE HAS A LARGE BEAST WITH HIM..."
"NO, I HEARD IT WAS A ROTUND CALICO ANIMAL..."
Hey!
Plop
"HM?"
SO THAT'S HOW IT GOES.

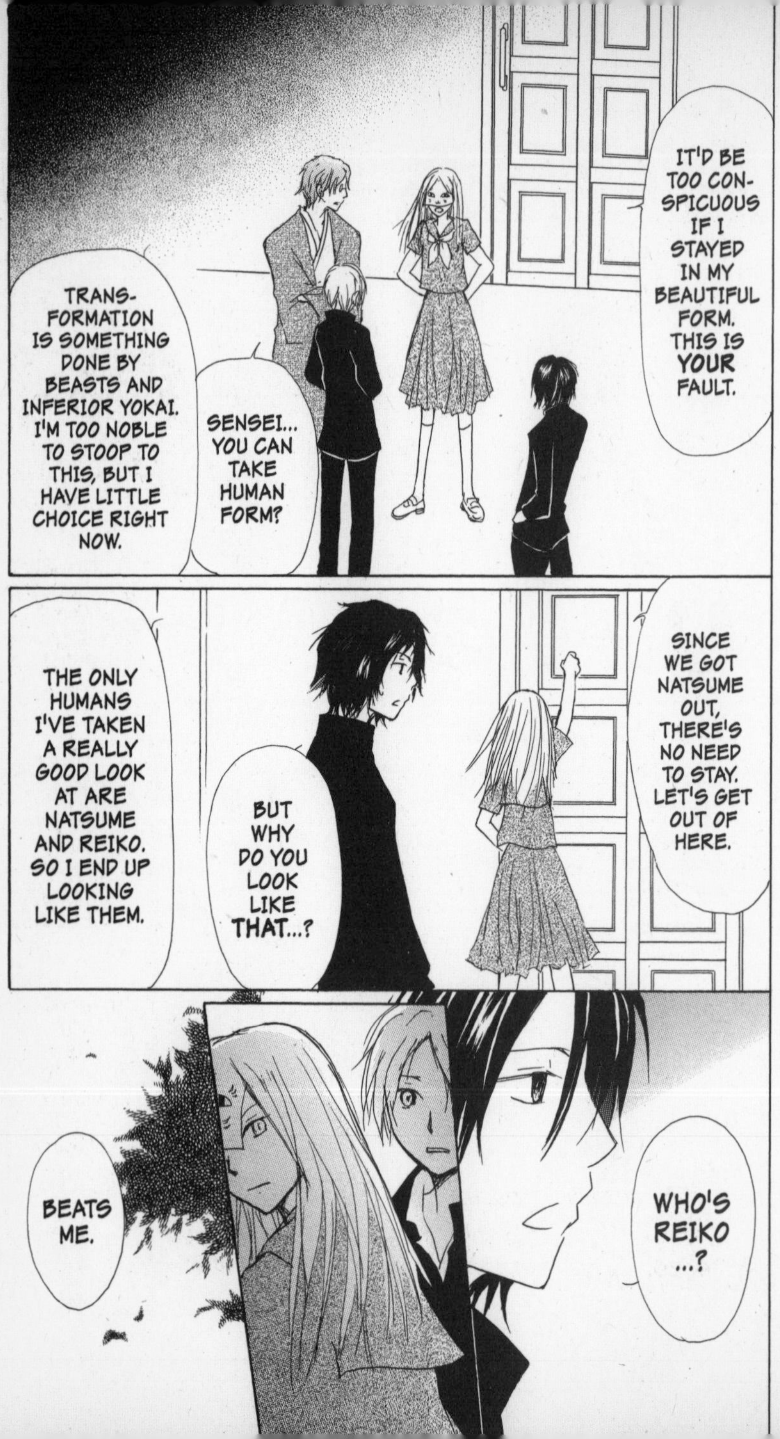
IT'D BE TOO CONSPICUOUS IF I STAYED IN MY BEAUTIFUL FORM. THIS IS YOUR FAULT.
SENSEI... YOU CAN TAKE HUMAN FORM?
TRANSFORMATION IS SOMETHING DONE BY BEASTS AND INFERIOR YOKAI. I'M TOO NOBLE TO STOOP TO THIS, BUT I HAVE LITTLE CHOICE RIGHT NOW.
SINCE WE GOT NATSUME OUT, THERE'S NO NEED TO STAY. LET'S GET OUT OF HERE.
BUT WHY DO YOU LOOK LIKE THAT...?
THE ONLY HUMANS I'VE TAKEN A REALLY GOOD LOOK AT ARE NATSUME AND REIKO. SO I END UP LOOKING LIKE THEM.
WHO'S REIKO ...?
BEATS ME.

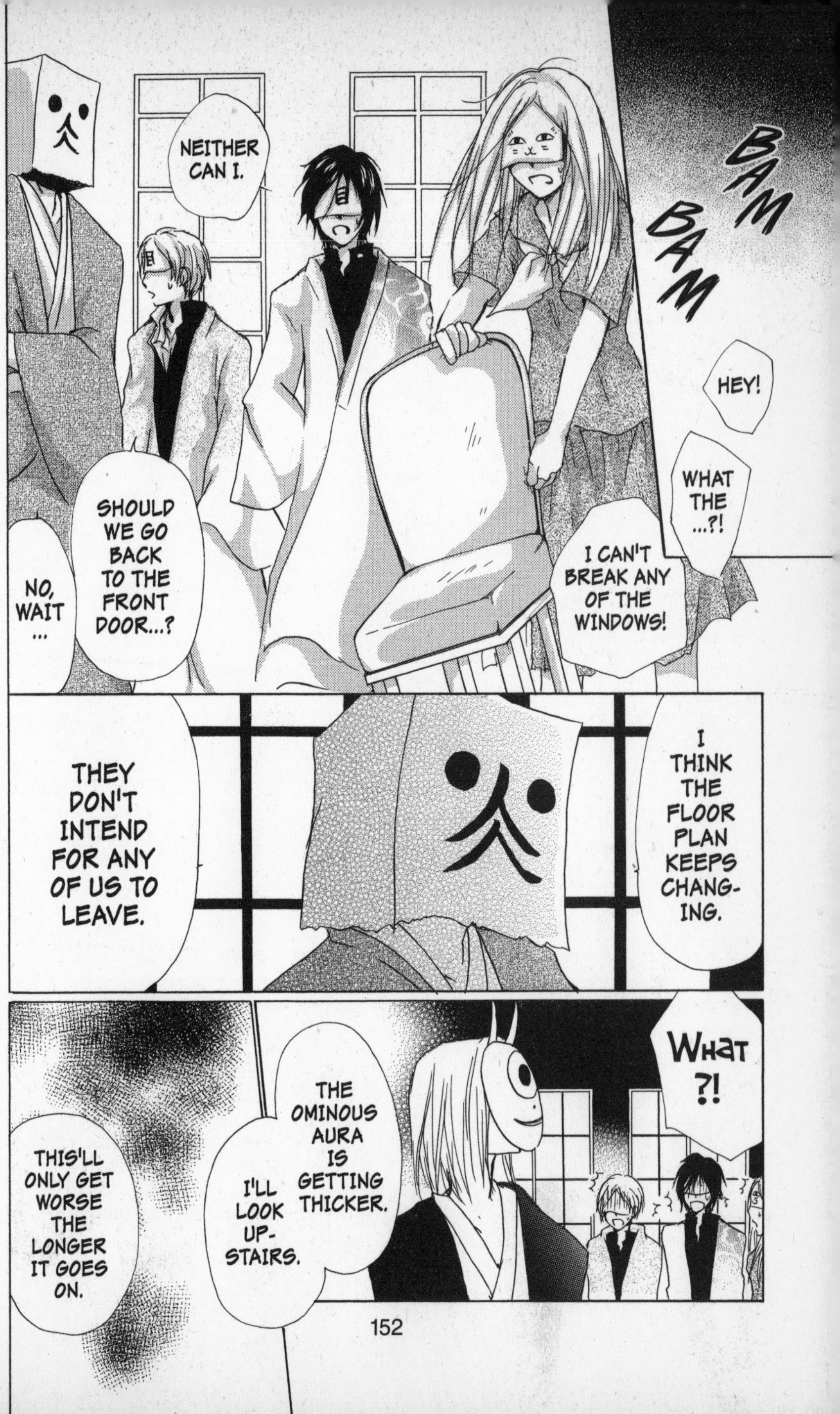
BAM BAM
HEY!
WHAT THE ...?!
I CAN'T BREAK ANY OF THE WINDOWS!
NEITHER CAN I.
SHOULD WE GO BACK TO THE FRONT DOOR...?
NO, WAIT ...
I THINK THE FLOOR PLAN KEEPS CHANG-ING.
THEY DON'T INTEND FOR ANY OF US TO LEAVE.
WHAT ?!
THE OMINOUS AURA IS GETTING THICKER.
I'LL LOOK UP-STAIRS.
THIS'LL ONLY GET WORSE THE LONGER IT GOES ON.

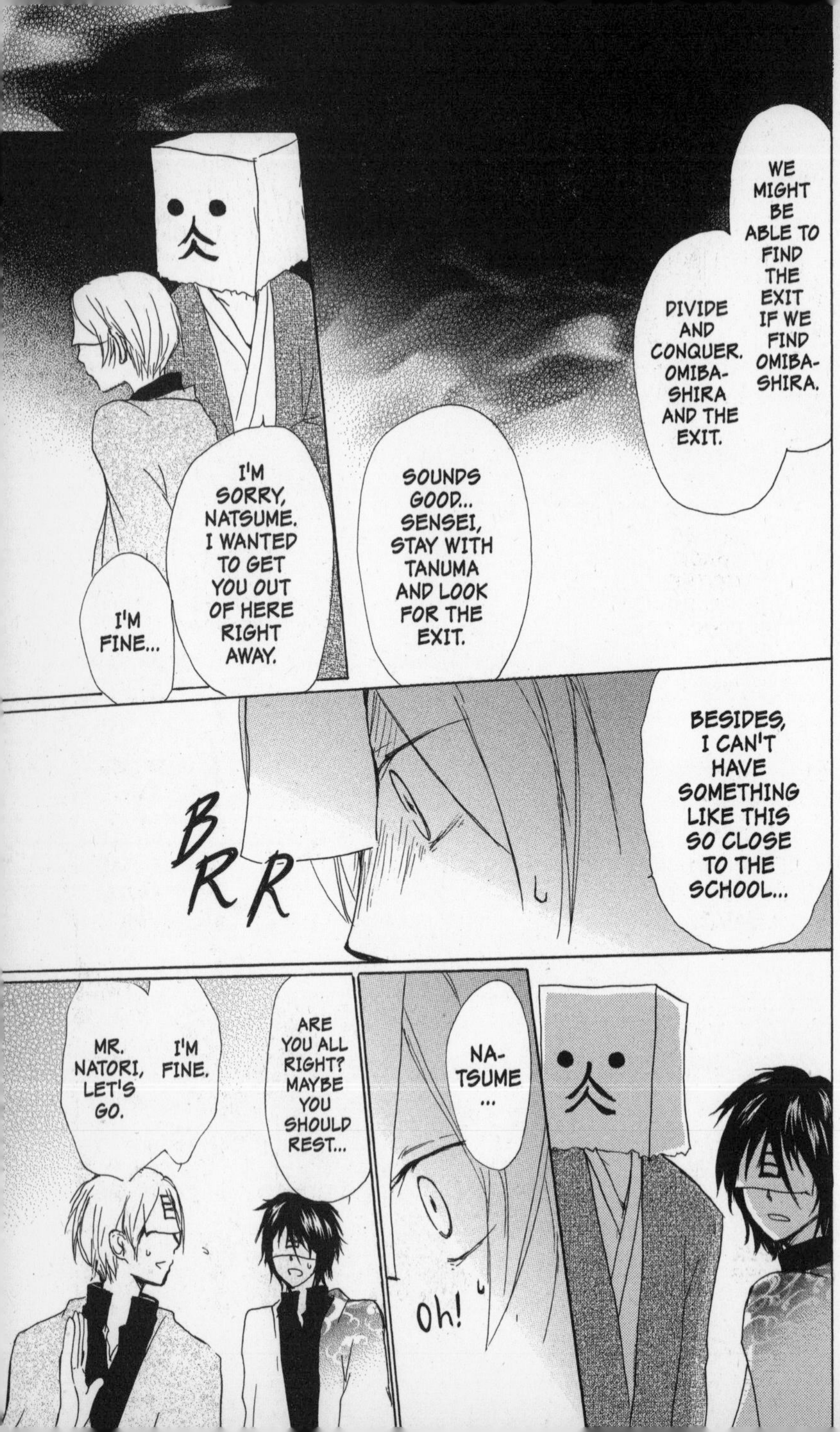
WE MIGHT BE ABLE TO FIND THE EXIT IF WE FIND OMIBASHIRA.
DIVIDE AND CONQUER. OMIBASHIRA AND THE EXIT.
SOUNDS GOOD... SENSEI, STAY WITH TANUMA AND LOOK FOR THE EXIT.
I'M SORRY, NATSUME. I WANTED TO GET YOU OUT OF HERE RIGHT AWAY.
I'M FINE...
BESIDES, I CAN'T HAVE SOMETHING LIKE THIS SO CLOSE TO THE SCHOOL...
BRR
NATSUME...
Oh!
ARE YOU ALL RIGHT? MAYBE YOU SHOULD REST...
I'M FINE.
MR. NATORI, LET'S GO.

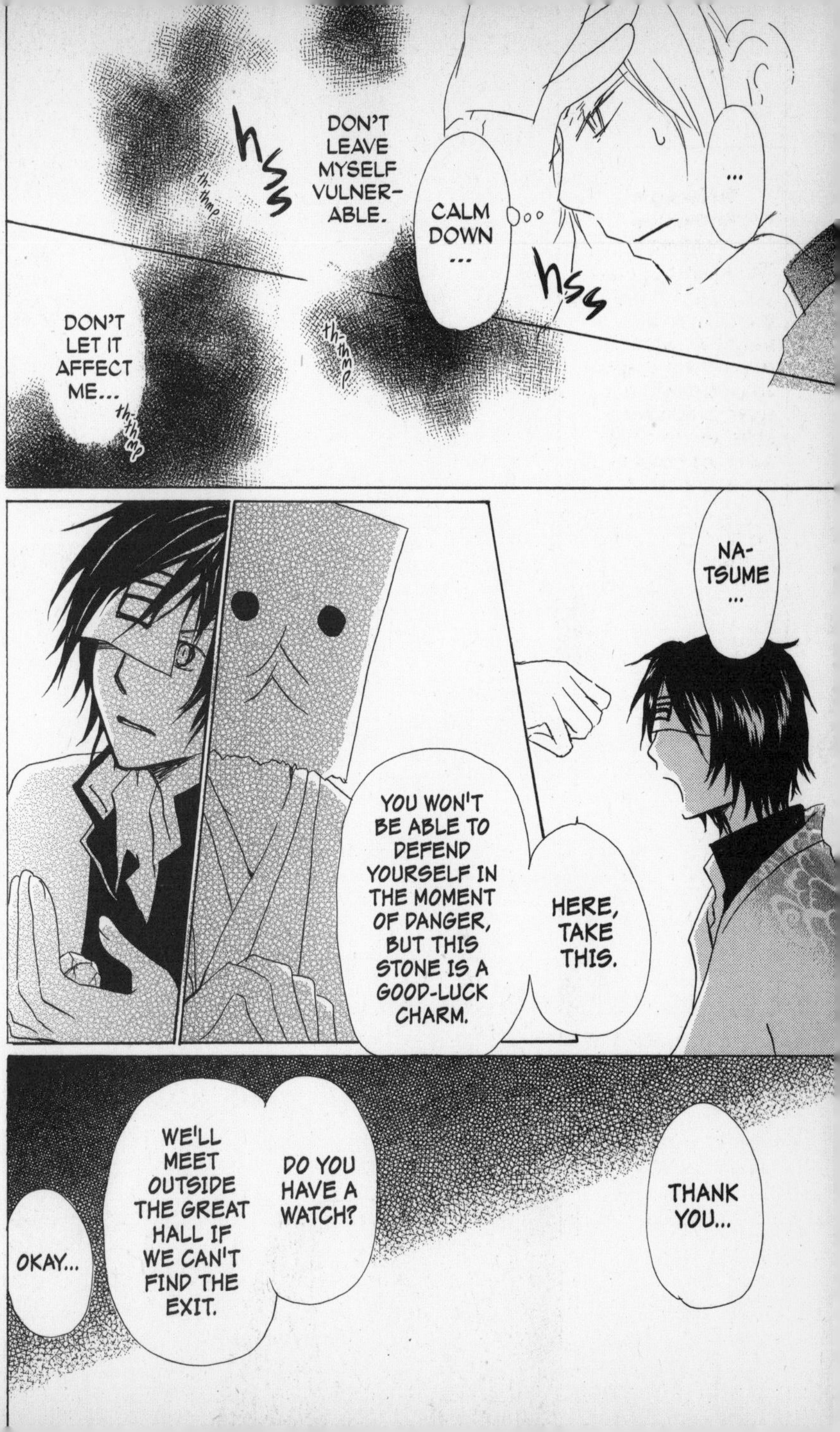
...
CALM DOWN...
hss
DON'T LEAVE MYSELF VULNERABLE.
hss
th-thmp
th-thmp
DON'T LET IT AFFECT ME...
th-thmp
NATSUME...
HERE, TAKE THIS.
YOU WON'T BE ABLE TO DEFEND YOURSELF IN THE MOMENT OF DANGER, BUT THIS STONE IS A GOOD-LUCK CHARM.
THANK YOU...
DO YOU HAVE A WATCH?
WE'LL MEET OUTSIDE THE GREAT HALL IF WE CAN'T FIND THE EXIT.
OKAY...

05

❋ Natsume Anthology: Summer

To commemorate the anime broadcast they're going to publish a collection of reprinted episodes from the manga, a super cute comic strip, and an original short story by the anime scriptwriter on July 8, 2011. I'm so deeply grateful.

End of 1/4 columns.

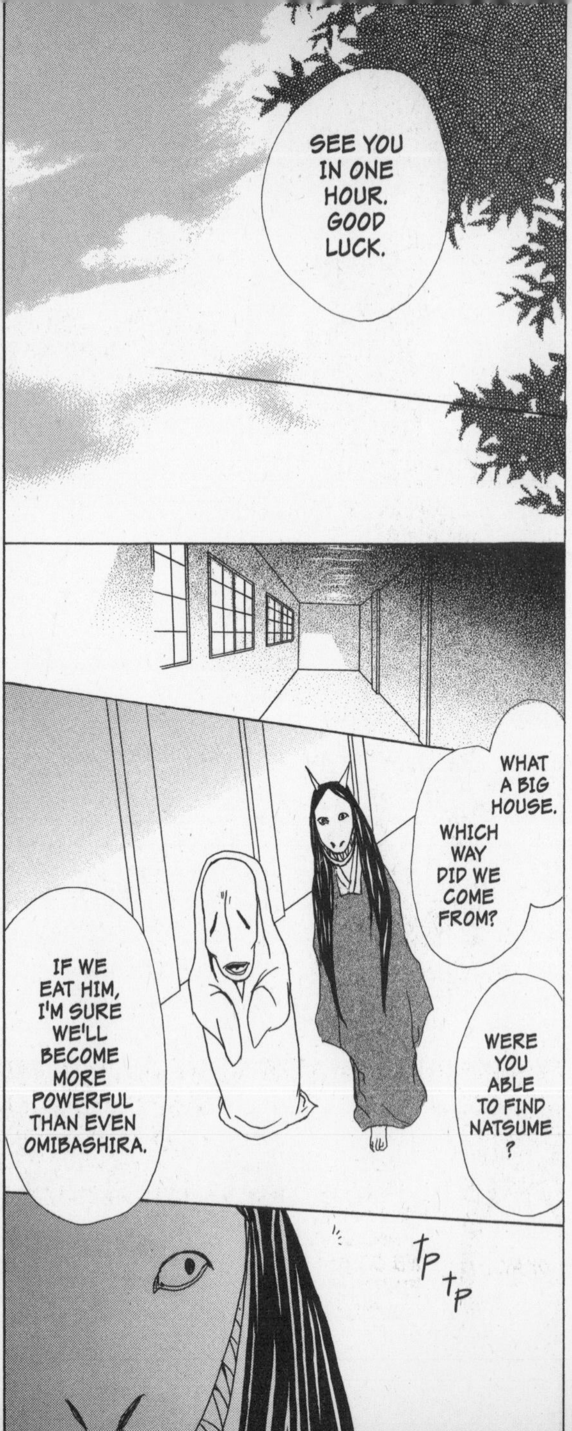
SEE YOU IN ONE HOUR. GOOD LUCK.
WHAT A BIG HOUSE.
WHICH WAY DID WE COME FROM?
WERE YOU ABLE TO FIND NATSUME?
IF WE EAT HIM, I'M SURE WE'LL BECOME MORE POWERFUL THAN EVEN OMIBASHIRA.
TP TP

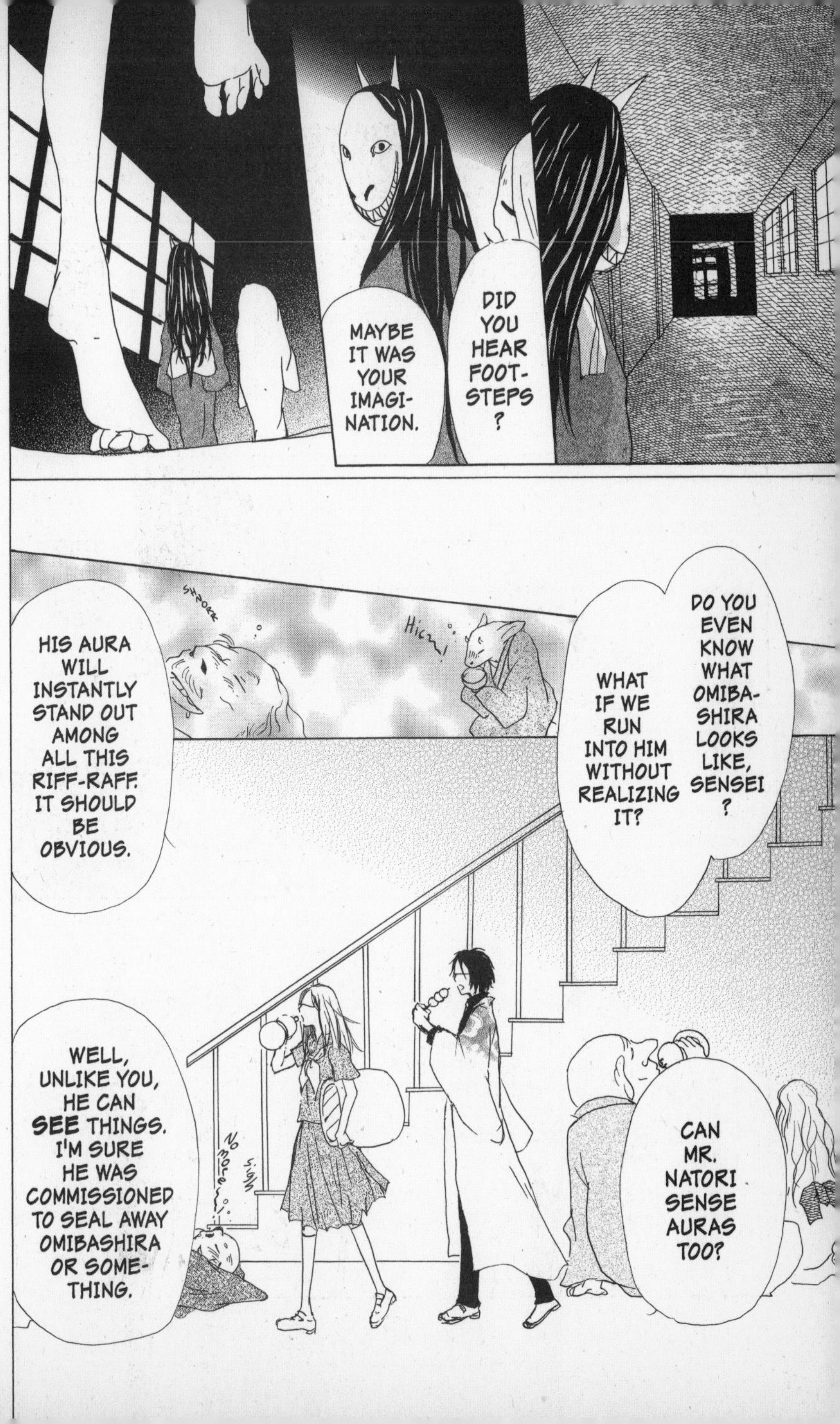
DID YOU HEAR FOOT-STEPS?
MAYBE IT WAS YOUR IMAGINATION.
Hic!
SHNORK
DO YOU EVEN KNOW WHAT OMIBA-SHIRA LOOKS LIKE, SENSEI?
WHAT IF WE RUN INTO HIM WITHOUT REALIZING IT?
HIS AURA WILL INSTANTLY STAND OUT AMONG ALL THIS RIFF-RAFF. IT SHOULD BE OBVIOUS.
CAN MR. NATORI SENSE AURAS TOO?
WELL, UNLIKE YOU, HE CAN **SEE** THINGS. I'M SURE HE WAS COMMISSIONED TO SEAL AWAY OMIBASHIRA OR SOME-THING.
sigh
No more~!

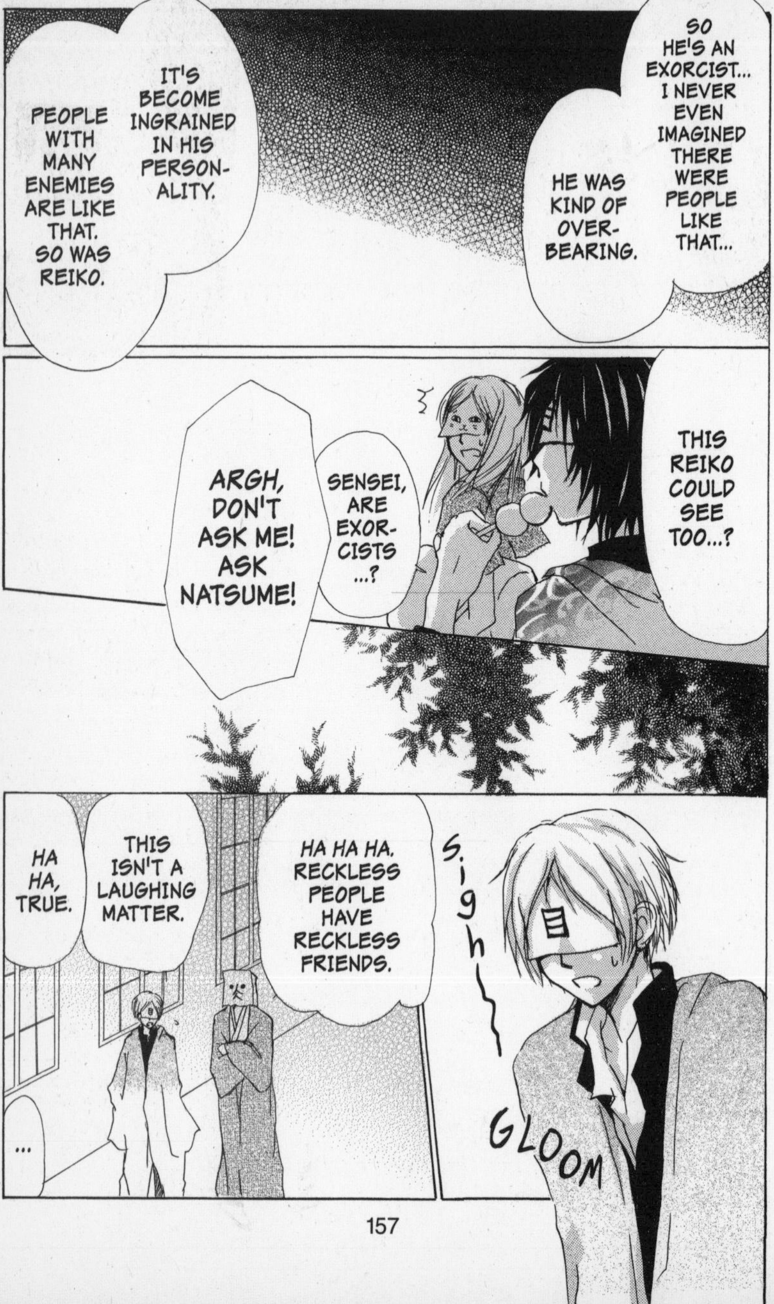
SO HE'S AN EXORCIST... I NEVER EVEN IMAGINED THERE WERE PEOPLE LIKE THAT...
HE WAS KIND OF OVER-BEARING.
IT'S BECOME INGRAINED IN HIS PERSON-ALITY.
PEOPLE WITH MANY ENEMIES ARE LIKE THAT. SO WAS REIKO.
THIS REIKO COULD SEE TOO...?
SENSEI, ARE EXOR-CISTS ...?
ARGH, DON'T ASK ME! ASK NATSUME!
SIGH
GLOOM
HA HA HA. RECKLESS PEOPLE HAVE RECKLESS FRIENDS.
THIS ISN'T A LAUGHING MATTER.
HA HA, TRUE.
...

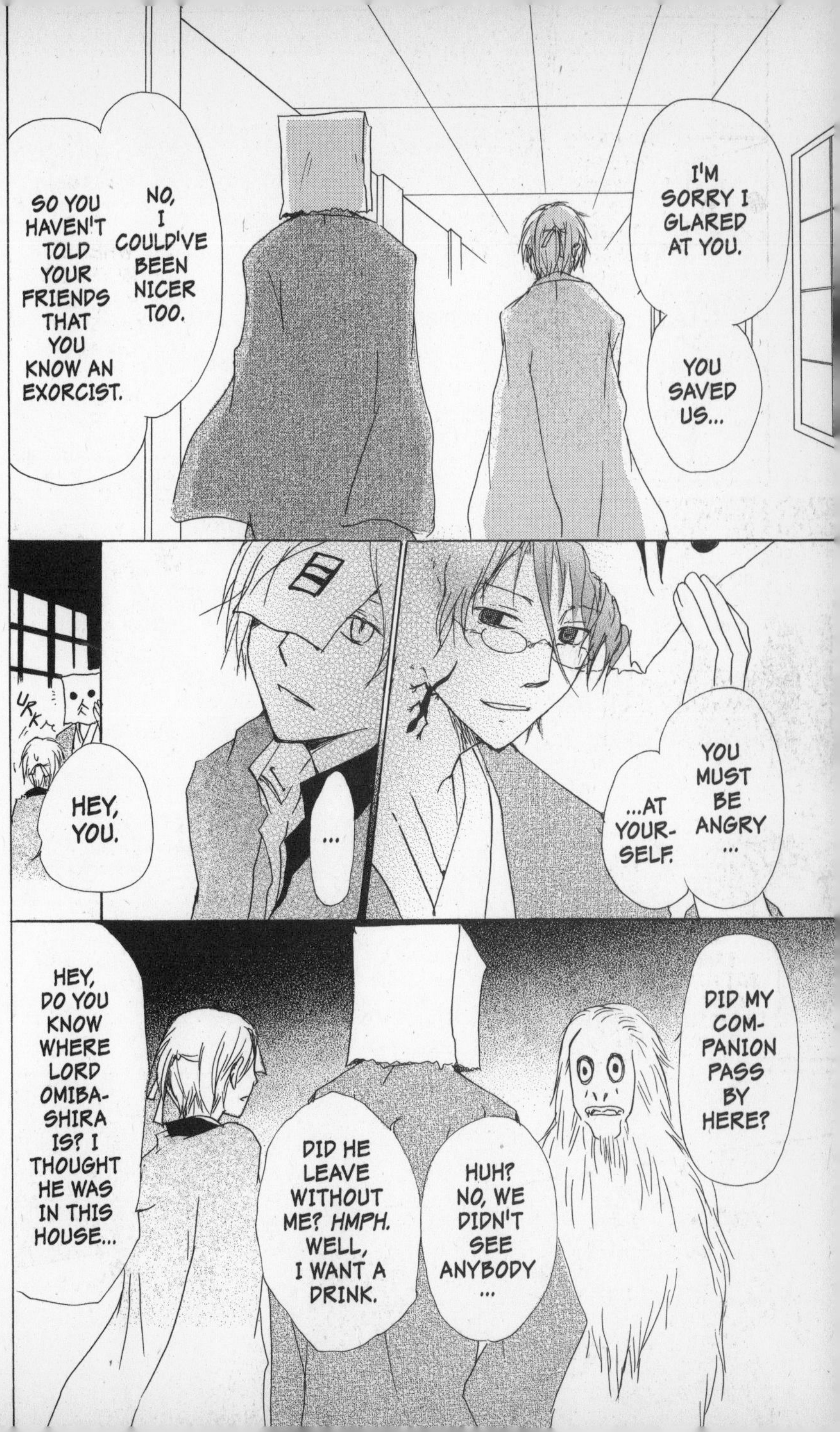
I'M SORRY I GLARED AT YOU.
YOU SAVED US...
NO, I COULD'VE BEEN NICER TOO.
SO YOU HAVEN'T TOLD YOUR FRIENDS THAT YOU KNOW AN EXORCIST.
YOU MUST BE ANGRY ...
...AT YOUR-SELF.
...
URK
HEY, YOU.
DID MY COM-PANION PASS BY HERE?
HUH? NO, WE DIDN'T SEE ANYBODY ...
DID HE LEAVE WITHOUT ME? *HMPH.* WELL, I WANT A DRINK.
HEY, DO YOU KNOW WHERE LORD OMIBA-SHIRA IS? I THOUGHT HE WAS IN THIS HOUSE...

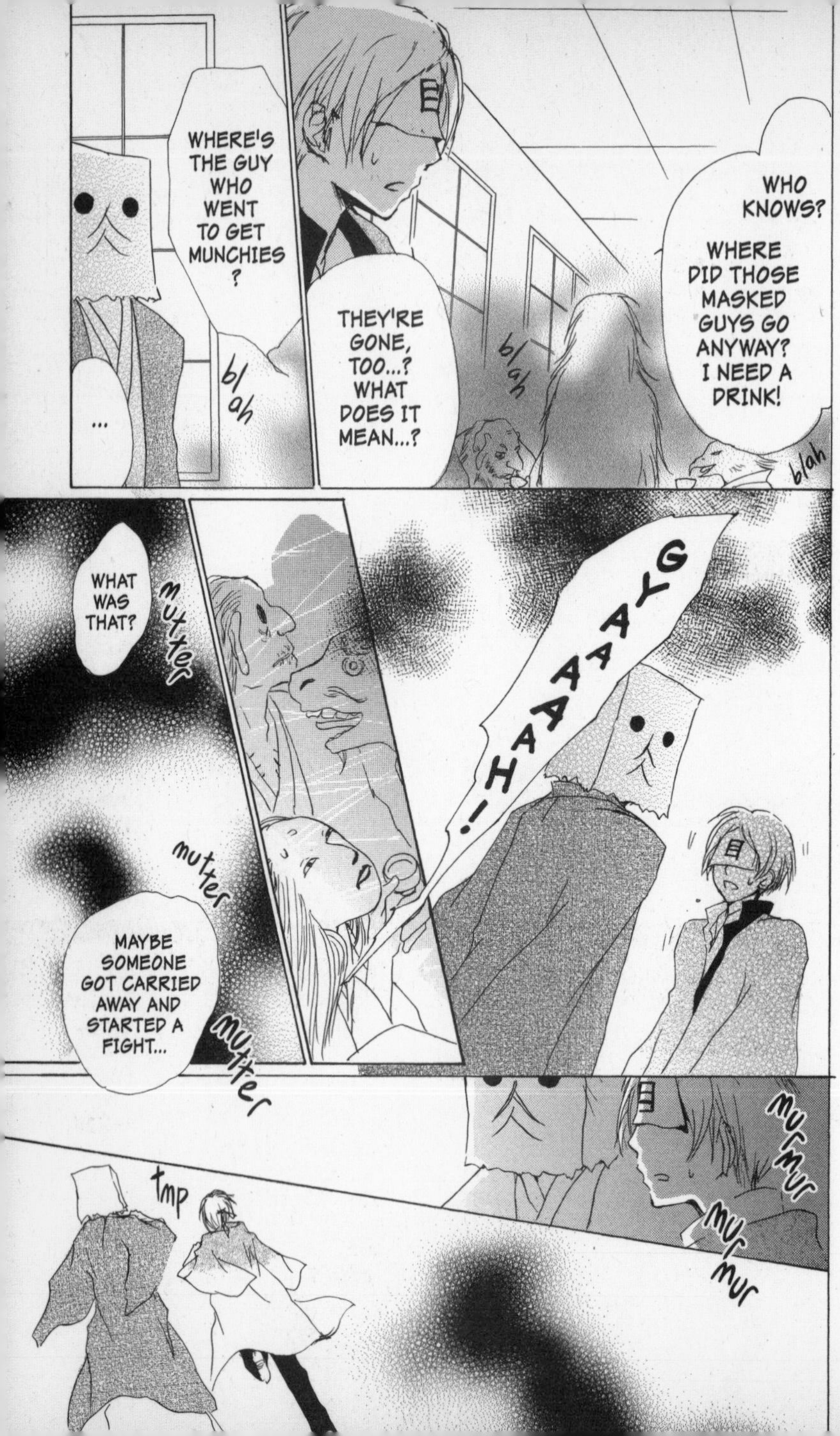
WHO KNOWS?
WHERE DID THOSE MASKED GUYS GO ANYWAY? I NEED A DRINK!
blah
blah
THEY'RE GONE, TOO...? WHAT DOES IT MEAN...?
WHERE'S THE GUY WHO WENT TO GET MUNCHIES?
blah
...
GYAAAAAH!
WHAT WAS THAT?
mutter
mutter
MAYBE SOMEONE GOT CARRIED AWAY AND STARTED A FIGHT...
mutter
murmur
murmur
tmp

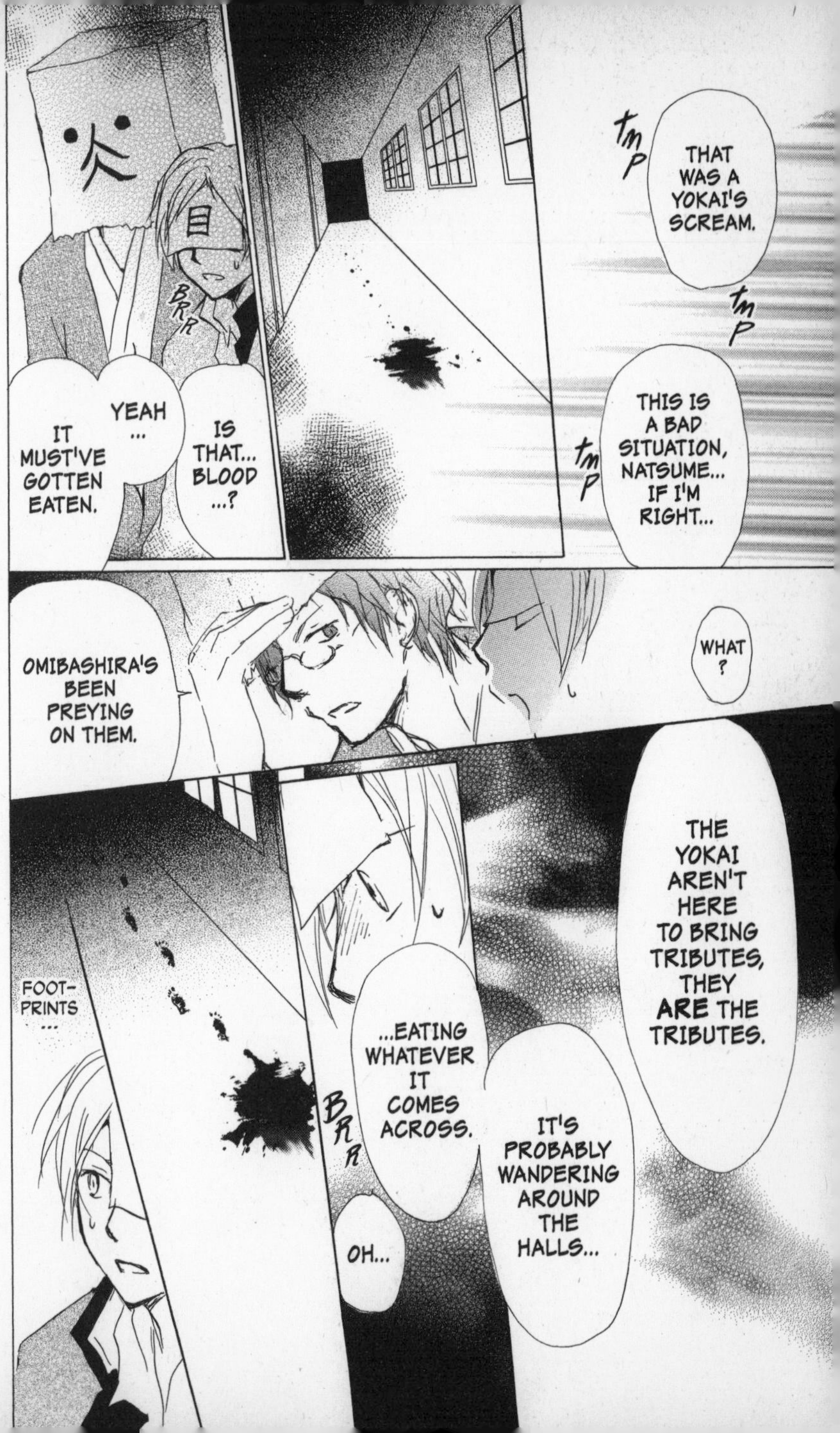

THAT WAS A YOKAI'S SCREAM.
TMP
TMP
THIS IS A BAD SITUATION, NATSUME... IF I'M RIGHT...
TMP
IS THAT... BLOOD ...?
YEAH ...
IT MUST'VE GOTTEN EATEN.
BRR
WHAT ?
OMIBASHIRA'S BEEN PREYING ON THEM.
THE YOKAI AREN'T HERE TO BRING TRIBUTES, THEY **ARE** THE TRIBUTES.
IT'S PROBABLY WANDERING AROUND THE HALLS...
...EATING WHATEVER IT COMES ACROSS.
BRR
OH...
FOOT-PRINTS ...

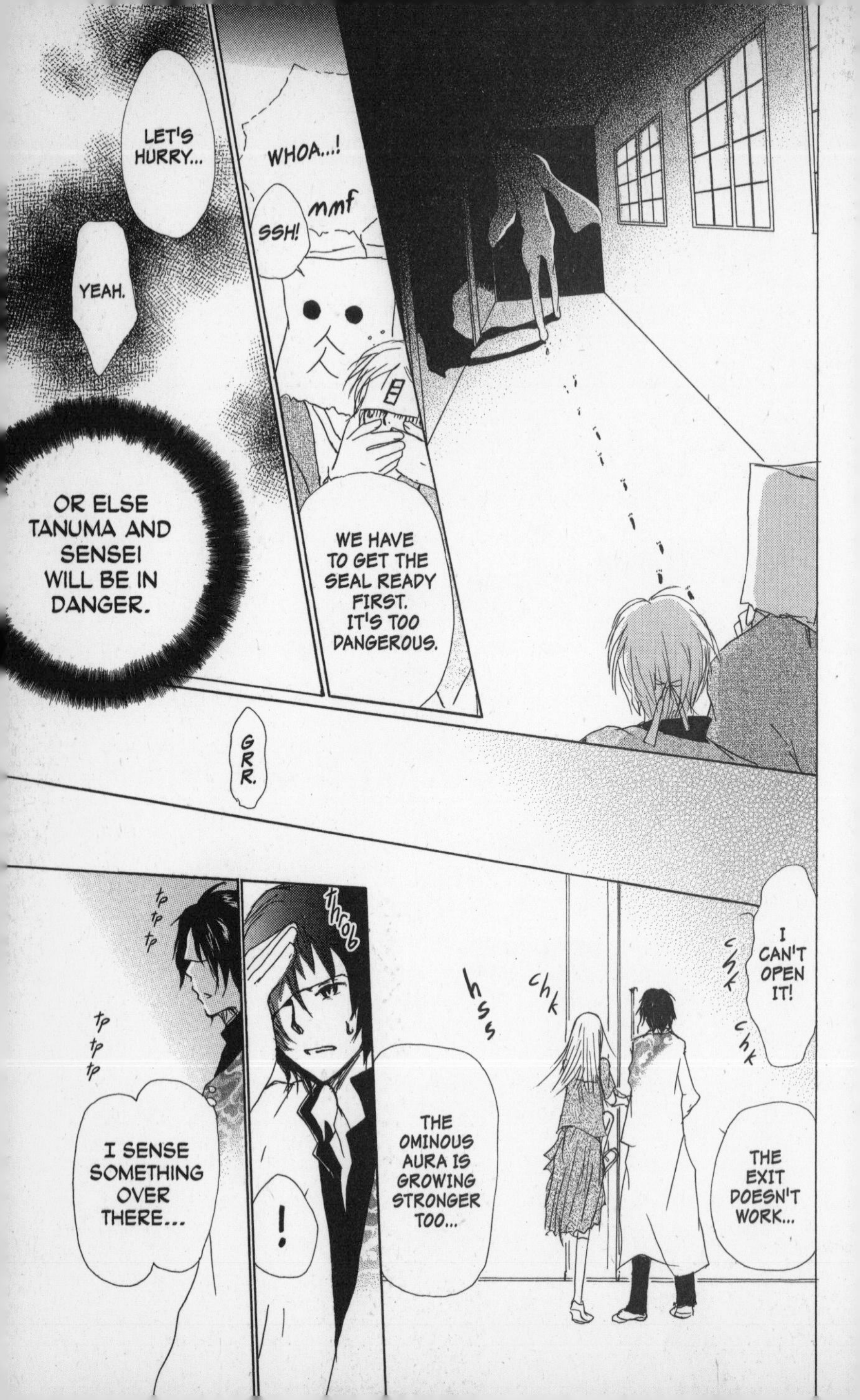
GRR.
WHOA...!
mmf
SSH!
WE HAVE TO GET THE SEAL READY FIRST. IT'S TOO DANGEROUS.
LET'S HURRY...
YEAH.
OR ELSE TANUMA AND SENSEI WILL BE IN DANGER.
I CAN'T OPEN IT!
chk
chk
chk
hss
THE EXIT DOESN'T WORK...
throb
THE OMINOUS AURA IS GROWING STRONGER TOO...
!
tp tp tp
tp tp tp
I SENSE SOMETHING OVER THERE...

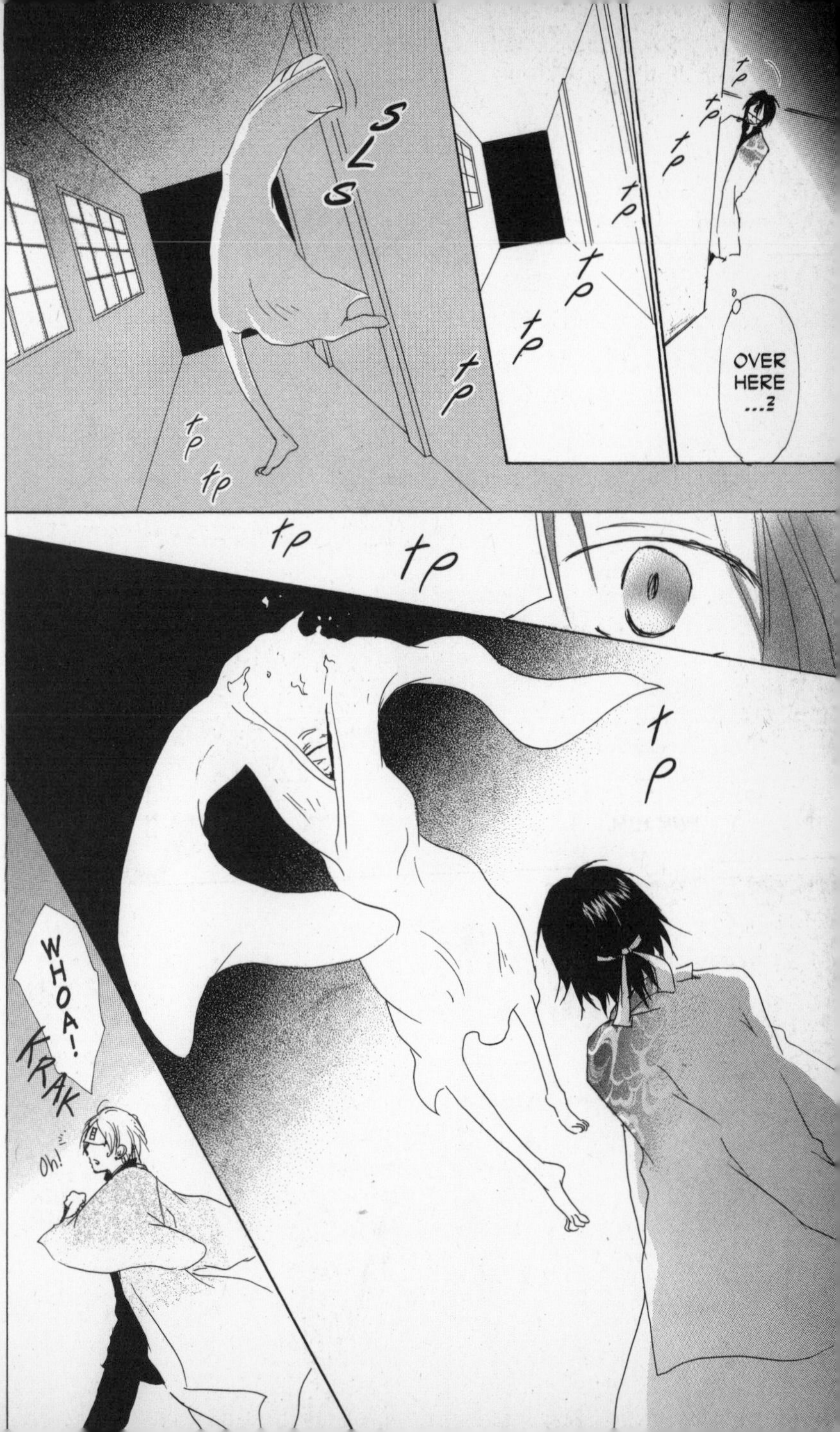
tp
tp
tp
tp
tp
tp
tp
OVER HERE ...?
SLS
tp
tp
tp
tp
tp
tp
WHOA!
KRAK
Oh!

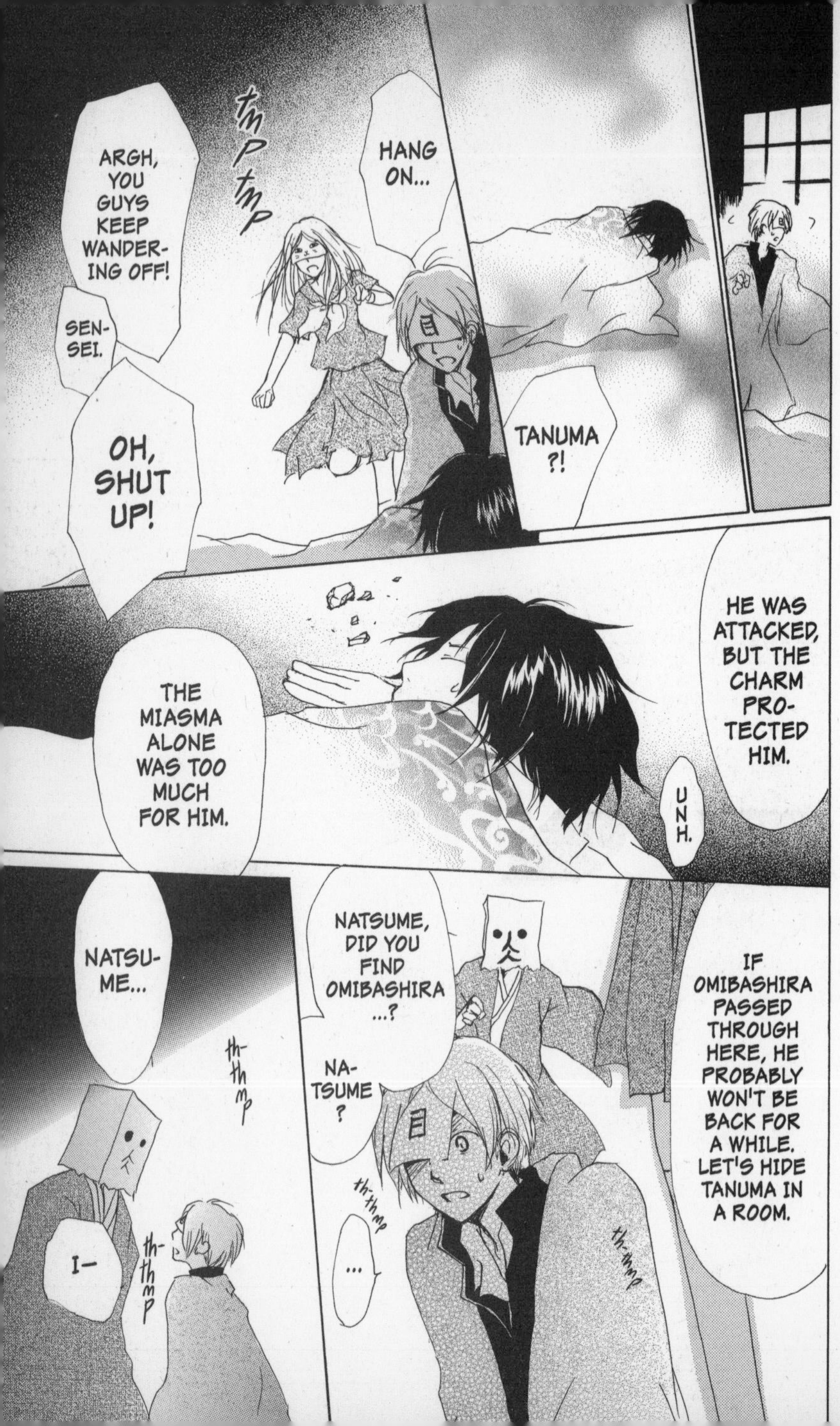
TANUMA?!
HANG ON...
tmp tmp
ARGH, YOU GUYS KEEP WANDER-ING OFF!
SEN-SEI.
OH, SHUT UP!
HE WAS ATTACKED, BUT THE CHARM PRO-TECTED HIM.
UNH.
THE MIASMA ALONE WAS TOO MUCH FOR HIM.
IF OMIBASHIRA PASSED THROUGH HERE, HE PROBABLY WON'T BE BACK FOR A WHILE. LET'S HIDE TANUMA IN A ROOM.
NATSUME, DID YOU FIND OMIBASHIRA ...?
NA-TSUME?
th-thmp
...
th-thmp
NATSU-ME...
th-thmp
I—
th-thmp

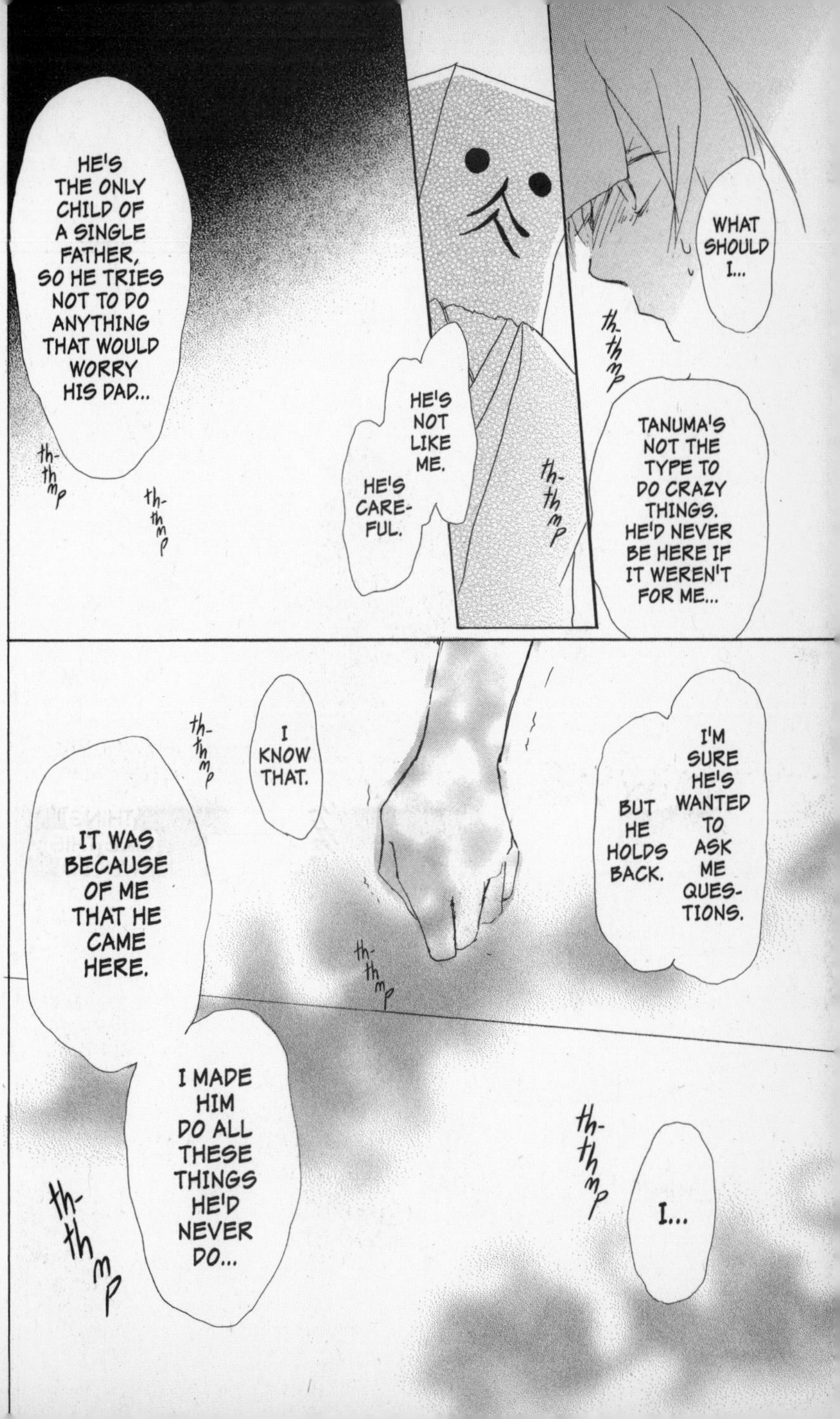

WHAT SHOULD I...
th-thmp
TANUMA'S NOT THE TYPE TO DO CRAZY THINGS. HE'D NEVER BE HERE IF IT WEREN'T FOR ME...
th-thmp
HE'S NOT LIKE ME.
HE'S CARE-FUL.
HE'S THE ONLY CHILD OF A SINGLE FATHER, SO HE TRIES NOT TO DO ANYTHING THAT WOULD WORRY HIS DAD...
th-thmp
th-thmp
I'M SURE HE'S WANTED TO ASK ME QUES-TIONS.
BUT HE HOLDS BACK.
th-thmp
I KNOW THAT.
th-thmp
IT WAS BECAUSE OF ME THAT HE CAME HERE.
I MADE HIM DO ALL THESE THINGS HE'D NEVER DO...
th-thmp
I...
th-thmp

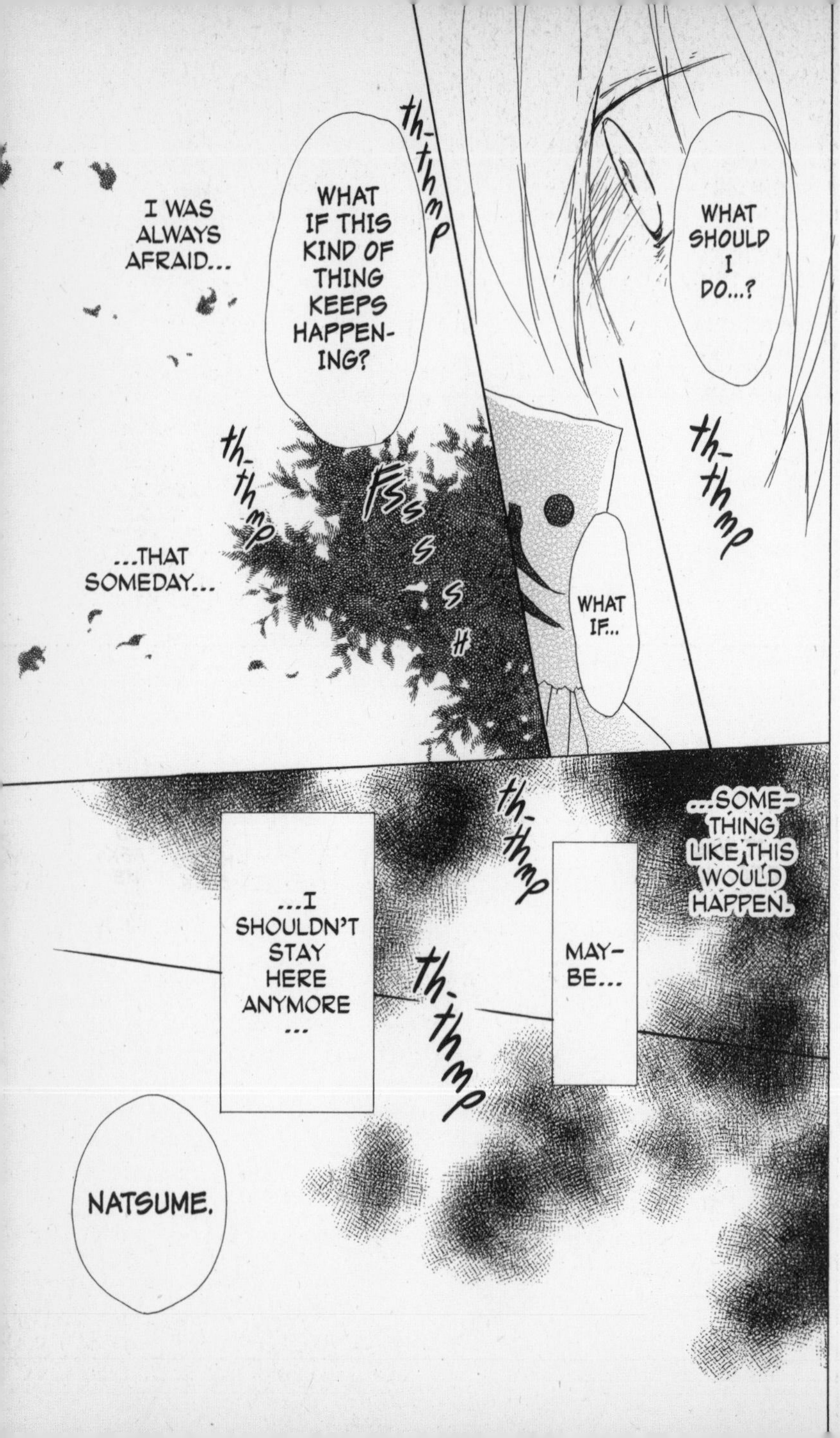
WHAT SHOULD I DO...?
th-thmp
WHAT IF...
th-thmp
WHAT IF THIS KIND OF THING KEEPS HAPPENING?
I WAS ALWAYS AFRAID...
th-thmp
Fssssh
...THAT SOMEDAY...
...SOMETHING LIKE THIS WOULD HAPPEN.
th-thmp
MAYBE...
th-thmp
...I SHOULDN'T STAY HERE ANYMORE...
NATSUME.

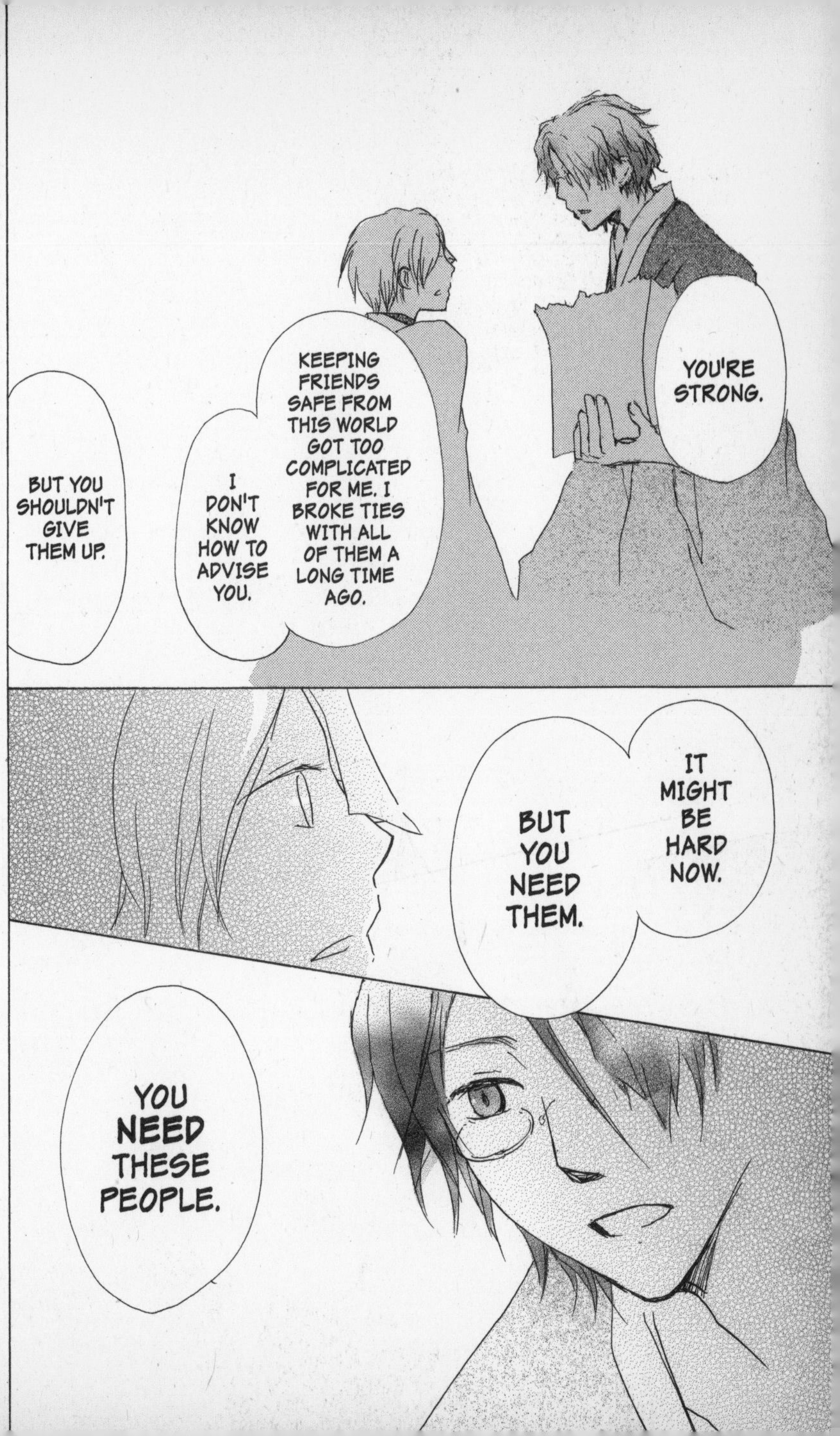
YOU'RE STRONG.
KEEPING FRIENDS SAFE FROM THIS WORLD GOT TOO COMPLICATED FOR ME. I BROKE TIES WITH ALL OF THEM A LONG TIME AGO.
I DON'T KNOW HOW TO ADVISE YOU.
BUT YOU SHOULDN'T GIVE THEM UP.
IT MIGHT BE HARD NOW.
BUT YOU NEED THEM.
YOU **NEED** THESE PEOPLE.

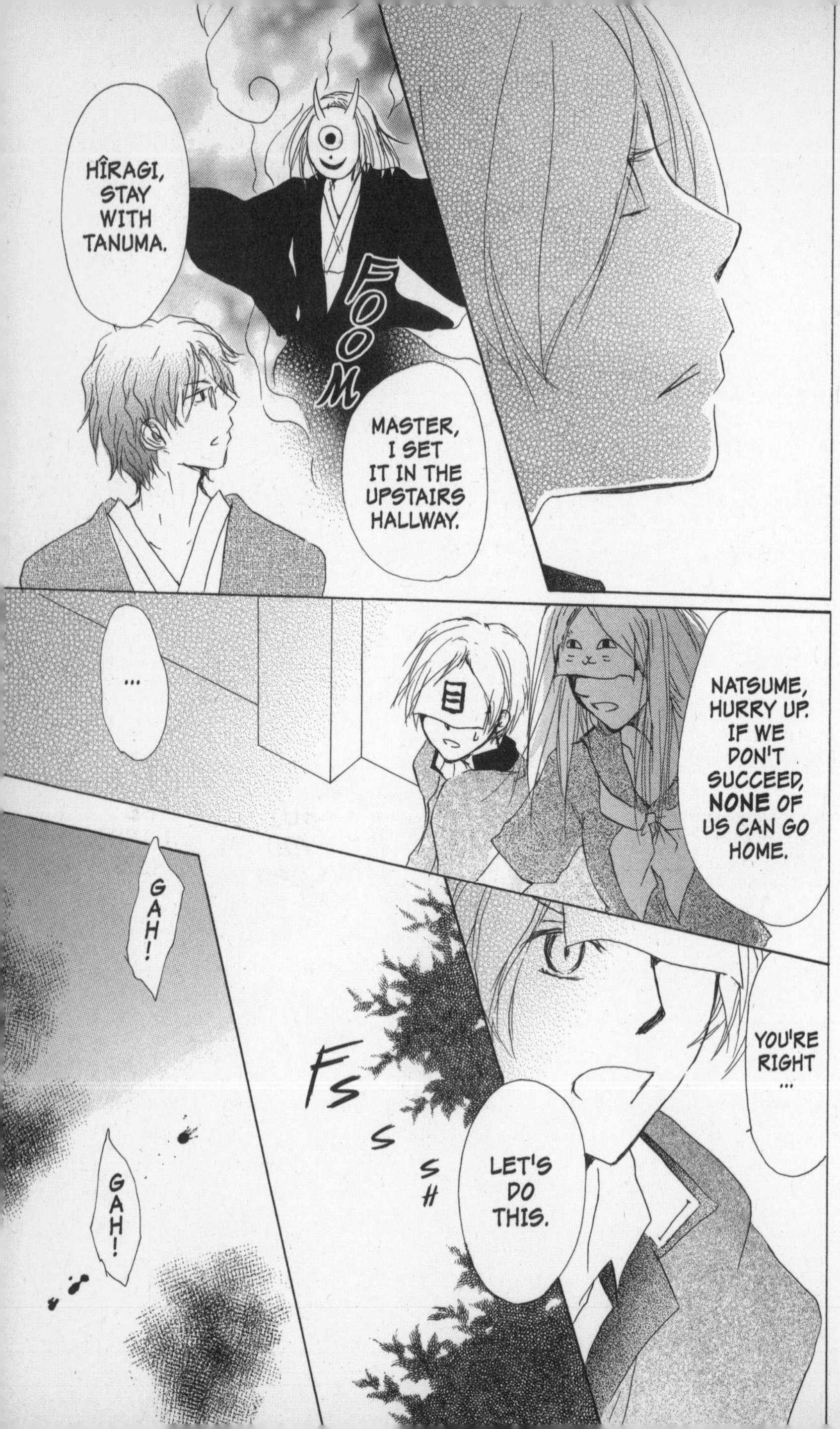
FOOM
MASTER, I SET IT IN THE UPSTAIRS HALLWAY.
HÎRAGI, STAY WITH TANUMA.
NATSUME, HURRY UP. IF WE DON'T SUCCEED, **NONE** OF US CAN GO HOME.
...
YOU'RE RIGHT...
LET'S DO THIS.
FSSSH
GAH!
GAH!

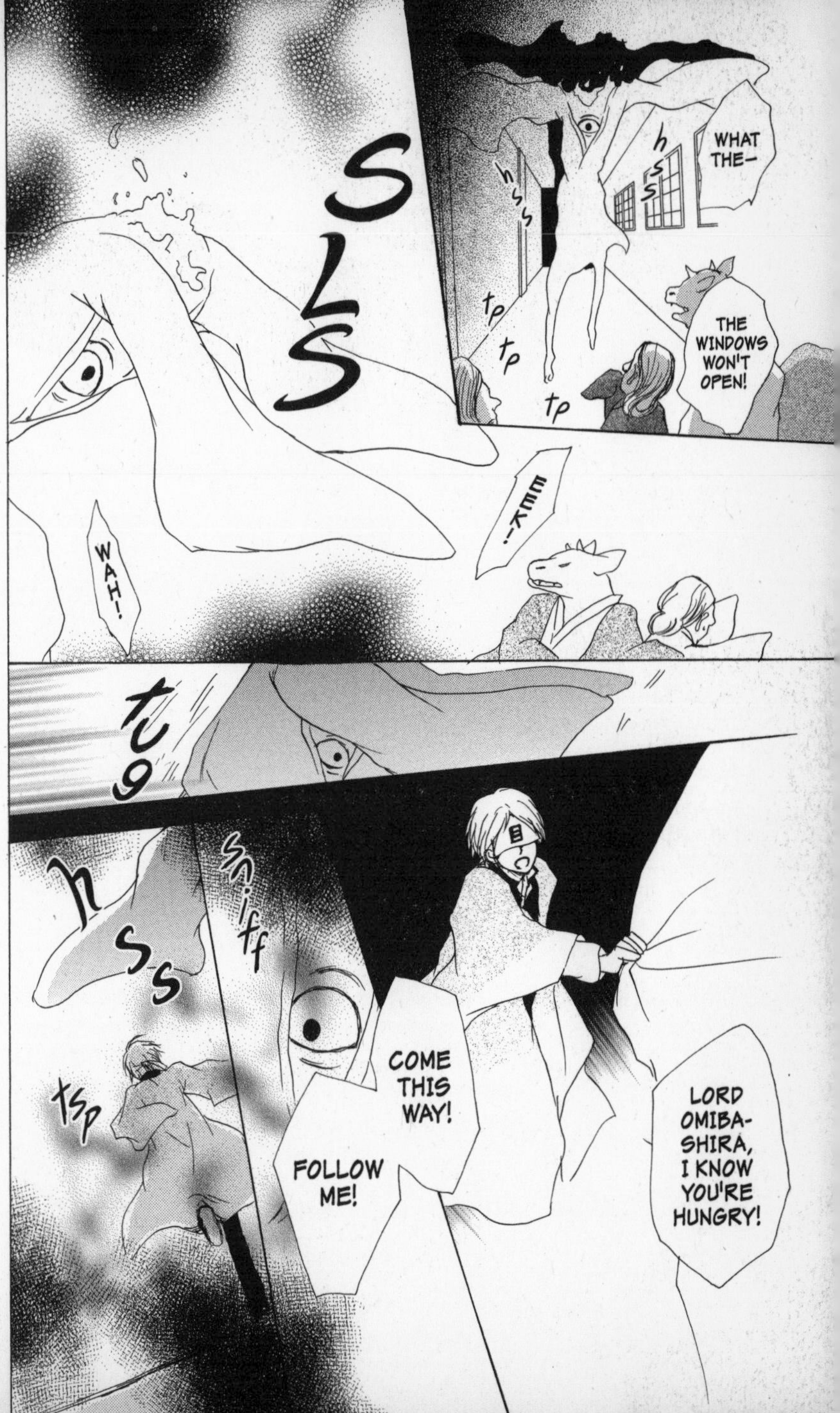
hss
WHAT THE—
hss
tp
tp
tp
THE WINDOWS WON'T OPEN!
SLS
EEK!
WAH!
tug
LORD OMIBA-SHIRA, I KNOW YOU'RE HUNGRY!
COME THIS WAY!
FOLLOW ME!
sniff
hss
tsp

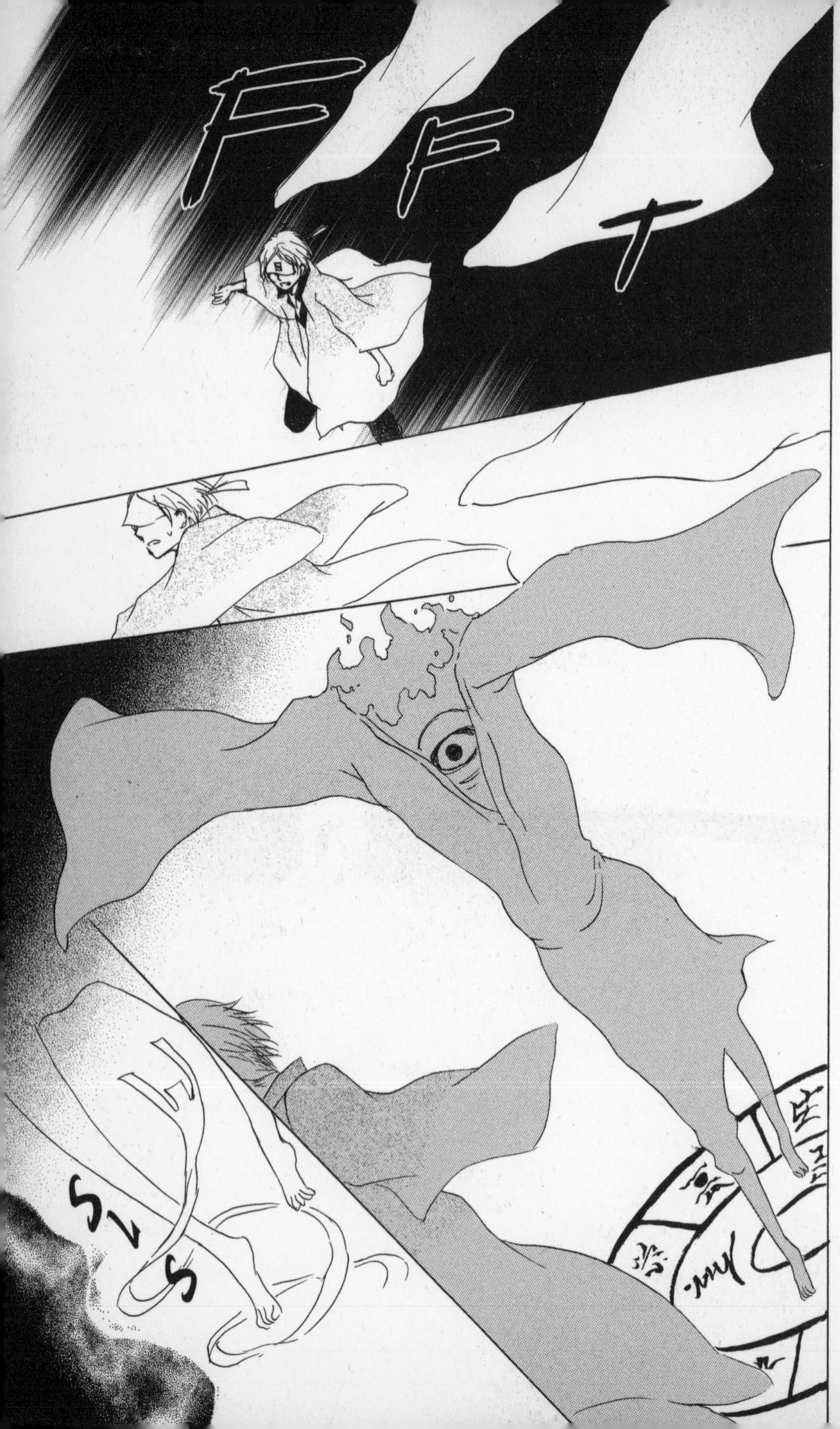
FFFT

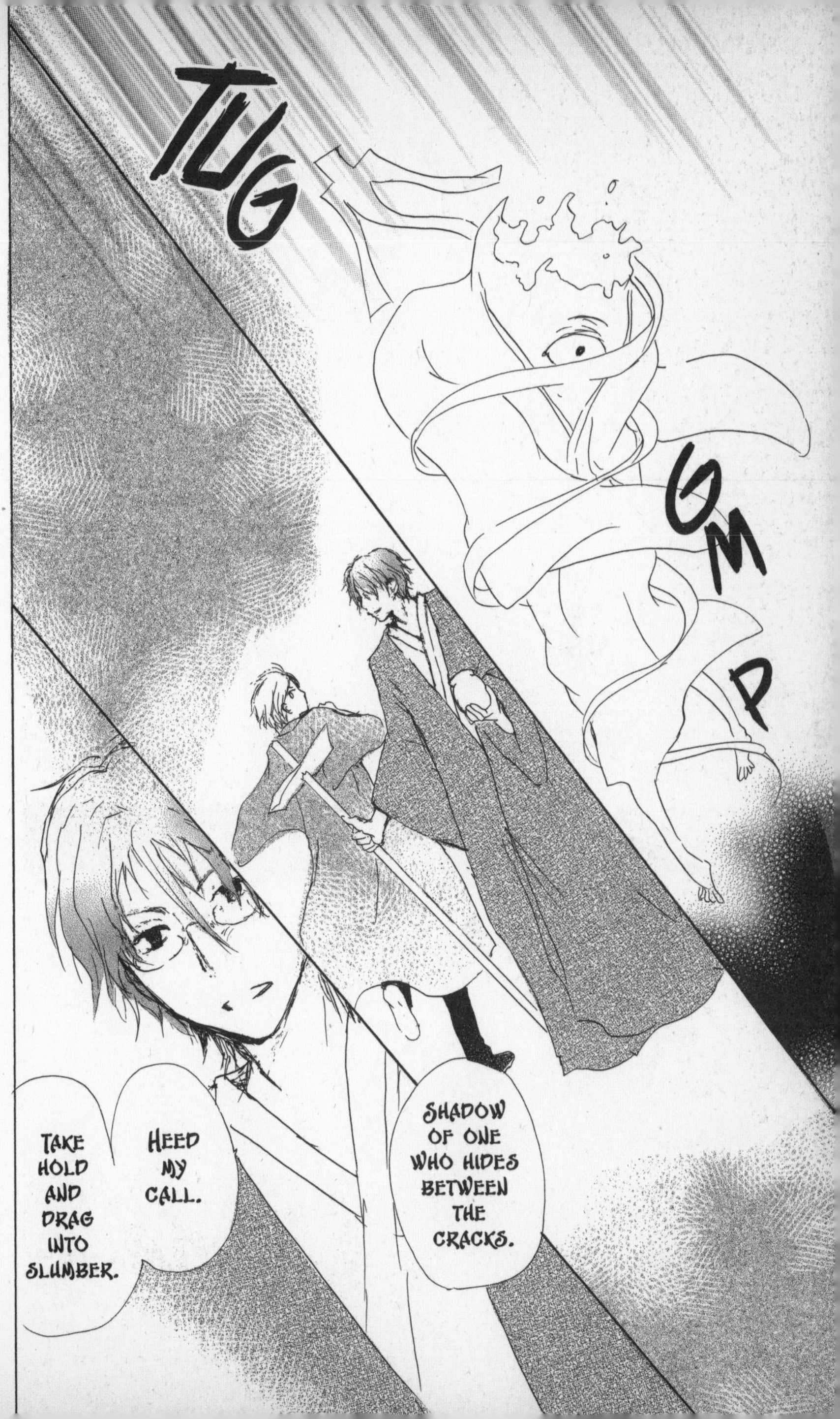
TUG
GMP
SHADOW OF ONE WHO HIDES BETWEEN THE CRACKS.
HEED MY CALL.
TAKE HOLD AND DRAG INTO SLUMBER.

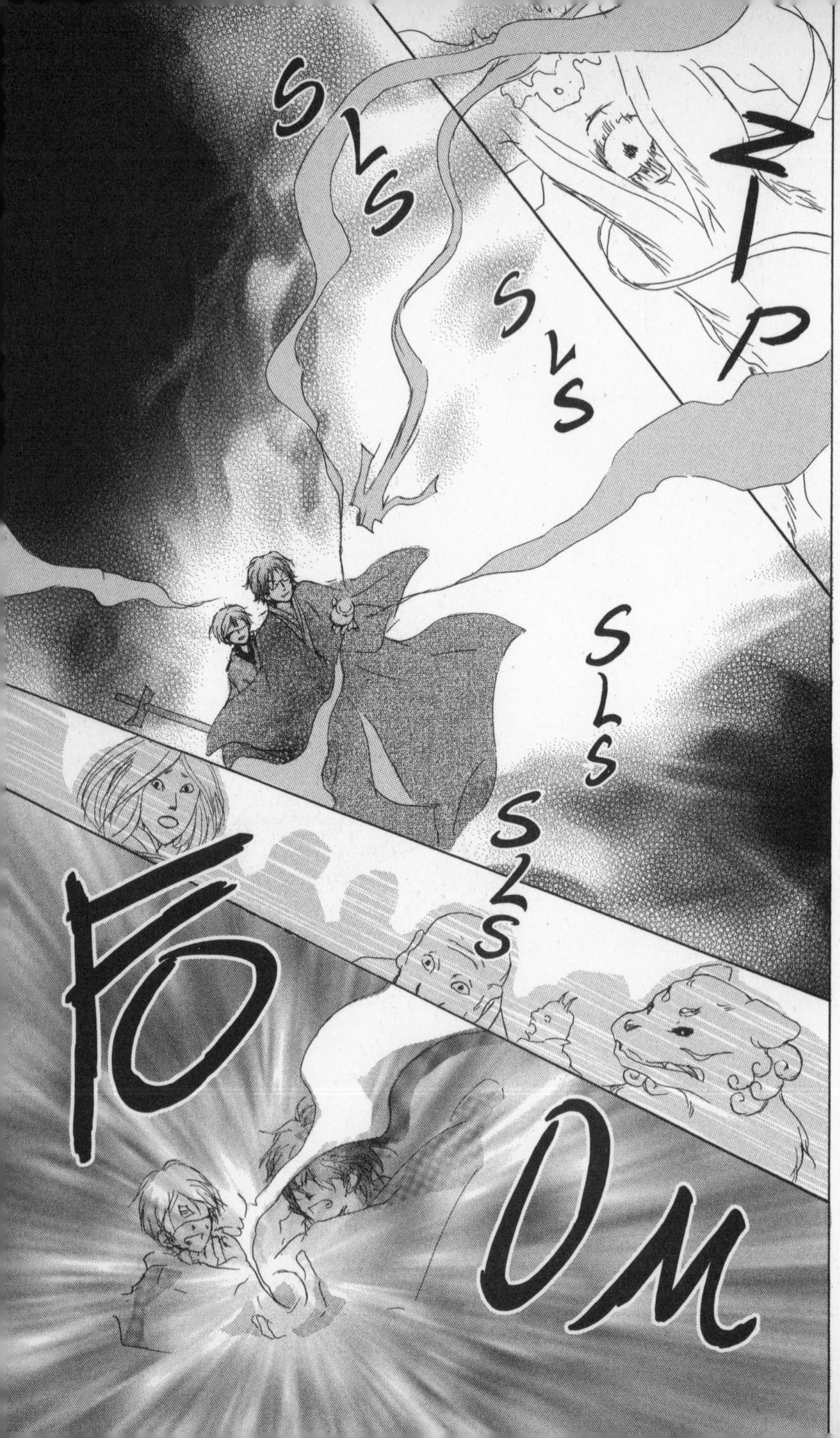
ZIP
SLS
SLS
SLS
SLS
FOOM

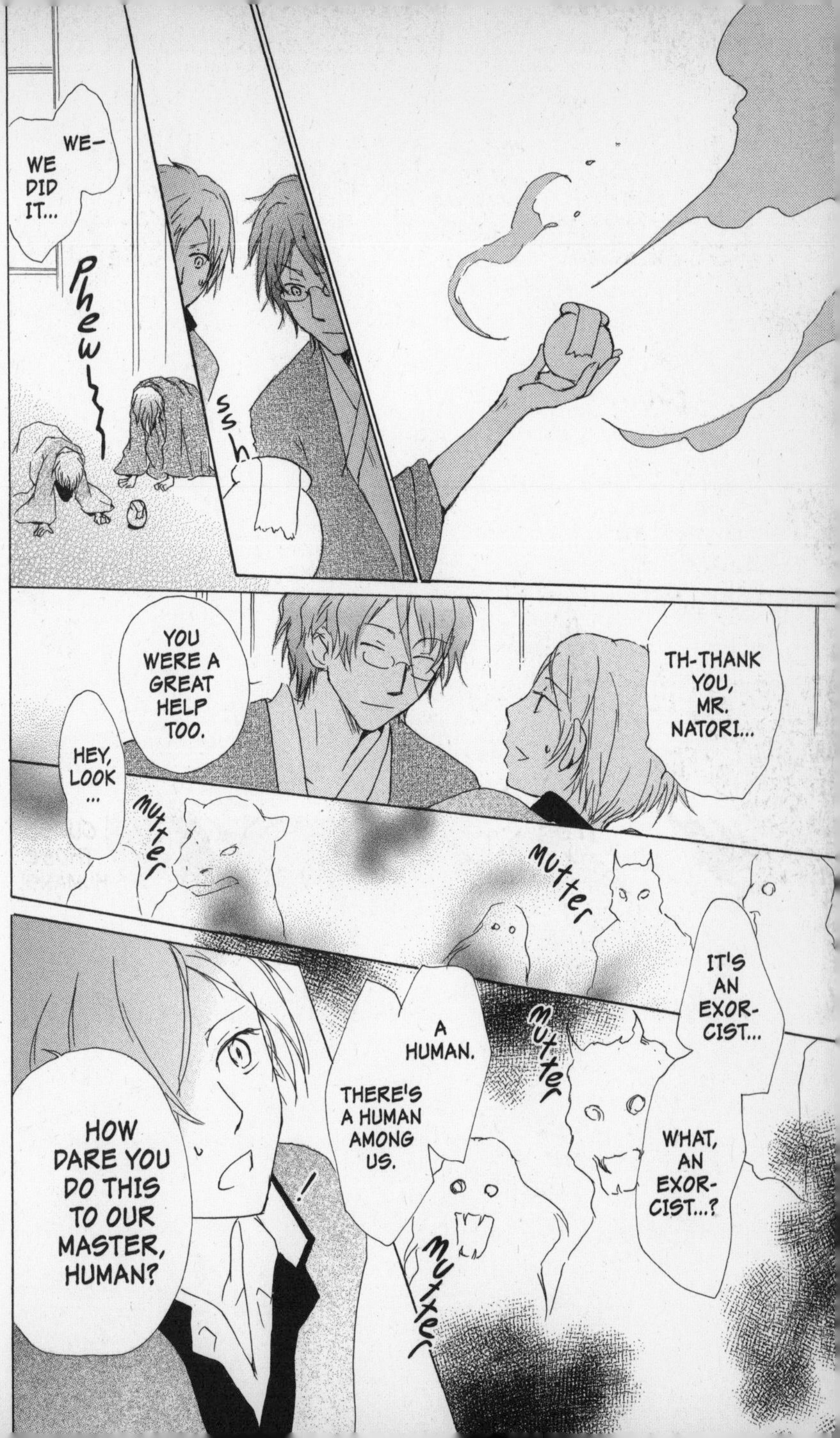
WE- WE DID IT...
Phew~
ssh
TH-THANK YOU, MR. NATORI...
YOU WERE A GREAT HELP TOO.
mutter
HEY, LOOK...
mutter
IT'S AN EXORCIST...
WHAT, AN EXORCIST...?
mutter
A HUMAN.
THERE'S A HUMAN AMONG US.
mutter
!
HOW DARE YOU DO THIS TO OUR MASTER, HUMAN?

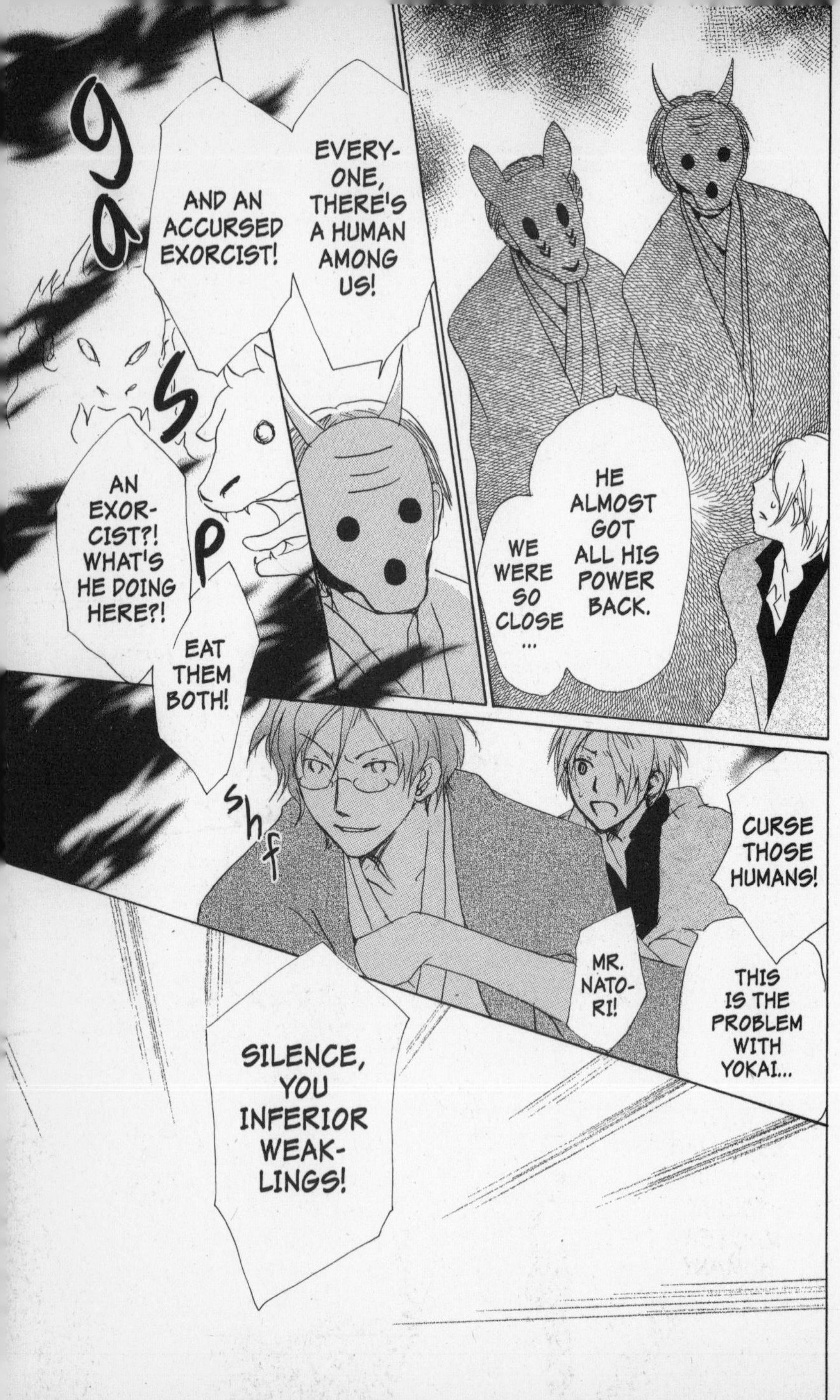
HE ALMOST GOT ALL HIS POWER BACK.
WE WERE SO CLOSE ...
EVERY-ONE, THERE'S A HUMAN AMONG US!
AND AN ACCURSED EXORCIST!
gasp
AN EXOR-CIST?! WHAT'S HE DOING HERE?!
EAT THEM BOTH!
CURSE THOSE HUMANS!
MR. NATO-RI!
shf
THIS IS THE PROBLEM WITH YOKAI...
SILENCE, YOU INFERIOR WEAK-LINGS!

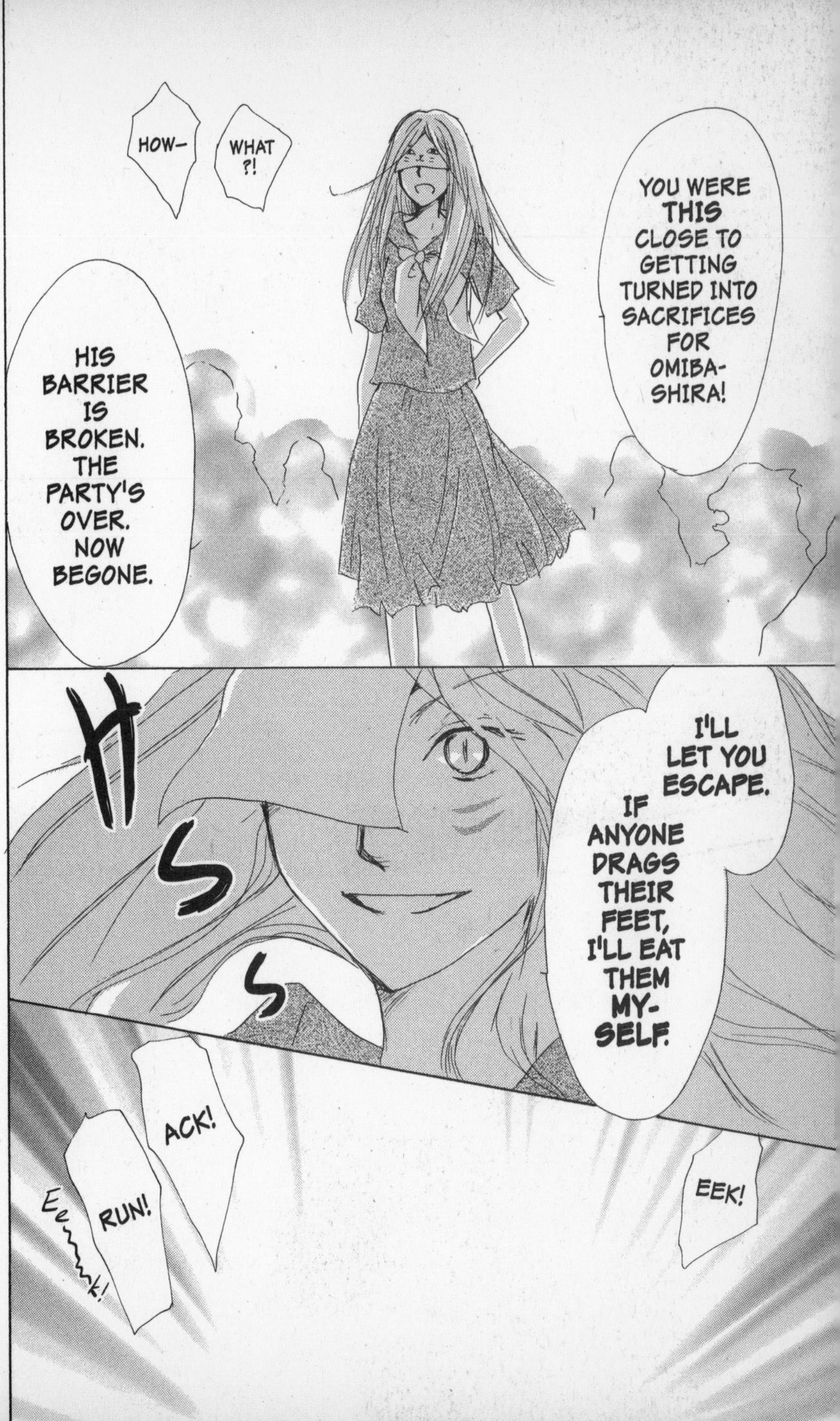
YOU WERE THIS CLOSE TO GETTING TURNED INTO SACRIFICES FOR OMIBA-SHIRA!
WHAT ?!
HOW-
HIS BARRIER IS BROKEN. THE PARTY'S OVER. NOW BEGONE.
I'LL LET YOU ESCAPE.
IF ANYONE DRAGS THEIR FEET, I'LL EAT THEM MY-SELF.
HSS
EEK!
ACK!
RUN!
Eeeek!

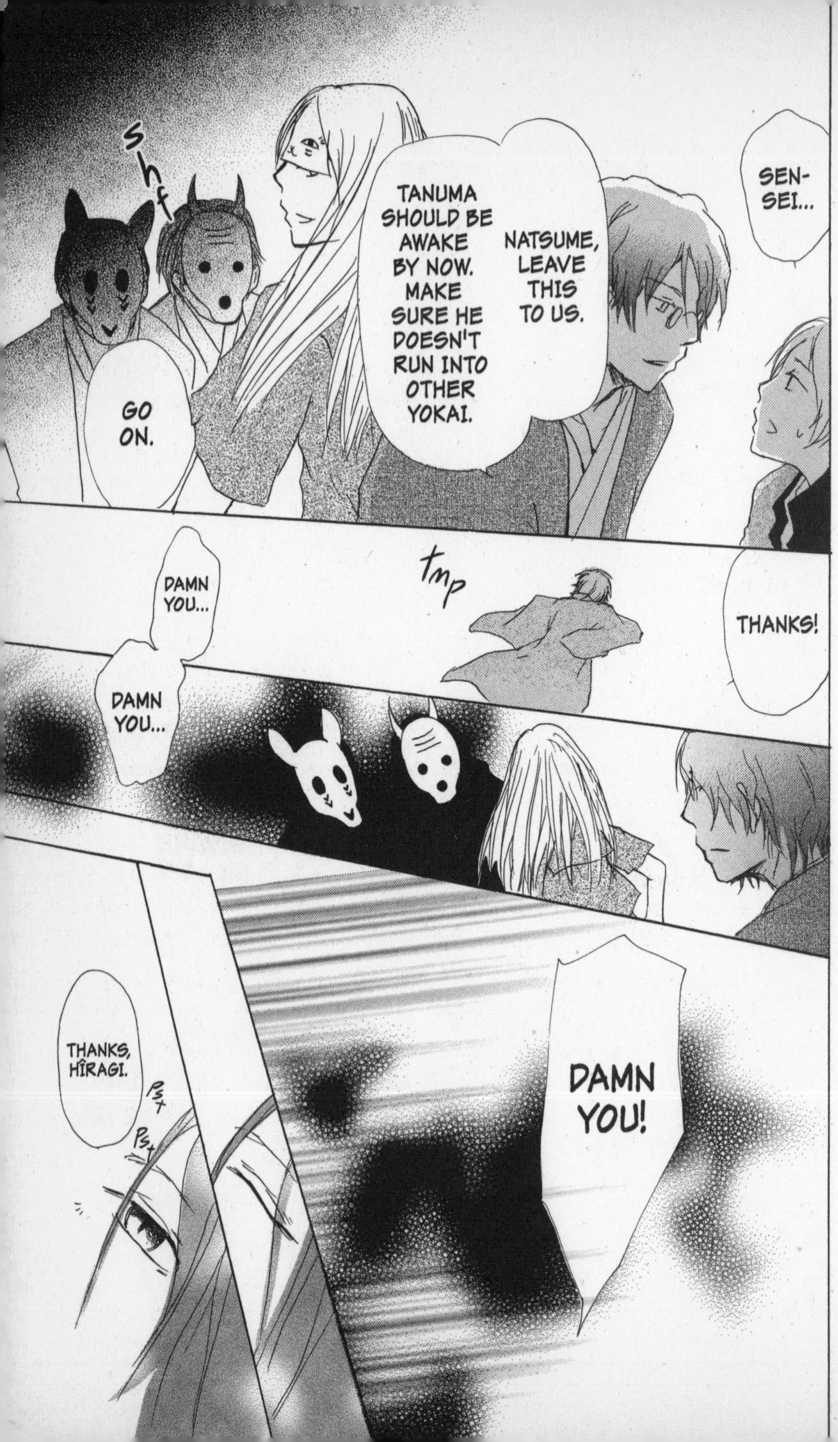
SEN-SEI...
NATSUME, LEAVE THIS TO US.
TANUMA SHOULD BE AWAKE BY NOW. MAKE SURE HE DOESN'T RUN INTO OTHER YOKAI.
shf
GO ON.
THANKS!
tmp
DAMN YOU...
DAMN YOU...
DAMN YOU!
THANKS, HÎRAGI.
Pst
Pst

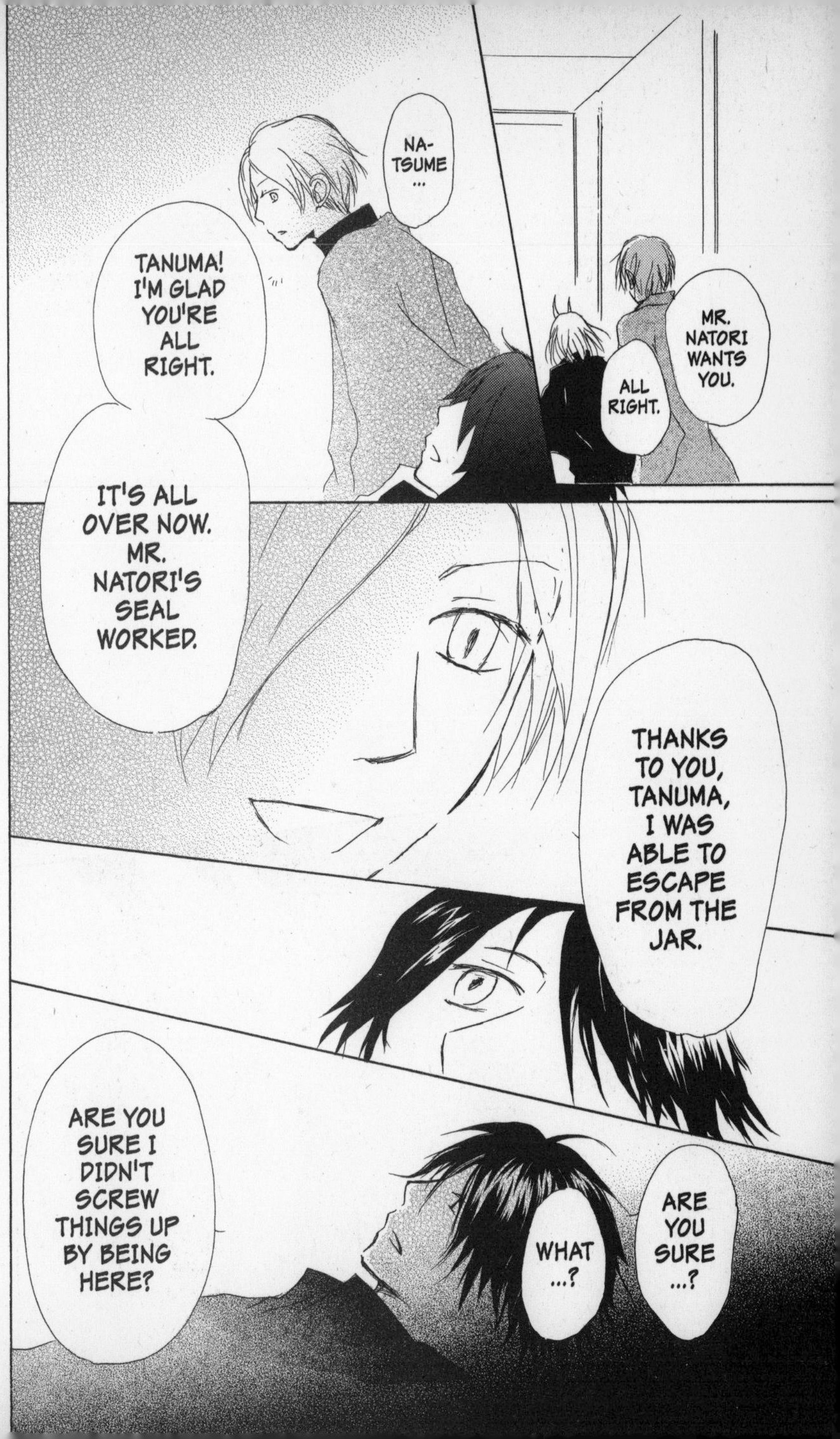
MR. NATORI WANTS YOU.
ALL RIGHT.
NA-TSUME ...
TANUMA! I'M GLAD YOU'RE ALL RIGHT.
IT'S ALL OVER NOW. MR. NATORI'S SEAL WORKED.
THANKS TO YOU, TANUMA, I WAS ABLE TO ESCAPE FROM THE JAR.
ARE YOU SURE ...?
WHAT ...?
ARE YOU SURE I DIDN'T SCREW THINGS UP BY BEING HERE?

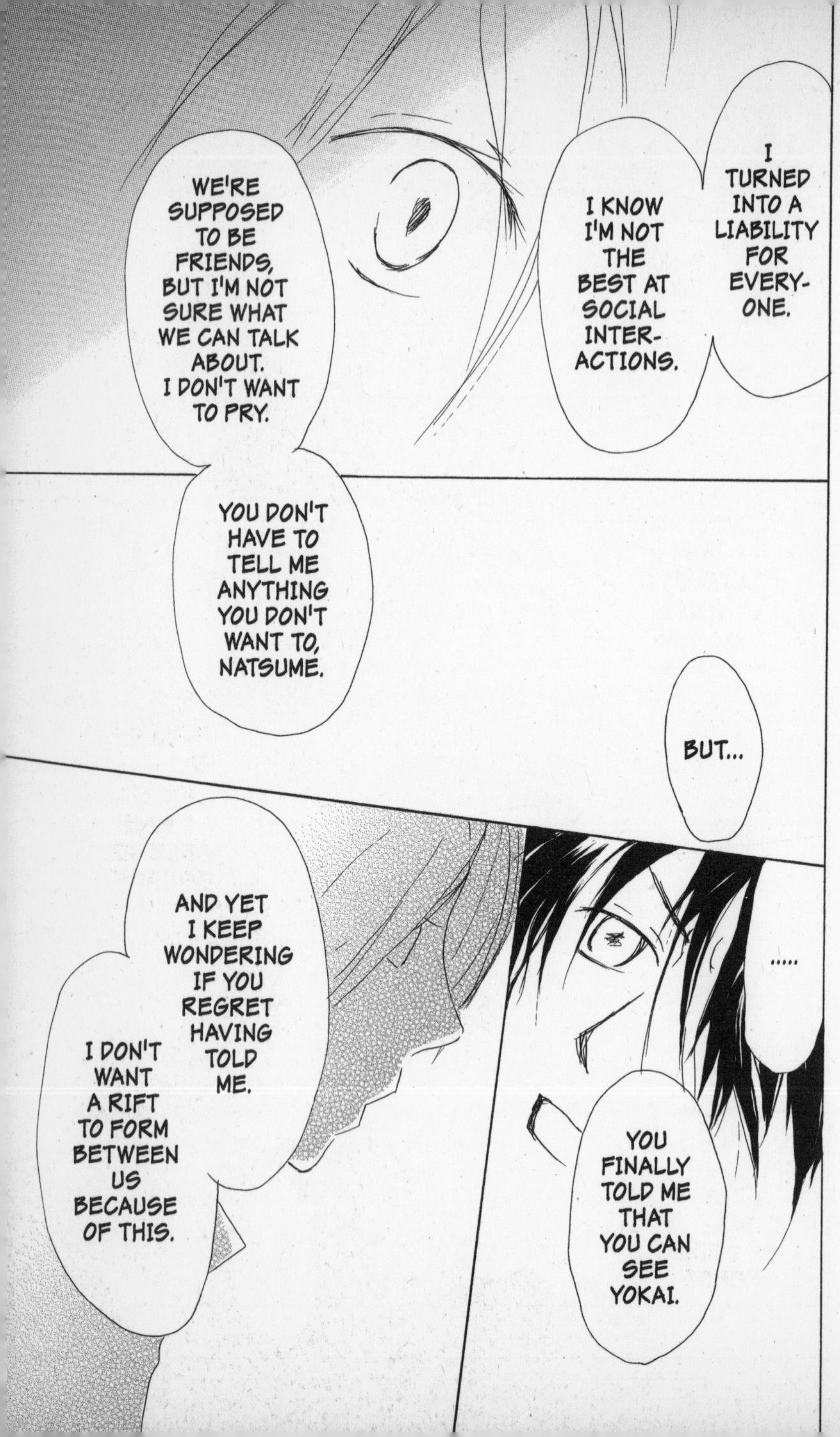
I TURNED INTO A LIABILITY FOR EVERYONE.
I KNOW I'M NOT THE BEST AT SOCIAL INTERACTIONS.
WE'RE SUPPOSED TO BE FRIENDS, BUT I'M NOT SURE WHAT WE CAN TALK ABOUT. I DON'T WANT TO PRY.
YOU DON'T HAVE TO TELL ME ANYTHING YOU DON'T WANT TO, NATSUME.
BUT...
.....
YOU FINALLY TOLD ME THAT YOU CAN SEE YOKAI.
AND YET I KEEP WONDERING IF YOU REGRET HAVING TOLD ME.
I DON'T WANT A RIFT TO FORM BETWEEN US BECAUSE OF THIS.

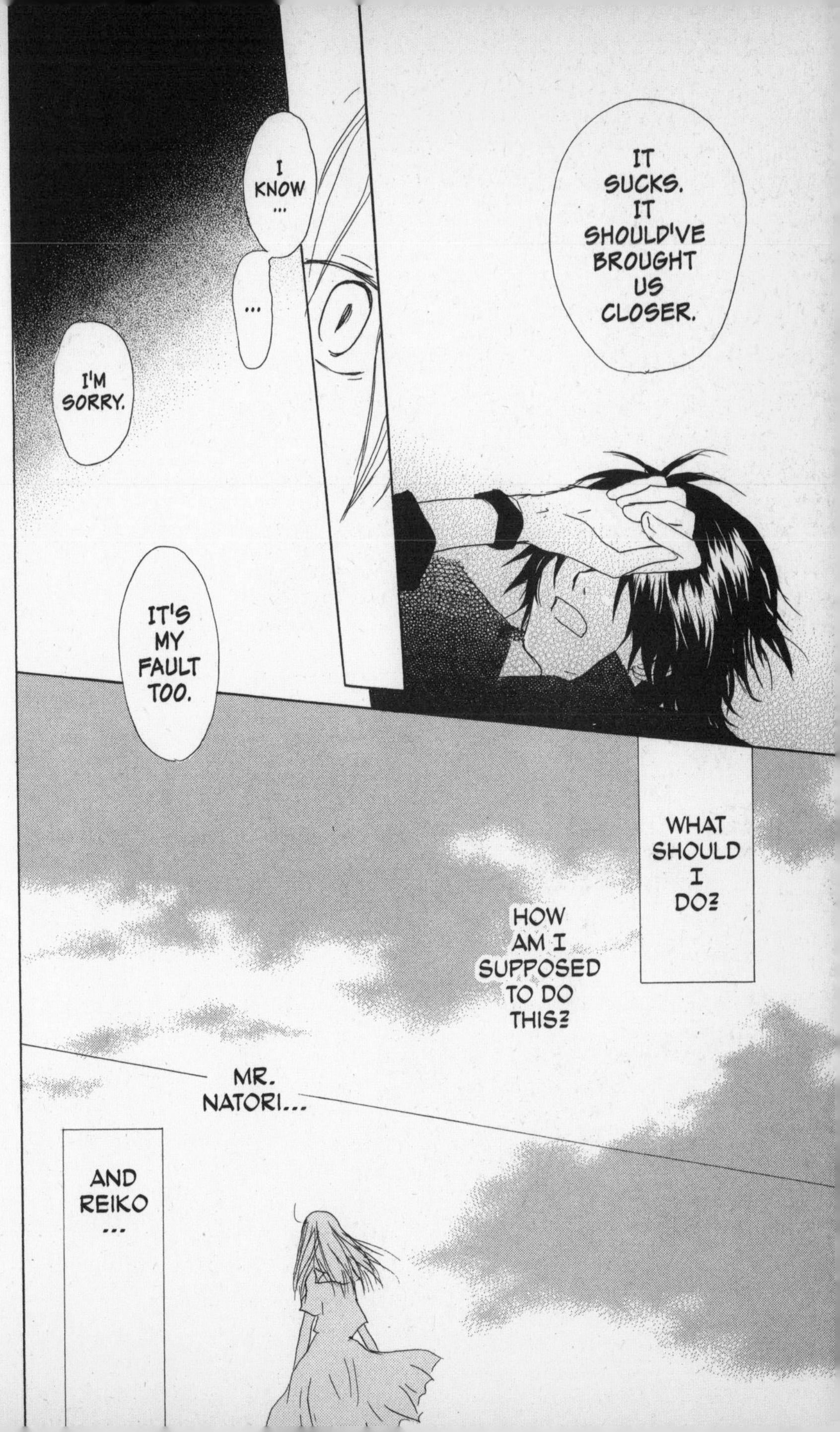
IT SUCKS. IT SHOULD'VE BROUGHT US CLOSER.
I KNOW ...
...
I'M SORRY.
IT'S MY FAULT TOO.
WHAT SHOULD I DO?
HOW AM I SUPPOSED TO DO THIS?
MR. NATORI...
AND REIKO ...

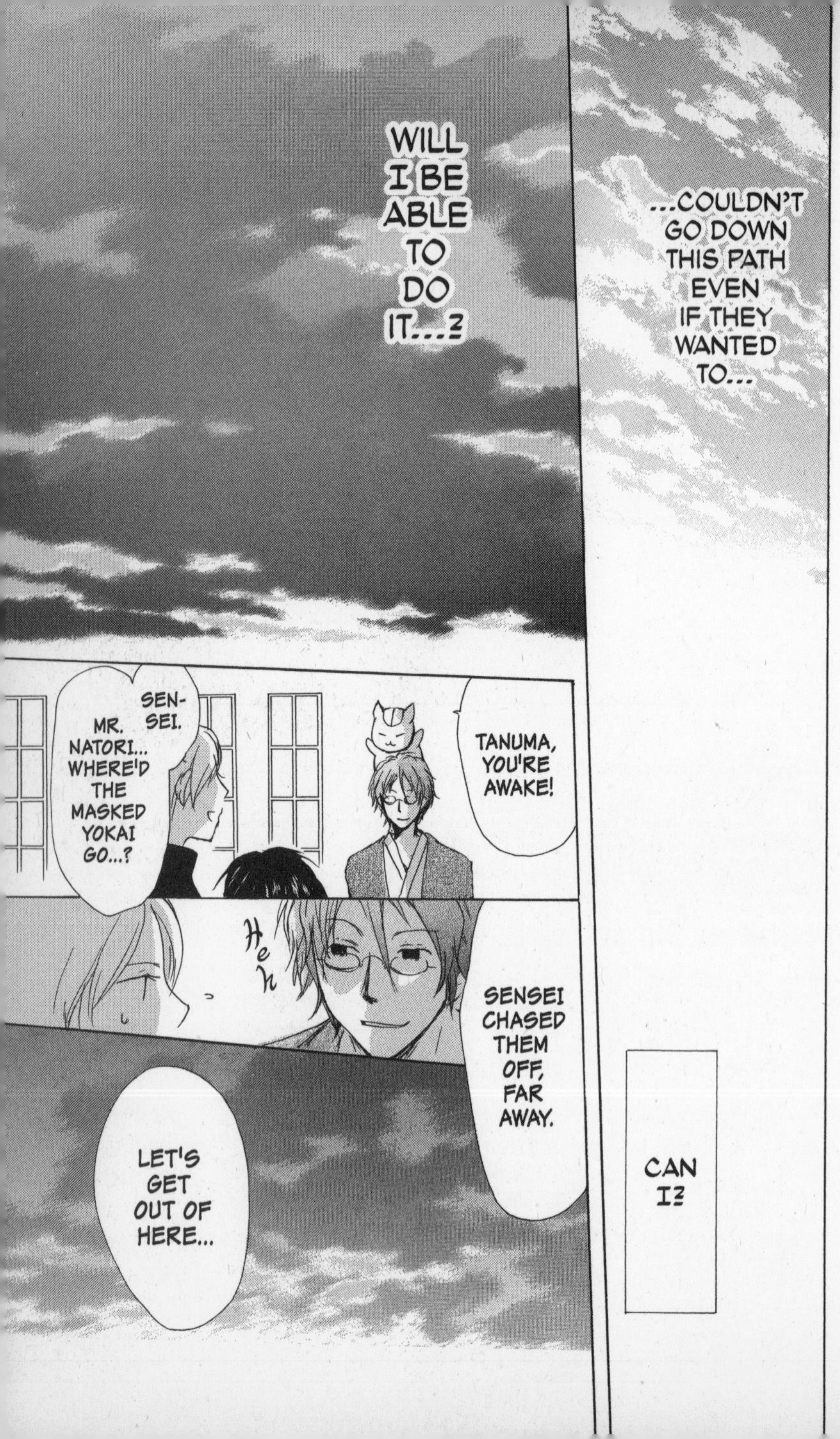
...COULDN'T GO DOWN THIS PATH EVEN IF THEY WANTED TO...
CAN I?
WILL I BE ABLE TO DO IT...?
TANUMA, YOU'RE AWAKE!
SEN-SEI.
MR. NATORI... WHERE'D THE MASKED YOKAI GO...?
Heh
SENSEI CHASED THEM OFF, FAR AWAY.
LET'S GET OUT OF HERE...

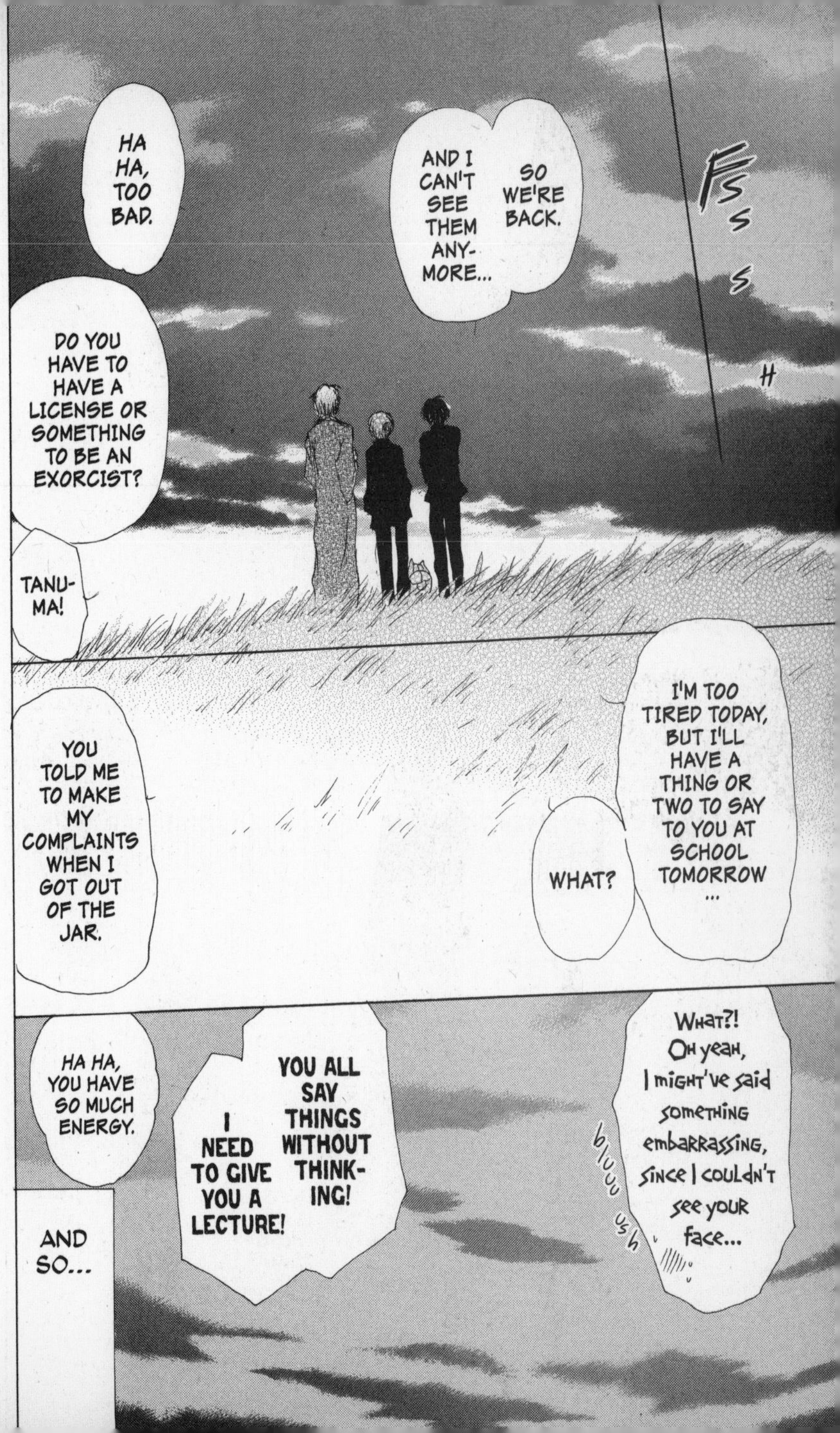
FSSSH
SO WE'RE BACK.
AND I CAN'T SEE THEM ANYMORE...
HA HA, TOO BAD.
DO YOU HAVE TO HAVE A LICENSE OR SOMETHING TO BE AN EXORCIST?
TANUMA!
I'M TOO TIRED TODAY, BUT I'LL HAVE A THING OR TWO TO SAY TO YOU AT SCHOOL TOMORROW...
WHAT?
YOU TOLD ME TO MAKE MY COMPLAINTS WHEN I GOT OUT OF THE JAR.
What?! Oh yeah, I might've said something embarrassing, since I couldn't see your face...
bluuush
YOU ALL SAY THINGS WITHOUT THINKING!
I NEED TO GIVE YOU A LECTURE!
HA HA, YOU HAVE SO MUCH ENERGY.
AND SO...

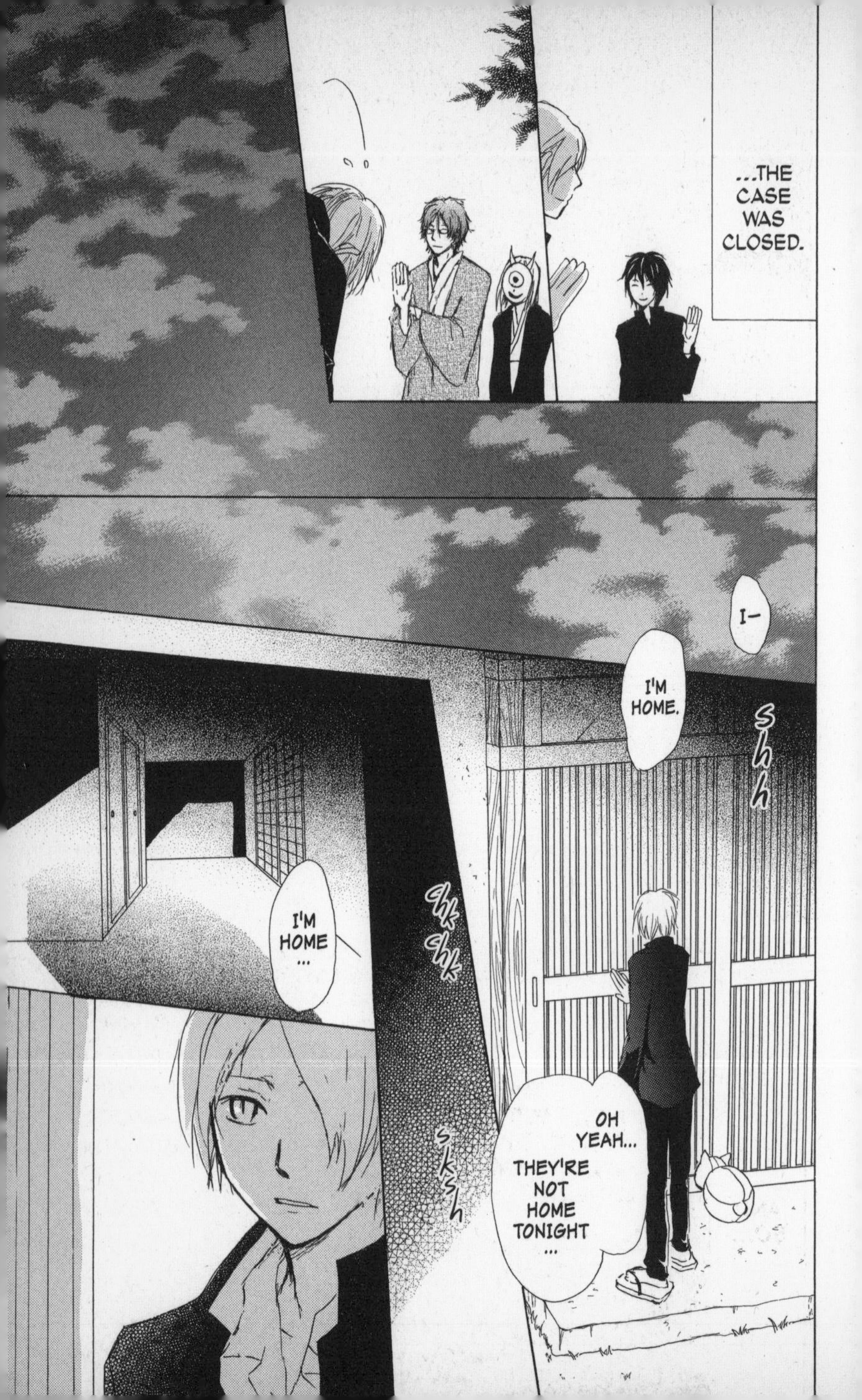
...THE CASE WAS CLOSED.
I—
I'M HOME.
shh
chk chk
I'M HOME ...
OH YEAH... THEY'RE NOT HOME TONIGHT ...
sksh

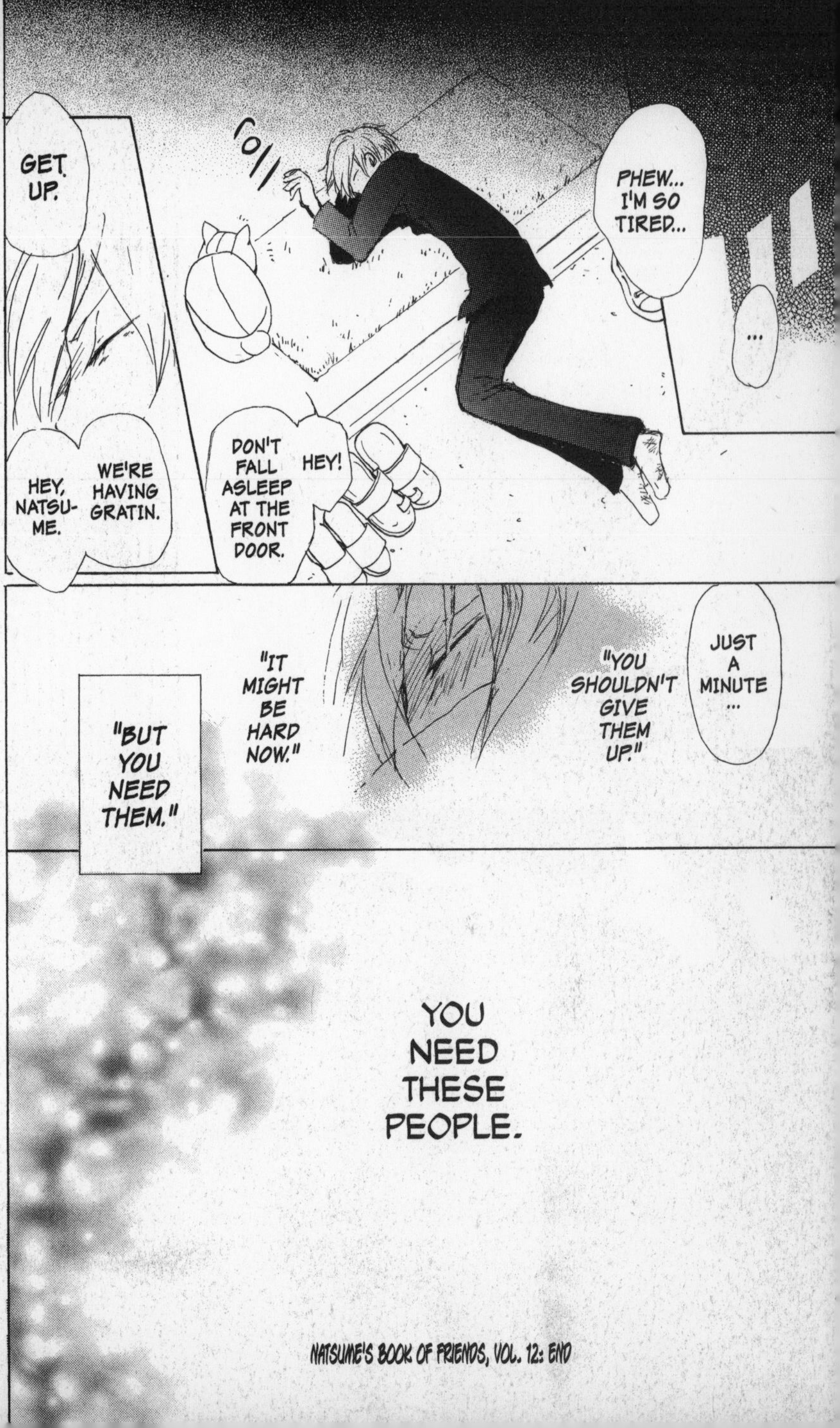
PHEW... I'M SO TIRED...
...
HEY!
DON'T FALL ASLEEP AT THE FRONT DOOR.
GET UP.
WE'RE HAVING GRATIN.
HEY, NATSUME.
JUST A MINUTE...
"YOU SHOULDN'T GIVE THEM UP."
"IT MIGHT BE HARD NOW."
"BUT YOU NEED THEM."
YOU NEED THESE PEOPLE.
NATSUME'S BOOK OF FRIENDS, VOL. 12: END

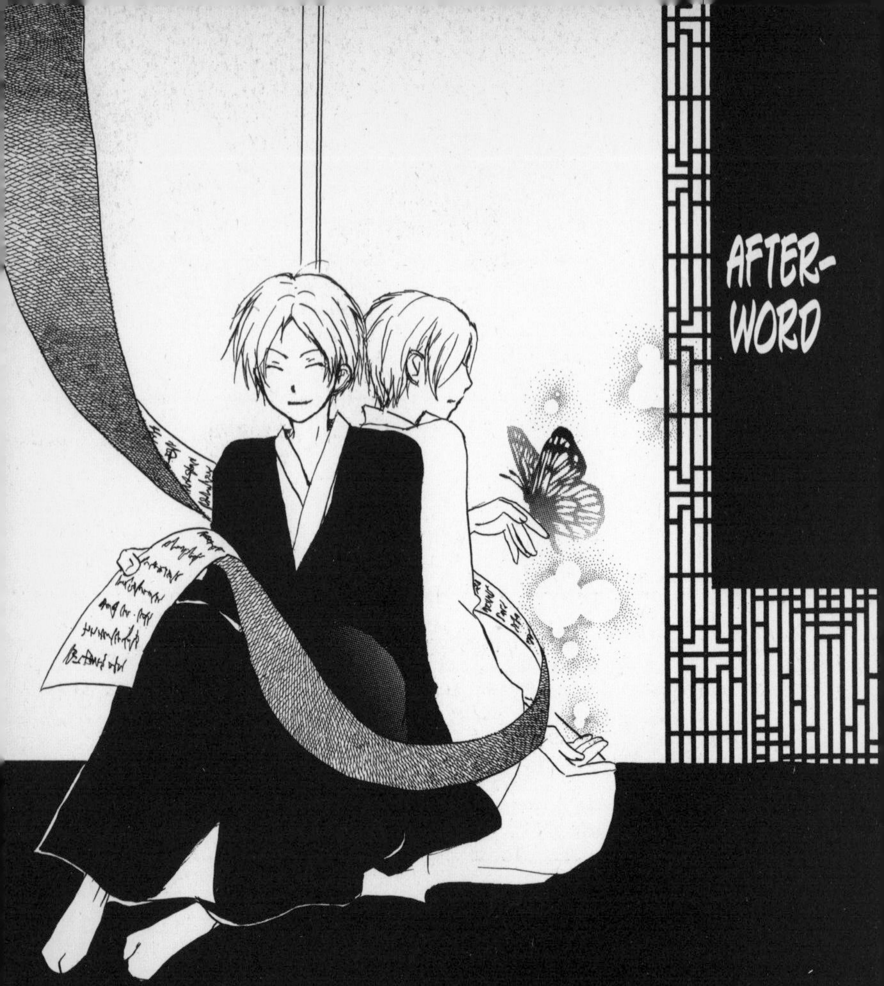
AFTER-
WORD

Thank you for reading.

Natsume went back to his childhood home in the previous volume, and now he's starting to be able to come face to face with his true feelings of loneliness. It's a joy to draw him. I think he's finally realized what most of us take for granted, that it's okay to show emotions. There's a sort of catharsis that comes from taking down these walls he's built, bit by bit. But the walls also kept some things safe all these years.

Please read the rest of this afterword only after reading the entire volume to avoid spoilers.

CHAPTER 47 Answer Instead

My original plan was to do the in-the-bottle episode as a two-parter, but then I was slated to do two one-shot stories. That made me quite nervous. Natsume met and then had to say goodbye to yet another yokai—he's grown so much more from his previous experiences. I felt strangely lonely and happy at the same time. I'm also quite fond of the way Karikami looks. If I saw this big pale thing standing in the dark forest, I think I'd faint.

CHAPTER 48 Name of the Mysterious One

They used this story as the first episode of the third season of the anime. The "ghost cup" was something I had come up with for my very first draft for the very first episode of this manga, but I had to edit it out at the time because I wasn't able to incorporate it well enough into the story yet. I had totally forgotten about it, but when I drew Natsume picking up the broken pieces, it reminded me that I started this manga precisely because I wanted to draw this kind of story. It made me feel so acutely grateful that I've been able to continue working on Natsume.

CHAPTERS 49-51 Beyond the Glass

Tanuma **wants** to help and **tries** to help, but he can't. The more he tries to take action, the more he comes up against this wall. Natsume gradually realizes that while he wants to talk to Tanuma, it also puts him in a dilemma. Seeing this, Natori wants to say, "I told you so," but he hopes that Natsume will be able to succeed where he failed. I was also excited that I could draw Sensei/Natsume with expressions that he doesn't usually make. Natsume is really not very expressive with his face.

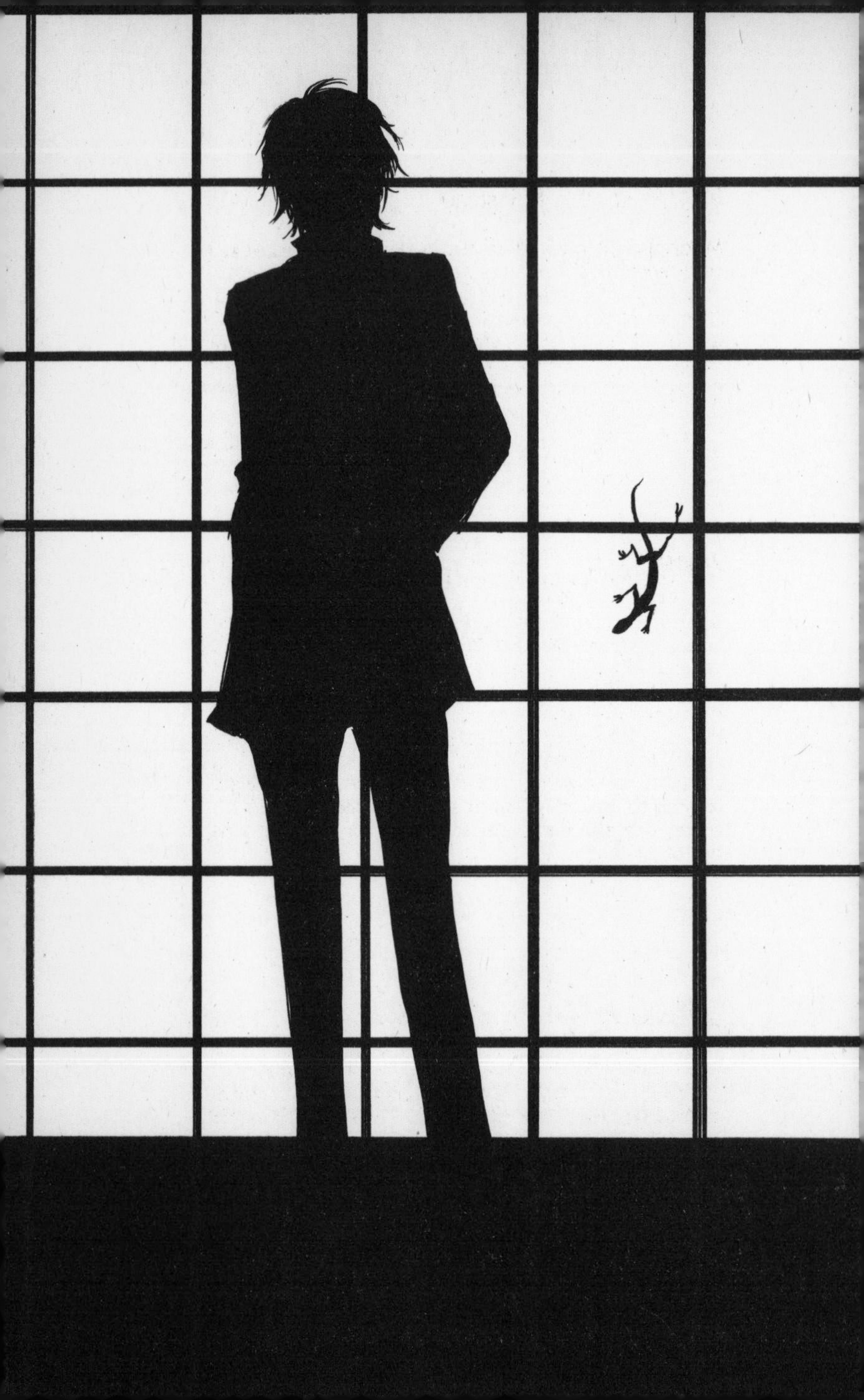

The third season of the anime is set to air late at night the day before this volume goes on sale in Japan. I would like to thank the director, the animation staff, voice actors, and all the fans and viewers who made the first two seasons possible.

And thank you so much to my dear readers. I've finally reached the fifty-episode mark. And I still have so many stories I want to write. I would like to continue writing them for you for a long time.

Thanks to:
Tamao Ohki
Chika
Mika
My sister
Mr. Sato
Hoen Kikaku, Ltd.
    Thank you.

AFTERWORD: END

Natsume's BOOK of FRIENDS

VOLUME 12 END NOTES

PAGE 39, PANEL 1: *Akebi*
A purple fruit that grows on vines. When ripe, the pod splits open to reveal seeds surrounded by sweet white pulp. The pod is also edible—it is often stuffed with ground meat and deep-fried.

PAGE 43, PANEL 5: *Winner*
Popsicle sticks are labeled "win" or "lose," and winning sticks can be traded at the store for a free popsicle.

PAGE 78, PANEL 2: *Shogi*
A Japanese board game similar to chess where the object of the game is to capture the opponent's king.

PAGE 79, PANEL 3: *Takoyaki*
Fried octopus balls, a popular festival food.

PAGE 95, PANEL 4: *Bento*
A lunch box that may contain rice, meat, pickles and an assortment of side dishes.

PAGE 108, PANEL 1: *New Year's postcards*
It is customary in Japan to send postcards with New Year's greetings. They are delivered on New Year's Day. Household members often lightheartedly compete to see who gets postcards from the most people.

PAGE 126, PANEL 3: *Tanuma's mask*
The character on the mask bears the character for "eye."

Yuki Midorikawa
is the creator of *Natsume's Book of Friends*, which was nominated for the Manga Taisho (Cartoon Grand Prize). Her other titles published in Japan include *Hotarubi no Mori e* (Into the Forest of Fireflies), *Hiiro no Isu* (The Scarlet Chair) and *Akaku Saku Koe* (The Voice That Blooms Red).

NATSUME'S BOOK OF FRIENDS
Vol. 12
Shojo Beat Edition

STORY AND ART BY *Yuki Midorikawa*

Translation & Adaptation *Lillian Olsen*
Touch-up Art & Lettering *Sabrina Heep*
Design *Fawn Lau*
Editor *Pancha Diaz*

Natsume Yujincho by Yuki Midorikawa
© Yuki Midorikawa 2011
All rights reserved.
First published in Japan in 2011 by HAKUSENSHA, Inc., Tokyo.
English language translation rights arranged with HAKUSENSHA, Inc., Tokyo.

The rights of the author(s) of the work(s) in this publication to be so identified
have been asserted in accordance with the Copyright, Designs and Patents Act 1988.
A CIP catalogue record for this book is available from the British Library.

Printed in Canada

Published by VIZ Media, LLC
P.O. Box 77010
San Francisco, CA 94107

10 9 8 7 6 5 4 3 2 1
First printing, July 2012

PARENTAL ADVISORY
NATSUME'S BOOK OF FRIENDS is rated T for
Teen and is recommended for ages 16 and
up. This volume contains fantasy violence.
ratings.viz.com

www.viz.com

www.shojobeat.com

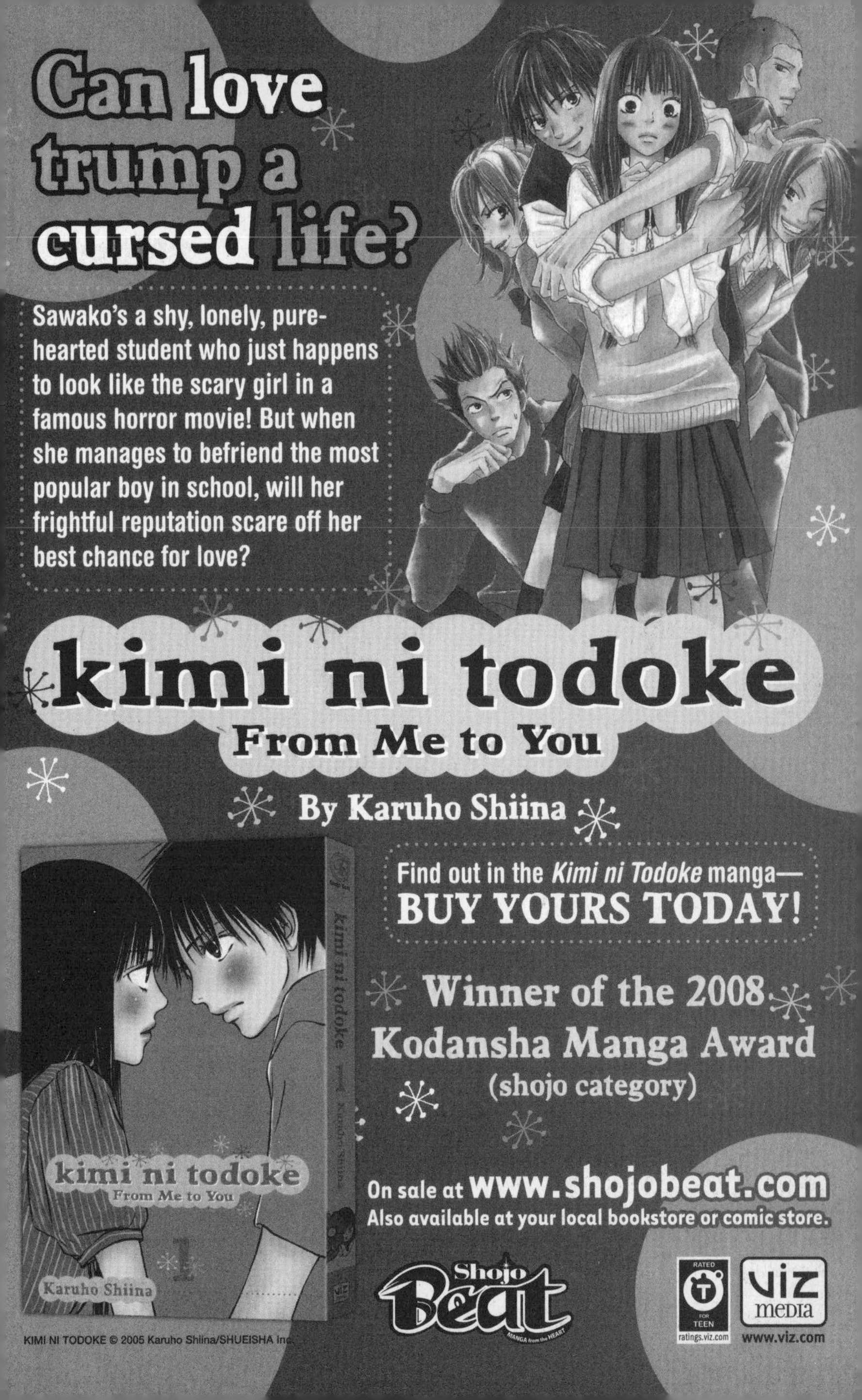
Can love trump a cursed life?
Sawako's a shy, lonely, pure-hearted student who just happens to look like the scary girl in a famous horror movie! But when she manages to befriend the most popular boy in school, will her frightful reputation scare off her best chance for love?
kimi ni todoke
From Me to You
By Karuho Shiina
kimi ni todoke
From Me to You
1
Karuho Shiina
Find out in the Kimi ni Todoke manga—
BUY YOURS TODAY!
Winner of the 2008
Kodansha Manga Award
(shojo category)
On sale at www.shojobeat.com
Also available at your local bookstore or comic store.
Shojo Beat
MANGA from the HEART
RATED T FOR TEEN
ratings.viz.com
VIZ media
www.viz.com
KIMI NI TODOKE © 2005 Karuho Shiina/SHUEISHA Inc.

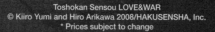

SURPRISE!

You may be reading the wrong way!

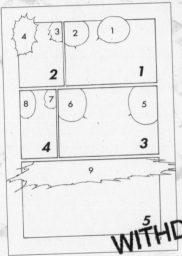

It's true: In keeping with the original Japanese comic format, this book reads from right to left—so action, sound effects, and word balloons are completely reversed. This preserves the orientation of the original artwork—plus, it's fun! Check out the diagram shown here to get the hang of things, and then turn to the other side of the book to get started!